FROM CREATION TO THE CROSS

Understanding the
First Half of the Bible

FROM
CREATION
TO THE
CROSS

*Understanding the
First Half of the Bible*

A revised and expanded edition of
On the Way to Jesus

Albert H. Baylis

ZondervanPublishingHouse
Grand Rapids, Michigan

A Division of HarperCollinsPublishers

From Creation to the Cross
Copyright © 1996 by Albert H. Baylis

A revised and expanded version of *On the Way to Jesus*

Requests for information should be addressed to:

📖 ZondervanPublishingHouse
Grand Rapids, Michigan 49530

Library of Congress Cataloging-in-Publication Data

Baylis, Albert H.
    From creation to the cross: understanding the first half of the Bible / Albert H. Baylis.
        p.   cm.
    Includes bibliographical references and index.
    ISBN: 0–310–49080–4 (hardcover)
    1. Bible. O.T.—Criticism, interpretation, etc. I. Title.
BS1171.2.B38 1996
221.6—dc20   96-1858
        CIP

This edition printed on acid-free paper and meets the American National Standards Institute Z39.48 standard.

Edited by Mary McCormick
Interior design by Sue Vandenberg Koppenol

Printed in the United States of America

---

97 98 99 00 01 02 / ❖ DH / 10 9 8 7 6 5 4

This book is dedicated to
AL III
Al, you are my Hero

CONTENTS

Part Four

LIFE IN THE LAND

Part Five

RESTORATION AND HOPE

ACKNOWLEDGMENTS

Special thanks are due to a great number of people for making this book possible. Certainly those editors at the old Multnomah Press who were close at hand to encourage me in my maiden effort with the first edition are still fondly remembered. Rod Morris, Steve Halliday, and Larry Libby encouraged me with their enthusiasm for both the content and style from the very beginning. Also, the interaction with John R. Kohlenberger III and John Johnson on significant sections was highly profitable. My daughter Elena, then a teenager, saved me much time by helping with the word processing. In this new expanded edition, she also gave me helpful suggestions for revisions in the chapters on Psalms and the two new chapters on the prophets.

In addition, my most faithful support and editor of *On the Way to Jesus* was my first Ally and Helper, Theota, who was taken into our Lord's presence following a tragic traffic accident. The book manuscript was completed by then, but not yet published. Her reward continues in this second volume, should our Lord continue to use it for his glory.

Also, this greatly expanded and revised work (from including fifteen Old Testament books to all thirty-nine), *From Creation to the Cross*, has increased the sphere of gratitude. The enthusiasm for republishing was first taken up by my friend Dick Sleeper and then by Ed van der Maas of Zondervan to an extent that would delight any author's heart. How encouraging to hear from a Senior Editor that the book was unique and needed to be republished, rather than trying to convince him! He also liked all my ideas for changes. In addition, Verlyn Verbrugge, Senior Editor, has faithfully guided the book to final publication. Thanks also to former teaching fellows, Bill Pruitt and Doug Peters, who aided in research and editing, and to my colleague at the seminary, Ron Frost, who provided insightful suggestions.

Finally, my new Helper, Barbara, deserves more reward than I can provide for her heroic efforts of support through a difficult time. Many of you who have waited through a delayed publication date know that my son, Al, came down with a rare bone cancer, Ewing's Sarcoma, just as I was beginning work on this edition. Al's needs, of course, took priority over publication. Through extensive periods of radical chemotherapy, long drives to Seattle at three- or four-week intervals for weeklong stays, full-time nursing at home (IVs, shots, and all), Barbara has lifted the load, encouraged and supported both Al and myself, and sought to create blocks of time for this work that she believed to be important for the kingdom. My special thanks to you, Barbi.

Al Baylis
Multnomah Biblical Seminary
Portland, Oregon
December, 1995

PREFACE

"Why do you want to write a book?"

A student of mine caught me up short with that question as we returned from Christmas break. As usual, I had spent the entire vacation writing. Why *did* I want to write a book? And why *this* book?

I have heard many a preacher say, "Christians know all they need to know about the truth. It's living it that is the problem." Yet year after year I discover that the students churches are sending to Bible college (some of their most dedicated) and even those coming to seminary do not know that much about their Bibles.

Certainly, living the truth we already know is a challenge. But it's hard to be challenged by truth we don't know! Too many of us are living on a subsistence diet of Scripture—and wonder why our strength is small. How do we receive motivation to live through difficulties, to face struggles, to avoid temptation, if it is not by a keen understanding of the Word of God?

Yet when it comes to the first part of the Bible, most people are lost. Oh, sure, they know and enjoy some individual stories such as those of David and Goliath, Joshua and the battle of Jericho, Noah and the flood; but few have put them together to understand what the Old Testament is all about . . . and where it is going.

I believe most Christians would like to know their Bible better. They would like to be motivated by its message. Yet, when they look for help to understand it, they are often weighed down with facts and dates and names and places. They conclude that understanding the Bible must be a dull and tedious task.

And then there is Jesus. Does the front half of the Bible relate to Jesus? How? Except for a few specific predictions, like Isaiah 53 and Isaiah 9, even most Christians aren't really sure. That is why I have spent my vacations writing on both the first edition and now the second.

Bible survey teachers responded postively to the first edition, *On the Way to Jesus*, but wished that it included a look at every single book of the Old Testament. Now this revised and expanded edition covers each book, stressing the message and theology of each. In addition, a number of charts and maps have been added with survey courses in mind.

Also, recognize that the book is written *on two levels*. For those who are first acquainting themselves with the flow of the Old Testament or for informal group discussions, I recommend reading only the text *without* considering the Notes and Comments section at the end of each chapter. Interpretational views as well as additional insights into biblical questions are discussed there. The text has been kept as readable as possible and sticks to what is important to grasp about the scope and outlook of Genesis to Malachi. For college classes, the Notes and Comments sections are not mere documentation of sources, but cover important academic debates and issues and are, therefore, essential reading as part of the text. The sections have been written so that students may read these comments for each chapter immediately *after* (not during) the reading of the chapter—no need to turn back and forth and interrupt the flow of reading the chapter itself. College students should appreciate not only the more readable style and cohesiveness of the text over the standard academic style, but also the Notes with their examination of academic issues.

So now you know what I've been doing with my vacations. I've been taking a trip through the heart of the Bible, thrilling to the dynamic of the Bible itself and plotting a road map for those who have not seen the best sights before. It's a journey that highlights the great themes of the Old Testament and shows how these themes do indeed lead to Jesus of Nazareth. I hope it opens up the larger portion of the Bible for you.

A Scripture reading guide as well as questions for personal or group interaction follow each chapter. Also attached are suggestions for further reading, primarily for the English reader rather than for the Hebrew scholar. But whether you are going to use the book for group study or personal enrichment, enjoy. The worst offense is to have a book about the Bible that makes it boring. I have done my best to capture the dynamic of the Bible itself.

My vacations are spent. Your trip is just beginning. I wish you Godspeed.

Maps, Charts, and Illustrations

ABBREVIATIONS

ANET	*Ancient Near Eastern Texts*, James B. Pritchard, ed. (Princeton, N.J.: Princeton Univ. Press, 1969).
AV	Authorized Version (King James Version)
BAGD	Walter Bauer, William F. Arndt, F. Wilbur Gingrich, and Frederick W. Danker, eds., *A Greek-English Lexicon of the New Testament and Other Early Christian Literature*, 2d ed. (Chicago: Univ. of Chicago Press, 1979).
BDB	F. Brown, S. R. Driver, and C. A. Briggs, *Hebrew and English Lexicon of the Old Testament* (Oxford: Oxford Univ. Press, 1959).
BSac	*Bibliotheca Sacra*
CBQ	*Catholic Biblical Quarterly*
CTM	*Concordia Theological Monthly*
EBC	*The Expositor's Bible Commentary*, Frank E. Gaebelein, ed., 12 vols. (Grand Rapids: Zondervan, 1975–91).
EQ	*The Evangelical Quarterly*
ICC	International Critical Commentary

Int	*Interpretation*
JBL	*Journal of Biblical Literature*
JETS	*Journal of the Evangelical Theological Society*
NASB	New American Standard Bible
NICOT	New International Commentary of the Old Testament
NIV	New International Version
NRSV	New Revised Standard Version
R&E	*Review and Expositor*
TB	*Tyndale Bulletin*
TDNT	*Theological Dictionary of the New Testament*, G. Kittel and G. Friedrich, eds., trans. G. Bromiley (Grand Rapids: Eerdmans, 1964–76).
TDOT	*Theological Dictionary of the Old Testament*, G. Johannes Botterwick and Helmer Ringgren, eds. (Grand Rapids: Eerdmans, 1978–).
TOTC	Tyndale Old Testament Commentaries
TWOT	*Theological Wordbook of the Old Testament*, R. Laird Harris, Gleason L. Archer, Jr., and Bruce K. Waltke, eds. (Chicago: Moody Press, 1980).
VT	*Vetus Testamentum*
WBC	Word Biblical Commentary
WTJ	*Westminster Theological Journal*
ZPEB	*Zondervan Pictorial Encyclopedia of the Bible*, Merrill C. Tenney, ed., 5 vols. (Grand Rapids: Zondervan, 1975).

The Holy Scriptures

Hebrew Names For The Books	Hebrew Arrangement And Classification		English Arrangement And Classification		Approximate Dates Concerned
In the beginning		Genesis	Genesis		
These are the names		Exodus	Exodus		
And He called	TORAH	Leviticus	Leviticus	LAW	The Beginning
In the wilderness		Numbers	Numbers	(Pentateuch)	to 1406 B.C.
These are the words		Deuteronomy	Deuteronomy		
Joshua		Joshua	Joshua		1406–1380 B.C.
Judges		Judges	Judges		1380–1050 B.C.
I Samuel	FORMER	I Samuel	Ruth		1200–1150 B.C.
II Samuel	PROPHETS	II Samuel	I Samuel		1100–1010 B.C.
I Kings		I Kings	II Samuel		1010–971 B.C.
II Kings		II Kings	I Kings	HISTORY	971–853 B.C.
Isaiah		Isaiah	II Kings		853–560 B.C.
Jeremiah		Jeremiah	I Chronicles		1010–971 B.C.
Ezekiel		Ezekiel	II Chronicles		971–539 B.C.
Hosea		Hosea	Ezra		539–450 B.C.
Joel		Joel	Nehemiah		445–410 B.C.
Amos	LATTER	Amos	Esther		483–474 B.C.
Obadiah	PROPHETS	Obadiah	Job		
Jonah		Jonah	Psalms	POETRY	No specific
Micah		Micah	Proverbs	and	historical period
Nahum		Nahum	Ecclesiastes	WISDOM	covered
Habakkuk		Habakkuk	Song of Solomon		
Zephaniah		Zephaniah	Isaiah		739–685 B.C.
Haggai		Haggai	Jeremiah	MAJOR	627–580 B.C.
Zechariah		Zechariah	Lamentations	PROPHETS	586 B.C.
Malachi		Malachi	Ezekiel		593–570 B.C.
Praises		Psalms	Daniel		605–530 B.C.
Job		Job	Hosea		760–720 B.C.
Proverbs		Proverbs	Joel		835 B.C.
Ruth		Ruth	Amos		760 B.C.
Song of Songs		Song of Solomon	Obadiah		845 B.C.
The Preacher		Ecclesiastes	Jonah		782 B.C.
How!	THE	Lamentations	Micah		737–690 B.C.
Esther	WRITINGS	Esther	Nahum	MINOR	650 B.C.
Daniel	(Hagiographa)	Daniel	Habakkuk	PROPHETS	609 B.C.
Ezra		Ezra	Zephaniah		640 B.C.
Nehemiah		Nehemiah	Haggai		520 B.C.
I The words of the days		I Chronicles	Zechariah		520 B.C.
II The words of the days		II Chronicles	Malachi		433 B.C.

John H. Walton, *Chronological and Background Charts of the Old Testament* (Zondervan, 1978), 13.

Old Testament Chronology

Creation	Fall	Flood	Babel
?	?	?	?

Old Testament Chronology

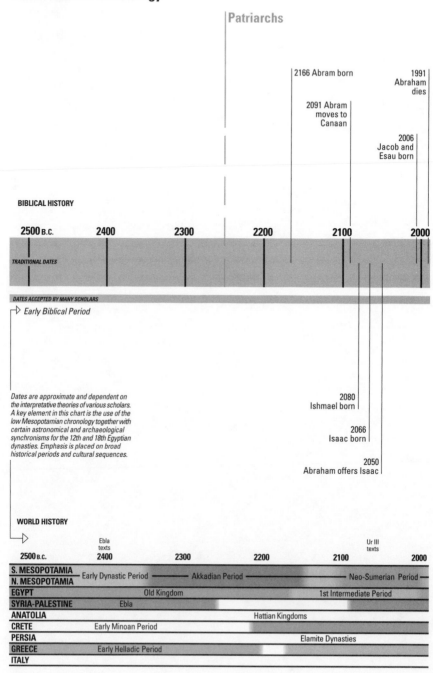

Patriarchs

2166 Abram born

1991
Abraham
dies

2091 Abram
moves to
Canaan

2006
Jacob and
Esau born

BIBLICAL HISTORY

| 2500 B.C. | 2400 | 2300 | 2200 | 2100 | 2000 |

TRADITIONAL DATES

DATES ACCEPTED BY MANY SCHOLARS

▷ *Early Biblical Period*

*Dates are approximate and dependent on
the interpretative theories of various scholars.
A key element in this chart is the use of the
low Mesopotamian chronology together with
certain astronomical and archaeological
synchronisms for the 12th and 18th Egyptian
dynasties. Emphasis is placed on broad
historical periods and cultural sequences.*

2080
Ishmael born

2066
Isaac born

2050
Abraham offers Isaac

WORLD HISTORY

▷

	Ebla texts			Ur III texts	
2500 B.C.	2400	2300	2200	2100	2000

S. MESOPOTAMIA	Early Dynastic Period ———		— Akkadian Period —		— Neo-Sumerian Period —
N. MESOPOTAMIA					
EGYPT		Old Kingdom		1st Intermediate Period	
SYRIA-PALESTINE	Ebla				
ANATOLIA				Hattian Kingdoms	
CRETE	Early Minoan Period				
PERSIA				Elamite Dynasties	
GREECE	Early Helladic Period				
ITALY					

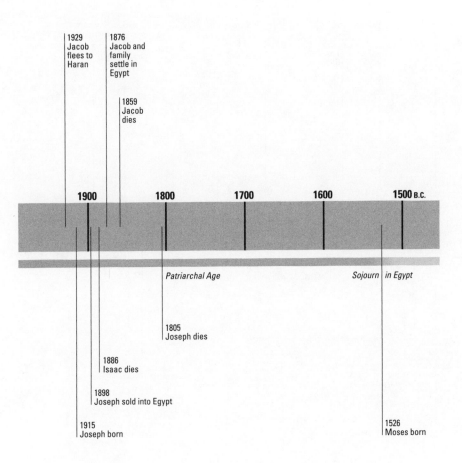

1929
Jacob
flees to
Haran

1876
Jacob and
family
settle in
Egypt

1859
Jacob
dies

1900   1800   1700   1600   1500 B.C.

Patriarchal Age   Sojourn in Egypt

1805
Joseph dies

1886
Isaac dies

1898
Joseph sold into Egypt

1915
Joseph born

1526
Moses born

	Cappadocian texts		Mari texts	Hammurapi texts		
	1900	**1800**		**1700**	**1600**	**1500** B.C.

Isin-Larsa Period	Old Babylonian Period

Middle Kingdom	2nd Intermediate (Hyksos) Period	New Kingdom

Amorite Period	Hyksos Period	Late Canaanite Period

Hittite Old Kingdom

Middle Minoan Period

Middle Helladic Period

Old Testament Chronology

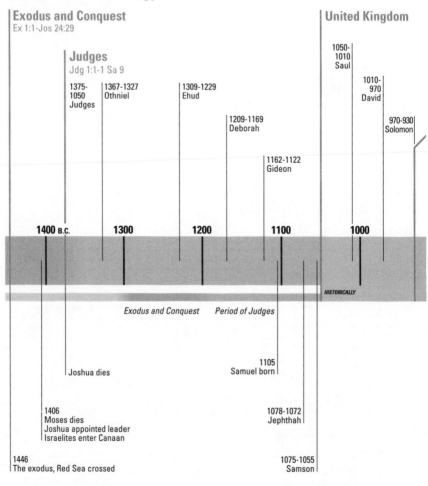

Exodus and Conquest
Ex 1:1-Jos 24:29

United Kingdom

Judges
Jdg 1:1-1 Sa 9

1375-
1050
Judges

1367-1327
Othniel

1309-1229
Ehud

1209-1169
Deborah

1162-1122
Gideon

1050-
1010
Saul

1010-
970
David

970-930
Solomon

1400 B.C.　　**1300**　　**1200**　　**1100**　　**1000**

HISTORICALLY

Exodus and Conquest　　*Period of Judges*

1105
Samuel born

Joshua dies

1406
Moses dies
Joshua appointed leader
Israelites enter Canaan

1078-1072
Jephthah

1446
The exodus, Red Sea crossed

1075-1055
Samson

Nuzi   Ugaritic
texts   texts
Amarna
texts
　　　　　　　　　Merneptah   Medinet Habu
　　　　　　　　　inscription   inscriptions
Shishak
inscription

1400 B.C.　　**1300**　　**1200**　　**1100**　　**1000**

S. MESOPOTAMIA	Kassite Period			
N. MESOPOTAMIA	◄—Mitannian Kingdom	Middle Assyrian Period		
EGYPT	New Kingdom			
SYRIA-PALESTINE	Late Canaanite Period	Sea Peoples	Phoenician,	
ANATOLIA	Hittite Empire	Phrygian Period		
CRETE	Late Minoan Period		Dorian States	
PERSIA				
GREECE	Late Helladic (Mycenean) Period	Dorian States		
ITALY				

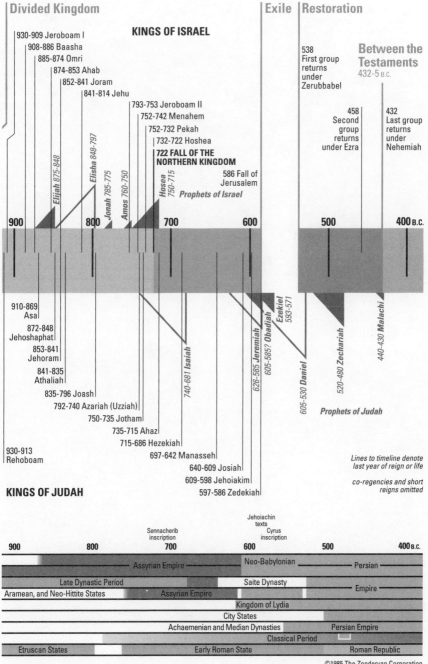

Divided Kingdom | **Exile** | **Restoration**

KINGS OF ISRAEL

930-909 Jeroboam I
908-886 Baasha
885-874 Omri
874-853 Ahab
852-841 Joram
841-814 Jehu
793-753 Jeroboam II
752-742 Menahem
752-732 Pekah
732-722 Hoshea
722 FALL OF THE NORTHERN KINGDOM
586 Fall of Jerusalem

Elijah 875-848
Elisha 848-797
Jonah 785-775
Amos 760-750
Hosea 750-715

Prophets of Israel

538
First group returns under Zerubbabel

Between the Testaments
432-5 B.C.

458
Second group returns under Ezra

432
Last group returns under Nehemiah

900   800   700   600   500   400 B.C.

910-869 Asa
872-848 Jehoshaphat
853-841 Jehoram
841-835 Athaliah
835-796 Joash
792-740 Azariah (Uzziah)
750-735 Jotham
735-715 Ahaz
715-686 Hezekiah
930-913 Rehoboam
697-642 Manasseh
640-609 Josiah
609-598 Jehoiakim
597-586 Zedekiah

740-681 Isaiah
626-585 Jeremiah
605-585? Obadiah
Ezekiel 593-571
605-530 Daniel
520-480 Zechariah
440-430 Malachi

Prophets of Judah

KINGS OF JUDAH

Lines to timeline denote
last year of reign or life

co-regencies and short
reigns omitted

Jehoiachin texts
Cyrus inscription

Sennacherib inscription

900   800   700   600   500   400 B.C.

Assyrian Empire — Neo-Babylonian — Persian

Late Dynastic Period — Saite Dynasty
Aramean, and Neo-Hittite States — Assyrian Empire — Empire

Kingdom of Lydia
City States

Achaemenian and Median Dynasties — Persian Empire

Classical Period

Etruscan States — Early Roman State — Roman Republic

Part One

Genesis 1 – 11

BASICS FOR UNDERSTANDING LIFE

chapter one

THE GOD OF CREATION
(*Genesis 1*)

Like many a modern parent faced with raising children in a confusing world of drugs, disasters, and mind-bending ideas, Moses must have had his concerns. Certainly God did. The book of Exodus tells us about the beginnings of the nation of Israel under the leadership of Moses, the man of God. It records their last-minute rescue through the sea and their camping trip in the desert of Sinai. But that is just the beginning. These former slaves must enter into a land inhabited by people who would make Hell's Angels seem like Sunday school teachers. As the patriarch lay down to sleep at night, he must have worried about this people he was leading. They had every mark of early adolescence about them, yet they needed a stability few adults ever achieve. Sure, they had witnessed God's power to plague and decimate the Egyptians. They had passed through the sea without muddying their feet. But had they really become the people of Yahweh in heart and mind?

How do you prepare a people to avoid the degrading tentacles of a deteriorated culture? How do you lay a foundation for a worthwhile life? What alloy do you use to strengthen their discernment and motivate them toward a better way? The answer is torah. *Torah* simply means instruction. *The Torah* came to be the name for the first five books of the Bible, Genesis through Deuteronomy. As we open the Bible we encounter that instruction—teaching given to prepare the Israelite people for their encounter with gross paganism. But oh, what teaching! No dull classroom recitation here. These are stories. And understanding the history in them is not the boring calisthenics of learning names, dates, and places but involvement with dynamic and crucial events giving us insight into life itself.

THE WORLD OF GENESIS ONE

So, let's join Israel in the desert. Pack up your tent. Leave your modernized campers behind. Come as you are—and bring an appetite for manna! As

Israelites, we owe our allegiance to Yahweh God in a world where many gods are worshiped. Their names are strange to our modern ears: Baal, Molech, Ashtoreth, Anath, and El. They have not survived the millennia, though they were drawing rave reviews in Palestine at the time. Stories about these gods form the belief-system of the world around us. These gods are like most people—and worse! They play and drink, and drink too much. They fight, deceive, and engage in licentious behavior. Just to give you the idea, let's take a quick X-rated look at El, the father of the gods. El is a brutal, bloody tyrant. He not only dethrones his own father (not an unknown temptation for king's sons) but also castrates him. He slays his own favorite son, and cuts off his daughter's head. He also has a reputation for seduction of women.[1]

But perhaps El is the exception. Certainly the goddesses must possess fine and gentle spirits! Well . . . no. Consider the goddess Anath, called the "queen of heaven" and "mistress of all the gods."[2] She, too, is sensuous and violent. Here is a description (not recommended for children) of gentle Anath at work:

> Anath hews in pieces and rejoices,
> her liver extends with laughter,
> her heart is filled with joy;
> for in Anath's hand is success;
> for she plunges her knees in the blood of the swift ones,
> her thighs in the gore of the fast ones.[3]

While the gods fight one another, Anath enjoys the carnage. If her father, the god El, does not grant Anath her request for a palace for Baal, then she assures us:

> I shall trample him down like a lamb to the ground;
> I shall bring down his hoary head with blood to the grave,
> the gray hair of his old age with gore.[4]

No doubt this tale did a lot to encourage honoring one's father and mother in Canaanite culture!

Intrigue and murder, deceit and incest are what you get from these gods.[5] Israel's Ten Commandments are broken without hesitation by these supposed divinities. These gods were not sterling examples. Could belief in them produce sterling civilizations?

THE NEED FOR THE TRUE CREATION STORY

These thoughts bring us face-to-face with a sobering fact. *People become like the gods they worship.* Their gods are their models. It would be disastrous if Israel thought Yahweh her God was like other gods. In fact, God warns his people that if they become as depraved as the people of Canaan, he will eject them from Palestine as well (Lev. 18:24–30). The Bible, then, begins with the most essential element of Torah—the real story about the true God—so the people of God may live a free and wholesome life.

But if we're trying to learn about God, why tell the story of creation? Doesn't that center on learning about the world? About origins? Geology? Not really. The Bible begins at the beginning not because Moses is a history buff obsessed with ancient chronology but because understanding God's creation of the world gives us a clear picture of what God is like.

Have you ever noticed that apart from spending time with someone in a number of situations, it is difficult to really know an individual? He or she could be described accurately to you over the telephone (generous, honest, enjoys tennis), but do you really have a clear picture? The best description would come by telling a number of stories about him. What did he do in a variety of situations? When confronted with a tough decision? When she was with her children? Now you understand and know the person better. The same is true for God. The Bible communicates what he is like by many, many events. By studying these carefully, we begin to understand and know God. And remember: People become like the God they worship. If we are going to learn about God through his activity, creation is the best place to start. It was and is the critical event for a person's worldview.[6] Knowing how God initiated my world helps me understand my own relationship to God more clearly. Then and now, the relationship (or non-relationship) of God to the world controls our total view of life.

Creator Most Worthy

As Moses sat in his tent and thought of the challenges ahead for the people he led, as he worried about their encounter with violent and sensuous paganism, his mind may have reviewed the creation stories of his neighbors—such as the famous Babylonian creation story *Enuma Elish*.[7] In this story one of the three original parents of the gods, Ti'amat, is identified as the ocean. Marduk, a younger god who becomes the chief Babylonian deity, kills her.

> *He split her open like a mussel into two parts;*
> *half of her he set in place and formed the sky therewith as a roof.*
> *He fixed the crossbar and posted guards;*
> *he commanded them not to let her waters escape.*[8]

Half of her corpse was used to form the sky, the other to make the earth[9] (a possible beginning for the expression "Mother Earth"?). The story continues:

Putting her head into position
he thereon formed the mountains.
Opening the deep which was in flood,
he caused to flow from her eyes the Euphrates and Tigris.[10]

Even the most superficial reading of Genesis one catches the far purer and more profound character of the biblical story. Could this people—could any people—prefer the violence of the gods over the majesty and purity of Israel's God? As Moses penned these words he must have fallen to his tent floor in adoration. The God of the Bible is more worthy than these gods. He is Most Worthy.

OVERVIEW OF THE CREATION STORY

The worthiness of God saturates the very structure of Genesis 1:1–2:3. As we look here, the first thing to notice is the tremendous beauty and order. Let me briefly summarize the layout.

It all begins with a topic sentence worthy of the most cloistered English teacher: "In the beginning God created the heavens and the earth." Nothing could be clearer than this. God created it all. "Heavens and earth" includes the universe as we know it—the land we live on, the sky and solar system we see.

The details of that creation follow. Verse 2 describes the desolate chaos present as God unleashes his creative word.[11] The planet was "formless and empty." It was desolate, without developed order, and it was uninhabited. Further, "darkness was over the surface of the deep [waters]." A dark watery chaos prevailed. Finally, "the Spirit of God was hovering over the waters." These three descriptions summarize the earth's desperate condition. The earth lacked productive energy. No life. No light. The only hope was the presence of the Spirit of God himself.[12]

The creative days which follow demonstrate that Israel's sovereign God is the one who makes creation out of chaos, a habitable earth out of a water-covered planet, and a dwelling place out of a desolate and foreboding atmosphere. But, more, he can do it in a beautiful pattern of harmony and wisdom. Note the order of events in figure 1.1.

The Master Designer is at work. An examination of the chart shows that Days 4–6 parallel Days 1–3. Days 1–3 provide the basic divisions necessary to a living environment. Darkness must be dispelled and limited to part of the day if there is to be life on the planet. The watery chaos must be penetrated and separated, with much of it removed to the heavens so the remaining sea can be limited to part of the globe. With this, dry land appears and vegetation can be brought into existence.

Day 4, however, returns to the subject of light. Particular lights now are created to bear the already created light, marking out time on earth—

Figure 1.1

Days 1–3	Days 4–6
Day 1: Creation of light & limitation of darkness (1:4–5)	**Day 4:** Lights created: sun, moon, stars (1:14–19)
Day 2: Creation of sky (heavens) by separation of the waters (1:6–9)	**Day 5:** Birds and sea creatures created (1:20–23)
Day 3: Creation of dry land by limiting sea; creation of vegetation (1:10–13)	**Day 6:** Domesticated animals, insects, wild animals created; man created in image of God (1:24–31)
Day 7	
God rests from his creative work (2:1–3)	

days, seasons, and years. Day 5 answers to Day 2 by providing inhabitants for sea and sky. Day 6 provides land creatures to inhabit the provisioned earth of Day 3. By the end of Day 3, the earth is no longer "formless." By the end of Day 6 it is no longer "empty." Day 7 is an unparalleled day—a day to commemorate the completion of creation.

When some scholars see this beautiful arrangement, they often jump to an unwarranted conclusion. To them the parallels prove that the account is symbolic, fictional, and mythological. But this suggestion ignores the very point of the account. The creation story is all about ordering. That God might create in an orderly fashion—even artistically arranged—is not surprising. Has anyone ever read about the symmetry of a snowflake or a rose or the designs on many reptiles and concluded that the writer must be inventing the order and beauty he describes? Israel's God is a God of order and beauty. More, he is a God of wisdom. To know the order of the universe and to have arranged that order is part of the wisdom of God (see Job 38–39; Ps. 104:24).[13]

But we have not exhausted this sublime account when we note its parallel structure. There is another thread woven through the passage. It is going somewhere. The trees bear fruit. For whom? The lights are created to mark out days, seasons, and years. But for whom? On the sixth day, the Creator's activity comes to a sudden time-out. A divine discussion is held. God's creative work is climaxed by the creation of a being distinct from all others, a creature made in the image of God and therefore able to rule as his vice-regent over the lower creation (Gen. 1:26–28).[14]

Mankind—male and female—is the peak of God's creation. All that went before was designed with man as the climax. Genesis 1:1 said it simply: "In the beginning God created the heavens and the earth." Genesis 1:2–2:3 said it profoundly: Out of desolation, emptiness and chaos, God creates order and beauty and makes a habitation fit for a king—his royal creation and representative, mankind.

Torah in Genesis 1

Many valuable concepts, vital to the Israelite entering the Promised Land, are taught in Genesis 1. It is not too much to say that Israel's success or failure will depend upon her understanding about God and his relationship to mankind and the material universe as taught in this chapter. Here are a few of these vital truths.

Concept #1: God is the transcendent, sovereign ruler of the creation. He is in complete control. He is not a part of it. Nor does it control him. It came into existence at his command.[15] The earth is not a dead, defeated god. There is no god of the sea.[16] For the pagan, the world was a fearsome place. The large sea creatures were feared as semigods. "Baal's adversaries were gods like himself, or demons to be propitiated."[17] But for Israel there is only one God. The productive earth, the seasons, and the light were all good gifts from the hand of God; provided in his original creation. These gifts are not dependent on cultic magic or the whim of gods, but are gracious provisions from the very first. This is why praise to the Creator is in order. This is Moses' very warning to the Israelites in Deuteronomy 8. They are ready to enter the land. They have seen God's direct, supernatural provision of food in the wilderness. But when they settle in the land and harvest abundant crops, they might say, "My power and the strength of my hands have produced this wealth for me" (Deut. 8:17). Such a viewpoint is rank heresy. They are to recognize God's hand in his provision for them even through these ordinary channels.

Centuries later, the apostle Paul would point out that failure to recognize the Creator and give him thanks was the critical first step toward the futility and darkness of idolatry and moral chaos (Rom. 1:18–23). The fallen culture around Israel believed that nature was nonregular, that it depended on the interaction of the gods and on human attempts to influence them. Today our culture has largely accepted the idea of regularity, but ironically it is a regularity originated by chance and upheld in randomness. The failure is the same: failure to honor God by recognizing the creation as a gracious, regular provision for which thanksgiving to the sovereign Creator is appropriate.

Concept #2: The surrounding gods are nonentities. Genesis 1 is one of the most remarkable put-downs ever administered. Without even mentioning them, this passage undercuts the false gods. Of course, the events of this chapter go back beyond the time when these false religions arose. But the wording of the passage leaves no doubt that it intends to snub them. Words and phrases are chosen that intentionally belittle claims existing at Moses' time. The idea that the sea is the kingdom of another god, as we have seen, is rejected.[18] It is just water. The earth is merely land that can be seen when the sea is removed from it. But what of the stars, the sun, and the moon? The stars also are created—nothing more. The sun and the moon are downgraded to being "two great lights," a "greater light" and a "lesser light." Even the names "sun" and "moon" are avoided.[19] These are not gods with personal names but mere functionaries. Though belief in the power of the sun and stars pervades history (Deut. 4:19; 2 Kings 23:11; Isa. 47:13), "in these few simple sentences the lie is given to a superstition as old as Babylon and as modern as a newspaper horoscope."[20] No, the sun and moon and stars, far from controlling us, are to function for humanity's benefit. They provide a measuring device for time, to mark off seasons. How ironic and shameful that what God created for human benefit and service has "ruled" man. For those who avoid subjection to the true Creator God, the human mind accepts almost any folly, even subjecting itself to lesser things in the creation.

Concept #3: God has a special interest in mankind. "In the Mesopotamian creation account man's creation is almost incidental. He is there to serve the whimsical pleasures of the gods, giving them food and satisfying their personal needs."[21] But in the Genesis record man is the apex of God's creative work. Earlier acts of creation anticipate man's needs. The step-by-step march of the narrative is broken by a divine conference before the final step is taken: "Let us make man in our image, in our likeness." Humanity is not special by accident. We bear a similarity to God that distinguishes us from all earlier creation. This similarity enables humanity to function as rulers of the earth under God's design. Because mankind images God and is at the pinnacle of God's creative work, people should recognize that it is entirely wrong to worship and serve images of the lower creation. It is a perversion of God's original calling for us to degrade our human position by setting material things and lower creatures in a higher position than ourselves. Sophisticated, twentieth-century Western cultures rarely bow before images of wood and stone, but often before creations of plastic, steel, and brick. Things of their own design control them (see Isa. 44:14–18). Men and women toil not as God's vice-regents but as a slaves to things.

FULFILLMENT OF GENESIS ONE

Creation does not stop in Genesis 1. Like many other concepts, it continues to develop as we journey to fulfillment of all God's purposes in Jesus—the author and completer of history. The teaching about the God of Israel as the true Creator God is a critical point in Israel's faith (see Ps. 33:6–11 and Isa. 42:5–9). This belief forms the groundwork for the first four commands of the

Decalogue (Ex. 20:1–8). Only the true Creator God deserves human worship and commitment, and he deserves it exclusively. Because of the profound wisdom evident in the creation, all people must bow in humble recognition of a sovereign and all-wise Creator, even when personal events and experiences go beyond man's ability to understand (cf. Job 38–39; Isa. 40:12–17).

Toward a New Creation

But the notion of creation does not stop there. It goes on to a final and glorious completion in a new creation. We have seen how God limited the fearful and negative elements of verse two and so made them a part of an ordered creation. The chaotic waters became the sea, which in turn became the habitat for the various forms of sea life. The total darkness becomes limited to nighttime and is further dispelled by the lesser light of the moon. Darkness and the sea, however, still hold for humanity a reminder of life as chaos—life apart from the Creator (see Pss. 107:10–14; 139:7–12; Isa. 60:1–3). But that is not the final story. This creation, marred by sin as recorded in Genesis 3, must yield to a new creation. It is not, however, simply a return to conditions of the original creation. It is an advance—a creation that does away with even the suggestion of original chaos. Compare the differences between the original creation and the new creation as prophesied in the book of Revelation.

Figure 1.2

Initial Chaos	Creation	New Creation
Darkness	Darkness limited to nighttime	No night (Revelation 22:5)
Darkness	Light and darkness controlled by sun and moon	No sun and moon (Revelation 21:23)
Covered by waters	Waters limited to the sea	No sea (Revelation 21:1)

This new creation is possible only because of the work of Jesus Christ, who as the Light of the world vanquishes both moral and physical darkness. There is a new "In the beginning" (John 1:1)—a new story of creation that begins with the Son of God who was with God in the beginning, created all things, and is life and light (John 1:1–5). Today as the light of the world he vanquishes darkness and provides life on an individual basis for his followers: "I am the light of the world. Whoever follows me will never walk in darkness, but will have the light of life" (John 8:12). In the future, he is also the one who will illumine the final habitation of believing men: "And the city does not need the sun or the moon to shine on it, for the glory of God gives it light, and the Lamb is its lamp" (Rev. 21:23).

The Journey to Humanity's Rulership

The special place of man, so central in the Creator's plan in Genesis 1, is celebrated elsewhere in Scripture. The most notable case is Psalm 8. Harking back to this creation account, King David marvels at the splendor and majesty of Yahweh in the creation. He sees the God of Creation as still able to show his strength through those regarded as weak (v. 2). But mostly the King praises God for the position God has given. Humanity is endowed with "glory and majesty"—a summary of the image of God. Man has been given rulership over God's creative work (vv. 6–8). Psalm 8 celebrates man's position but does not explore the problem of sin and man's subsequent failure to appropriately exercise that rulership. New Testament writers quote the psalm a number of times, in each case tying the truth about man's rule to the work of Jesus. The writer of Hebrews is bold to note (2:5–10) that though the psalmist says God has subjected all things under humanity, "Yet at present we do not yet see everything subjected to him [mankind]." There is a problem. God as Creator subjected all things to man—male and female. That was the original commission. But in practice, complete subjection has never taken place. The answer? "But we do see Jesus, who for a little while was made lower than the angels, now crowned with glory and honor" (2:9 NRSV). Jesus became man in order to bring to pass God's plan for mankind—a plan that could never come to pass under fallen humans who are unable to bring the earth into a state of righteous rule under God.

Jesus is the perfect man who becomes the perfect author of salvation for humanity through his death on the cross. Because of this, he alone is able to bring man to the place of honor and glory that God intended for him (Heb. 2:9–10). Even so, we do not yet see this full subjection. Jesus has been given authority over everything, and in that sense God already has put "all things under His feet" (Eph. 1:22; quoting Ps. 8:6). But we still live in a fallen world where injustice and man's inhumanity to mankind too often prevail. We await Christ's return when "he must reign until he has put all his enemies under his feet" (1 Cor. 15:25). Under the rule of Jesus Christ, the perfect man, God will bring all things into the order and design he originally intended. Jesus himself will present this harmonious kingdom back to the Father. Then everyone will recognize that there is no God besides Yahweh, the God of Israel. God will be all in all (15:28). Creation will be complete.

SUGGESTED SCRIPTURE READING:
Genesis 1:1–2:3
Job 38:4–21
Psalm 8
Revelation 21:1–4 and 22:1–5
Hebrews 2:5–9

For Interaction and Discussion:

1. What problems were solved for the Israelites by understanding God's creation of the world?

2. Check out each of the following mythical beliefs. Is each mostly "ancient" or "modern"?

- astrology
- materialism
- polytheism
- idolatry
- sun worship
- belief in the irregularity of nature
- culturally approved perversion and violence
- "chance" as the cause of life

3. Why is thanksgiving an important response to God as Creator? What is the result of failing to be thankful?

4. What importance is given in Genesis to the creation of humanity? Why is being created in the image of God significant? What is our place in the creation? What does this mean regarding human responsibility and the environment today?

5. Why is everything not in subjection to mankind now? What has been accomplished by Jesus to advance God's program for human rule?

6. Why do you think light and darkness have become synonymous with truth and error? In what sense is Jesus the light (John 1:1–18)?

For Further Reading:

Derek Kidner. *Genesis*. Downers Grove, Ill.: InterVarsity, 1967. Solid, insightful commentary on Hebrew text for the English reader.

Allen P. Ross. *Creation and Blessing*. Grand Rapids: Baker, 1988, 101–16. Helpful with structure and theology.

Gerhard Hasel. "The Polemic Nature of the Genesis Cosmology." *EQ*, 46 (1974): 82–88.

Ronald Youngblood. *The Genesis Debate*. Nashville: Nelson, 1986.

Gordon J. Wenham. *Genesis 1–15*. WBC. Waco, Tex.: Word, 1982. Academic commentary on the Hebrew text.

Notes and Comments:

[1]See W. F. Albright, *Archaeology and the Religion of Israel*, 5th ed. (Baltimore: Johns Hopkins Press, 1968), 73.

[2]U. Cassuto, *The Goddess Anath*, trans. by Israel Abrahams (Jerusalem: Magnes Press, 1971), 65.

[3]*Epic of Baal*, Tablet V AB, 2nd section, lines M, N, as translated in Cassuto, *The Goddess Anath*, 89.

[4]Ibid., Tablet V AB, 5th section, lines O, P, 99.

[5]For examples of deceit and murder among gods see "A Babylonian Theogony" in *ANET*, 517–18. For intrigue among the gods see *Enûma Elish*, Tablet 1. For a more detailed coverage of pagan cosmology as the background of Genesis 1 see Gerhard F. Hasel, "The Significance of the Cosmology of Genesis 1 in Relation to Ancient Near Eastern Parallels," *Andrews University Seminary Studies*, 10 (1972): 19.

[6]Most ancient and modern philosophies recognize the necessity of starting with some concept of God and his relationship to the world. Some recent philosophies, however, have attempted to start with a denial of any reality beyond the natural. These lead inevitably to nihilism, despair, or a denial of rationality. For a helpful analysis of worldviews see James W. Sire, *The Universe Next Door*, 2d ed. (Downers Grove, Ill.: InterVarsity, 1988).

[7]We have called *Enûma Elish* "the Babylonian creation story." This should be qualified with the reminder that pagan "creation stories" were not attempts at historical cosmologies but were intended primarily for magical, ritual recitation to influence natural events. Cf. Alexander Heidel, *The Babylonian Genesis* (Chicago: Univ. of Chicago Press, 1951), 10–11, 16–17; and Bruce K. Waltke, "The Creation Account in Genesis 1:1–3," *BSac*, 132 (1975): 327.

[8]*Enûma Elish*, Tablet IV, lines 137–40, as translated in Heidel, *The Babylonian Genesis*, 42. To make the quotation easier to read, I have omitted the indicators for supplied and partially missing words.

[9]Heidel, *The Babylonian Genesis*, 9. Other views of creation in the ancient Near East are summarized in Gerhard F. Hasel, "The Polemic Nature of the Genesis Cosmology," *EQ*, 46 (1974): 87–88.

[10]*Enûma Elish*, Tablet V, lines 50–60, translated in *ANET*, 501–2. The translator's editorial marks have been omitted.

[11]A variety of interpretations have been suggested for verses 1–3. These are discussed in Bruce K. Waltke, "The Creation Accounts in Genesis 1:1–3," 25–36, 136–44, 216–28, 327–42; and Mark F. Rooker, "Genesis 1:1–3: Creation or Re-Creation?" *BSac*, 149 (1992): 316–23, 411–27. The articles debate the two main views. The precreation chaos view (Waltke) sees the arrangement of Genesis 1:1–3 as parallel to that of the beginning of the next account in 2:4–7: 2:4 is a summary statement, similar to 1:1; 2:5, as in 1:2, gives a description of the prevailing conditions as the action begins; 2:7 begins the details of the story, as does 1:3 (Day One).

This parallel pattern shows that 1:2 should be understood as providing the background conditions that exist and for which the creation (summary statement) of 1:1, creative details in 1:3 ff., is the Creator's response.

Rooker defends the traditional view that sees 1:1, not as a summary of the chapter but as the first creative act producing the desolate, water-covered planet of 1:2. Genesis 1:3 begins a second stage of creation that builds on the first stage of 1:1–2. Rooker describes this traditional view (held by Calvin, Luther, etc.) as "the initial chaos view," meaning that the initial stage of God's creative activity in 1:1 involves the creation of the earth as described in 1:2—chaos. This is in contrast to the "precreation chaos view" of Waltke, so labeled because the chaos of verse 2 precedes the creative activities of 1:3ff. and therefore the summary of that activity in 1:1 as well. Von Rad agrees that 1:2 speaks of such a "preprimeval period," but insists that verse 2 nonetheless comes under the general truth of verse 1. Cf. Gerhard von Rad, *Genesis*, rev. ed. (Philadelphia: Westminster, 1972), 50–51.

Figure 1.3

Initial Chaos (Traditional) View	
Stage 1: 1:1–2	**Stage 2: 1:3–31**
Original Creation out of nothing announced and described (desolate & empty)	Creation continues over six days
Precreation Chaos View		

1:1	1:2	1:3–31
Summary statement	State of planet as God begins creative activity (chaos)	Details of the creation of "heavens and earth"

Variations on these two views abound. Cf. John Sailhamer, "Genesis," *EBC*, 2:19–34, who follows the traditional reading of verse 1, but argues that the creation of the heavens in verse 1 necessarily includes the creation of the sun as does the division of day and night on day 1. This, along with the creation of the expanse and naming it "heavens" ("sky," NIV) on day 2 raises some interesting questions about duplication for the traditional view.

It is not within the scope of this survey to evaluate the strengths and weaknesses of these two predominate views. My conclusions regarding the theology of the account can be accepted by both views.

[12]Von Rad, *Genesis*, 49, takes *Elohim* in a figurative sense—meaning "great" as in the expression, "mountains of God" for great mountains. This combined with translating *Ruah* ("spirit") by its alternate meaning as "wind" produces the idea of a great wind as an additional element of chaos in 1:2. As it would be difficult, however, to expect the readers to take *Elohim* as figurative here when it is used in its normal sense for God in 1:1 and throughout the chapter, the traditional translation

"Spirit of God" is preferable. Cf. U. Cassuto, *A Commentary on the Book of Genesis*, I (Jerusalem: Magnes Press, 1961), 24, who concurs.

[13]Those holding that the account is presenting Israel with a true, inspired synopsis of the Creator's work divide into three camps concerning the days of Genesis. (1) The days are represented as normal temporal days and present a chronological order of God's creative activity. Cf. Robert C. Newman, "Are the Events in the Genesis Creation Account Set Forth in Chronological Order? Yes," *The Genesis Debate*, ed. Ronald Youngblood (Nashville: Nelson, 1986), 36–55; Henry M. Morris, *The Genesis Record* (Grand Rapids: Baker, 1976), 53–81. (2) The days as longer periods of time that overlap (Day-Age Theory), so roughly matching modern geology, combined with a view of progressive creationism, roughly matching the spread of development espoused by modern paleontology while rejecting the method of evolution (cf. Kidner, *Genesis*, 54–58). (3) The account is a distinct literary genre—a literary-artistic presentation of God's creation. In this case days are normal, but figurative, nonchronological, and form the structure for an almost hymnic presentation of God's complete creation. God's wise ordering is said to be graphically but not literally communicated by this highly patterned and structured presentation of creation. Cf. Mark A. Throntveit, "Are the Events in the Genesis Creation Account Set Forth in Chronological Order? No," *The Genesis Debate*, 36–55; Henri Blocher, *In the Beginning* (Downers Grove, Ill.: InterVarsity, 1984); Gordon J. Wenham, *Genesis 1–15*, WBC (Waco, Tex.: Word, 1987), 1:39–40.

Interestingly enough, Cassuto, *Genesis,* 1, 12–16, 42–43, is usually cited by those taking a symbolic literary approach for the numerous literary features (in addition to the pattern of days), which for him shows the high ordering of the account for theological purposes (10 commands, patterns of 7s and 3s); yet he also explains any supposed chronological contradictions within this account and between this account and Genesis 2. These are differences upon which these scholars built the argument that the days are meant to be understood as figurative by the author. He also observes that the normal pattern for pairs of days in Akkadian and Ugaritic literature is 1 with 2, 3 with 4, then 5 with 6, not as here.

[14]Cf. F. Delitzsch, *New Commentary on Genesis,* trans. Sophia Taylor (Edinburgh: T. & T. Clark, 1888–89), 100; and von Rad, *Genesis*, 59. The image of God in man is not dominion itself. The dominion is the result of the image. Neither is "male and female" the image, but rather an indication of the scope of the image. Most Old Testament scholars relate the idea of "image" to the practice of kings in setting up their statues in lands over which they were claiming dominion. Man, then, is to be God's representative, proclaiming and implementing God's rule over earth. Cf. Hans Walter Wolff, *Anthropology of the Old Testament* (Philadelphia: Fortress, 1974), 159–65. That man was given the creative capacities (mental, emotional, moral) to operate as God's regent, of course, follows. Many Hebrew scholars prefer to translate "as the image of God" rather than "in the image of God."

[15]This creation by the word of God (Ps. 33:9; 2 Peter 3:5) is distinctive. The closest parallel is the use of words in Egypt in a superstitious way to repeat a magical

formula. The commanding of creation and naming of the elements of creation demonstrate God's sovereignty and distinguish him from the material world.

[16]The use of the term *têhom* in Genesis 1:2 for the "deep" has been seen by some to be a link to the Babylonian creation story where Ti'amat is the primordial saltwater ocean goddess. Hasel, "The Significance of the Cosmology of Genesis 1," 7, points out that though the words derive from a common Semitic root, there is no direct borrowing. In fact, "the description of the depersonalized, undifferentiated, unorganized, and the passive state of *têhom* in Genesis 1:2 is not due to any influence from non-Israelite mythology but is motivated through the Hebrew conception of the world. In stating the conditions in which this earth existed before God commanded the light should spring forth, the author of Genesis 1 rejected explicitly contemporary mythological notions." Cf. Hasel, "The Polemic Nature of the Genesis Cosmology," 82–85.

[17]Derek Kidner, *Genesis* (Downers Grove, Ill.: InterVarsity, 1967), 49. See Hasel, "The Polemic Nature of the Genesis Cosmology," 85–87, for the discussion of myths regarding sea monsters. In Genesis 1:21 and Psalm 104:25–26, the large sea creatures are simply creations of God—nothing more. Waltke discusses this sea monster motif as found in the rest of the Old Testament in *BSac*, 132 (1975): 32–36.

[18]See previous note 17 for the rejection of Genesis 1 of the mythological notion of the sea.

[19]Von Rad, *Genesis,* 55.

[20]Kidner, *Genesis,* 49.

[21]R. Dennis Cole, "Foundations of Wisdom Theology in Genesis One to Three," (unpublished Th. M. thesis; Portland, Ore.: Western Conservative Baptist Seminary, 1978), 14. Cf. Hasel, "The Significance of the Cosmology of Genesis 1."

chapter two

THE STORY OF HUMAN RELATIONSHIPS
(Genesis 2–3)

Blood will I form and cause bone to be;
Then I will set up lullû, *"Man" shall be his name!*
Yes, I will create lullû: *Man!*
Upon him shall the services of the gods be imposed
    that they may be at rest.[1]

"Who am I?" is a modern question, but the need to know our place in the world is as old as creation. According to the Babylonian creation legend above, Marduk creates people to make life easier for the gods. The God of the Bible, however, does not need food and drink. Rather than being a taker, God is a giver. As Paul puts it, God "is not served by human hands, as if he needed anything, because he himself gives all men life and breath and everything else" (Acts 17:25).

Genesis 1 featured a sovereign Creator who shaped the material world for humankind, male and female. Our story provides a second dimension to the picture of life as God intended it. As before, *telling the story* communicates most effectively human place and significance.

THE STORY OF HUMANITY

Like Genesis 1, our story opens with a summary title (2:4) followed by the prevailing situation (2:4–6)—which God's action will change.

TITLE: "This is the account of the heavens and the earth when they were created."

SITUATION: "When the LORD God made the earth and the heavens, no shrub of the field had yet appeared on the earth and no plant of the field had yet sprung up; the LORD God had not sent rain on the earth and there was no man to work the ground, but streams came up from the earth and watered the whole surface of the ground."

The problem is clear. Certain things have not occurred because man's creation is still future.[2] This story, then parallels the sixth day of the initial creation account. It is written, however, not to fill in details or make corrections, as if something were left out of the majestic account of Genesis 1, but to give us information designed to help us understand our place and situation in the world in which we find ourselves.

God's Care and Provision

If you want to know about relationships you need to understand events and interaction. I can give you facts about my children—current height and weight, birthdays, physical characteristics. But you still know nothing of my relationship to them. You would learn better by hearing or seeing normal or significant events in our lives—glimpses of play, of tucking them into bed as youngsters, scenes of discipline, stories of working together, times of laughing together, crying together.

Figure 2.1

The *Toledoths*

The Book of Genesis begins with the prologue of creation (1:1–2:3). This is followed by 11 divisions, which are introduced by the Hebrew word *Toledoth,* as follows:

Creation (1:1–2:3)
Toledoth of the heavens and earth (2:5–4:26)
Toledoth of Adam (5:1–6:8)
Toledoth of Noah (6:9–9:26)
Toledoth of the sons of Noah: Shem, Ham, & Japeth (10:1–11:9)
Toledoth of Shem (11:10–26)
Toledoth of Terah (11:27–25:11)
Toledoth of Ishmael (25:12–18)
Toledoth of Isaac (25:19–35:29)
Toledoth of Esau (36:1–36:8)
Toledoth of Esau (36:9–37:1)
Toledoth of Jacob (37:2–50:26)

The term *Toledoth* is variously translated in the versions as "the generations of," "the line of," "the account of," "the story of." The stories that follow each title often include a genealogy of descendants or the story of the descendants.

Our story gives us those scenes that are necessary for the ancient Israelites to understand who they are and what their relationship to God can be. They learn that humans, like the animals, are created from the ground (2:7, 19) and are physical beings. In Genesis 1 this was indicated by creation on the same day as the animals. Physically, humans are like the animals . . . some more than others! But people are also more than animals. Mankind was created in the image of God. In Genesis 2 the special nature of humanity is marked out by the personal way God gives to man the breath of life. By this direct transfusion, Adam becomes a "living being."[3] Though Adam is not deity, he has a special tie to God—the tie of personal relationship initiated by God himself.

But this tie of a personal creation is not the only indication of God's special relationship to humanity. What follows in the account is a series of actions in which God's special care for the man is demonstrated. First, God's care is evident by God's provision of a "paradise" (2:8–17). Adam's home is a bountiful, parklike garden. This new inhabitant of earth will not have to scrap and scratch for food. Unlike the image many have of Eden's garden, this is no Walden Pond. No placid creek with pond here but a massive and mighty river, suitable for wide-scale irrigation. It is superior to the rivers later civilizations relied on. Northwesterners should think bigger than the Columbia. Midwesterners, the Mississippi. Egyptians, the Nile. In this magnificent setting the human species could begin exercising creativity and rule by cultivating, pruning, and otherwise caring for the garden. There is no rush to subdue the whole earth. No one's in a hurry. Yahweh has provided a productive beachhead from which to start. As the human race grows, the model garden can be creatively extended.

Additionally, in his great kindness Yahweh designates all the trees in the garden as sources for food. Adam need not ask divine permission. He does not have to pray about it. This is his realm by God's sovereign appointment. Of course, there is a minor restriction (2:17), but it is the *abundance of provision* that is stressed here. "The prohibition (v. 17) is completely embedded in the description of God's fatherly care for man."[4] Even the prohibition of this one fruit must be for good. Its mention along with the penalty prepares us for future events that are equally important for understanding ourselves.

The climax of God's care is the gift of the creative counterpart. The creation of humanity, both male and female, was the high point of Genesis 1. Likewise, in recounting God's care for the man in Genesis 2, the provision of the woman is the final and most special provision. Only in this context do the words "not good" appear in describing God's creation. The announcement "It is not good for the man to be alone" does not contradict the "very good" of Genesis 1:31. Creation is "very good" *after* the creation of both male and female in that account. But man without his female counterpart forms an incomplete humanity—lacking true companionship and the ability to procreate (cf. Gen. 1:28). So crucial is this creation of the woman that it is preceded by a heavenly discussion (2:18). Only creation in the image of God merited such a discussion in chapter 1.

Now comes a parade! The heavenly discussion is followed, not by woman's creation as we might expect, but by a parade of the animals created by God.[5] Adam initiates rule over the creation by naming them. In the ancient world the right to name indicates rule.[6] As God's agent, Adam begins to organize and order the creation. Yet, there is a more basic reason for this zoo-in-motion in the narrative: "But for Adam no suitable helper was found" (2:20). Of course, there wasn't. God was not surprised. Remember verse 18? But now Adam knew his need.

And so God creates the woman. His "fanciful" method displays his wisdom. By using a part of the man to create the woman, there can be no doubt that the woman is on the same level as Adam.[7] To deny her is to deny himself. Commitment to each other and dependence on each other must be total. Adam recognizes the significance of God's action, but even more, celebrates the unique value of the gift of God. The first preserved words of human history are not the primeval grunt of a narrow-browed Neanderthal, but poetry:

> This is now bone of my bones
>   and flesh of my flesh;
> She shall be called "woman,"
>   because she was taken out of man (Gen. 2:23).[8]

Poetry in recognition of woman! Poetry in recognition of marriage—of two, male and female, becoming one flesh to propagate and rule. Of two whose transparent relationship did not include shame.

And so, here is our first answer to "Who am I?" The Babylonian myth would answer, "You are a product of the gods to make their life easier." Modern myth would assert, "You are a product of random chance in a purposeless universe." The Bible says, "You are a personal creation of Yahweh, who cares for you, has created you male and female, and has placed you in an orderly and good creation as his representative ruler." This knowledge of God's order and created relationships is considered obsolete by many today. As a result, our age suffers the anxiety of enjoying no secure place or significance in the world.

The Temptation and Fall

The earlier prohibition against eating from "the tree of the knowledge of good and evil" was introduced as the only restriction in an overwhelming and abundant provision by God (2:16–17). What kind of a tree was it? Certainly *not* an apple tree. Its name is provided: a "knowledge-of-good-and-evil" tree.

But what was its significance? Why was it there? First, we should note that this was not a sinister tree. All of God's creation was pronounced "good" by the divine author himself. The name "good and evil" does not brand the tree as partially evil. As in English when we say we "searched high and low," two opposites are chosen to include everything in between. In Genesis 1:1, "heavens and earth" includes the whole solar system. In Psalm 139:2, David says that God knows him when he sits down and rises up. This does not limit God's knowledge only to those two occasions but to those actions and all others in between. The knowledge of good and evil then involves knowing the whole moral spectrum, just as the tree of life related to living forever. This tree, then, has to do with moral knowledge.[9]

Though participating in both good and evil is not good, moral knowledge is good. And Genesis confirms our conclusion, for God himself knows good and evil: "The man has now become like one of us, knowing good and evil" (3:22). The New Testament understands this expression in the same way, describing the spiritual person as marked by this very quality: "But solid food is for the mature, who because of practice have their senses trained to discern good and evil" (Heb. 5:14 NASB). Infants lack this discernment (Deut. 1:39), and King Solomon prays for it as part of the wisdom he desires (1 Kings 3:9).

It is good to be able to make moral distinctions—to tell right from wrong. We can only conclude that God in some way intended to use this tree and its presence in the garden to bring the man and woman to a mature level of moral perception. Would they have been commanded to partake after a trial period of willingly abstaining? Or would abstaining from the tree's fruit itself be the key ingredient to learning the main issue in moral discernment? We cannot say. We can know only that God's creation of the tree was for a positive purpose.

The introduction of the serpent in 3:1 begins the temptation narrative. Here is another conundrum. The text informs us that the serpent was "more crafty than any of the wild animals the LORD God had made." This immediately alerts the Israelite reader that a real serpent is in view—not a serpent as found in many of the myths.[10] But this leaves us unprepared for the remainder of the narrative. As much as any Israelite of Moses' time, we are surprised to read of a talking serpent. Not only does the serpent talk, but it reasons—to a degree that is convincing to a human! Beyond all this, the serpent knows about the prohibition. And, the serpent is already bent toward evil purposes—how so in a good creation?

No answers to this dilemma are provided. We are forbidden by the passage to make the scene mythical. We seem forbidden by the conversation to make the serpent one of God's good creatures and nothing more.[11] It is clear from the narrative that a sinister mind is at work in the serpent. The ancient

Israelite readers were aware of the use of the serpent as a god.[12] They also recognized that false gods were demonic (Deut. 32:17). All of this agrees with the view of New Testament writers who identify the serpent with Satan (see John 8:44; Rev. 12:9; Rom. 16:20; 1 Cor. 10:20). Our account of the entrance of sin into human experience assumes an already fallen intelligence—devilishly so![13]

The serpent approaches the woman, who already knows about the forbidden tree, though the command not to eat of it was given prior to her creation (2:16–17). Perhaps Adam was responsible for communicating this to her. As is typical to the present day, the temptation calls into question the reality of the word of God: "Did God really say . . ." Beyond this, the serpent wants to *focus on the restriction*: "Did God really say, 'You must not eat from any [literally, 'every'] tree in the garden?'"

Though the woman is quick to the defensive, her reply shows that the serpent succeeded in directing her to focus on the single prohibition. Eve's reply differs in at least three ways from the original command.[14]

Figure 2.2

Original Command	Eve's Reply
"You are free to eat from any [every] tree in the garden."	"From the trees of the garden, we may eat."
Tree of life is in the middle of the garden (cf. 2:9, NRSV).	Tree of knowledge of good and evil is in the middle.
"You must not eat from the tree of the knowledge of good and evil."	God did say, "You must not eat … and you must not touch it."

Some of these distinctions may be insignificant. In the first, the original command emphasizes the generosity of God's provision of every tree for food—the restriction is seen as slight. Eve's response fails to emphasize the generosity but states it only as simple permission: "We may eat . . ." Her answer is truthful, but lacks the enthusiasm for God's goodness.[15] The second comparison may also be insignificant. Here the restricted tree is identified as being in the center. The original description places the tree of life as in the center (cf. NRSV on 2:9). Eve's geography may not be that poor. The forbidden tree is closely associated with the tree of life and may also be with it toward the center of the garden (cf. NIV on 2:9). But, even so, Eve's identification of the tree of the knowledge of good and evil as in the middle overlooks entirely the tree of life with its positive appeal. Again, the serpent has been successful at focusing her thoughts on the restriction.[16]

The third distinction, however, seems very significant. Eve adds to the original restriction against eating. Not only are they not to eat from the tree, but they are not to *touch it*. Again, the restriction looms larger than it really is.

At this point, the serpent's reply becomes more bold (3:4–5). Now that the woman is focusing on the restriction, he contradicts God's warning about the penalty in the most direct way possible. Where God had said, "You will surely die" (2:17), the tempter literally says, "You shall surely not die" (3:3, author's translation).[17] He must relieve Eve of the idea that she will suffer the announced penalty. He says in effect, "You won't reap what you sow." To make this contradiction of God's word seem reasonable, Satan invents a false motive for God. God, he says, has really invented a nonexistent penalty to keep you in your place. He is afraid you will rise to his level. If you knew as much as God knows, you would become a threat to him.

Eve's response is fatal. She divorces her God-given reason from God's word and relies instead on her own limited experience. The tree looks good. And it was, wasn't it? Eve eats and gives to Adam who also eats, and so disobedience is invented. Here is one case where necessity is not the mother of invention.

The Immediate Results of Sin

Here comes the clothes! Earlier the narrative described the original couple as naked and not ashamed (2:25). Now they immediately recognize their nakedness *as a source of shame* and attempt to clothe themselves. This is remarkable when one considers that they were the only humans around! A Jewish commentator summarizes the original view of nakedness before the Fall: "They looked upon the sexual organs in the same way as we regard the mouth, the face and hands."[18] This has not been true since. Adam and Eve quickly set about to remedy their sense of shame with temporary garments. This partial remedy was continued by God with more substantial clothing (3:21) that has remained a social necessity. Throughout the Scripture the concept of nakedness and shame are connected (cf. Ezek. 23:29; Rev. 3:17–18). It was not so from the beginning.

A second experience previously unknown was a sense of fear arising from guilt. The human pair hide themselves from God—as best they can. God comes and graciously directs a discussion in a way that gives them opportunity to recognize and fully confess their sin.[19] Adam admits to fear (3:10). This fear, arising out of his sense of shame, separates him from an open, transparent relationship with God. So he hides. "Fear and shame are henceforth the incurable stigmata of the Fall in man."[20]

If these first two responses sound as modern as a page in the local psychiatrist's notebook, the third reaction of man does nothing to lessen the impression. The man attempts to avoid personal responsibility by shifting blame to the woman and ultimately to God himself: "The woman you put here with me—she gave me some of the fruit, and I ate it" (3:12). The woman shifts responsibility to the serpent (3:13).

A close look at the order of this interrogation plus the order of the cursing that follows suggests again the theme of the divine order of creation. The order is called a chiasm. It involves a mirror-imaging arrangement, starting and finishing at the same place. It goes like this:

A: The man is addressed (3:9–11)
    B: The woman is addressed (3:13)
        C: The serpent is cursed (3:14–15)
    B': The woman is cursed (3:16)
A': The man is cursed (3:17–19)

A few observations are in order. The series begins with the man and ends with the man. Eve's answer indicates a clear reversal of the divine order: Male and female were to have dominion over the beasts (1:26). God does not accept Adam's excuse either (3:17). Listening to his mate rather than submitting to the divine order is soundly rejected. The serpent is not interrogated—another indication that this is a previously bent personality.

At this point it is possible to suggest a reason for the temptation coming in the form of a serpent as well as why the woman was tempted first. The order of temptation is a reversal of the divine order: A beast tempts the woman and the woman decides apart from and for the man. The theme of the divine order and the satanic desire to incite rebellion against God's rule makes this format for the temptation especially potent. It is a satanic *coup d'etat!* Satan not only incites them to sin in direct disobedience and rebellion against a divine command, but the sin also directly flouts the divine order. Humanity's charge to rule over the beasts is violated, and Adam capitulates his moral leadership.[21]

According to 3:22, what the serpent said came true. They became like God. They knew good and evil. Their eyes were opened (3:7). But all this occurred in the most perverse way, rather than in the way God intended. They learned good and evil by adding sinful experience to the good creation they had already known. But one thing the serpent said was not at all true: Death surely did come to the first human couple on the day they ate. Adam had been created from the ground with the capacity to die; he was mortal— though as long as he remained faithful to God death could not touch him. But as soon as he sinned, death came. Adam, like Paul in Romans 7:11, could say, "Sin . . . put me to death"—though both men were still breathing. Death was first seen in man's guilt and fear before God. It would ultimately send man's body back to the dust (Gen. 3:19).

A THEOLOGY OF RELATIONSHIPS

The story of Genesis 2 and 3 is a theology of relationships. It is here to provide a theological anthropology for the ancient Israelite.

> The creation of humans includes the living space (the garden), the means of life (the fruit of the garden), the occupation or work (cultivate and preserve), and the community (man and woman) and, as a medium of the community, language. This complex understanding of the creation of human life has largely been overlooked. . . . [It] is a matter—in the relationship to God as well—of people in all their relationships . . .: living space, nourishment, work, and the social realm.[22]

Relationship to Yahweh God

Our story of the heavens and earth (2:7) is the story of relationship to the Creator and his care for his creation. It is not enough to know that God is the sovereign Creator. The Israelite must realize that Yahweh cares. Knowing God as Creator calms our fears about a hostile and irrelevant world. Knowing that God initiates and desires personal relationship and fellowship with those created to image him motivates love and response. God's personal commitment to man began by personally breathing into man life itself and by providing a productive environment. But most striking to the Israelite must have been God's immediate presence in the garden. There was direct fellowship with God at the very first (cf. 3:8–9). If Eden were England, teatime would have been anticipated with great delight!

Moreover, God is called *Yahweh* in Genesis 2. Genesis 1 used the title *Elohim*, the general title for the Supreme Being—"God" in English. Genesis 2 adds the name *Yahweh* to the title *Elohim*. Yahweh is the personal name for God and stresses his covenant relationship to his people.[23] Its presence here supports the central theme: *Yahweh, the true Creator God and God of Israel, created humanity personally and desires only good for them.*

Of course, this original fellowship was ruined by sin, but this does not make our story of the original relationship irrelevant for later readers. The same Yahweh revealed here is the Yahweh who delivered the Israelite readers from Egypt. His care and concern have not changed though the ideal circumstances have. He still wants to be with his people. This same Yahweh wants to give Israel a bountiful land "flowing with milk and honey." To enjoy this land—and God's fellowship as well—Israel, like Adam and Eve, must be faithful.

Our story, however, also answers the question of why things are not ideal—why bad things happen in the creation of a good Creator. The answer is that the creation *became fallen* due to human rebellion. Like the ancient Israelites we still witness a creation that clearly has strong elements of order, beauty, wisdom, and goodness—and yet also has elements of disorder, evil, ugliness, and folly.

Relationship to Order and Sovereignty

A major theme in our story is God's sovereignty over mankind. In turn, the animals are under human sovereignty. The order of male and female, however, is more complex—and has been ever since! The narrative clearly emphasizes the equality of the woman with the man, as has been noted. The word *helper* is often used of military allies as well as of God as man's helper (Hos. 13:9; Ps. 115:9–11). It does not imply inferiority. It is almost as if in the light of then current practices, the account is saying to each husband of ancient Israel: "Recognize your wife as an equal ally in the ruling of the earth. Rejoice in her as Adam did. Leave father and mother to cling to her"—a notion which certainly provides a note of balance to the prevailing practice. "The woman is not described as man's servant, his valet, his little errand girl whom he needs for this or that, but as the help equal and adequate to him."[24] The woman is misused if she is not treated as an equal ally in the human calling.

Yet there are also indications that seem to suggest a male/female functional order as well. The account starts with the male, and the counterpart is provided for him. Could it have been the other way around, or is there a significance to the fact that the woman is a gracious provision for the man (cf. 1 Cor. 11:8–9)?[25] The man names the animals, signifying rule. Both parents name children, an appropriate indication of the order of creation (4:25; 5:3). God names mankind (5:2). Does Adam's naming of his wife also signify an order within marriage (2:23; 3:20)? We have already suggested that the satanic attack is an attempt to reverse the divine order. This, as well as the order of God's confrontation and judgment, suggests that the narrative views Adam as having the final responsibility for moral leadership and accountability.[26]

Relationship to Evil

It is this entire arrangement that comes under satanic attack. A number of satanic strategies are evident. Earth clearly has become a battlefield between the good Creator and a sinister yet intelligent foe of God. Much like the story of Job, the enemy of God and humanity is out to show that God's creatures will not recognize his sovereignty nor will they abide by the wise order he lays upon his creation. Our story provides a model for the ancient reader and for us to recognize and counter such temptation. The apostle Paul told believers at Corinth, "We are not unaware of his [Satan's] schemes" (2 Cor. 2:11; cf. Eph. 6:11). No doubt this Scripture contributed greatly to that awareness! The temptation of Eve gives flesh and blood reality to the effectiveness of these several strategies:

Scheme #1: Satan attempts to have us view God's standards as unreasonable restrictions. The command not to eat of the tree of moral discernment involved no hardship for Adam and Eve. They did not go to bed hungry. There was no nutritional lack in their diet. There was even ample variety to avoid dietary boredom without this tree. Yet the temptation to focus on a limitation worked. The lesson is clear: God's people should focus on all the evidence that God has been gracious rather than on limitations that have not been explained. Doubting God's goodness, even in restrictions, sets us up for this failure. That the restriction was incidental and involved no sacrifice brings a further reflection: The more insignificant and unimportant the restriction, the more useful it may be for inspiring human rebellion. Two decades as a teacher and parent have confirmed the suspicion. Point out that the restriction (read, "injustice") being denounced is so small as to be hardly worth the effort and the reply most often will be: "That's what makes me so upset!"[27] Counting blessings one by one to rehearse the goodness of God is still good advice (1 Thess. 5:16–18; cf. Phil. 4:4–7).

Scheme #2: Satan questions what God has said. Eve may well have received her information secondhand from Adam. But even those who received it first-hand have found room to doubt it. Because God has spoken through selected individuals, it is always possible to doubt that the message of prophet and apostle is the message of God. In addition, there are always charlatans looking for a following or a full collection plate. To further complicate the picture, Satan often produces counterfeit or false prophets. So even for people of faith it is impossible to accept just anyone's word that he is speaking for God. Because of this, God provided strict objective tests for his people (Deut. 18:14–22). God's word will stand up to the tests that God himself has instructed his people to use. In this way they will avoid being duped by false claims.

When Eve was ready to judge the situation by her own limited understanding, the battle was all but over. The tree *looked* like a good tree, both nutritionally and aesthetically. And didn't it hold out the promise for greater wisdom, as its name suggested? From her perspective and with the facts in hand, it was *reasonable* to try this experience—if she allowed herself to become the judge of God's instruction. For us, the prophets and apostles of Scripture have already been clearly vindicated by miracle and fulfilled prophecy as spokesmen for God. To proclaim our own omniscience and reject their instruction can be a fatal mistake.

Scheme #3: Satan asserts that people will not reap what they sow. "God's restrictions are just attempts of formal religion to hold you in line," Satan repeats with defeating regularity, "God just doesn't want you to have fun." Just as many cigarette smokers believe they will be the exception to the health problems associated with tobacco smoke, so men and women seem ready to believe that somehow they will be exempted from the results of sin outlined in the Bible. What difference can this one sin make? God's limits are advance notices concerning how the creation works best. When we violate the divine blueprint, we learn by hard experience the tragic effects on ourselves, our futures, our families, and our fellowship with God.

Scheme #4: Satan encourages dissatisfaction with our God-appointed role. Ambition is noble if its antonym is laziness. But ambition can be destructive if it is based on dissatisfaction with how God has made me, his gifting of me, and the role in which I serve him. The serpent hooked Eve into the desire to not be limited by God. The tendency of mankind, male and female, is to "break their chains" and "throw off their fetters" (Ps. 2:3) when it comes to following any God-ordained leadership. Each of us finds ourselves in positions of both leadership and submission throughout our lives (cf. Rom. 13:1; Eph. 5:21–6:9). Scriptural leadership does not imply superiority. Too many men get all tangled up in the telephone booth trying to uncover their costume with the "S" on the chest. Nor does scriptural leadership suggest having one's own way. Giving up rights for others is a central concern of Scripture and this is to be most evident of those in leadership roles (cf. Phil. 2:1–13). Success is not measured by superior roles but by obeying God and following the divine order and responsibility in whatever servant role we find ourselves.

To discover God's created order and live by it is a major theme of the Old Testament. In Proverbs it is called "the fear of the LORD," and it is the beginning of wisdom itself. The narrative of Genesis 2–3 provides a model of order and relationships essential to understanding who we are and what we have become.

Relationship in Marriage

The initial male and female design, we are told, is God's plan for marriage (2:24). Though every man's wife is not formed from one of his ribs, God's design is that men seek a counterpart in life. When a man and woman come together in this way, they—like the first man and woman—become one in God's order.

This prescription for marriage was surprising for the ancient world. A man is to *leave* his father and mother and cling to his wife. The instruction is clear. The new unity is to be foremost—surpassing even the former loyalty to parents. In the patriarchal world no stronger affirmation could be made about commitment in relationship.[28]

Though sexual union is a significant part of this "clinging," sexual union by itself does not qualify as marriage. Even the betrothal contract is stronger than sexual union as a marriage claim (Deut. 22:23–27). Sexual union apart from public leaving is fornication. The backseat of a chariot is not an acceptable place to initiate marriage. The mother's tent, after public arrangements, is (Gen. 24:67). Fornication and adultery are perversions of the "one flesh" pattern of marriage, for they experience a "one flesh" physical experience without the commitment of marital unity and so stand condemned (cf. 1 Cor. 6:15–18).[29] Moderns may regard marriage as only "a piece of paper," but the created order is clear and the toll of social consequences for violation becomes clearer as we go.

Relationship to Vocation

Popular ideas of Eden's garden often include the picture of no responsibilities—as if Adam and Eve spent all their days on the beach. If Eden is no Walden, neither is it Sun City, Arizona. As we have seen, God gave humanity certain tasks. In 1:28 they are to subdue the earth. Even the garden God prepared is to be tilled, pruned, and cared for. Adam and Eve, created in God's image, like God himself engage in meaningful, creative activity. He is not made to graze all day without a creative thought, plan, or responsibility. Mankind, even in "paradise," has tasks and goals—and the freedom to carry them out creatively.

Keeping the wolf from the door, however, was not a concern. There was an abundance of food and a magnificently large river. Famine was not on the horizon. Work became a burden due to the tragedy of humanity's own making. But even after sin's entrance, work can be positive. Appropriately subduing and ruling the earth are still a human responsibility. As the Old Testament wisdom books (Proverbs, Ecclesiastes, and Job) clearly teach, "Man is meant for an orderly role in an orderly cosmos. His rightful duty is to discern that order and find his responsible share in it. Scientific endeavors, therefore, in the fields of biology, chemistry, geology, mathematics, forestry, and others, should be looked upon as honorable as they seek to discern the order of the universe."[30]

FULFILLMENT OF RELATIONSHIPS

Fulfillment of God's Presence

Why tell the Israelite of a time when life was lived in a much finer setting, when mankind had direct contact and fellowship with God? Sacrifice was not offered in the garden. No temple was needed as a place to approach God. No priesthood had been appointed. God himself visited Adam and Eve in the garden. The contrast with the daily experience of the normal Israelite is remarkable.

One reason this wonderfully open past relationship to God is recorded is to allow every man to understand why God does not communicate openly and directly today. Surely all serious people have wondered why God seems so difficult to talk to—and even more, to hear from! The Scriptures confirm that God hides himself from man. God's direct revelation to Moses was considered exceptional (Num. 12:6–8). Other prophets received their messages in dreams and visions (Num. 12:6), and the people received God's message through these prophets. Moses is said to have spoken "face to face" with God, and yet the same passage makes clear that he did not directly and fully view God (Ex. 33:11–23). In Eden, God communicated directly with man because man was perfect from God's creative hand. But, as we have seen, that perfection is no longer the case.

Though our story begins to explain why God's presence is hidden, there is another reason for it. It also points with hope to the future. The story of man's *formerly* open communication with God helps us understand the relationship God desires with man *now*. And so the story builds the foundation for what God will do in the future. In progressive stages, God is bringing to pass his plan in history for restoring man to direct fellowship with himself. With Christ, a new level beyond the revelation to Moses was reached (John 1:17–18). The instruction that came through Moses was direct, but the grace and truth revealed by the one who is God among us outshines Moses in glory. After the Day of Pentecost, every believer experiences a new level of fellowship with God (2 Cor. 3:18). Believers enjoy that restored relationship through Jesus Christ (Eph. 2:11–18).

But there is still *more to come*. One day we shall know *fully* just as we are fully known by God (1 Cor. 13:12). Then we shall be like our Savior, Jesus Christ, because "we shall see him as he is" (1 John 3:2). Then will come to pass the future blessing Jesus promised: "Blessed are the pure in heart, for they shall see God" (Matt. 5:8).

Fulfillment of Temptation

Before it is possible for humanity to fully experience God, the book on rebellion and sin must be closed. The beginning of the end of Satan's deception of mankind occurs in the life of Jesus of Nazareth. The original creation and humanity were victimized by the original liar and murderer, the Devil (John 8:44). God's plan for restoring humanity involves the victory of Jesus Christ over the Devil, temptation, and sin.

It is not surprising, therefore, to find that Jesus also faces satanic temptation in a one-on-one encounter. The Bible records only two temptations in which actual conversation takes place between the Devil and people. The first is in Eden. The other is with Jesus Christ. This is not coincidental. Neither is it coincidental that this second temptation follows the voice from heaven that declares Jesus to be the chosen Son with whom the Father is well pleased (Matt. 3:17; Luke 3:22). To make the point clearer, Luke even inserts the genealogy of this chosen Son at this very point in his narrative—between the heavenly announcement and the temptation account—tracing Jesus' lineage all the way back to . . . Adam![31]

Jesus, unlike Adam and Eve, is actually hungry, but he refuses to violate God's will and mission for him by making life easy through the misuse of supernatural power. He is willing to submit to the divine order and plan. There is no rebellion against his assigned and difficult role here!

Satan also tempts Jesus to seek rule and position independent of God (Luke 4:5–7). The Devil has always tempted people to think of themselves as captains of their own fate and souls. Those he has deceived always boast, "I will be like God," whether they are a king of Babylon (cf. Isa. 14:14), the director of a bank, or a hardworking grease-monkey. Jesus rejects this temptation and affirms the command of God. Though kingship will eventually be his, he will not take a shortcut by disobeying God's commands.

Jesus maintained his complete subjection to God's role for him throughout his earthly life, even though that role involved not only temptation but also suffering (Phil. 2:5–11). This qualified him as the author of salvation for all who follow him (Heb. 2:10; 5:8–10).

Not only did Jesus' death qualify him as the one to lead humanity into God's presence, it also marked the place of Satan's judgment. Spliced neatly into Jesus final instruction to his disciples on the way to the cross is a significant notation: "The prince of this world now stands condemned" (John 16:11). Because the usurper of the rule of this world would meet his judgment in Jesus' crucifixion, the disciples would be able to proclaim a message of freedom from the fear of death. Jesus died to "destroy him who holds the power of death—that is, the devil" (Heb. 2:14; cf. Col. 1:13).

With Satan judged at the cross, it's all over but the shooting. Real battles still occur. But, lest there be any doubt of the victory, Jesus was raised from the dead and ascended to the right hand of the Father. By this, his authority over every other power is guaranteed (Eph. 1:18–21). Those powers against which the Christian struggles in spiritual battle and temptation (Eph. 6:10–18) may be withstood in the might of the conquering King. The armor here is the armor that Isaiah predicted would be worn by the victorious King at his coming (cf. Isa. 11:5; 52:7; 59:17). *The believer may wear it now!* And we need to wear it, for the battle still rages all around us. When Paul heard of the obedience of the Roman Christians, he encouraged them with the fact that "the God of peace will soon crush Satan under your feet" (Rom. 16:20; cf. Gen. 3:15). Fellowships of believers, when obedient, may expect to fulfill the work of Jesus himself, extend his kingdom, and implement his victory over Satan even now.

Yet bullets are still flying. Sin and temptation have not been finally eradicated. The ammunition is live, and a person can still be wounded if he fails to follow orders. These battlefield conditions are not a New Eden. When the Corinthians were acting superior, Paul chided them with these words: "Already you have all you want! Already you have become rich! You have become kings—and that without us! How I wish that you really had become kings so that we might be kings with you!" (1 Cor. 4:8). The time to reign as kings over the earth—God's original intention for man—is still future for believers. Today we live as aliens and pilgrims in a world that still tempts with sinful desires (1 Peter 2:11). Today we walk in humility and subjection, that God may exalt us "in due time" (1 Peter 5:5–6).

Fulfillment of Creation

The New Testament emphasizes this plan to restore humanity by announcing a new creation that we can experience *already* (2 Cor. 5:17). As believers we participate already in the new order of living—*eternal life*. As citizens of the kingdom (Col. 1:13) we have a whole new set of relationships and a totally new identity—"If anyone is in Christ, he is a new creation; the old has gone, the new has come!" (2 Cor. 5:17). Old identities are severed; a new relationship with God is what counts (Eph. 2:10–13).

But the full implementation of this new creation is still future. As the apostle John describes his vision of the future in Revelation 21:1–22:5, the theme of a restored world is announced. We saw earlier that this coming new world has no hint of the original chaos in Genesis 1:2. Now compare the new order with the scene in the garden of Eden, and note the similarities:

- No need for a temple.
- God is directly present.
- There is a river.
- The tree of life is there.

Yet the new creation is not a return to the gracious provisions of the garden. It is an *advance*. Note the differences from the garden:

- The presence of God and Christ is continuous.
- The throne of God is there. His perfect order and rule is guaranteed.
- Eternal life is secured.

What was lost in Eden is more than regained. For those redeemed by Christ, a new humanity has begun!

Fulfillment of a New Humanity

For a new creation there must be a new humanity. God began the old creation with one man. Adam was it. He was humanity. Eve was created as his complement, and together they were "man" (Gen. 5:2). In starting a new creation, God begins it with the man Christ Jesus.

Paul compares these two men in 1 Corinthians 15:45–49. He calls Adam the "first man" and he calls Christ the "second man" and the "last Adam." How many men does that leave between Adam and Christ? How many men does it allow after Christ? For Paul there were *only two real men*. Only these men are heads of humanity. Adam was humanity as God created it. But by his sin he placed all of his future progeny out of fellowship with God (Rom. 5:12–19). The new human race begins with Christ as head. All who are his by God's grace and through faith in him become part of this new humanity. Under Adam we suffered the results of sin. Under Christ we enjoy the accomplishments this Son of God has brought. We are counted righteous before God. We have life and have entered into Christ's righteous reign (Rom. 5:16–19; 8:1–10).

Though severed from our citizenship in the old creation, as a new creation we still live in it[32] and still experience in these physical frames the results of the failure of our original Old Man. We often struggle with temptation and groan with the rest of a creation out of gear (Rom. 8:22–23). But believers eagerly anticipate a final redemption out of this creation (8:29) and the changeover when we shall wear the likeness of the New and Last Man (1 Cor. 15:49; Rom. 8:29).

> Now the dwelling of God is with men, and he will live with them. They will be his people, and God himself will be with them and be their God. He will wipe every tear from their eyes. There will be no more death or mourning or crying or pain, for the old order of things has passed away (Rev. 21:3–4).

SUGGESTED SCRIPTURE READING:

Genesis 2:4–3:24
Luke 4:1–13
Romans 5:12–21; 8:12–39

For Interaction and Discussion:

1. From what you know about (a) ancient pagan beliefs, (b) modern secular beliefs, and (c) biblical teaching, compare what each one says about the purpose of life and human relationship to God or gods.

2. How does understanding "life in Eden" help the reader who is not living in Eden? How does understanding how humanity left Eden help in understanding life today?

3. In what ways are "fear and shame . . . the incurable stigmata of the Fall in man"?

4. What events in Genesis 2 and 3 show the full equality of man and woman as God's creation? Does a distinction such as the author made about the husband's moral responsibility violate the notion of equality of persons?

5. What cultural practices do you think violate male and female partnership and equality and which do you think are appropriate as part of a biblical model? Which are cultural practices that are neither condemned nor approved by the biblical teaching?

- The husband usually drives the car when they go places together.
- Only the wife wears a wedding ring.
- The wife takes her husband's last name in marriage.
- The wife is the primary caretaker of children.
- The husband is the primary "breadwinner."
- The man walks on the street side of the sidewalk when walking with a woman.
- The man holds the door for the woman to enter.
- When walking together, the wife walks a short distance behind the husband.
- The husband makes all the financial decisions.
- The family will move to follow the husband's employment, and the wife will seek new employment at the new location.

6. Why is sexual union not an adequate definition of marriage? Does modern society experience any social problems when the marriage pattern of Genesis 2 is set aside?

7. How can people learn "good and evil", both positively and negatively, today? What is the ultimate temptation? What mental attitudes are important in facing temptation?

8. What is the importance of God's presence to the history of humanity?

For Further Reading:

Gerhardus Vos. *Biblical Theology*. Grand Rapids: Eerdmans, 1948, 39–45.
Older, but solid discussion of the temptation and fall.

Derek Kidner. *Genesis.* TOTC. Downers Grove, Ill.: InterVarsity, 58–72.

Allen P. Ross. *Creation and Blessing.* Grand Rapids: Baker, 1988, 117–38.

Hans Walter Wolff. *Anthropology of the Old Testament.* Philadelphia: Fortress, 1974, 159–76. Summary of Old Testament outlook and practices of marriage.

Notes and Comments:

[1]A. Heidel, *The Babylonian Genesis,* 46 (Tablet VI), 1, lines 5–8. The editorial marks of the translator have been omitted from this quote.

[2]The apparent contradiction with Genesis 1—that vegetation came before man, but in 2:5–6 has not yet sprouted because man is not available to cultivate it—is due to the more limited reference in Genesis 2. The verse is not speaking of all vegetation but about cultivated fields as indicated by the switch from "earth" in Genesis 1 to "field in the earth" in 2:5. "Field" may refer to a particular field (as here and 37:7; 47:24) or a pastureland (29:2) or open country (25:29). See BDB, 961. The "plants of the field" refer to "wheat and barley and other kinds of grain from which *bread* is made" (U. Cassuto, *Genesis,* 1:102). See Genesis 3:18–19 for the same phrase. Cf. *TWOT,* 700–701.

[3]Nahum M. Sarna notes other ancient Near Eastern parallels to creation of man out of "clay." Yet he sees a distinct difference in the biblical account: "Man, alone, has the breath of life blown into his nostrils by God Himself. Only by virtue of this direct animation did man become a living being, drawing directly from God his life source," *Understanding Genesis* (New York: Schocken, 1966), 14–15.

[4]Von Rad, *Genesis,* 82.

[5]Another apparent difficulty arises in comparing Genesis 2 with Genesis 1. It appears that 2:19 teaches a creation of animals and birds *after* man's creation. As Keil points out, this is due to Hebrew style: "The writer, who was about to describe the relation of man to the beasts, went back to their creation, in the simple method of early Semitic historians, and placed this first instead of making it subordinate; so that our modern style of expressing the same thought would be simply this: 'God brought to Adam the beasts which He had formed.'" (C. F. Keil and F. Delitzsch, *The Pentateuch,* [Grand Rapids: Eerdmans, 1971], 1:87). This literary practice of "starting over" with the sequence of events and bringing it up to the present time of the narrative is, of course, not our common Western pattern. To place it in sequence the verb must be translated in English, "had formed" as in the NIV. Similarly, see 2:7–8; when was man formed? The NIV, NASB, RSV, and NRSV all translate "had formed" in 2:8.

The grammars deny, however, that the construction of 2:19 (*waw* plus the imperfect should be translated as a pluperfect, "had formed" as in 2:19 NIV), though they allow the perfect to be so translated as in 2:8. Yet in Genesis 31:34 both the perfect and the *waw* plus the imperfect are used for pluperfect actions of Rachel that involve a flashback prior to the action of the ongoing narrative. Cassuto rejects the above but offers another solution. Noting that only the beasts and birds among the groups of original creation are said to be "formed" here by God, yet the domesticated animals ("livestock," NIV) are included in the naming; Cassuto concludes that this is a special creation of wild animals only, as they would not be available to Adam like the domesticated animals would be. These are formed especially for the purpose of Adam's naming them. This event, therefore, need not be a conflict with the initial creation of all creatures (Cassuto, *Genesis*, 1:128–29).

[6]For the significance of naming as an indicator of ruling see Cassuto, *Genesis*, 1:130. As Cassuto notes, this emphasis on man's rule is clear from 2:19 where Adam's work is accepted as final. God's rule is also indicated by naming in Genesis 1:5, 8, 10; and 5:2. Parental rule is exercised by Eve in 4:25.

[7]The absurd deduction that God's "surgical operation" on Adam produced an *inherited* shortage of one rib per man is an obvious *non sequitur*, but has had an interesting history. See the summary by Paul K. Jewett, *Man As Male and Female* (Grand Rapids: Eerdmans, 1975), 121–22. But why does Jewett then himself use this faulty deduction to support the notion that a literal reading of Genesis contradicts modern biology?

[8]The play on the words *ish* for "man" and *ishah* for "woman" comes out well in English translation. That *ishah* may not be derived directly from *ish* in the Hebrew language is beside the point. Assuming Hebrew was not the original language of the garden, it follows that Adam derived her designation from his in whatever language was spoken. The closest parallel in Hebrew was *ish* and *ishah*. English is blessed with two sets of acceptable terms to convey the idea: man/woman and male/female.

[9]Cassuto, *Genesis*, 1:112, takes "knowledge of good and evil" as "objective awareness of all things, both good and bad." Von Rad takes it as omniscience (*Genesis*, 1:81). But 3:22 certainly eliminates both of these suggestions. Man has not become omniscient. It is best to follow Gerhardus Vos, *Biblical Theology* (Grand Rapids: Eerdmans, 1948), 39–43, who shows that the tree functions as a tree of probation intended to teach man moral discernment at the highest level—obedience to God. See also H. C. Leupold, *Exposition of Genesis*, 2 vols. (Grand Rapids: Baker, 1942), 1:120–21. "Good and evil," if developed positively, may well be equivalent to "wisdom" in the Old Testament (see chap. 11).

[10]Both Cassuto, *Genesis*, 1:139–43, and Sarna, *Understanding Genesis*, 26, recognize that the text explicitly rejects a mythological interpretation by identifying the serpent as one of the beasts of the field. Both, however, ultimately see the existence of a serpent myth as the reason for the choice of a serpent as the tempter. Cassuto takes the serpent to be allegorical for the slyness of Eve's own mind as she seeks to discover the reason for the prohibition. But this makes the shift of blame in 3:13 meaningless and the curse upon the serpent (3:14–15) even more so. In spite of his own interpretation, Cassuto also notes that the Pentateuch avoids allegory. It would be more consistent to see the serpent-myth tradition as getting its start here as a distorted memory of the real event of the fall of mankind.

[11]Vos, *Biblical Theology*, 43–44, rightly rejects any allegorical interpretations that reduce the events recorded here to nonhistorical representations of everyman's temptation. Walter Kaiser, *Toward an Old Testament Theology*, 77–78, has suggested a grammatical solution to the problem of the serpent. He takes "serpent" as only a

title for Satan—not a designation of an animal or the form in which Satan came. According to Kaiser, 3:1 ("more crafty than any beast of the field") compares Satan with the beasts of the field, rather than includes the serpent as one of them.

[12]Sarna, 26, summarizes the serpent imagery available. "This reptile figures prominently in all the world's mythologies and cults. In the Near East the serpent was a symbol of deity and fertility, and the images of serpent-goddesses have been found in the ruins of many Canaanite towns and temples."

[13]Vos, *Biblical Theology*, 44–45; Leupold, *Genesis*, 1:141–42.

[14]The three differences between Eve's response and the original form of the commands and description are distinguished by Bruce K. Waltke, "The Fall of Man," Bueermann-Champion Lectures, Western Conservative Baptist Theological Seminary, Portland, Ore., October 1974, who sees them all as significant departures.

[15]Waltke sees the difference in the grammatical form as indicating a shift from command ("You shall surely") to optional permission ("We may") and, therefore, a modification of emphasis on God's goodness. Leupold, *Genesis*, 1:148, finds no difference in meaning due to the grammatical differences but does see the omission of "all" (every) as significant. "She was beginning to lose sight of the goodness of God."

[16]Waltke takes Eve's identification of the tree being in the middle of the garden as a direct geographical error caused by a faulty focus on the restriction. Leupold, *Genesis*, 1:149, argues that both trees are in the middle and sees no problem with Eve's statement identifying the tree of knowledge as being in the middle. But Cassuto here agrees on a shift of focus: "Although there was in the *center* of the garden also the tree of life, and possibly there were other trees as well, her interest is focused at the moment on the *forbidden tree,* and for her it is *the tree*—with the definite article—in the center of the garden" (*Genesis* 1:145).

[17]Cassuto disagrees that "You shall not surely die" is intended to be the opposite to the "you shall surely die" of 2:17. He argues that it is too distant from 2:17 and that "you" is plural here, but singular in 2:17 (*Genesis*, 1:145). That change, of course, is necessary to include the woman. Otherwise it is a direct contradiction.

[18]R. Obadiah Sforno, quoted in Cassuto, *Genesis*, 1:137.

[19]As Cassuto notes, ibid., 155–56, to assert that God's question, "Where are you?" (3:9), is an indication of some lack in God's omniscience is to fail to note the purpose of the question. God was not seeking information but was seeking them out. See Genesis 4:9 for a similar question followed by the already known answer.

[20]Von Rad, *Genesis*, 91.

[21]Some have suggested that Paul's point in 1 Timothy 2:12–14 is that the women of Ephesus should not teach, not because of divine ordering, but because like many first-century women, they were untaught and so should not teach. If so, Paul's citation of Genesis 3 is not to show an order of responsibility or creation, but the "orders of education"—the need for qualification (cf. Walter C. Kaiser, Jr., "Shared Leadership or Male Headship?" *Christianity Today*, 30, 14 [March 1986]: 12-I). As appealing as this conclusion might be, this is a difficult reading of Genesis. Eve knows something. She must have heard it from someone—either God or Adam. If from God, then she is not untaught. If her changes in the command and

its focus come from Adam, then the man is a poor teacher and advocating that women not teach would hardly be the appropriate conclusion. The parallel simply will not work, because Eve must have been taught by someone. She is not unaware of the command. And, there is not a lot of learning to do with one prohibition!

[22]Claus Westermann, *Elements of Old Testament Theology*, trans. Douglas W. Stott (Atlanta: John Knox, 1982), 95.

[23]We will discuss the meaning and significance of the personal name for God, *Yahweh*, more fully in chapter 5.

[24]Jewett, *Male and Female*, 124. As quoted, Jewett rightly rejects the role of menial servant for the woman and emphasizes her as an equal ally and completion of humanity. The unproven assumption of Jewett's book, however—that equality of person cannot exist alongside of complementary or differentiation of role or responsibility—does not necessarily follow. Cf. Hans Walter Wolff, *Anthropology of the Old Testament*, 159–65, where differentiation of role is seen as part of the human mandate. Dominion requires the whole community of mankind. "They are to be able to generate children and thus to increase mankind. The increase of mankind and dominion over the earth and the beasts are directly linked together" (162).

[25]Some think that Paul is misinterpreting the account when he argues from the man being created first. They point out that being created last meant the highest level of creation in the Genesis 1 account. Cf. Jewett, *Male and Female*, 126–27; Letha Scanzoni and Nancy Hardesty, *All We're Meant to Be* (Waco, Tex.: Word, 1974), 27–28. Of course, the order of any account does not have a predetermined significance. In Genesis 1 the order was ascending with humanity as the climax—and order was not the only indicator of this. In Genesis 2 the distinctive context of gracious provision for the newly created man who has needs (including a mate) on his level is often overlooked. Order is actually climactic here, too. As Adam affirmed in poetry, last is best. In Genesis 2—the greatest provision was the woman—a creation appropriate to him.

[26]Again, this raises the issue of the legitimacy of Paul's use of the order of the creation account. My point is that, though the account is primarily one indicating equality, there are some features of the narrative itself (apart from reading Paul) that lend support to Paul's appeal to a functional order. Cf. Ann L. Bowman, "Women in Ministry: An Exegetical Study of 1 Timothy 2:11–15," *BSac*, 149 (1992): 204–5. Bowman follows Ross [cf. Allan P. Ross, "The Participation of Women in Ministry and Service," *Exegesis and Exposition*, 4 (Winter, 1989): 76–77] in concluding that Paul is arguing by analogy as did the rabbis. Bowman finds features in the Genesis narrative and theology that grounds the analogy in actual significance found in Genesis, whereas Ross seems to believe that such an order is true because it is declared by the apostle, but we could not have been sure of it from the simple narrative of creation order. For a full and careful treatment of the significance of these narratives and the biblical pattern that follows, see Bruce K. Waltke, "The Role of Women in the Bible," *Crux*, 31 (September 1995): 29–40.

[27]My comments about rebellion against insignificant rules should not be taken as approval of operating by a rules-oriented approach that is condemned in Colossians 3:21 and 2:20–23.

[28]The strength of the statement that a man leave his father and mother to be joined to his wife, coupled with no mention of the wife leaving her parents, have led some to suggest that the earlier marital practice was for the couple to live with the wife's family. In contrast with this is the patriarchal family pattern of the rest of Genesis. It is likely that the stress on the man's leaving is to balance the current patriarchal pattern so as to stress the commitment to the wife as stronger even than parental ties.

[29]Paul's quotation of Genesis 2:24 in 1 Corinthians 6:16 is often read as if it equates the sex act with the one-flesh arrangement God ordained in Genesis 2. But if that is the case, why would Paul call it fornication? It is, therefore, not the "one flesh" as intended by Genesis but a distorted "one flesh." This is what makes it fornication and a misuse of God's original intention. It takes what God made as part of the "one flesh" of marriage and uses it in a way that sins against God's design for mankind.

[30]Cole, "Foundations of Wisdom Theology," 133.

[31]Regarding Jesus' temptation by Satan, Matthew seems to be most concerned with its parallel to Israel's temptation in the wilderness—a theme we will address in a later chapter. Luke, however, with the inserted genealogy that takes us back to Adam, seems to be making the comparison which we develop here—Jesus as the Man qualified to save.

[32]The way a believer is to live in the old creation with its original institutions of marriage and labor as well as with its fallen realities of increased pain and institutions such as slavery, takes up a significant segment of Paul's letters and can only be addressed briefly here. The ongoing debate over the place of male and female, in my judgment, frequently misses this tension that Paul teaches between living as part of the old creation order at the same time as already being part of a new creation. In the future new creation many of these old creation institutions will pass away or be distinctively different—marriage being an obvious example. To fail to see this tension creates the danger of removing it by eliminating one side of the tension or the other. Some choose Galatians 3:28, which clearly states the new creation equalities, and then proceed to effectively eliminate Paul's applicationary passages to living in the old order (1 Cor. 11:1–11; 14:25; 1 Tim. 2:12–15; and to a lesser extent Eph. 5:18–6:9) as temporary applications and restrictions for very local situations. In that way these passages have little normative application today. On the other side of the issue, some reduce Galatians 3:28 to mere positional truth with few earthly implications, focus on defending the restrictions in the applicationary passages as normative for male/female order and design, and seem to lose Paul's stress on new creation concerns for those situations. Paul's concern that believers find ways of living out the new order in the midst of old-order realities is a balance often missing in the current debate. Its loss dulls the vitality of Christian witness in our society. The church either becomes defenders of the traditional status quo or simply mirrors prevailing cultural trends.

chapter three

THE EFFECTS OF SIN:
LOSS OF ORDER
AND BALANCE
(Genesis 3–11)

Travel in ancient times was no Boy Scout expedition. In an account of his traveling the coast of Palestine and Phoenicia during the time of the biblical judges, Wen-Amon, an official of Egypt, spells out some of the difficulties he encountered. He is robbed. His ship is tied up in harbors. He is caught in a storm and is forced to land and face attack by local townspeople.[1]

Perhaps an even less peaceful scene prevailed inland. The Bible pictures the danger.

> In the days of Shamgar son of Anath,
>   in the days of Jael, caravans ceased,
>   and travelers kept to the byways (Judg. 5:6 NRSV).

The Israelites of Moses' time had their problems too, not only from outsiders but also from their own ranks. There was rebellion against Moses (Num. 16). There was idolatry (Ex. 32:4; Amos 5:25–26). The caseload of disputes between Israelites required Moses to get help by appointing judges (Ex. 18). This world is no Eden.

In the Fall, every level of creation was thrown into imbalance. Our first parents introduced into human history the principle of basing moral choices on limited human perception and experience rather than on the Word of God. Following this introduction, the invasion of sinful dysfunction and death is swift and total. The harmony between mankind and the ground, between animal and human creation, between man and woman, and between mankind and God are turned upside down. Like Humpty Dumpty of nursery fable, humanity has not been able to get it together since.

Ever since the Fall, people have been attempting to conduct business as usual, convinced that we can solve society's problems on our own. Some optimistically proclaim that life is on an upward trek. If only it were so! But the tragic results of that word, *sin*, will not go away. A society may avoid the word and occasionally wonder aloud, "Whatever happened to sin?" But, the results won't go away. New labels such as "alternate lifestyle," "termination of pregnancy," and "significant other" will not hide our shame. The effects and reduplication of this ancient malady remain. Fallen society fails to recognize the inner deterioration of its own civilization.

Genesis 3:14–11:9 announces the results of the Fall in a curse formula and then traces the deterioration of two successive civilizations following sin's successful invasion of the human homeland.

THE CURSE: PREDICTIONS OF STRUGGLE IN RELATIONSHIPS

The remainder of the temptation account of Genesis 3 sketches in reverse order the results of sin for each of the participants. The official interrogation by the Creator (3:11–13) led from the man to the woman to the serpent. Then each appropriate judgment is announced in reverse (chiastic) order—heightening the stress on the divine order which had been successfully upset by the serpent's *coup d'etat*.

Struggle with the Serpent

First, the serpent is addressed (3:14–15). The penalty is announced in language appropriate to the animal used but applies more specifically to the demonic personality involved. This curse does not involve a change in the digestive system of reptiles so that dust suddenly becomes nutritionally beneficial. The dust is not its regular diet but an unpleasant effect of the previous line: "You will crawl on your belly." Though the animal used was classed as having the highest mental capacity among the wild animals, much as dolphins and great apes are viewed today, the tempter will experience another feature of the animal: crawling in the dust. This is common language for defeat and demotion to a place of dishonor (cf. Mic. 7:17 for this idiom).

More critical is the point that the struggle that began at the temptation between the serpent and the woman would continue into the future. To limit the struggle to snakebites is to cancel out the significance of the initial interchange between the serpent and the woman. Just as the original encounter involved a demonic intelligence, so the curse of the serpent involves Satan. Satan himself will meet his demise through the action of the woman's offspring. But, as with many curses, the words are cryptic and can be fully understood only upon the fulfillment of the curse. Here the significance of the woman's seed as part of God's ultimate plan to overcome the effects of the Fall through one who will be called Messiah is just beginning to unfold.[2]

Struggle with Multiplying and Marriage

As with the previous struggle, this struggle introduces no new function on the part of the woman. Childbearing was part of God's original intention (1:28). The Fall has increased the pain of an event that was to be totally beautiful.

Those who, like myself, have participated with their wives in classes designed to help control the labor process and have invaded the labor and the delivery rooms of hospitals can testify that childbirth is still awesomely beautiful. Yet there is pain. The husband can be there to encourage, but he cannot truly share any of that pain. Modern medicine can and should relieve it as much as possible, yet it has been integrated into the process itself. As with all human functions, the Fall has made the task more difficult. And the pain of childbearing is only the initial pain for the woman because of the children she brings into the world.

In addition to this struggle with multiplying, the woman will face tension in the very relationship that was the hallmark of her creation—her marriage: "Your desire will be for your husband and he will rule over you" (3:16). This verse, like all personally threatening verses in Scripture, has been interpreted in many ways. Some understand it to mean that the woman has a physical and emotional tie to her husband that makes it *easy* for him to exercise his leadership role in the family. But that view weakens the idea of *judgment* that is part of this context. None of the rest of the statements ease the situation between the participants.

Another view holds that these words teach a desire for harmony and rest in the husband, but that his response is harsh rule instead. This fits the context of a curse very well, but the word *rule,* when used without other qualifiers, does not suggest harshness. It is used of both God's rule and man's rule.

A third view has the advantage of fitting both the context and the use of the words elsewhere. This view asserts that the woman's desire will be to dominate her husband, yet he is to rule over her. This view is supported by a look at the parallel wording in the very next chapter involving God's discussion with Cain. In 4:7 God informs Cain that sin's "desire is for you, but you must master it" (NRSV). Sin wanted to overcome and dominate Cain, but he had the responsibility to rule over it.[3]

Likewise in 3:16, the woman desires to dominate her husband (as sin did Cain), but it is the husband's moral responsibility to maintain leadership. This involves no new arrangement, as we have seen, but rather a difficulty brought on by the Fall. What was formally a highly compatible arrangement will become beset by the difficulties of fallenness on both sides. Here is a struggle that the woman will lose, just as the serpent will lose the struggle with the woman's seed and man will lose the struggle with the ground.

This is not to say that the account gives *carte blanche* to man's rule—no matter how it is implemented. This is a curse on the woman and not a vindication of the man. The history of man's leadership is also the tragedy of the Fall. His failure to recognize his mate as his divine complement and equal is notorious. He has often failed to follow the model of Yahweh's love to Israel, and for New Covenant believers, Christ's love for the Church. So in Ephesians 5, Paul reminds the woman to voluntarily follow and respect her husband's moral leadership and exhorts the husband to love his wife. Each emphasis meets the particular temptation for each of the partners.[4]

This does not mean that every wife is bent on undermining her husband, any more that it indicates that all husbands are unthoughtful and abusive. Yet the Fall introduced this particular weakness and temptation that will occur regularly in marriages generally. Just as there is discord between man and the ground in the next curse, so discord has entered the most intimate and fulfilling of relationships. Yet the message of Genesis 2 concerning God's best gift to the man is still true: "He who finds a wife finds what is good and receives favor from the LORD" (Prov. 18:22).

Struggle in Subduing the Earth

The curse for the male reduces the joy of creative lordship over the earth by adding a struggle with the ground (3:17–19). Woman's intermittent pain is paralleled by this constant pain for the man. Again the contrast with the pre-Fall situation is not complete. Work did not begin at the Fall. Satisfaction with work is still a gift of God (Eccl. 3:13). Yet, as in the previous two pronouncements, the struggle will be lost by the man. The ground will win and man will return to the dust.[5]

SIN'S PROGRESS

The next events in Genesis graphically catalog the Fall's impact upon the race. These stories focus on curse and judgment. The story of the first family (Gen. 2:4–4:26) ends in the violence of Cain and Lamech. Such is repeated in the stories (*Toledoth*) that follow. All of these judgments highlight the scope of failure that dogs the human family as a result of the Fall. Yet there is also the alternating theme of blessing and grace from a faithful Creator that also punctuates the narrative of human failure. The following chart catches the pattern.[6]

Figure 3.1

Story	Sin/Curse/Judgment	Blessing/Grace
Story of heavens & earth (2:4–4:26)	The Fall; curse on serpent, woman, man, violence of Cain & Lamech	Birth of Seth; calling on the name of Yahweh
Story of Adam's descendants (5:1–6:8)	Continual evil; Yahweh repents that he made man	"But Noah found favor in the eyes of Yahweh"
Story of Noah & descendants (6:9–9:29)	Earth corrupt & filled with violence; the Flood; curse on Canaan	Blessed Noah (9:1); but ends with Noah's drunkenness & curse on Canaan
Story of descendants of Shem, Ham, & Japeth (10:1–11:9)	Tower of Babel	None. The next two stories narrow the field of vision to provide the grace/ blessing necessary.
Story of descendants of Shem (11:10–26)		Narrows to Terah, the father of Abram, through whom blessing will come.

A Family Album

Not only was the marriage relationship affected by the Fall (Gen. 3:16), but so was the relationship between brothers (Gen. 4). Here we see all those vile monsters that have been the daily companions of our fallen humanity: envy, hypocrisy, malice, and guile (cf. 1 Peter 2:1, a remarkable agreement with our story).

Why was Cain's sacrifice not acceptable to God? The text does not say. Some believe that it was not acceptable due to the fact that no blood was shed. This could be the case if a sin offering is in view. Yet, the specific word for that type of offering is not used here. In the Mosaic Law, or Torah, there are other sacrifices besides animal sacrifice when other purposes are in view. Others have suggested that we have here the original distinction between external religion and true devotion. In other words, Abel came with the right motivation and the best of his flocks, while Cain came grudgingly. This may be supported by the observation that Abel brought the firstborn of the flock, not simply any animal. Cain's offering is merely described as from the fruit of the ground.[7]

But notice the point of the passage. Whatever the cause, Cain's offering is unacceptable. Yahweh warns Cain that he must act properly toward God. Cain has the option to respond appropriately and correct his failure. If he does not, he is responsible for his sin (Gen. 4:7).[8] Cain, however, in this second temptation, fails to respond humbly before God. His failure to control his anger leads to murder, and *God's sovereignty proves undiminished by man's fall*. The point: as Creator, God is still in charge and acts as judge against injustice on the earth.

The episode of the "sons of God" and the "daughters of men" in 6:1–3 adds to the theme of human decline. Yet interpreters differ on what kind of event is in view. The following chart summarizes the main options.

Figure 3.2
Identity of the "Sons of God" in Genesis 6:1–2

Items	Theory No. 1	Theory No. 2	Theory No. 3
Sons of God	Fallen angels	Godly line of Seth	Dynastic rulers
Daughters of men	Mortals	Line of Cain	Commoners
Sin	Marriage between supernatural and mortal	Marriage of holy to unholy	Polygamy
Supporters	Philo, Josephus, Justin, Ambrose, Apocrypha (Enoch), Delitzsch, Driver, Cassuto, H. Morris, von Rad, Speiser	Leupold, Stigers	Aramaic targums, Rashi, Ramban, Jacob
Evidence	1. The term "sons of God" refers only to angels (Job 1; 38:7; Pss. 29:1; 89:7). 2. Jude 6–7 perhaps refers to this incident. 3. It is the clear reading of the text. 4. The Septuagint in Job 1 reads "angels of God." 5. Christ says angels do not marry; doesn't say "cannot."	1. The concept of a holy line is seemingly established. 2. Hebrew indicates continuity from the previous chapter. 3. The sin here becomes a common theme throughout the Pentateuch.	1. Magistrates or rulers often referred to as gods (Exod. 21:6; 22:8, 9, 28; Ps. 82:1, 6). 2. Kings sometimes called sons of deities.
Problems	1. Lends mythological tone. 2. Angels were not previously mentioned. 3. Why is man punished by the Flood for the wickedness of angels? 4. New Testament support is questionable.	1. The term "sons of God" never means this elsewhere. 2. No evidence that the lines are kept totally separate. The theory does not account for Adam and Eve's other children. 3. God has not yet begun working through one line. 4. The term for "men" is general. It would need further classification to be understood otherwise. 5. In Noah's time he alone was holy.	1. Kingship is not expressed in any way. 2. Scripture never considers kings to be sons of deity (possible exception: Ps. 2:6–7). 3. Needs the connection of v. 4, but the "mighty men" are the Nephilim, not the children of the union.

John H. Walton, *Chronological and Background Charts of the Old Testament* (Zondervan, 1978), 35.

And so the album of the first family closes. One son is banished. The other's blood has wet the dust to which all men will return. Though man is able to advance in the arts and technology after the Fall (4:21–22), Abel's blood is not the last emblem of violence and strife on the earth (4:23).

A Civilization Falls

The Bible next records the progress of the first civilization from Adam to Noah. It is a story marked by a dismal conclusion. In contrast to the Babylonian flood story, in which the gods destroy mankind because they were making too much noise, the Bible cites the moral failure of man. "The LORD saw how great man's wickedness on the earth had become, and that every inclination of the thoughts of his heart was only evil all the time" (Gen. 6:5). Man's inner life has gone the wretched limit. So ends the story of Adam's descendants (5:1–6:8) with the announcement that Yahweh who had made humanity has decided to unmake mankind.[9] The Story of Noah (6:9–9:29) thus begins with the tragic results for society of this moral breakdown: "The earth is filled with violence" (6:13).

Once again the sovereign God judges the moral failure of man, and this time destroys the ancient world by flood. Civilization must start anew through a single family whose head "walked with God."[10] But what happens as soon as that family gets off the boat and resettles? The family patriarch gets drunk and one of his sons acts shamefully toward him in his drunken and naked state.[11] Depravity was not eliminated by the Flood, only judged.

The subsequent curse upon Canaan, the son of Ham, is not a curse on the Negroid race but on the Canaanites—the very people Israel would expel from the land for their wickedness. Why is the curse not on Ham himself, rather than one of his sons? If it were, it would be experienced by all of his sons. God graciously limits the curse to only a portion of Ham's descendants—and that portion that will develop a propensity toward the same perversity as Canaan's father. The curse is fully vindicated when the Canaanites actually practice again the indecencies that brought on the curse.[12]

The New Civilization—Genesis 10–11

Let's check the score. Following the fall of Adam and Eve, Cain kills Abel. *Failure in the first family.* Score: 1 to 0. Eventually that whole civilization fails (2 to 0), Noah's family settles in again and before you know it, 3 to 0. But what of the civilization that arises after the Flood? The answer: 4 to zip. The movement from family failure to failure of the society is Genesis' way of showing the pervasiveness of the movement away from the Creator's blessing in the ancient world.

No better example could be found of this universal deterioration than the rebellion of Babylon. Here arises a plot against God's instruction. These men are *not* trying to create the ancient world's forerunner to Skylab—the passage doesn't condemn space exploration or skyscrapers! The violation here is pure and simple. It is rebellion against God's instruction which came immediately after the Flood: "Be fruitful and increase in number and fill the earth" (Gen. 9:1, 7; cf. the original blessing of 1:28).

The men found the plain where Babylon was built and decided to build a city with a tall tower that could be seen from miles around in order that they might not be spread out over the earth. Yahweh takes a decided interest in this building program, insignificant as it is compared to him. He has to "come down" to see this oh-so-tall edifice—generally considered a Babylonian ziggurat or temple-tower.

But God does seem worried, doesn't he? After all, he says that "nothing they plan to do will be impossible for them" (11:6). The passage, however, is not speaking of technology but of *morality*. Yahweh concludes (my paraphrase): "If I let them get away with this, they will stop at nothing." And so, he initiates a judgment to counter their rebellion. The introduction of languages makes this rebellious unity of mankind a practical impossibility. Yahweh scatters them throughout the earth.

Conclusion

But what of all this failure?

Why recount these ancient events for the benefit of the Israelites who so newly have become a people under God? Their ancestry, of course, has been traced through Shem to Noah and back through Noah and Enoch to Seth. It has not been a perfect ancestry, but it has been preserved by God's grace and has been the object of his special selection. The theme of the promised seed continues. But the theme of moral rebellion has been even more center stage. Moral rebellion is the reason the Canaanite nations are being dispossessed (Lev. 18:24–25). Israel's own success in the land is dependent upon her recognition of the need for submission to God's sovereign rule (18:26–30).

Not all the descendants of Noah are blessed by God. The moral sin of the Canaanites is anticipated in the sin of Ham and predicted in the curse on Canaan. Just so, the selection process would continue. Not all the sons of Abraham would secure God's blessing. And so, within Israel it could be assumed that God would judge and discard those who insist on the route of rebellion.

The first eleven chapters of Genesis stand as a monument to Israel's solemn privilege as God's current standard-bearers in the midst of general rebellion—but also as a monument of warning that the human tendency is to rebel and allow society to deteriorate. If this happens, the Creator will judge.

FULFILLMENT IN THE HUMAN FAMILY

Like a well-fought tennis game in which the competitors power the ball from one side of the court to the other, the themes of judgment and blessing alternate throughout the Bible. In both themes God is seen to be the sovereign Lord of the universe.

But God's ultimate purpose is not limited to displaying his sovereignty in a world that continues to burst open at the seams. *Reversal* of this process is God's ultimate plan. Judgment must culminate. Grace and blessing must conquer.

Reversal of Babel

The judgment of different languages that came at Babel forced man to move out to populate and exercise dominion over the earth as God had commanded. But it also introduced a barrier to the unity of the human race. As long as man is in a state of rebellion against God, unity would be dangerous. God would use national desires and interests to control the rise of evil in various populations (cf. Acts 17:26–27).

In the Old Testament, foreign speech or tongues is always a judgment. It is at Babel. It is in Isaiah 28:11 where the language that God promises to speak to Israel is the language of the Assyrian invader. Because they have rejected the clear message of the prophet, God's next message to them will be captivity. Hearing foreign tongues was promised in Deuteronomy 28:49 as God's judgment on Israel for rebellion against his covenant with her. A century after Isaiah, Jeremiah would predict a similar judgment of unknown language and exile for Judah (Jer. 5:15).[13] Paul censures the Corinthians for using the gift of tongues in an Old Testament manner (1 Cor. 14:20–25). Used in a setting in which the people do not understand, tongues should only be used when judgment is intended. Yet under the gospel, the Corinthians are attempting to be an instrument of grace to their unbelieving neighbors. Only words that can be understood should be used, so that divine conviction and God's grace would result.

This is the context of Acts 2—the Day of Pentecost, a day on which a distinct signpost was given. Christ's death fifty days earlier brought judgment to climax. The critical battle was won. The victory was sure. The tide of defeat had been stemmed, and now God was bringing his program to completion. All humanity would come to unity under Christ. This first signal of ultimate unity and the clear indication that we have entered the last phase of God's program was the overcoming of the language barrier at the coming of the Holy Spirit.

In Revelation 7:9–10, what was signaled at Pentecost comes to harmonious completion before the throne of God and before the Lord Jesus as a great multitude from "every nation, tribe, people, and language" cry out in unison: "Salvation belongs to our God, who sits on the throne, and to the Lamb."

Unity in Christ

The creed of religious liberalism earlier in the century was captured in the slogan: "The Fatherhood of God and the brotherhood of man." Undoubtedly they were right. All men owe their existence to the sovereign Creator. And all men are related. As the apostle put it, "From one man he made every nation of men, that they should inhabit the whole earth" (Acts 17:26).

But these ancient stories show us that the physical brotherhood of humanity has not produced a spiritual unity of peace, harmony, and love. Cain and Abel were brothers, but just as surely as this initial brotherhood cracked under the weight of envy, jealousy, and strife, so sin continues to fracture the hope of universal brotherly harmony.

The Old Testament theme of the unity of mankind does not find resolution until we come to the New Testament. To achieve a true unity of peace and love, mankind needs intervention from the outside, as the Old Testament prophets predicted. That help arrived when the sovereign Creator became the sovereign Redeemer. In a demonstration of both judgment and grace, the Author of Life died (Acts 3:15).

But what did he achieve in death? He achieved that very unity that has eluded humanity. No greater spiritual division existed in the first century than between Jew and Gentile. Yet the Gentile who had no covenant with God receives the news: "But now in Christ Jesus you who once were far away have been brought near through the blood of Christ. For he himself is our peace, who has made the two one . . . thus making peace" (Eph. 2:12–15). What *Good News*! By faith in Christ alone, men are able to enter God's redeemed family (Eph. 2:8–9).

But that unity, achieved by Christ, must be maintained and implemented by Christ's church. This is the force of the apostle's instruction in the last half of Ephesians. Those who are Christ's are to preserve and manifest this unity by dropping the old ways of life in which we serve ourselves and implementing the new life received through Christ. It is significant that Paul mentions the characteristics of humility, gentleness, patience, forbearance, peace, and love in connection with preserving this unity (Eph. 4:1–3).

The foundation for unity was destroyed at the Fall with the entrance of sin. That foundation for unity was restored at the death and resurrection of Christ through divine forgiveness, cleansing, and power for living a life of love, sacrifice, and true humility. The church exists to model this kind of reality in a fallen world. Jesus said it plainly: "By this everyone will know that you are my disciples, if you have love for one another" (John 13:35 NRSV). Ultimately the unity that God desires will be achieved fully when Christ returns to reign over the earth and all nations will worship the true God as the prophets predicted.

SUGGESTED SCRIPTURE READING:
Genesis 3:14–6:22; 9:18–27; 11:1–9
Ephesians 4:1–16

For Interaction and Discussion:

1. In what ways do these biblical accounts help us understand the problems of human relationships?

2. When so many people desire peace and happiness, what makes this world a place of war, divorce, estrangement, violence, and perversion? Do you think a personal devil is necessary to explain our failure?

3. How can a Christian have a positive attitude in the light of all that is wrong with the world? Are ideals like peace, justice, and unity unrealistic?

4. What kind of reversal does the New Testament see for temptation, sin, and disunity? How much of this reversal can we experience now?

For Further Reading:

Victor P. Hamilton. *Handbook on the Pentateuch*. Grand Rapids: Baker, 1982, 49–85. See especially the discussion of the Flood narrative as a literary unit.

Nahum M. Sarna. *Understanding Genesis*. New York: Shocken, 1966, 37–80. See for discussion of ancient parallels, mythological and historic.

Allen P. Ross. *Creation and Blessing*. Grand Rapids: Baker, 1988, 139–252. Helpful for structure and emphasis of each story.

George W. Coats. "Strife and Reconciliation: Themes of a Biblical Theology in the Book of Genesis." *Horizons in Biblical Theology*, 2 (1980): 15–35. The theme of strife and reconciliation, begun with the Fall, continues throughout Genesis.

Jack Lewis. "The Woman's Seed (Gen. 3:15)." *JETS*, 34 (1991): 299–320. Covers messianic views and history of interpretation.

R. A. Martin. "The Earliest Messianic Interpretation of Genesis 3:15." *JBL*, 84 (1965): 425–27.

O. Palmer Robertson. "Tongues: Sign of Covenantal Curse and Blessing."
WTJ, 33 (1975): 43–53.

Notes and Comments:

[1]"The Journey of Wen-Amon to Phoenecia," *ANET*, 25–29.

[2]The first revelation of human victory as part of the curse of the serpent begins a growing and developing theme that will ultimately lead to human victory through God's representative King (Messiah). The history of its interpretation shows widely different opinions about how much detail was clear to Adam and Eve about the future history of redemption. Some as Victor P. Hamilton, *Handbook on the Pentateuch* (Grand Rapids: Baker, 1982), 50, even see a clear reference to the Virgin Birth as it is the "seed" of the woman, not the man. This is the only place in the Old Testament that the Hebrew word for "seed" or "descendant" occurs with a third-person, feminine, pronominal suffix—"her seed." Yet, Jack Lewis argues: "A look at the texts about Hagar and Rebekah in Genesis [16:10, Hagar's "seed" with Abraham as natural father; and 24:60, Rebekah's "seed" with Isaac as natural father] could have safeguarded interpreters from the whole misguided exegetical effort" of proclaiming this a prediction of a virgin birth ("The Woman's Seed [Gen. 3:15]," *JETS*, 34 [1991]: 299–320). The development of the theme of "seed" or "offspring" is a key theme of the rest of the book, bringing us to the seed of Abraham and to ultimate blessing through him (Gen. 12:1–7; 15:5), and so Genesis 3:15 is ultimately Messianic. Cf. R. A. Martin, "The Earliest Messianic Interpretation of Genesis 3:15," *JBL*, 84 (1965): 425–27. Others see 4:1 as reflecting an expectation by Eve of an incarnation of Yahweh, as this may be translated (with Luther): "I have brought forth a man, Yahweh." But most versions prefer to translate "with the LORD." Cf. the discussion in Sailhamer, "Genesis," 62, nn. 1–2. Such an understanding would make Eve right about incarnation (which was not predicted in 3:15), not expecting a virgin birth with Adam's being the father (which advocates of this view often see predicted in 3:15) and mistaken in all other aspects of her statement.

[3]For a detailed analysis of the parallels in wording and grammar of 3:16 as well as a consideration of other views, cf. Susan T. Foh, "What Is the Woman's Desire?" *WTJ*, 37 (1975): 376–83. An alternate interpretation of 4:7 is found in *Matthew Henry's Commentary*, 6 vols. (Old Tappan, N.J.: Revell, n.d.), 1:39. This alternate view sees the rule as Cain's position as firstborn. Cf. John Calvin, *Commentary on the First Book of Moses Called Genesis*, (Grand Rapids, Baker, n.d.), 1:203–4. The context of a curse or penalty in 3:16 that announces the effects of entering a fallen state with its struggles in relationships and goals, makes Foh's interpretation most compatible with both contexts. Ronald B. Allen, *The Majesty of Man* (Portland, Ore.: Multnomah, 1984), 145–49, has produced a combination view. Though he accepts Foh's argument based on the parallel to 4:7 to define "desire," he does not follow her in seeing the grammar of the last line as also parallel ("But you/he must . . ."), a statement stressing moral obligation. He takes the "rule" in 3:16 as a harsh rule by the husband. Though this would fit nicely in a context of difficulties to the woman, Allen's view is weakened by the observation that the word "rule" does not imply by itself a harsh or improper rule elsewhere in the OT, even

being used of God's rule. It simply indicates a function of authority. Another idiom is used for harsh rule (cf. Lev. 26:43, 46). The verb of this idiom for harsh rule is also frequently used by itself to connote harsh dominion. However, he is undoubtedly correct in his understanding that, since the Fall, man has distorted his pre-Fall leadership function. Allen P. Ross, *Creation and Blessing* (Grand Rapids: Baker, 1988), 146, also indicates that the word "rule" can have a harsh usage but provides no references to such. Even in a reference such as Isa. 19:4, it is not the word for "rule" that connotes harshness. It is the fact that it is a "fierce king" and "hard master" who is ruling that suggests a difficult time.

[4]This rationale was suggested to me by my late colleague at Multnomah School of the Bible (now Multnomah Bible College), Edward Goodrick.

[5]In spite of the main emphasis being judgment and penalty on the man and woman in Genesis 3:16–20, Hamilton (*Handbook on the Pentateuch*, 48) sees a redemptive purpose in these penalties. "Like a surgeon who cuts with his scalpel only that he may heal, God initiates a means of redemption to reclaim the prodigals. His plan? To place at the respective point of highest self-fulfillment in the life of a woman and a man problems of suffering, misery, and frustration. These 'sentences' are not the prescribed impositions of a volatile deity. Rather, they are gifts of love, strewn in the pathway of man, to bring him back to God."

[6]Ross has pointed out the movement toward chapter 12 and grace in the last two sections of Genesis 4–11, as well as the difference in emphasis of the two genealogies. "Genesis 5:1–6:8 stressed that death prevailed in the race; but Genesis 11:10–26 stresses a movement away from death toward the promise, and it stresses life and expansion, even though longevity was declining. The tone of this list, then, is different. It actually starts with Shem, who was blessed, and concludes with Abram, who was called to receive the blessing" (*Creation and Blessing*, 252, emphasis deleted).

[7]Cf. the discussion by Sailhamer, "Genesis," 61–62, and Ross, *Creation and Blessing*, 157. Also see N. H. Snaith, "Sacrifices in the Old Testament," *VT*, 7 (1957): 308–17; Bruce K. Waltke, "Cain and His Offering," *WJT*, 48 (1986): 363–72. Jack P. Lewis, "The Offering of Abel (Gen. 4:4): A History of Interpretation," *JETS*, 37 (1994): 481–96, provides a summary of the wide range of views on the nature of the offense of Cain. Ross also charts the literary movement of the passage from Cain to Abel, then Abel to Cain, and so on, which strengthens the contrast being made (154).

[8]Modern translations have preferred to find sin "crouching" at Cain's door rather than the AV's "couching." The term, however, simply means "lying" and not necessarily a crouching position. A study of the other occurrences of this term suggest that the animal would be more likely resting after a meal than ready to pounce on one (Ex. 23:5; Gen. 49:9, 14; Isa. 11:6), cf. BDB, 918. "Lying" or "couching" pictures the responsibility that rests at Cain's door, if he does not do well. More recent commentators have appealed to an Akkadian cognate term used for a type of demon to suggest a deeper significance to the term. Normal Hebrew usage should be preferred.

[9]For an interesting attempt at dealing with the great ages in the genealogy of Genesis 5 by ancient parallels, cf. R. K. Harrison, "A Reconsideration of the Antediluvian Patriarch's Ages," *JETS*, 37 (1994): 161–68.

[10]The qualification of Noah as righteous is another contrast with the Babylonian flood stories in which personal favoritism is the basis for the choice. Cf. Sarna, *Understanding Genesis*, 51.

[11]The description of Ham's sin includes, as a minimum, parental dishonor. Calvin says: "Ham, by reproachfully laughing at his father, betrays his own depraved and malignant disposition. . . . This Ham, therefore, must have been of a wicked, perverse, and crooked disposition, since he not only took pleasure in his father's shame, but wished to expose him to his brethren" (I, 302). Cassuto, *Genesis*, II, 152, defines it as "looking with unclean intent." It could involve more than mockery. The idiom used can involve more direct actions than "seeing" (Lev. 20:17). Allen P. Ross, "The Curse of Canaan," *BSac*, 137 (1980): 223–40, examines these options and rejects any greater sin than viewing Noah's nakedness, yet he adds: "To the writer of this narrative this viewing nakedness was apparently serious enough to incur the oracle on Canaan (who [the Canaanites] might be openly guilty in their customs of what Ham had been suspected of doing)" (230).

[12]In addition to the article above, Ross has discussed the place of Canaan and the function of the table of nations in "The Table of Nations in Genesis 10," *BSac*, 137 (1980): 340–53.

[13]Sarna, *Understanding Genesis*, 70–74, has gathered evidence for the accuracy of the Babel account regarding ancient Mesopotamian building practices and terminology.

GOD'S
PLAN
FOR
REVERSAL

chapter four

A New Beginning
(Genesis 12–50)

Do you remember when zoom lenses first came out? I can remember sitting down to home movies made with a zoom lens. Before that, all we had for entertainment was the projector's reverse switch. Now we were entranced by the wide-angle shot which gradually—after practice—narrowed the field of vision until what was previously a small detail now took up the entire screen.

In much the same way the camera of Genesis narrows our field of vision to a single individual. Suddenly the screen is filled with the craggy Semitic face of one man. In Genesis 1–11 we were faced with cosmic issues: the sovereign Creator, the divine order for life, the destructive and debilitating effects of sin, God as sovereign moral ruler, and man as God's designated regent—yet unable to rule himself. Genesis 12 builds on these themes, but focuses our vision on the cosmic importance of one person's life. Genesis 1–11 crunched more than 2000 years of human history—perhaps much more—into less than twenty percent of the book. Genesis 12–50 deals with only four generations. God has focused on one family before. He began with Adam and Eve, but the account quickly moves on through generations to the Flood. He began all over again with Noah and his family. But again, from a few critical incidents in their lives the camera scans to the failure of civilization.

With Abraham we are beginning again.[1] Abraham—initially "Abram"—is God's chosen instrument for starting his program of reversal. The development of God's program of redemption begins to take shape in the story of Abraham. God intends all the world to be in proper relationship with himself. This universal redemption, however, will come about by selecting not everyone, but a few—initially one. While previously we were given a broad, panoramic understanding of life as it is, now we focus on God's special work that makes *history* into *his story* . . . the Story of Reversal.

THE PROMISE TO ABRAHAM, ISAAC, AND JACOB

God's selection is announced to Abraham in the form of a promise:

I will make you into a great nation
 and I will bless you;
I will make your name great,
 and you will be a blessing.
I will bless those who bless you,
 and whoever curses you I will curse;
and all peoples on earth
 will be blessed through you (Gen. 12:2–3).

This promise forms the backbone to the rest of Genesis. It is repeated with each succeeding generation. Isaac receives it in Genesis 26 (twice). Jacob receives it in Genesis 28 and Genesis 35. Only one string is attached to the promise. It is stated in Genesis 12:1: "The LORD had said to Abram, 'Leave your country, your people and your father's household and go to the land I will show you.'" Abraham took up the offer God had made and came to the land of Canaan (Gen. 12:4).[2] Abraham has made his decision, and though he has much to learn about the life of faith, the promise is his. God is only too willing to reassure Abraham about this, even when the old patriarch struggles with problems and doubts.

The promise to Abraham is reaffirmed by God on at least five occasions. It includes the following elements:

- The promise of a great nation through Abraham (12:2; 18:18)
- The promise of a great name (12:2)
- The promise of innumerable offspring (13:15–16)
- The promise of the land of Canaan (12:7; 13:14–17; 15:18–21; 17:8)
- The promise of universal blessing through Abraham (12:3; 18:18; 22:18)
- The promise to be the sovereign Protector of Abraham and his descendants (15:1; 17:8)

This last element holds good even when Abraham himself causes the problem by not wholly trusting God's protection (12:10–17; 20:1–7). God confirms this promise to Abraham by going through a covenant or contract procedure used in the culture of the time (Gen. 15:12–21). Animals were split apart and those making the contract would pass between the pieces. God, in symbolic form—"a smoking firepot with a blazing torch"—passed between the divided animals by himself. By this God bound himself irrevocably to his promise.[3] Abraham was the passive recipient of an irrevocable covenant. Or as the biblical writer puts it, "On that day the LORD made a covenant with Abram, saying, 'To your descendants I have given this land, from the river of Egypt as far as the great river, the river Euphrates'" (Gen. 15:18).

THE FAITH OF ABRAHAM

But let's face it . . . Abraham walked around in that land for twenty-four years with nothing but promises. Well, promises plus verbal assurances whenever he was depressed enough to ask. Abraham gets a lot of ceremonies but no offspring. What is God up to? Why is he taking so long?

It appears God wants to do more with Abraham than drop promises on him. Abraham had received an irrevocable promise from God. But being God's candidate for blessing is not a trip to Disneyland. Because God is going to bless Abraham, he's going to make him into a man of faith. Because God is going to make Abraham a blessing, God will take whatever time is necessary. And God has never let time bother him.

Blessing or Difficulties?

Abraham arrives in the land. No doubt he expects only good times now. Yet he encounters famine. He heads for that perennial haven from crop failure, Egypt, with its dependable Nile. This unforeseen development leaves Abraham insecure. He finds it difficult to appropriate God's promise of protection: "I will bless those who bless you, and whoever curses you I will curse" (Gen. 12:3). He is afraid for his own life and allows Sarah (still known as Sarai) to be taken into the harem of Pharaoh. He even accepts wealth in his new role as brother-in-law to Pharaoh.

But in spite of Abraham's lack of faith, God still acts as his Protector. "The LORD inflicted serious diseases on Pharaoh and his household because of Abram's wife Sarai" (Gen. 12:17). Abraham is a Typhoid Mary to Pharaoh. He is hustled out of the country by military escort—gently, no doubt. Abraham is being stretched. And foreign kings may well hope he learns to trust more. They will be blessed or cursed based on their treatment of him.[4] And even if Abraham is weak, God will not fail in achieving his promise of descendants through Abraham and Sarah.

Two Steps Forward—Genesis 13

The next snapshot of Abraham catches an entirely different picture. Abraham is magnanimous toward his nephew Lot, allowing him to choose the best pasturage in this land that had been promised to Abraham. To this giant step of faith, God responds in kind. Abraham had given Lot his choice:

"If you go to the left, I'll go to the right; if you go to the right, I'll go to the left" (13:9). Yahweh now says to Abraham, "Lift up your eyes . . . north and south, east and west. All the land that you see, I will give it to you and your offspring forever. . . . Go, walk through the length and breadth of the land, for I am giving it to you" (13:14–17). *Abraham couldn't give the land away.* In this walk through the land—another ritual of his culture—he symbolically lays legal claim to it (cf. Josh. 1:3–4). This high point of faith is followed by the building of another altar of worship (Gen. 13:18; cf. 12:7–8).

The next challenge to Abraham's faith is brought on by his nephew Lot's association with Sodom (Gen. 14). As the result of an ancient military conflict, Lot and his household are carried away. In a lightning military strike which brings to mind the later activity of the judges—compare Gideon with his three hundred men—Abraham rescues Lot as well as the goods and people of the Sodom coalition. Here Abraham's faith nearly orbits. He is blessed by an ancient Priest-King of the Most High God, Melchizedek.[5] Abraham confesses Yahweh as the Most High, the Owner of heaven and earth, who is his Protector, Savior, and Provider. He tithes the confiscated booty in recognition of the victory given by God and refuses to take anything from the king of Sodom lest the king be able to say, "I made Abram rich."[6] Abraham has confirmed his commitment to Yahweh as his Provider, the one who is *God Most High*, Possessor of heaven and earth (14:22). God has demonstrated his ability to give military victory to Abraham and his descendants.

God's Response—Genesis 15

The Lord again appears to Abraham in a vision (Gen. 15) in response to Abraham's act of faith above. God's response is to affirm Abraham's stand and encourages him in it (15:1).[7]

> Do not be afraid, Abram,
> I am your shield,
> your very great reward.

Abraham is undoubtedly encouraged by this, but quite naturally he wonders when God will get started on fulfilling the promise. How will there be a great nation, a multitude of offspring who will inherit this land, if Abraham is childless? When will he receive a son? Lot has left, and according to the custom of his time, a servant named Eliezer would inherit everything. For his part, the servant would be responsible for giving Abraham and Sarah a proper burial—a fine prospect for the promise![8]

God repeats only the promise itself—that Abraham's descendants would be as uncountable as the stars (15:5). *And that satisfies Abraham.* God's clearly stated word was enough for Abraham. Here the biblical writer makes it plain that God was pleased. This is the writer's only comment in the whole of the text about God's view of things: "Abram believed the LORD, and he credited it to him as righteousness" (15:6).

God's clear word about descendants and the mention of the land (15:7) prompts another question from Abraham. True to human experience, the resolution of one troubling item prompts the raising of another that has been stirring beneath the surface. "As long as my doubts are getting addressed without censure," Abraham must have thought, "What about the land?" Again God deals with Abraham in a way that encourages his faith and certifies God's promise in the strongest terms. He gives him that irrevocable covenant in a form that could not be misunderstood by Abraham. Nor could its clear intention be later doubted (Did God really say, "You will possess this land"?). In addition, God clarifies the delay in receiving the land and declares centuries in advance the trials and deliverance ahead for his descendants (15:13–16).[9]

One Step Backward—Genesis 16

But even if God's word is clear, human frailty has a way of finding alternate routes apart from the path of faith. Sarah comes up with such a route. It was quite acceptable in the culture of the time but was not what God intended by his promise. She suggests that her servant be her substitute to overcome her barrenness. As the ancient Nuzi tablets indicate, this was a legal procedure by which the child of Hagar would be born as Sarah's. Sarah then could "obtain children by her" (16:2 NRSV).[10] Though humanly acceptable, this approach brings its own problems when Hagar tries to use the pregnancy as a means of elevating her own status (a Prov. 30:23 situation).[11] As in the situation with Pharaoh, even this failure comes under the protective hand of God. Even this substitute son is Abraham's descendant and receives God's protection and a promise of future greatness (Gen. 16:9–12; 21:13–21).

Beginning of Fulfillment—Genesis 17

Thirteen years elapse after the attempt at do-it-yourself fulfillment. Abraham now is ninety-nine and Sarah only ten years younger (17:1, 17).[12] After these apparently silent years, God comes to Abraham as God Almighty—the one who is not limited by human agendas. He has come to signal the beginning of fulfillment! He does this by announcing three changes: Abram's name is changed to Abraham. This signals that God intends to bring to pass his covenant with Abraham, but not through Ishmael. Abraham could see himself as "Abram" ("exalted father") through Ishmael; but God strains his faith by renaming him Abraham ("father of many").

Ishmael would be blessed, but the nation possessing the land of Canaan will come not through Ishmael but through Isaac (17:7–8, 21).

A second alteration is introduced—the physical sign of circumcision. It was common in the ancient Near East to have a sign to indicate a covenant's existence. The sign of the covenant with Noah was the rainbow (Gen. 9:12–16). The sign of the Mosaic Covenant would be keeping the Sabbath day (Ex. 20:8–11; 31:12–17). For Abraham and his descendants, circumcision is the sign of God's covenant with him. To refuse this sign and to fail to practice it as a family would be to reject that covenant. When Moses later postpones the circumcision of his son, God's judgment is aroused even though God had called him to lead the Exodus (Ex. 4:24–26).

A third change indicating that God was about to begin fulfilling the promises in his own supernatural way is the renaming of Sarai as Sarah ("princess"), and the announcement that she will be blessed by becoming the mother of nations and kings. Abraham's reaction is a mixture of reverence (he fell facedown) and bemused astonishment (he laughed). If only God Almighty could be realistic and recognize Ishmael as the way of fulfillment! Twenty-three years earlier there was some hope, but now barren Sarah is eighty-nine! God, however, is unmoved by human "realism." He will bless Ishmael,[13] but the covenant will come through Isaac.

Sodom Revisited—Genesis 18–19

The first episode of Lot and Sodom marked the high point of Abraham's faith during the initial period in the land. A second episode with Sodom again marks Abraham's development as a man who is a prince with God. The judgment on Sodom reminds us of God's continuing sovereignty as judge of all the earth (as in Gen. 4–11). Abraham's descendants ultimately would receive the land when God again brings judgment on the nations of Canaan (Gen. 15:16). But for now, Sodom and all the surrounding cities have reached the point of injustice necessary for Yahweh's formal investigation. As in the tower of Babel incident, Yahweh says, "I will go down and see" (Gen. 18:21; 11:5).

Much like the story of Noah, this setting of judgment becomes the scene for God's choice and blessing. Yahweh, present in appearance as a man, announces the approaching conception of Isaac. Sarah laughs, but Yahweh—in line with his previous announcement as God Almighty (Gen. 17)—rebukes them: "Is anything too hard for the LORD?" (18:14).

Another mark of Abraham's standing with God is Yahweh's own recognition of Abraham as the father-designate of a nation chosen to model his justice (18:17–19). "Shall I hide from Abraham what I am about to do? Abraham will surely become a great and powerful nation, and all nations on earth will be blessed through him." The status God himself has given to Abraham through the promise gives Abraham a legal standing in the land—a standing significant enough that Yahweh should honor him by informing him of his plans and allowing Abraham to plead the cause of as few as ten innocents in Sodom.[14]

The incident with the two supernatural visitors confirms the injustice of Sodom. Sodom is destroyed, but God's grace in providing a saving plan is present as well. At the Flood, Noah was God's means of salvation for the future. After the waters accomplished their judgment, "God remembered Noah" (Gen. 8:1). After the burning sulfur has exacted the divine penalty on the cities of the plain, "He remembered Abraham" (Gen. 19:29) *and delivered four people*.

Failure Revisited—Genesis 20

The prince-designate of Palestine does it *again*. Abraham once more becomes his own worst enemy by placing the promise in jeopardy. In Genesis 12 he allowed Sarai to enter Pharaoh's harem. In Genesis 20 he allows Sarah to enter Abimelech's harem. Sarah, renamed "Princess" because the promise will come through her womb, is threatened with violation by a Canaanite king immediately after Abraham is told that she will give birth to Isaac within a year.

But if Abraham is his own worst enemy, he has God Almighty for a friend. God keeps Abimelech from violating her and allows him to repent of his sin of ignorance. God requires him to make intercession through Abraham. How different this is from the episode with Pharaoh. There God allowed an indignant Pharaoh to hustle Abraham away. Here, Abraham is no doubt as embarrassed, but God forces Abimelech to honor him anyway.[15]

Sarah will become a nation's mother through the promise in spite of Abraham's weakness. So sure is God's promise that Abraham cannot give her away. And now that God has begun to implement his promise, kings will recognize the status of Abraham even in his weakness.

The Son of Promise

Laughter has come to the house of Abraham, because Isaac (which means "He laughs" or "May He [God] smile"), son of promise, is born. Abraham laughed at the absurdity (17:17), Sarah laughed at the impossibility (18:12). Now she laughs with rejoicing, and others will laugh with her (21:6). But a difficult decision has also come to Abraham. Following Isaac's weaning, the prospect of a rivalry and divided inheritance arises. Abraham is concerned for his son Ishmael but is directed by God to follow Sarah's wish to send him away.

God assures Abraham that Ishmael will also achieve nationhood because of Abraham, but the promised line must come through Isaac.

Climax of Testing

The story could have ended with the birth of Isaac. The issue of descendants and God's method of fulfilling the promise is resolved. But the story stretches to an even higher climax. There can be no doubt now that Abraham is blessed of God—as even the local king now recognizes: "God is with you in everything you do" (Gen. 21:22). The nations seek out Abraham for a friendship treaty in order to assure their own future blessing. But just as the story settles down for a smooth landing, the promise is in jeopardy again—this time by God himself.

The final issue to be branded into the mind and soul of Abraham and our Israelite readers is the necessity of faith. Is Yahweh the God of Abraham? Or is the promise the god of Abraham? To paraphrase Satan's accusation against Job: "Does Abraham serve God for nothing? You have blessed him with flocks and herds and provided him a son through his barren wife. You protect him against kings even when he is less than honest. Just ask him to give up his son, and he will curse you to the face" (cf. Job 1:9). Abraham has had the faith to live with the promise in view. Does he have the faith to put the promise on the altar? He is asked to cancel out the only concrete fulfillment he has experienced.

Words are sparse on the way to the altar as the story becomes painfully slow and detailed (Gen. 22). Caring to the end, Abraham carries the dangerous items himself. The boy, as all children, is observant and inquisitive: "Where is the lamb?" The heartbroken father's explanation answers a question too painful to face: "God will provide the sacrifice." It seemed he had—in the son who was to be the heir. More prophetic than he knew, Abraham spoke only what he had experienced of God. *God provides.* He always does. *Sometimes he waits until the raised knife has removed all question of divided motive.*

The Father of Israel has shown future descendants that commitment to God ("I know that you fear God," Gen. 22:12) is the whole duty of man. This leads to a new affirmation of the covenant of promise heightened by Yahweh's taking an oath in his own Name (22:15–18).

Two final duties remain for the patriarch. First, to bury Sarah (Gen. 23)—thereby gaining the only property in Canaan he ever owned. He looked not for property he could buy at discount rates but looked forward to the fulfillment of the promise. Other kings had their cities, but Abraham looked ahead to the city that would come from God.[16] A second duty was to find a wife for Isaac. God is faithful in this as well. Abraham's servant carries back to the eastern relatives the story of Yahweh's blessing on Abraham and receives Yahweh's aid in finding Isaac's bride, Rebekah.

The Blessing Goes On

The remainder of Genesis confirms that the covenant God made with Abraham continues on to his descendants, Isaac and Jacob. These men also become the fathers of the nation of Israel. The Abrahamic Covenant with its many features (blessing, descendants, nationhood, the land of Canaan) is repeated to Isaac and Jacob (Gen. 26:2–5 and 26:24 for Isaac; Gen. 28:10–15 and 35:11–13 for Jacob).

FAMILY TREE OF THE PATRIARCHS

In fact, Isaac's experiences of Genesis 26 are a microcosm of the events we have seen in Abraham's life. He experiences famine—but is told not to go to Egypt. He encounters a Canaanite king, Abimelech, and tries to pass off Rebekah as his sister. (This is not the same king Abraham encountered; "Abimelech" is a hereditary title like "Pharaoh.") But God blesses him to the extent that the Canaanite king recognizes his need for a covenant with Isaac.

God's choice of Jacob as heir of the promise is announced at the birth of the twins—from a previously barren wife. The story of Jacob becoming heir takes up the balance of the *Story of Isaac's Descendants* (Gen. 25:19–35:29). Acting like divine bookends, Jacob's diary of heir-apparent in a strange land is enclosed by two repetitions of the covenant (28:15; 35:9–13).[17] The first includes a promise of protection for the time he is out of the Land of Promise (28:15). Though Jacob's actions and plots are far from defensible, the recognition that God is blessing him is required by all involved (30:27; 31:24–29).

The critical midpoint of this story finds Jacob wrestling with God and being renamed (Gen. 32). Like the stereotypical used-car salesman, this man has "worked the angles" all his life. He encountered and ultimately prevailed over one of his own kind in Laban. But he cannot go back. In front of him is Esau, a victim of earlier plotting. He can only pray to the God of the covenant, acknowledge God's grace, and lean on his promise (32:9–12). What other security is there? Jacob wanted more than anything else to be blessed of God (32:24–29). He struggles all the way into what God wanted to give him—and prevails.

The story of Jacob as patriarch in the land (Gen. 37–50) is mainly about sons Joseph and Judah. Joseph's own summary of his experience capsulizes the major theme: "God sent me ahead of you to preserve for you a remnant on earth, and to save your lives by a great deliverance. So then, it

Figure 4.1
Patriarchal Family Tree

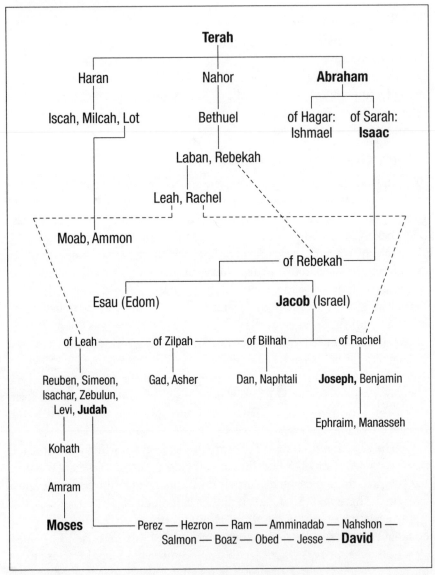

John H. Walton, *Chronological and Background Charts of the Old Testament* (Zondervan, 1978), 41.

was not you who sent me here, but God" (Gen. 45:7–8). Jacob heads out of the land in a different direction than he traveled in his youth. As he nears the borders of Canaan, God confirms the covenant with him and again promises to bring Israel back into the land (46:1–3). What God had explained to

Abraham (Gen. 15:13–16)—that they would be strangers in a foreign land from which they would return to take possession of Canaan—is under way.

The blessing goes on. It cannot stop. God has sworn by himself to Abraham.

FULFILLMENT OF THE ABRAHAMIC COVENANT

The Foundation for God's Developing Plan

The Abrahamic Covenant is the spring from which the rest of God's plan of redemption flows. In the Old Testament it is the foundation for the rest of the covenants.

The Law, or *Mosaic Covenant*, marks the beginning of the nation that was promised to Abraham, Isaac, and Jacob. And the entrance into the land under Joshua is the beginning of God's fulfilling the promise of land (cf. Josh. 1:6). The kings promised as part of Abraham's descendants include first Saul, but later David and his line. God's promise to David in 2 Samuel 7:8–16, the *Davidic Covenant*, promises his descendants will have perpetual rulership over the land and nation promised to Abraham.[18]

Even when Israel becomes a nation in exile because of her unfaithfulness to God, God promises restoration. Note those elements of Jeremiah 30:18–22 that correspond to the elements of the Abrahamic Covenant,

Figure 4.2

Abrahamic Covenant	Jeremiah 30:18–22
Blessing and land	"I will restore the fortunes of Jacob's tents and have compassion on his dwellings; the city will be rebuilt on her ruins, and the palace will stand in its proper place …
Descendants	I will add to their numbers, and they will not be decreased;
Great name	I will bring them honor, and they will not be disdained.
Nation	Their children will be as in the days of old, and their community will be established before me;
Protector	I will punish all who oppress them …
God	So you will be my people, and I will be your God."

This notion of restoration of the nation introduces the *New Covenant*, a future covenant to be given to the nation as an improvement over the Mosaic Covenant that the nation consistently violated (Jer. 31:31–37). This New Covenant will include inner enablement for living in God's ways—a covenant which will be written on the heart. God will not only provide the instruction but the change of heart necessary to follow his teaching.

The progression of God's plan through the Old Testament is traceable by following these covenants which are all based on the Abrahamic Covenant. See the chart below.

Figure 4.3

	Mosaic Covenant – Nation formed.
Abrahamic Covenant – God is faithful.	**Davidic Covenant –** Line of kings over nation.
	New Covenant – Enablement for blessing.

God Is Faithful

Our survey of God's work with Abraham shows that God sovereignly gave the covenant to him in the clearest terms that language and culture allowed as an irrevocable covenant. From entering the land onward, Abraham's obedience or disobedience did not change God's decision to work through Abraham. Of course, Abraham's great acts of faith bring from God a reiteration of the promise and statements of approval and acceptance (Gen. 15:6; 22:15–18). But statements of God's intention to fulfill the promise are just as clear after Abraham's failure to act in faith (Gen. 17:17–22). And after Abraham's death it is God's dealings with Abraham, not Isaac's activity, that are given as the basis for confirming the promise to Isaac (Gen. 26:3–5; 26:24).[19]

The prophets also proclaim God's faithful determination, even while Israel stands under God's judgment for near-continuous disobedience:

> Thus says the LORD,
>> Who gives the sun for light by day,
>> And the fixed order of the moon and the stars for light by night,
>> Who stirs up the sea so that its waves roar;
>> The LORD of hosts is his name:
>> "If this fixed order departs from before me," declares the LORD,
>> "Then the offspring of Israel also shall cease
>> From being a nation before Me forever" (Jer. 31:35–36 NASB).

Clear enough? If not, turn to Malachi 3 where some have returned to the land from the Babylonian captivity. They have not been obedient. But what does God promise? To send his messenger to bring chastening so Israel's worship might be pleasing to the Lord once again. And he finishes with these words: "I, the LORD, do not change. So you, O descendants of

Jacob, are not destroyed" (3:6). Yahweh does not change. He cannot bless unrighteousness, but he also cannot—he will not—change his promise with Abraham, Isaac, and Jacob.

And this is the point that confuses many readers of the Old Testament. God promised Abraham a nation, land, and blessing for himself and the world. He will fulfill his promise, but not when the nation is disobedient. Perhaps an illustration will help. I could promise to buy my son a new sports vehicle. I could make that promise in unconditional and irrevocable terms. We could even split a few animals on the front yard and I could walk between them. Or, as a more recent substitute, I could sign my name in blood. The bargain is clear. He will get the truck. But when? I may find that the tender age of sixteen, when he first receives his license, is not the time to fulfill my contract with him. Having a new vehicle then may do him more harm than good. I may decide to give him the wheels at age seventeen because he seems to exhibit a special maturity for his age. But within six months, I find he is having problems fulfilling other responsibilities because he is spending so much time with his truck. I exile it to the garage indefinitely, putting it on hold until I believe he is ready. Have I violated or canceled my contract? No, I have not. In terms of the Abrahamic Covenant, this means God is committed to fulfilling his promise to Abraham, but he is not obligated to do it all at once, or to bless every generation no matter how rebellious they are. God's promise to Abraham does guarantee the conclusion of the matter. *It will come to pass.* It does not guarantee the nation unrestricted blessing at all times.

Jesus, the Son of Abraham

The New Testament immediately introduces Jesus as "the son of David, the son of Abraham" (Matt. 1:1). Tracing the line of Jesus back to Abraham is important because God had already indicated it was through Abraham that blessing for all the nations would come. God was bound to his own oath. "Because God wanted to make the unchanging nature of his purpose very clear to the heirs of what was promised, he confirmed it with an oath" (Heb. 6:17).

Several announcements mark the significance of Jesus' birth. Among them is the *Magnificat* of Mary (Luke 1:46–55). She finishes with these words:

> He has helped his servant Israel,
>   remembering to be merciful
> To Abraham and his descendants forever,
>   even as he said to our fathers.

The promise is not dead, but very much alive in the child within her womb! Is anything impossible for God? The child who will fulfill the promise is not the son of a barren woman, but the son of a woman who has not had sexual intercourse at all. What a way to mark out the special nature of this Son of Abraham!

Zechariah, the father of John the Baptist, prophesied concerning Jesus:

> Praise be to the Lord, the God of Israel,
>> because he has come and has redeemed his people.
> He has raised up a horn of salvation for us
>> in the house of his servant David
> (as he said through his holy prophets of long ago),
> salvation from our enemies
>> and from the hand of all who hate us—
> to show mercy to our fathers
>> and to remember his holy covenant,
>> the oath he swore to our father Abraham (Luke 1:68–73).

Israel expects restoration to full nationhood, and Zechariah by the Holy Spirit predicts it will come through Jesus. Such restoration is confirmed by the apostle Paul who emphatically denies that God has cast away his people, the physical descendants of Abraham (Rom. 11:2). He points out that there has always been a faithful minority, a "remnant," who truly knew God in Israel.[20]

This is true in the present age as well. There is a remnant of faithful Israelites who are now participating in the church (11:5), Paul himself being a prime example (11:1). Paul sees the blind state of most of Israel at the present time as "a partial hardening" that "has happened to Israel until the fullness of the Gentiles has come in; and thus all Israel will be saved" (11:25–26 NASB). He then splices quotes of Old Testament promises for Israel's restoration: "The deliverer will come from Zion, He will turn godlessness away from Jacob. And this is my covenant with them, when I take away their sins" (11:26–27; cf. Isa. 59:20–21; 27:9).

In 1939 Ross Parker and Hughie Charles wrote the song, "There'll Always Be an England." It encouraged hope at a time when England needed her spirits lifted. It's a fine national sentiment, especially for those with English blood in their veins. But only one people really have such an assurance. There'll always be children of Israel—not because Israel is faithful, but because God has given his word to Abraham.[21]

Jesus, the Seed of Abraham

The seed, the descendants of Abraham, would also be the mediators of blessing to all the nations of the earth (Gen. 22:18; 12:3). This also comes to pass through Jesus. Jesus is the Seed—the descendant of Abraham *par excellence*. Just as at a later time the Israelite king would represent the whole nation, so Jesus is God's chosen representative for the nation.

The good news of Jesus Christ—that God would justify the Gentiles by faith—was proclaimed to Abraham, Paul says, in the promise: "All nations will be blessed through you" (Gal. 3:8). Jesus, in fact, came under God's judgment on the cross "in order that the blessing given to Abraham might come to the Gentiles through Christ Jesus, so that by faith we might receive the promise of the Spirit" (Gal. 3:14). But the full extent of this Gentile blessing is revealed only in the New Testament. The Old Testament foresees ultimate Gentile redemption but does not foresee the nature of the church—a body in which there is no distinction between Jew and Gentile. Both are fellow members in the Body of Christ, the church (Eph. 3:6).

Paul reminds his Gentile readers of their relationship to God before they came to believe in Christ (Eph. 2). No more desperate condition could be described than that of Ephesians 2:12: "Remember that at that time you were separate from Christ, excluded from citizenship in Israel and foreigners to the covenants of promise, without hope and without God in the world." But God has done something new. He has made a "new man" (2:15), the church, which includes both Jew and Gentile.

The Gentile experiences not only the blessing through Abraham's Seed as originally promised, but more: Since God has placed all who believe, whether Jew or Gentile, as equal members in Christ, the Gentile finds himself a part of Christ, the Seed of Abraham. This is the essence of Paul's proclamation of the gospel—that "the Gentiles are heirs together with Israel, members together of one body, and sharers together in the promise in Christ Jesus" (Eph. 3:6). "If you belong to Christ, then you are Abraham's seed, and heirs according to the promise" (Gal. 3:29). You can't do better than that. What was previously a very narrow spot on the screen—one man—has now opened up to a glorious, wide-angle vista. For Israel it's because of God's faithfulness to his promise. For Gentiles like myself, it's called GRACE.

SUGGESTED SCRIPTURE READING:

Genesis 12:1–7; 18:1–15; 22:1–19
Ephesians 2:8–3:6

For Interaction and Discussion:

1. Abraham was God's choice to bring blessing to the world. Did Abraham have an easy life? What advantages did he experience? What difficulties and frustrations? What about Isaac and Jacob?

2. What factors in God's working with Abraham do you see as similar to God's working today? What factors are unique to Abraham's special calling? What makes Abraham a man of faith?

3. What do Abraham's failings and God's response to them tell us about God? What do they tell us about Abraham? Is Abraham a hero—more "human" than the rest of us? Or less?

4. How does Genesis see Abraham become accepted as righteous before God? How does a person do this today?

5. Imagine yourself living in the tent next to Jacob's. Would you like to be his neighbor? What was Jacob's attitude toward God's promise?

6. What makes the Abrahamic Covenant so important to understanding the Bible? Do you think the survival of the Jewish people relates to this covenant?

7. What is the "good news" for Gentiles? Why was Jesus' work necessary to achieve this good news?

For Further Reading:

Walter C. Kaiser, Jr. *Toward an Old Testament Theology*. Grand Rapids: Zondervan, 1978, 84–99. Discussion of the theology of the Abrahamic Covenant.

Derek Kidner, *Genesis*. TOTC. Downers Grove, Ill.: InterVarsity, 1967, 113–224. Commentary accessing the Hebrew text for the English reader.

Nahum M. Sarna. *Understanding Genesis*. New York: Schocken, 1966, 81–163. Helpful with archaeological background and customs, though speculative regarding numbers.

Notes and Comments:

[1]When we point out that we are beginning again with one man, this is not to suggest an absolute break with the previous section. The introduction of Abraham was anticipated in the selection of earlier material. The genealogies are leading toward Abraham. The comments about Shem also anticipate God's choice of Abraham.

[2]Some, using the ages given, criticize Abraham for an apparent delay in coming to Canaan. The text (12:4) gives no hint of censure. See Kidner's appropriate remarks (*Genesis*, 113–14).

[3]Sarna, *Understanding Genesis*, 126–27, should be consulted for the significance of the ritual of Genesis 15. He says, "The covenant completely lacks . . . mutuality. It is a unilateral obligation assumed by God without any reciprocal responsibilities being imposed upon Abraham. The use of established legal forms of treaty-making to express such a situation is a dramatic way of conveying the

immutable nature of the divine promise." For an interesting symbolic interpretation of the ritual cf. Gordon J. Wenham, *Genesis 1–15*, WBC (Waco, Tex.: Word, 1987), 1:332–33, where, concerning the covenant, Wenham writes: "Throughout the Abrahamic stories there is an implicit comparison with the later experience of Israel, and it has therefore been supposed that the patriarchal and Sinaitic covenants were similar. But this is not so. The Sinaitic and Deuteronomic covenants were agreements imposing obligations on both God and Israel: their closest extra-biblical analogy is found in the ancient international treaties made by great powers with their vassals. This covenant with Abraham is different: it is a promissory oath made by God alone. Weinfield (*JAOS* 90 [1970], 184–203; *TDOT* 2:270–72) says the nearest parallel to this form is the royal land grant, made by kings to loyal servants. These grants were typically made to a man and his descendants in perpetuity. In form and content they thus run in parallel to the patriarchal promises."

⁴We should not miss the additional lesson that the story of Abraham's lack of faith in Egypt teaches. "If Yahweh did not go astray in his work of sacred history because of the failure and guilt of the recipient of promise, then his word was really to be believed" (von Rad, *Genesis*, 170). This again shows that the point of these narratives is the certainty of the promise.

⁵The appearance of Melchizedek in Genesis 14 is not a theophany or an appearance of an angelic being as we find in Genesis 18 with the "three men." Melchizedek represents the reality of true worship in the nations outside of Israel before the Exodus. Moses' father-in-law, Jethro, is also viewed as a true priest. The choice of Abraham and his descendants was necessary because true worship was declining and the nations were turning away from God. Melchizedek is represented as an earthly king of an earthly city, Salem, who is also a priest. David, after conquering Jerusalem, seems to have been aware of this ancient line and ascribes it to his final successor (cf. 2 Sam. 6:14; Ps. 110:4).

⁶Von Rad, *Genesis*, 180, finds an inconsistency in the account of Abraham's not accepting anything of the booty, yet tithing it. The inconsistency is possible only if the order of the account is reversed. Abraham tithes the booty as appropriate for the deliverance, then refuses the offer to take something for himself.

⁷As here in Genesis 15, visions often follow actions of faith in the narrative. See 12:7 following the entrance into the land; 13:14 after allowing Lot his choice of land; and, most notably, 22:11 after Abraham's willingness to sacrifice Isaac. Additionally, Yahweh's speaking to Abraham introduces new steps: 12:1; 17:1; 18:1; 22:1.

⁸The Nuzi Tablets, dated only slightly later than Abraham, illumine the nature of Eliezer as heir. The Nuzi texts include actual legal documents of such adoptions. One document reads: "As long as Nashwi is alive, Wullu [the adoptee] shall provide food and clothing; when Nashwi dies, Wullu shall become the heir. If Nashwi has a son of his own, he shall divide (the estate) equally with Wullu, but the son of Nashwi shall take the gods of Nashwi," *ANET*, 219.

⁹Sarna, *Understanding Genesis*, 121–22, finds four connections of this renewed promise of land for Abraham in Genesis 15 to the previous context dealing with the booty of the kings. One connection is the "possessions" that Abraham's descendants

would have, corresponding to the possessions (14:21, same word) which Abraham refused from the king of Sodom.

[10]Marrying a slave from the land of Lullu is specified as the way to guarantee an heir if the wife is barren, *ANET*, 220. If this is done, the original wife "may not send the offspring [of the slave-wife] away." Cf. Sarna, *Understanding Genesis*, 128–29. It is clear from the Rachel story that when the slave is the wife's, the children are to be counted as the wife's (Gen. 30:3—"that she may bear on my knees, that through her I too may have children" NASB). "The slave was born 'on the knees' of the wife, so that the child then came symbolically from the womb of the wife herself (cf. 30:3, 9)!" (von Rad, *Genesis*, 191). Talk about surrogate motherhood!

[11]Sarah's statements in 16:5 are confusing since she, not Abraham, had suggested Hagar as a substitute. How could Abraham be responsible? Von Rad, *Genesis*, 191–92, points out that the maintenance of justice was the husband's responsibility. The allowance of the new "wife" to despise her mistress was an injustice. Sarah utters this legal formula calling for redress of the wrong. Abraham's verdict is to reassert Hagar's status as Sarah's personal servant and her right to do what she wished with her. Hagar flees after Sarah's rough treatment but is sent back by God with directions to submit. A similar case appears in the Code of Hammurabi (#146) with the same verdict (*ANET*, 172).

[12]The summary of 16:15–17:1 informs us of a thirteen-year time gap. Is this gap due to Abraham's desire to use Ishmael as a substitute? Is it significant that it is thirteen years—long enough for Ishmael to grow out of childhood? The summary also appears to act as a hinge in the movement of the narrative. Following this summary and prior to the birth of Isaac, earlier threads are picked up. Another incident with Lot and Sodom, another encounter with a king involving Sarah, and the reaffirmation of the promise are renewed themes.

[13]Note the language similarity in the blessing on Ishmael and the wording of the original blessing of Genesis 1:28.

[14]Abraham's recognition by God in the Sodom account is impressive. It is heightened by the fact that Abraham realizes he is pressing his point as he arbitrates, and so is presuming upon God's patience (18:27–32). God's willingness to allow Abraham to press the issue highlights Abraham's position. A second point is observed by von Rad, *Genesis*, 213–14. Abraham's objections are really questions of justice. He believes it unworthy of God that a significant minority should die with an admittedly perverse majority. Additionally, the account shows that he misjudged God's grace. He bargained all the way down to ten, but God exceeds his request and delivers the four who "qualify" anyway! This has its relevance to the Israelites. They are to understand that their invasion of Canaan was under a God who was not just eliminating the whole nation because the majority were perverse. No. God would have saved even a small minority of morally good citizens (cf. Gen. 6:5).

On the sin of Sodom see Sarna, *Understanding Genesis*, 144–46. C. F. Keil argues that it is not Abraham's position but the object lesson for his descendants that is the primary reason for God's consultation (*The Pentateuch* [Grand Rapids: Eerdmans, 1971], 229–30).

[15]As Kidner, *Genesis*, 117, points out, this second incident of Sarah being desired for a king's harem is not due to beauty as was the first at a younger period in her life but probably represents a desire by Abimelech to enhance his own position by an alliance with Abraham who is now well-off.

[16]In stating that Abraham was looking forward to a city, the writer of Hebrews demonstrates an understanding of the culture of the land of promise in Abraham's time (Heb. 11:10). The city he was looking forward to was not heaven. Further discussion of the interpretation of Hebrews on this point is found in chapter 8.

[17]The narrative of "Jacob out-of-the-Land" is enclosed by the two events at Bethel, one on the way out and the other on the way back in. For some literary observations see: Steve McKenzie, "You Have Prevailed," *Restoration Quarterly*, 23 (1980): 225–31; also, Michael Fishbane, "Composition and Structure in the Jacob Cycle (Gen. 25:29–35:22)," *Journal of Jewish Studies*, 28, 15–38.

[18]Kaiser, *Toward an Old Testament Theology*, 153, includes a revealing comparison between the language of the Davidic Covenant and the Abrahamic. Our discussion of the Davidic Covenant comes in chapter 9.

[19]Some maintain that the Abrahamic Covenant was revocable all along and could be canceled for disobedience. Cf. Daniel Fuller, *Gospel and Law* (Grand Rapids: Eerdmans, 1980), 121–45. Fuller fails to recognize the distinction between an unconditional, irrevocable covenant in which enjoyment of the covenant at any point in time is conditioned on faithfulness, and a conditional, revocable covenant, which can be entirely canceled out for unfaithfulness and, therefore, allow no future fulfillment. Thus he turns the whole issue on its head and declares all the covenants conditional and revocable. It will still turn out the same, he assures us, because both Ezekiel 36 and Genesis 18 make "certain both the end that God would unite Israel in the land, and the means necessary for achieving this end, namely, that Israel be godly" (143). He finds one passage, Genesis 18:18–19, which, unlike other passages, seems to have a condition attached. He reads the passage's final (result) clause—"so that the LORD will bring about for Abraham what he has promised him"—as if it is stating a condition. Yet both verses are clearly a prediction and guarantee that God's covenant will surely come to pass for Abraham. One must simply ask of the verses: Do they indicate God has promised something to Abraham? Do they indicate God will bring it to pass? What else do we mean by irrevocable or unconditional? The last clause merely reaffirms the assured result. These things will occur so that God will establish his covenant. On the other hand, to make the covenant totally conditional ignores all of the contextual indicators that the covenant is totally guaranteed on God's part. To introduce a condition as late as chapter 18 is to destroy the significance of the earlier narrative. Cf. Kaiser, *Toward an Old Testament Theology*, 91–94. Fuller's treatment might imply that seeing the Abrahamic Covenant as unconditional or irrevocable is an interpretation unique to dispensationalism. Such is far from the case. Cf. Sarna, *Understanding Genesis*, 127; John Bright, *A History of Israel*, 3d ed. (Philadelphia: Westminster, 1959), 102–3; Leupold, *Genesis*, 1:489; Wenham, *Genesis 1–15*, 1:333.

[20]It is important to recognize that Paul uses the term "Israel" here for physical descendants of Abraham, whether in or out of the church. "All Israel shall be saved" (Rom. 11:25–26) cannot, therefore, be referring to those not physically Israelites.

[21]A wider array of scholars is recognizing that a future is predicted for Abraham's physical seed in Romans 11. Cf. Anthony A. Hoekema, *The Bible and the Future* (Grand Rapids: Eerdmans, 1979), 144–47, though he takes Israel's salvation to be an ongoing process not distinct from the present remnant; and Gordon J. Wenham, *The Book of Leviticus* (Grand Rapids: Eerdmans, 1979), 333. It is a credit to God's grace that he gives covenant benefits to those with whom he had no promise (Gentiles), but it is an unworthy accusation that God has cast away those to whom the promise was given originally.

chapter five

A REDEEMED PEOPLE
(Exodus)

Thanks to the efforts of Cecil B. De Mille in his screen spectacular *The Ten Commandments*, much of the English-speaking world has no difficulty picturing the drama of the Exodus. We can relive the emotions of a mass of all-too-common people with their doubts, complaints, and hopes, who at last scurry between two walls of water in an escape to freedom. Though we know the plot, we feel the tension as the Egyptian chariot force hesitates momentarily before literally taking the plunge.

But the Exodus is more than a mass movement of tons of water. More, in fact, than the beginning of freedom for an oppressed people. The Exodus is truly a creation—a creation of that nation which would be distinctively God's people. The Exodus for Israel is not the "luck of the draw," nor is Moses the George Washington of a new democracy. Step by step, the book of Exodus records for us the process of God redeeming this enslaved people. Like most of God's operations, it seems exceedingly slow—especially for those who cry out to God for help. Why does he take so long? When will God answer? These are questions Abraham asked ... questions asked again by the descendants of Abraham ... and questions still asked today. The book of Exodus has answers to these questions. For it recounts not simply a spectacular miracle or even a score of them, but a revelation of Yahweh, the true God. The goal of God's activity here is to have his people learn to know Yahweh.

THE REDEMPTION FROM EGYPT
Egypt, the Artificial Womb—Exodus 1–2

God does his creating in the most unlikely wombs. A great nation was promised out of Sarah's barrenness. The descendants of her womb become a people through the surprising hospitality of Egypt. Oh, it started out well enough with Joseph being sent ahead by God. In fact, Egypt continued to be a positive birthing station: "The Israelites were fruitful and multiplied greatly and became exceedingly numerous, so that the land was filled with them" (Ex. 1:7). It is no accident that these words repeat God's blessing given originally to Adam (Gen. 1:28), to Noah (9:7), and to Jacob (35:11).

The text is telling us that *the Creator God is the God of this people*. The people of Abraham experience blessing originally intended for all mankind because they have come into relationship with God through his covenant with Abraham, Isaac, and Jacob.

But the artificial womb turns hostile. New leadership first tries harsh labor, then infanticide. Finally, being born a male Hebrew becomes a capital offense. Yet none of these steps can stem the blessing of God (Ex. 1:12, 20). Out of this last, most oppressive step, God raises up a deliverer. Oppression was Egypt's fatal mistake. It placed Egypt in a hostile relationship with Yahweh because of his covenant with Abraham: "I will bless those who bless you, and whoever curses you I will curse" (Gen. 12:3). By perverting its role as host, Egypt fell from the place of being blessed to the place of being cursed.

Pharaoh[1] has taken on an awesome Opponent who delights in proving his strength out of weakness. From the desperation and pain of a powerless Hebrew mother, God raises up a deliverer. Moses rides in a frail mini-ark to safety,[2] and God rears his leader with Pharaoh's groceries.

But if Israel's hopes were riding on having an inside man at the Kremlin, these hopes are dashed as Moses must flee to the wilderness. Here again there is irony in God's providence. The very taunt thrown up to Moses by his own fellow Hebrew becomes the reason Moses must go to the desert. "Who made you ruler and judge over us?" (2:14) stands as a concise summary of Moses' need and as a clear pointer to the focus of the Exodus—Who indeed?[3]

But to the Hebrews in bondage, the signs of God's concern must have seemed minimal. Ignorant of God at work behind the scenes, they could only cry out in their misery. Let us not forget that this was real groaning and without knowing the purpose for it.[4] How much of life is like this—where the reasons for present pains will become clear in God's purposes generations later?

God has not forgotten, however. "God heard their groaning and he remembered his covenant with Abraham, with Isaac and with Jacob. So God looked on the Israelites and was concerned [knew] about them" (Ex. 2:24–25). God heard . . . God remembered . . . God looked . . . and God knew. All terms of involvement. For God to remember is not to imply prior absent-mindedness. God's "remembering" is a way of saying he is about to act. God remembered Noah and acted by causing the flood waters to recede (Gen. 8:1). God promised to remember his covenant with Noah to never again destroy the earth with a flood (9:15–16). God remembered Abraham and his concern for his nephew and so delivered Lot from Sodom (18:29). God remembered Rachel and her request for a son by causing her to conceive (30:22). God is now ready to act on the basis of his covenant with Abraham, Isaac, and Jacob. This guarantee of God's impending intervention switches the scene back to the preparation of Moses.

Yahweh Encounters Moses—Exodus 3–4

To date, God has been in the background. But now God begins an outright program of revealing himself to this people nurtured in the womb of idolatrous Egypt. His revelation to the deliverer comes first. From the middle of a burning bush, God identifies himself as "the God of your father, the God of Abraham, the God of Isaac, and the God of Jacob." This is not empty repetition or even name-dropping. It announces God's intention to keep his covenant made with the fathers. He will rescue Israel[5] and bring her into the land promised to Abraham. Moses will be his prophetic spokesman to lead Israel out of Egypt.[6]

Moses' questions and problems provide the background for the critical themes of this book. Moses' first problem is his own inadequacy for the task. He has no current standing in Egypt. The answer is that God will be adequate: "I will be with you" (Ex. 3:12). This leads to Moses' second problem: Who is the God of Abraham? What is his Name? If Moses is to represent Yahweh in polygamous Egypt, he would need more than the title, God, in a country that had multitudes of gods under various names. These two questions introduce the major theme: the name *Yahweh*. Up to this point in Exodus the name *Yahweh* has not been used. The title *Elohim* (translated "God") has indicated the Creator's interest in Israel to bless them. But the rest of the book is the story of Israel's and Pharaoh's increasing understanding of God as Yahweh.[7] The statement, "I am Yahweh," makes its imprint on each unfolding episode which follows.

But why does this name make a difference? What's in a name, anyway? In most of our naming, the answer is "Not much." Sometimes, as in our family, the first son will be named after his dad. For our second son we chose the name Mark. No, not because it is a biblical name. We just liked it! Many biblical names also have little ultimate significance. Some, like "Moses," are a wordplay of the situation at birth. Others reflect a renaming, as in Jacob's case, to reflect a change of status.[8] But the name of God? Surely God's self-chosen name must be significant. It is, therefore, not merely the name but the meaning of the name that is being emphasized here. And what is God's name? It appears in the Hebrew Bible as יהוה, which transliterated into English would read YHWH. In most English Bibles this name is not given but is represented by the word LORD, printed with all capitals. Some Bibles use the

Figure 5.1
Comparison of Chronological Systems

Early Exodus Long Sojourn	Early Exodus Short Sojourn	Late Exodus	Reconstructionist
The Patriarchs 2166-1805		**2100**	
Migration to Egypt 1876		**2000**	
		1900	
	The Patriarchs 1952–1589	**1800** The Patriarchs 1950–1650	
Egyptian sojourn 1876–1446	Migration to Egypt 1660	**1700** Migration to Egypt 1650	
Slavery 1730–1580		**1600**	
	Egyptian sojourn 1660–1446 Slavery: 1580	**1500** Egyptian sojourn 1650–1230	The Patriarchs 1500–1300 Gradual migration
		1400 Slavery 1580	Egyptian sojourn 1350–1230
Wandering 1446–1406	Wandering 1446–1406	**1300**	
Conquest and Judges 1406–1050	Conquest and Judges 1406–1050	**1200** Conquest and Judges 1230–1025	Conquest and Judges 1230–1025
		1100	
United Kingdom 1050–931	United Kingdom 1050–931	**1000** United Kingdom 1025–931	United Kingdom 1025–931
		900	
Early date for Exodus and 430-year sojourn in Egypt per Masoretic reading of Exod. 12:40	Early date of Exodus and 215-year sojourn in Egypt per LXX reading of Exod. 12:40	Late date of Exodus and belief in historicity of patriarchal events	Late date of Exodus and reconstruction of biblical history through use of form criticism
*L. Wood, J. Davis, M. Unger, and G. Archer	J. Free and S. Schultz	R. K. Harrison, G. E. Wright, K. A. Kitchen, and W. F. Albright	A. Alt, M. Noth, C. Gordon, and H. H. Rowley

*The authors named may vary as to the exact dates, but they fall generally in the given school of thought.
John H. Walton, *Chronological and Background Charts of the Old Testament* (Zondervan, 1978), 25.

name Jehovah, but this is not really accurate. Because of its tie with the verb "I AM" (Ex. 3:14–15), most Hebrew scholars are convinced the name ought to be pronounced "Yahweh."[9]

But again we must ask, What does it mean? The explanation to Moses is, "I AM WHO I AM. This is what you are to say to the Israelites: 'I AM has sent me to you.' "God also said to Moses, "Say to the Israelites, 'Yahweh, the God of your fathers—the God of Abraham, the God of Isaac and the God of Jacob—has sent me to you.' This is my name forever, the name by which I am to be remembered from generation to generation" (Ex. 3:14–15).[10]

Tomes have been written on the meaning of this Name. But our best clue is the use of the same word for "I am" in this very discussion with Moses. For God has given as his first answer to Moses' objections the promise, "I will be with you" (3:12). The word for "I will be" is the same word translated "I am" and it has the same significance.[11] God answered Moses' objection that he had no standing with Pharaoh by assuring him that his own Presence would be enough standing for both of them. God was assuring Moses: "I am present with you when you stand before Pharaoh. Go, for I am with you." So in the name YHWH is wrapped up the notion that God is present to help. In other words, God is faithful. He is there to act on behalf of those who know him. "I am who I am" means: "I am there, wherever it may be ... I am really there."[12] Furthermore, the name Yahweh is associated with the fulfillment of his promise. As Yahweh he has promised to bring Israel out of her misery in Egypt and bring her into the land of the Canaanites. The repeated "I am YHWH" in this book will continue to emphasize the One who has come into relationship by covenant with this people and so is committed to faithfulness to them.

A second theme introduced by Moses' objections is the theme of plagues and the response of the Pharaoh (Ex. 3:18–20). Moses is commissioned to approach Pharaoh about Yahweh's right to demand worship from his people. Pharaoh, Yahweh predicts, will reject Yahweh's sovereignty, thus setting up the confrontation between Yahweh and Pharaoh over the rights to the sons of Israel.

Moses' concern that he might be rejected as a prophetic spokesman for God is answered when God turns the staff of Moses into a serpent as a sign of his commission. Don't miss the humor of it. The sign Moses so desperately wants chases him around. Two other signs also are provided (Ex. 4:1–9). With these three signs Moses' status as a spokesman for Yahweh will not be in doubt. Following the answer to Moses' objection that he is not an adequate orator, another theme is introduced—the theme of the firstborn.

> When you return to Egypt, see that you perform before Pharaoh all the wonders I have given you the power to do. But I will harden his heart

so that he will not let the people go. Then say to Pharaoh, "This is what Yahweh says: 'Israel is my firstborn son, and I told you, "Let my son go, so he may worship me." But you refused to let him go; so I will kill your firstborn son'" (Ex. 4:21–23).

The firstborn son had the place of privilege and responsibility in the family. He was also granted an extra share of the inheritance. Israel as Yahweh's firstborn was to stand in the place of privilege. Israel was his designated leader among the family of nations. If Pharaoh was not willing to recognize this special relationship, the justice of correspondence ("eye for eye") would come into play. Pharaoh's firstborn would not be recognized by Yahweh.

But the next event involves Moses' firstborn (Ex. 4:24–26). This is not accidental, though its meaning is not totally clear. What is clear is that Moses comes under Yahweh's judgment. Why would Yahweh try to kill his chosen spokesman? The answer is tied to the fact that Moses' firstborn had not been circumcised. How can Moses represent Yahweh, the God of Abraham, Isaac, and Jacob, when he has not circumcised his own son? This would be like the president of Chrysler Corporation appearing in a television commercial for Chryslers, then driving a Toyota home. Circumcision is the sign of faith in what God promised to Abraham (Gen. 17:9–14). Zipporah, Moses' wife, and perhaps part of the problem, circumcises Gershom to save Moses.[13]

Yahweh claims the right of his firstborn to serve him. And he claims the right to Moses and Moses' son. Yahweh's right to all of Israel will become an institution in the redemption of every firstborn son as a mark of the Exodus (Ex. 13:11–16).

Who Is Yahweh?—Exodus 5–6

The people of Israel accept Moses as spokesman for Yahweh with a demonstration of the signs, but Pharaoh, as predicted, is adamant in his refusal to let the people obey Yahweh by going into the wilderness to sacrifice (Ex. 5:1–3). Now, a festival in the wilderness certainly looks suspicious. Are they really going to have the ancient equivalent of a Sunday school picnic and return to Egypt as good slaves? Isn't this idea of a religious retreat simply an attempt at escape? Pharaoh thought so. Wouldn't you?

You might, until you recognized that all Yahweh is trying to establish at this time is his right to receive worship as Israel's God. If Pharaoh will recognize this right, then Pharaoh can come under the blessing of those who bless Abraham's descendants. But of course, Pharaoh has already violated Yahweh's people by continuing to hold them under the yoke of slavery and worse. Abraham's descendants will come to birth as a nation, even if God has to use caesarean section or worse on Egypt. Much better for Egypt if she is cooperative with the divine program. The program will not suffer. Those who don't submit, will. Some things never change!

But Pharaoh has had his chance, and he has now formally rejected Yahweh with the haughty answer: "Who is Yahweh, that I should obey him and let Israel go? I do not know Yahweh and I will not let Israel go." Because Pharaoh reacts by increasing the workload, and the people of Israel respond by accusing Moses and Aaron of causing their ruin, Moses complains to God. God's response? A reaffirmation of his activity as Yahweh. In these eight verses the expression "I am Yahweh" is repeated for emphasis four times and is both the opening and closing statement. Because he is Yahweh, his promise will be fulfilled. He not only makes covenants, he establishes them by his active intervention.

A Plague or Ten—Exodus 7–14

There are ten plagues and twelve miracles in this section. The ten plagues are preceded by a miracle of authentication and followed by a final miracle of judgment. Prior to all the plagues, Yahweh announces the certainty of Pharaoh's obstinacy:

> I will harden Pharaoh's heart that I may multiply my signs and my wonders in the land of Egypt. When Pharaoh will not listen to you, then I will lay my hand on Egypt, and bring out my hosts, my people the sons of Israel, from the land of Egypt by great judgments. And the Egyptians shall know that I am Yahweh. When I stretch out my hand on Egypt and bring out the sons of Israel from their midst (Ex. 7:3–5 NASB).

The Plagues and Pharaoh. But what about hardening Pharaoh's heart? Was it right for God to harden it? Did Pharaoh harden it first? Much of the discussion on this issue misses the point of these events. Egypt has *already* violated her privilege as host to Yahweh's covenant people. She has enslaved them, murdered them, and now rejected any claim of Yahweh to their service for even a few days. Egypt is already due for judgment. Attempts to prove that this Pharaoh hardened his heart first are less than convincing.[14] Yahweh has hardened Pharaoh's heart so he would do something no sane ruler would ever contemplate: encourage Yahweh to multiply the evidence of his power at Egypt's expense.

As you read through these plagues, think of yourself as a businessman running Egypt. Surely you would like to hold on to such a workforce as the Israelites. But how many plagues would it take before you reconsider whether this was such a good bargain? The land is decimated step by step. Cut your losses, Pharaoh, and let them go! Don't be a fool.

The magicians are no fools. By hook or crook they duplicate the first three miracles. But don't miss the irony here. They make more blood from water when water that isn't blood is nearly impossible to find. They produce more frogs when the land is crawling with the squishy things. When Yahweh is making blood out of water and producing frogs, almost anyone can do it! If these magicians were so great an answer to Moses and Aaron, why couldn't they reverse the plagues? And don't forget the first miracle where they lost their serpents.

But, these magicians are not fools. Following the third plague, they advise Pharaoh: "This is the finger of God." But guess what? "Pharaoh's heart was hard and he would not listen, just as Yahweh had said" (Ex. 8:19). Yahweh didn't want Pharaoh to do the reasonable thing once he saw he was out-plagued. If Pharaoh just used his judgment, cut his losses, and let the people go, the crucial place of the Exodus in Israel's history would not have been so clear. What is it that Yahweh says to Pharaoh before the seventh plague?

> By now I could have stretched out my hand and struck you and your people with a plague that would have wiped you off the earth. But I have raised you up for this very purpose, that I might show you my power and that my name might be proclaimed in all the earth (Ex. 9:15–16).

And again, what reason does Yahweh give to Moses for Israel not yet being free?

> Go to Pharaoh, for I have hardened his heart and the hearts of his officials so that I may perform these miraculous signs of mine among them that you may tell your children and grandchildren how I dealt harshly with the Egyptians and how I performed my signs among them, and that you may know that I am Yahweh (Ex. 10:1–2).[15]

And again, following the announcement of the culmination of plagues—the death of the firstborn:

> Pharaoh will refuse to listen to you—so that my wonders may be multiplied in Egypt (Ex. 11:9).

Pharaoh had said, "Who is Yahweh?" Before Yahweh is finished with Egypt, God declares concerning the crossing of the sea:

> I will harden the hearts of the Egyptians so that they will go in after them; And I will gain glory through Pharaoh and all his army, through his chariots and his horsemen. *The Egyptians will know that I am Yahweh*, when I gain glory through Pharaoh, his chariots and his horsemen (Ex. 14:17–18).[16]

The Plagues and the Gods. Not only does Yahweh want the full extent of wonders to be performed, but he wants to make clear who the true God is.

These plagues vindicate Yahweh as the true God in a land of gods, a land ruled by a Pharaoh regarded as the incarnate son of the god Re. Pharaoh is to learn that the earth is Yahweh's (Ex. 9:29). So Yahweh announces, "I will bring judgment on all the gods of Egypt; I am Yahweh" (Ex. 12:12).

In fact, many of the individual plagues directly demonstrate Yahweh's power over the gods. The Nile River was considered sacred, yet it was turned to blood. Associated with the river were the gods Khnum, Hapi, and Osiris (for whom the Nile served as his bloodstream).[17] The goddess Heqt, the wife of Khnum, was represented as a frog. "The frog was one of a number of sacred animals that might not be intentionally killed, and even their voluntary slaughter was often punished with death."[18] And where was the sky goddess Nut, from whose domain came the hail? Isis and Seth, responsible in part for agricultural crops, seem to have been overwhelmed. A number of gods are identified with the sun, including the sun god Re. Certainly these gods failed in allowing a heavy darkness to blanket Egypt for three days.

Yahweh and Israel on the Move—Exodus 12–18

But if the plagues are to teach the Egyptians that Yahweh is the true and living God, the Israelites themselves are not so far ahead in their own understanding of Yahweh. Yes, they initially accept Moses (with signs in tow) as God's prophet. But even that attitude changes when Pharaoh does not immediately respond to Moses' demands. The Israelite foremen actually call a curse on Moses and Aaron for the increased workload: "May Yahweh look upon you and judge you!" (Ex. 5:21). Yahweh's people have little faith or endurance. God's purpose in the plagues was not simply to force the Egyptians to let Israel go, nor even to punish them for their injustice to Israel, but to bring about a climactic deliverance to be remembered by Israel "that you may tell your children and grandchildren how I dealt harshly with the Egyptians and how I performed my signs among them, and that you may know that I am Yahweh" (Ex. 10:2). To really know God as Yahweh was a goal not yet achieved among Israel. The events following the plagues are intended to increase their faith and leave a clear message for their children.

Ceremonial Beginnings. Ceremonies can be either stale ritual or vital reminders. Certainly this initiation of Passover at the front end of Israel's annual calendar was not stale ritual. The lives of their firstborn sons depended upon its observance! God commanded a number of ceremonies for Israel's annual calendar so the meaning of the Exodus would not be lost to future generations (Ex. 12:40–13:16). The Passover meal would be Israel's annual reminder of the final plague when Israel's firstborn were passed over by the angel of death. Just as a lamb was consumed on that first Passover night when its blood marked the doorposts of Yahweh's people and protected their firstborn sons, so a lamb would be eaten yearly to commemorate the deliverance they experienced. Passover initiated the longer Feast of Unleavened Bread. Going without yeast for a full week would remind the people of the quick flight from Egypt—too quick for baking normal bread. And the giving of each firstborn animal and son to God keeps alive the memory that God delivered his firstborn, Israel, from Egypt at the cost of Pharaoh and Egypt's firstborn. The judgment of the final plague on Egypt is summarized in a few sentences (12:29–30). What was to be remembered in future celebration for Israel was only "loud wailing in Egypt" that night.

The Crossing of the Sea. Finally comes the event associated most with the Exodus—crossing the Red Sea or more literally, the "Sea of Reeds."[19] Popular conception has it that the Israelites unwittingly got caught up against the sea. Not so, says the Bible. Yahweh instructed them to camp there to draw Pharaoh into his trap!

> Pharaoh will think, "The Israelites are wandering around the land in confusion, hemmed in by the desert." And I will harden Pharaoh's heart, and he will pursue them. But I will gain glory for myself through Pharaoh and all his army, and the Egyptians will know that I am Yahweh (14:3–4).

For the Egyptians this would be a final lesson. For Israel it would be a tremendous test. As the encamped Israelites see Pharaoh's mighty army approach, they are terrified. They are forced to cry to Yahweh for help, but they attack Moses with their sharpest tongue-lashing: "Was it because there were no graves in Egypt that you brought us to the desert to die?" (Ex. 14:11). The test: to wait and see Yahweh deliver. They need do nothing but learn this lesson: "Yahweh will fight for you" (Ex. 14:13–14). Oh, the lesson they learned! The Song of Moses reflects their newfound reverence for this powerful God who had delivered them in the face of "impossible" odds.

> Yahweh is my strength and song;
>   he has become my salvation;
> He is my God, and I will praise him,
>   my father's God, and I will extol him.
> Yahweh is a warrior;
>   Yahweh is his name. . . .
> Who among the gods is like you, O Yahweh?
>   Who is like you—
>   majestic in holiness,

> awesome in glory,
> working wonders? . . .
>
> Yahweh will reign
> for ever and ever (Ex. 15:2–3, 11, 18).

On the Way to Sinai. Now they have surely learned who Yahweh is. But Yahweh, who sees the heart, knows that a consistent response of faith is not achieved by one experience—no matter how impressive. The ingrained habit of squealing when squeezed is too near the surface in all of us. The inconsistency of this motley crew is obvious on the pages of this book. Our own is safely tucked away in the folds of minds practiced at focusing on finer moments.

But let us document the trek nonetheless. The lessons here loom clear. Yahweh is faithful. Yahweh is patient. Yahweh responds in grace.

Yahweh tests them as he tests all—not to tempt to sin but to cause increasing recognition of his ways. At Marah it is bitter water. At Elim they are short of food. In the Desert of Sin it is no water at all. Finally, they face war with Amalek.[20] None of these experiences seem like easy street. And this group knows how to grumble! Yet they must learn that Yahweh is sufficient for their need. He was sufficient for repulsing Pharaoh's army and he is sufficient again for the attack by Amalek. In between, their faith must recognize that Yahweh provides. "Give us this day our daily bread." Yahweh puts up with their testing, an indication that he still considers that they do not fully know him.

Their peace, safety, and survival are threatened but are never in doubt. The hardships they meet along the way are to teach them that Yahweh saves from each one. Praise comes to Yahweh as others see his power to save (Ex. 18:8–12).

Yahweh and Israel at Sinai

The Challenge at Sinai. All this experience with Yahweh was designed with one goal in mind: that Israel might commit herself unreservedly to following Yahweh. How does God summarize Israel's journey? "You yourselves have seen what I did to Egypt, and how I carried you on eagles' wings and brought you to myself" (Ex. 19:4). God has been carrying them the whole time! But are they ready to obey? Are they ready to trust Yahweh unreservedly as the One Who Is Present to carry out his covenant with Abraham, Isaac, and Jacob? If so, they can take their unique place among the nations: "Now if you obey me fully and keep my covenant, then out of all nations you will be my treasured possession. Although the whole earth is mine, you will be for me a kingdom of priests and a holy nation" (Ex. 19:5–6).

The people believe they are ready to take on that commitment which has eluded them so far. "The people all responded together, 'We will do everything Yahweh has said' " (19:8).

Figure 5.2
The Route of the Exodus

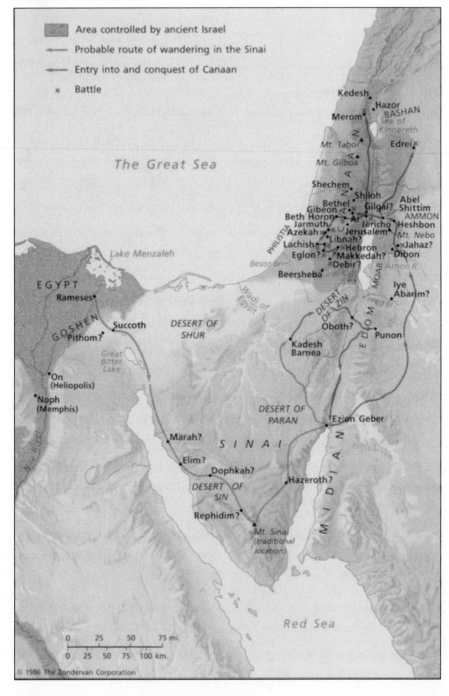

The Covenant with Yahweh. Again, as Yahweh takes this people as his own by entering into covenant with them at Sinai, the emphasis is on Yahweh's Presence. He draws near in cloud, smoke, and fire announced by thunder and lightning, trumpet blast and earthquake on the mountain itself. God speaks the Ten Commandments as the people tremble with fear and ask that Moses be the spokesman, lest they die (20:1–20). Thus begins the unfolding of the Mosaic Covenant.

UNDERSTANDING EXODUS

Yahweh As the Sovereign God

The Exodus, as we have seen, involved a complex series of events more than just the miraculous crossing of the sea. It involved God hearing the prayers of distressed sons of Israel, raising up a deliverer, judging Egypt and Pharaoh, and Israel celebrating the Passover and Feast of Unleavened Bread. But primarily it involved God demonstrating himself to be Yahweh—so all would know that Yahweh is the true God of the whole earth (Ex. 9:29). His sovereign control of events in order to bring about his purposes is everywhere evident. At times God's purposes seem to ride on something as fragile as papyrus coated with pitch, and even the odd, selective pity of Pharaoh's own daughter. But if we think this is really the case we have missed the point. The sovereign Creator God is able to bring about his purposes as easily through insignificant persons and incidental events as he is through massive use of natural forces. Yahweh was present with them even when they did not know it.[21] God's sovereign control of circumstances produced deliverance out of the most calculated oppression. The darkest hour was the hour closest to success. It is then that God must remember because he is Yahweh—the one who has promised and the one who will fulfill. It is he who finally causes all things to work together for his good purposes.

Yahweh As Creator of Israel

Not only is Yahweh the sovereign Creator God, but he is the one who in the Exodus created the nation of Israel. This is especially indicated by the pronouncement, "I will take you as my own people, and I will be your God" (Ex. 6:7). Yahweh, much later through Isaiah, reminds the people of the Exodus in these terms:

> I am Yahweh, your Holy One,
> Israel's Creator, your King (Isa. 43:15).

The tie between Yahweh as Creator and Yahweh as Israel's God and King is so close that the sign of Israel's covenant with Yahweh is the keeping of the Sabbath day:

The Israelites are to observe the Sabbath, celebrating it for the generations to come as a lasting covenant. It will be a sign between me and the Israelites forever, for in six days Yahweh made the heavens and the earth, and on the seventh day he abstained from work and rested (Ex. 31:16–17; cf. 20:10–11).

But for what purpose did Yahweh create Israel by redemption from Egypt? Israel's place in God's program is stated in 19:5–6.

Now if you obey me fully and keep my covenant, then out of all nations you will be my treasured possession. Although the whole earth is mine, you will be for me a kingdom of priests and a holy nation.

Just as Yahweh created this nation from Abraham as he promised (Gen.12:2), so they are to be the means of blessing to the world (12:3) by demonstrating in their national life the true Creator God and being intercessors for the world. Even Pharaoh recognizes something of this as he finally exhorts Israel to leave after the death of the firstborn. He adds: "And also bless me" (Ex. 12:32).

Yahweh As Judge

We do not appreciate too much the *lex talionis*: "an eye for an eye and a tooth for a tooth." But it is simply a formal way of stating that the punishment ought to fit the crime. In other words, it is a call for simple justice. We saw in Genesis that God retains his sovereign right to judge even after man's fall into sin. Remember Cain? Remember the Flood and Babel? Remember Sodom and even Lot's wife? So here at the Exodus, God demonstrates his rule as judge by hardening Pharaoh and decimating the land of Egypt. These are not simply great miracles, they are great "judgments" (Ex. 7:4; also 6:6; 12:12). The hardening of Pharaoh is necessary to provide the opportunity for this judgment (Ex. 7:3), though God could have obliterated Egypt in one swipe (Ex. 9:15–16).

Yahweh As Yahweh

"Be yourself" is frequently good advice—though not for social misfits! Surely the major theme of this book, a theme that includes all the previous themes, is that Yahweh is being himself. He is Yahweh—and that is good news indeed! He promised Abraham a great nation to whom he would give the land of Canaan. As Yahweh he is going to establish the covenant he made with Abraham by consolidating this people into a nation and by bringing them into the land. Childs puts it beautifully: "The name of Yahweh functions as a guarantee that the reality of God stands behind the promise and will execute its fulfillment."[22] He is Yahweh because he is faithful, even though the people are slow to respond. Psalm 78 reminds us of this negative side to the Exodus:

> He did miracles in the sight of their fathers . . .
> He divided the sea and led them through . . .
> He guided them with the cloud by day . . .
> He split the rocks in the desert . . .
> He brought streams out of a rocky crag . . .
> But they continued to sin against him,
>   rebelling in the desert against the Most High.
> They willfully put God to the test (vv. 12–18).

Psalm 105 praises Yahweh for being faithful to his covenant without mentioning the failure of the people:

> Egypt was glad when they left,
>   because dread of Israel had fallen on them.
> He spread out a cloud as a covering,
>   and a fire to give light at night.
> They asked, and he brought them quail
>   and satisfied them with the bread of heaven.
> He opened the rock, and water gushed out;
>   like a river it flowed in the desert.
> For he remembered his holy promise
>   given to his servant Abraham (vv. 38–42).

What's in a name? All God's promises are in his Name because HE IS and HE IS PRESENT to bring them to pass. And God himself proclaimed his Name before the people. Listen to our God and know him:

> Yahweh, Yahweh, the compassionate and gracious God, slow to anger, abounding in love and faithfulness, maintaining love to thousands, and forgiving wickedness, rebellion and sin. Yet he does not leave the guilty unpunished (Ex. 34:6–7).

THE COMPLETION OF THE EXODUS

The Exodus marked out God's choice of Israel to bring restoration to mankind. As such, it marks out the truth that God is acting in history to bring to pass his promise to Abraham—and through that promise, universal blessing to the world. It also provides a working model or pattern for God's future activity in completing that restoration.

Passover and Firstfruits

Paul observes that Christ is our Passover (1 Cor. 5:7). Crucified at Passover, Jesus was God's Passover Lamb. The shedding of his blood, accepted by faith, delivers men from the judgment of death. It was at the celebration of the annual Passover that Jesus announced his death and its significance for his followers: Taking the cup of wine, he proclaimed it symbolic of his blood to be shed for his followers. And using the unleavened bread of the feast, he proclaimed it symbolic of his body to be given in death (Luke 22:13–20). Jesus thereby initiated a new and greater Passover out of the celebration of the original Passover. This New Passover would do more than bring deliverance from a local plague of death in Egypt. It celebrates the continuation of God's program of blessing and deliverance for the world through his promise to Abraham. It signifies ultimate deliverance of his people from the death that plagued all mankind since humanity broke their relationship to God.

The New Exodus and Firstborn Son

Israel, as Yahweh's firstborn, would represent Yahweh to the world. Yet history showed her failure to live as a kingdom of priests. After various measures of lesser judgment failed to consistently revive the nation, Yahweh finally removed his people from the land he had promised. At the time of this exile to Babylon, Ezekiel the prophet writes and again draws on the theme of the Exodus: "I am Yahweh." Just as Moses announced that Pharaoh, Egypt, Israel, and the world would know who Yahweh is by the plagues on Egypt and the deliverance of the Hebrews, so Ezekiel announces that Israel and the nations will again "know that I am Yahweh." This recognition of Yahweh as the true God of Israel, however, would come through judgment and destruction of the land God gave to Israel. Not unlike Egypt, "their land will be stripped of everything in it" (Ezek. 12:19–20). The false gods would again be overcome—but this time they are idols Israel herself has set up (Ezek. 6:1–7). The people would die by plague, sword, or famine, though some would be spared and taken into captivity (Ezek. 6:8–14).

But this is not the end of Ezekiel's proclamation of Yahweh. Yahweh is judging his people, but he is not deserting them. They still have a future. Just as he initially proved himself to be Yahweh, he will again bring them into the land promised to Abraham:

> This is what the Sovereign LORD says: "When I gather the people of Israel from the nations where they have been scattered, I will show myself holy among them in the sight of the nations. Then they will live in their own land, which I gave to my servant Jacob. They will live there in safety and will build houses and plant vineyards; they will live in safety when I

inflict punishment on all their neighbors who maligned them. Then they will know that I am Yahweh their God" (Ezek. 28:25–26).

This return to the land would involve a restoration to nationhood as God's covenant people (Ezek. 34:25–31; 20:36–44). A new inner motivation to live under Yahweh's rule will be given by Yahweh. Cleansed and renewed, Yahweh will be able to bless his people (Ezek. 36:24–38). Again, Yahweh will dwell with them (Ezek. 37:24–28). Yahweh restores them because of his Name (Ezek. 20:44; 36:22–23). He is faithful to his promise. He cannot deny himself.

Isaiah also pictures a New Exodus and entrance into the land. Just as Yahweh created the nation by deliverance through the sea the first time, so now he will make a supernatural way through the wilderness (Isa. 43:14–21). This New Exodus is marked out by the announcement, "In the desert prepare the way for Yahweh" (Isa. 40:3), and by the expectation of the Servant of Yahweh—the New Israel who will achieve Israel's original mandate of universal blessing (Isa. 42:1–9).

Jesus, New Israel, and Firstborn

It is not surprising that the New Testament recognizes the appearance of Jesus as the one who will achieve God's plan for Israel. Matthew's Gospel raises the curtain on Jesus' role as Yahweh's Servant-Son who will achieve for Israel what she failed to achieve for herself. Matthew sees Jesus' return from Egypt as a fulfillment of Hosea 11:1: "Out of Egypt I called my son" (Matt. 2:15). In Hosea, this description refers to the Exodus by Israel. The verses which follow note Israel's consistent failure to follow God:

> When Israel was a child, I loved him,
>   and out of Egypt I called my son.
> But the more I called Israel,
>   the further they went from me.
> They sacrificed to the Baals
>   and they burned incense to images (Hos. 11:1–2).

Israel failed as God's firstborn son. But now God had sent his Son and Servant, Jesus, to represent Israel and achieve for her and the world what she had never achieved on her own. Matthew returns to this theme both by identifying John the Baptist as announcing the New Exodus of Isaiah 40:3 and by the identification from heaven itself of Jesus: "This is my Son, whom I love; with him I am well pleased"—a quotation of Isaiah 42:1 (Matt. 3:1–3, 16–17).

Almost immediately, as if to test the heavenly announcement, Jesus is led by the Spirit into the wilderness to be tempted (Matt. 4:1–11). And what were the tests? Hunger, testing God, false worship. Because Jesus answers the Tempter with Old Testament Scripture, it is common to make the application that believers are to be ready to give answers from the Bible when they are tempted. This is certainly a good idea, but it misses the real point of Jesus' answers. Christ's answers came not from scattered locations in God's Word, but from Deuteronomy 6–8. And what is Deuteronomy 6–8? It is Moses' reminder to Israel's second generation about the sins of the first generation in the wilderness. They are to learn from these failures to live by obedience to the word of God without complaining or testing God or yielding to false worship.

Jesus, Matthew is telling us, achieved what Israel regularly failed to achieve because of disobedience. As Yahweh's Son and Servant he will not only bring Israel's restoration but also light to the Gentiles.

SUGGESTED SCRIPTURE READING:

Exodus 1:1–6:9; 12:1–13; 14:1–31
Matthew 3:1–4:11

For Interaction and Discussion:

1. What is the significance of Israel's being "fruitful and multiplying" (Ex. 1:7)?

2. What was Egypt's fatal mistake? Why? Are there similar fatal mistakes in modern history?

3. How do you explain the suffering of the Israelites in Egypt? Why does God allow the killing of innocent babies, even among his own people? Was God at work during this period?

4. Does the phrase "God remembered" imply that God had forgotten? What kind of a relationship does God's remembering imply?

5. What is the significance of the name "Yahweh" and in what ways is it central to understanding the book of Exodus? Do you think we should use this name today?

6. What right of Yahweh is debated in Exodus 5? How does Pharaoh's rejection of this right bring the plagues on Egypt? Does Yahweh have this right today?

7. Was it right for God to harden Pharaoh's heart? Do you agree that God should bring this moral judgment on Egypt? Do you think God hardens the hearts of national leaders today?

8. What did God plan to teach Egypt through the plagues?

9. How do the magicians' actions and responses provide insight into God's greatness?

10. What three common worries are dealt with in Exodus 15:22–17:7? What does Israel learn about Yahweh in facing these concerns? Does God's view of these difficulties differ from the view of the people?

11. How is Jesus' crucifixion related to the Passover? Compare the function and importance of each to Old and New Testament believers.

12. How did Israel fail as God's firstborn? What is Jesus' role here as God's firstborn Son? Do believers today have a similar role?

For Further Reading:

John J. Davis. *Moses and the Gods of Egypt*. Grand Rapids: Baker, 1971. A good solid treatment for the English reader.

Nahum Sarna. *Exploring Exodus: The Heritage of Biblical Israel*. New York: Schocken, 1986.

Brevard S. Childs. *The Book of Exodus*. Philadelphia: Westminster, 1974. Academic with theological and literary insights when dealing with the meaning of the canonical text as it stands.

Notes and Comments:

[1] I have not attempted to identify individual Pharaohs in the account, following the pattern of the book itself. For discussion of the possible identifications and dating see the commentaries.

[2] I have used the term "mini-ark" intentionally to bring to mind Noah's ark. Apparently the writer wants us to compare the two boats. As Cassuto notes, "The word *ark* . . . occurs in only two sections of the Bible: here and in the section of the Flood. This is certainly not a mere coincidence. By this verbal parallelism Scripture apparently intends to draw attention to the thematic analogy. In both instances one worthy of being saved and destined to bring salvation to others is to be rescued from death by drowning. In the earlier section the salvation of humanity is involved, here it is the salvation of the chosen people," *A Commentary on the Book of Exodus*, trans. Israel Abrahams (Jerusalem: Magnes, 1967), 18–19. Also the use of this term at this point in the narrative with its suggestion of Noah continues the emphasis on God's providence without explicitly stating it.

[3] The fellow Hebrew's statement "Who made you a prince or judge over us?" is not the only statement of "providential irony" in the passage. Moses also names his son Gershom (meaning "an alien there"), explaining that he, Moses, has become an alien in a foreign land. Undoubtedly we readers are to raise the question: What land is not foreign to Moses and the Israelites? Which land would be considered home? Egypt or Canaan?

[4] In light of the rest of the book, the purpose for the suffering of the Hebrews seems to be to allow the iniquity of the Egyptians to become full (cf. Gen. 15:16 for the Amorites as a parallel). God does not bring judgment—and with it relief for his people—at the first injustice. God's patience toward the ungodly often involves allowing his people to suffer. Paul seems to have this in mind in Romans 8:31–39

where he quotes Psalm 44:22, "For your sake we face death all day long; we are considered as sheep to be slaughtered."

[5]The use of the term "come down" (Ex. 3:8) indicates God's intervention to bring justice on earth as we saw in its earlier usage in Genesis for Babel and Sodom (Gen. 11:7; 18:21). Here it is connected to deliverance that will take place in the context of judgment on the Egyptians (cf. Cassuto, *Exodus*, 34).

[6]The call of Moses becomes the pattern for the call to the office of prophet. Cf. Brevard S. Childs, *The Book of Exodus* (Philadelphia: Westminster, 1974), 56.

[7]Ibid., 119. Childs notes that by chapter 6 "the whole focus falls on God's revealing of himself in a majestic act of self-identification: I am Yahweh. . . . To know God's name is to know his purpose for all mankind from the beginning to the end."

[8]Scholars argue about the derivation of names. Do they actually derive from the words used to explain them and the meaning given in the text? Or are they names chosen because of a similarity, but not a direct linguistic connection, to the significance attached? It does not matter. The name was given to imply a significance whether by direct derivation or by similar sound.

[9]Because Hebrew is a consonantal language, only the consonants *YHWH* are provided. Later Jewish readers, who did not want to pronounce the name YHWH lest they use it in vain, most often substituted their word *Adonai* (translated "Lord") whenever they came to the name YHWH in the text. Due to this practice, the correct pronunciation of YHWH is in doubt. Because the name is built on the verb meaning "I am," most scholars conclude that it should be vocalized as Yahweh. The spelling JeHoVaH was mistakenly produced by combining the transliterated consonants (YHWH or JHVH) with the vowel sounds of Adonai.

[10]I have substituted "Yahweh" in the biblical quotations for "the LORD" in this quotation and in many others throughout the rest of this chapter in order to bring out the full emphasis on the Name. Unless otherwise noted, the rest of the Scripture quotation follows the NIV.

[11]The Hebrew tense represented may be translated as either "I will be" or "I am." The suggested translation "I cause to be" is impossible in 3:12, and therefore should be rejected for 3:14. Cf. *TWOT*, 1:211.

[12]T. C. Vriezen as quoted in Childs, *Exodus*, 69. The LXX (Greek Septuagint) translates the Hebrew: "I am the One who is." Though we have taken the meaning of Yahweh to represent primarily his presence and faithfulness along with many other interpreters, it seems a bit hasty to dismiss the notions of eternality and independent existence as further potential implications of "I AM" as well (cf. John 8:58; Rev. 1:8). Certainly the use of "I am he" for the exclusive existence of the true God against all other gods is common (Deut. 32:38; Isa. 48:12). Cf. *TDNT*, 2:343–54; Childs, *Exodus*, 82–83; *TWOT*, 1:210–12.

[13]The grammar itself is not clear about who the Lord sought to kill, Moses or his son, nor even whose feet were touched in 4:25. Many theories have resulted (cf. Childs, *Exodus*, 95–101). The view I have taken is that of both Jewish tradition and the history of Christian interpretation.

[14]Many attempt to show that Pharaoh first hardened his own heart because they want to avoid a doctrine of predestination or the accusation that God is unjust. On the other hand, those who find predestination here often fail to see that this hardening is preceded in the book of Exodus by the moral failure of Egypt in mistreating God's people. God has determined to judge Egypt; therefore, he has hardened Pharaoh's heart. Many have followed the explanation of Kaiser who places God's hardening after Pharaoh's hardening of his own heart. Cf. Walter C. Kaiser, Jr., *Toward Old Testament Ethics* (Grand Rapids: Zondervan, 1981), 252–56; Nahum Sarna, *Exploring Exodus* (New York: Schocken, 1986), 64–65. This explanation succeeds only by reducing statements of God's announced determination to harden Pharaoh's heart to mere predictions, rather than statements of intention that form the background and explanation of Pharaoh's response (Ex. 4:21; 7:3). In fact, when the text states that Pharaoh hardens his heart or that his heart was hardened prior to the sixth plague it repeatedly points us backward to these announcements of God's intention to harden Pharaoh's heart (7:13, 22; 8:15, 19). God did not predict that Pharaoh would harden his own heart: rather, God predicted that he himself would harden Pharaoh's heart, and we are told that Pharaoh's hardening his heart is the fulfillment of this. Exodus 4:21 and 7:3 are, therefore, not predictions about what would come at the sixth plague and later but state Pharaoh's response and God's control of it from the very beginning.

This creates an ethical problem only if we do not see Pharaoh and Egypt as deserving this judgment before Exodus 9—if we picture Pharaoh as an innocent participant who deserves a chance to respond before God hardens him. But if we understand the picture provided by our book that Egypt's cup of iniquity is already full, that God is determined to bring a judgment against her, and that Pharaoh as head of Egypt must be hardened so as not to let the people go before God has decimated Egypt—then we have no ethical difficulty with the Pharaoh's hardening.

[15]The emphasis is mine and not that of the version quoted.

[16]Again, the emphasis is mine.

[17]For these identifications of Egyptian gods see John J. Davis, *Moses and the Gods of Egypt* (Grand Rapids: Baker, 1971), 100. Cf. Sarna, *Exploring Exodus*, 60, for possible connections of Moses' serpent-rod to Pharaoh and the gods.

[18]Davis, *Moses and the Gods of Egypt*, 100.

[19]The *Yam Suph* or "Sea of Reeds" has been traditionally translated, following the Greek Septuagint, as the "Red Sea." Many scholars have rejected that identification because reeds only grow in fresh water and, therefore, this sea should be identified with one of the marsh areas farther to the north. However, such logic fails to note that the same term is definitely used of the Red Sea itself (reeds or not!) in Exodus 23:31; Numbers 21:4; Jeremiah 49:21; and 1 Kings 9:26. Sarna, *Exploring Exodus*, 107–8, has suggested that the term is applied indiscriminately to the network of lakes in the Delta and the gulfs of Aqaba and Suez. Whatever the outcome, the sea must meet the requirements of the ancient narrative and be sufficient for significant water movement and drowning of Pharaoh's army (cf. Ex. 15:4–5).

[20]Cf. John R. Kohlenberger III, *Jonah and Nahum* (Chicago: Moody, 1984), 113–14. Kohlenberger suggests a chiastic arrangement of this material with the protection in battle by Yahweh being recognized at the beginning and end (15:1–21 and 17:8–16) and the incidents of provision being in the center.

[21]Childs, *Exodus*, 13, puts it: "Direct theological statements concerning God's activity are used sparingly." Cf. pp. 17, 24–25 for Childs' helpful discussion of providence which I have largely followed here.

[22]Ibid., 115.

chapter six

A NEW NATION: THE LAW
(Exodus–Numbers)

God's plan for reversal began with the covenant with Abraham—a single individual. It now has grown to include a people delivered out of Egyptian slavery. They have been transported by God's grace "on eagles' wings" to Mount Sinai. What is God's next step? The giving of the Law—otherwise known as the Mosaic Covenant.

Christian thinking about the Law in the past has popularized certain ideas. Check these to see if they fit your notion of the Law:

- The Law is a step backward from living by faith as Abraham did.
- The Law is opposed to God's grace.
- The Law is good only for showing us we're sinners.
- The Law introduces salvation by works.

The Law has received a bad press. It has always been a difficult subject for Christians, and there has been widespread disagreement on how to understand the Law and its place in God's program. The Law in general has been treated like a white elephant gift from a relative. It can hardly be thrown out, yet no one wants it in a prominent place. Of course, many do not mind displaying the Ten Commandments suitably framed. But what about those other laws—clean and unclean, dietary restrictions, special festivals and new moons, "an eye for an eye." What to do with them? How can they be part of the Scripture that Paul recommends as profitable for instruction in righteousness (2 Tim. 3:16–17)? Only by understanding the place of the Law as given at Sinai can we hope to properly understand its place in the Scripture.

WHAT WAS THE LAW?
A Gracious Gift of Yahweh

The introduction to the Law begins with these words: "I am Yahweh your God" (Ex. 20:2). We have seen already how important this identification is in the book of Exodus. According to Exodus 6:6–8, there are three stages for God's gracious action as Yahweh. The first stage, deliverance from Egypt, is complete, and the third stage is yet to come: possession of the land promised to Abraham. At Sinai, stage two has arrived: "I will take you as my own people, and I will be your God." The Law is not a bogus door prize. It is the opportunity of a lifetime. These people are about to become the people of God. They have been chosen to enter into a covenant with God in which Yahweh commits himself to them as his people and they recognize Yahweh as their God.

Let us make clear that they are not entering this relationship by works. What works have they done? Crossing the sea when God opened its waters? Complaining about lack of food and drink? Beating the Amalekites when God was their warrior? What have these people done to qualify themselves? The answer is clearly, "Nothing." "Israel certainly had demonstrated in her past actions no qualifications for this undeserved favor."[1] They have simply received God's gracious promise to Abraham and were graciously delivered from Egypt. Now, as a people chosen of God, they are to become his nation. "Blessed is the nation whose God is Yahweh, the people he chose for his inheritance" (Ps. 33:12).

A Constitution for a Nation

Israel does not reject the opportunity to become God's nation (Ex. 24:3–8). They covenant with God to keep his Law. The Law becomes their constitution and national legislation.

Part of the Christian's confusion over the Law comes from expecting to find only *spiritual* things in the Bible. But the Bible here records God's purpose of starting a nation. Nations need laws.[2] And, these laws must include statutes that cover criminal as well as civil cases. A recent court case in Oregon involved a public school teacher who wore a religious turban to work. Oregon law covered this situation and the instructor's teaching certificate was removed when she refused to abide by the law. It is not only the Mosaic Law that covers seemingly incidental things such as dress. Our modern building codes and public health laws also have their counterparts in the Mosaic Law (Lev. 13:12–17; 14:33–42; Deut. 22:8).

But let us recognize a great difference between our laws and the Mosaic Law. Our laws are the *efforts* of men to legislate justice for the common good. The Mosaic Covenant was given by God and therefore is "holy, righteous and good" (Rom. 7:12). All legislation is legislated morality, but all legislation is not good. Is a progressive income tax right? Is it right to imprison a man who owes debts? Should victims of crimes be compensated? The difference between our laws and the Mosaic Law is that the Israelites need not debate these questions.

God gave them a legal code which, if kept, would ensure his blessing on the nation (Ex. 15:26; 23:25–26). What a privilege to have your national laws given by God! The psalmist rejoices over Israel's unique place:

> He has revealed his word to Jacob,
>> his laws and decrees to Israel.
> He has done this for no other nation;
>> they do not know his laws (Ps. 147:19–20).

A Covenant with Yahweh

The study of ancient Hittite treaties reveals a similar pattern to the arrangement in the Mosaic Covenant.[3] This has had significant impact on confirming the historical validity of the Law. It has also helped us gain further insight into the nature of the covenant. Of course, the biblical material itself tells us this is a covenant (Ex. 24:7). But understanding covenant forms of the time helps us recognize the importance and significance of various features. For instance, the Hittite king-vassal covenants always started with an *identification of the king* who was extending the covenant. This was followed by the *gracious actions and provisions* that the king had given in the past, and that call for a response of gratitude and loyalty. The *requirements* that follow are those that the covenant names as the appropriate, grateful response. This is the very pattern we find in Exodus 20. The king is named: "I am Yahweh your God" (20:2). The benefits the king already has provided, though they were undeserved, are named: " . . . who brought you out of Egypt, out of the land of slavery" (20:2). This gracious action is the basis for a response of loyalty (20:3–17). Just as the king of the Hittite treaties expected loyalty to him, so Yahweh, the one who delivered them from bondage and to whom they owed their very lives, expected undivided loyalty—"no other gods." That the New Testament operates as well on this "first grace, then response of gratitude" pattern confirms again that Yahweh is the gracious God who abounds in love and faithfulness (Ex. 34:6).[4]

A Guarantee of Yahweh's Presence

The revelation of the name Yahweh indicated the promise of his presence with his people. This is guaranteed in the Mosaic Covenant by the tabernacle. The tabernacle is the place of worship and accountability to God. But even more important, there Yahweh "will meet with the Israelites" (Ex. 29:43). He says, "I will dwell among the Israelites and be their God. They will know that I am Yahweh their God, who brought them out of Egypt so that I might dwell among them" (29:45–46). While God informs Moses about construction of the tabernacle and its furniture, the Israelites make a calf idol and worship it as the God of the Exodus (Ex. 32). Because of this demonstrated tendency toward disobedience, the Lord proposes that Israel would be better off without him. He will give them the land as promised, but without his presence, for otherwise he will have to judge them more strictly (Ex. 33:1–5). But Moses recognizes the significance of Yahweh's presence for the choice of Israel as his nation. They not only need the Exodus and the land. To be recognized as uniquely Yahweh's, they must have his presence (Ex. 33:12–16). Yahweh relents so easily and quickly that we know he also sees his presence as necessary to Israel—not only a presence of judgment, but a presence of compassion, grace, and faithful love (Ex. 34:5–7). Among these people he will do wonders "never before done in any nation in all the world" (34:10). The book of Exodus closes with the glory of Yahweh coming to inhabit the tabernacle. What privilege! What grace!

Opportunity to Be a Blessing

What responsibility! A linkup with Yahweh is a powerful opportunity but also a dangerous one. Judgment always begins at the house of God (1 Peter 4:17). To be a son is always to invite chastening (Heb. 12:7). And what was their opportunity as the People of God? "Now if you obey me fully and keep my covenant, then out of all nations you will be my treasured possession. Although the whole earth is mine, you will be for me a kingdom of priests and a holy nation" (Ex. 19:5–6). A priest is one who intercedes for others. Just as Abraham was God's route for intercession for Abimelech (Gen. 20:7, 17), so Israel would be a nation through which the world would find Yahweh.[5] Her success at this, however, is totally conditional. By entering this gracious covenant with Yahweh, she gets favored-nation status. But her own experience of blessing as well as her ability to be a blessing to the world is based on her obedience—as the promises of blessing or cursing in Leviticus 26 so clearly announce.

UNDERSTANDING THE LAW

Laws and the Law

To fully appreciate the Mosaic Law, we must compare it with available law codes from the ancient Near East. Many biblical laws resemble those found in earlier codes such as the Code of Hammurabi, the Middle Assyrian Laws, and the Laws of Eshnunna. Common circumstances dictate that many of the same issues be covered. But there are differences, and they are significant.

Biblical law places a primary concern on human life. The destruction of human life, unless accidental, always requires capital punishment. Other law codes allow monetary compensation, especially in cases involving the death of a lower member of society.[6] The Bible allows compensation only in the case of death by a dangerous animal. Even there, if a bull has the habit of goring, both the bull and the owner must die. The family of the deceased could substitute payment, if they wish.[7] Capital punishment for human life is applied even to animals, continuing the directive of Genesis 9:5–6.

Biblical law involves "eye for eye, tooth for tooth" (Ex. 21:22–25). Though it sounds violent, this biblical formula does not advocate barbaric justice, but rather, equal justice for all.[8] Those with money do not get off with mere fines. Additionally, the Bible does not allow children to be punished for the wrongs of a parent. In the Code of Hammurabi, if a man strikes another man's daughter and she dies, the murderer's daughter is put to death.[9] Sounds fair . . . unless you were the daughter! In the Bible, the murderer is put to death.[10] A slave receives even better than an eye for an eye if he suffers at the hand of a master: He receives his freedom (21:26).[11]

Biblical law judges crimes against property more leniently. Though the Bible judges crimes against people more strictly than earlier laws did, it is less strict than those laws in judging crimes against property. The Mosaic Law normally requires double restitution for theft (Ex. 22:4, 7). Hammurabi requires ten- to thirty-fold. If the thief cannot pay the restitution, Hammurabi has him killed. Exodus allows him to work it off as a slave (22:3). If you are a thief, you would rather be one under the Mosaic Law. If you're caught tunneling through someone's mud wall, the homeowner can kill you and ask questions later, but only if it happens at night (22:2–3). Hammurabi will punish you with death day or night, and the hole you made would be filled with your corpse and plastered over.[12] The Laws of Eshnunna let you off with a fine during the day but requires your death at night.[13] Biblical law regards even the life of a thief as worth something and tries to protect it!

Without a prison system, options for punishment in the ancient world are fewer; they include capital punishment, fines, and mutilation. In Assyria, a wife can lose her nose or ear for varying degrees of unfaithfulness—no doubt an effective way to cut down on her desirability![14] If you are a surgeon, Hammurabi requires that your hand be cut off if anyone dies under your knife. But the Bible avoids using bodily mutilation as a penalty.

Biblical law includes worship practices as part of its law. Other codes do not, because they are understood to be the product of a king seeking to please his god by formulating just laws. Since Israel's Law is directly from God, there is no distinction between civil and religious law. All law is religious. "What other nation," Moses asked, "is so great as to have such righteous decrees and laws as this body of laws?" (Deut. 4:8). The question was rhetorical. The answer is obvious.

The Lay of the Law

But it is not enough to see how well the Mosaic Law compares to other law codes. This would be like comparing your farm to one in another country by talking about the type of soil, the annual rainfall, and farm equipment used but never staying home enough to recognize and enjoy the landscape. If we are to understand the Law, we need to know a little bit about the lay of its land. If we are to understand the Law, we need to study its own inner workings.

It is so common to divide the Law into the moral, civil, and ceremonial that many are surprised to find out Moses did not outline it that way! Actually, the Law comes out in ever-widening circles, as represented in the chart below:

Figure 6.1

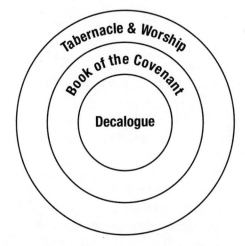

First comes the Decalogue (Ex. 20:3–17). These Ten Commandments are often understood as the abiding moral law that Christians should keep, while the rest of the Law does not apply. Certainly, the Decalogue has primacy of place and so emphasizes essential standards to mark out the holiness of God's chosen people. Yet, this popular conception does not work for at least two reasons. First, great moral laws are found elsewhere in the Law. Christ said the second greatest commandment is: "Love your neighbor as yourself." Reference? Don't look for it in the Ten Commandments. You'll find it in Leviticus 19:18, bumper to bumper with such commands as: Do not mate different kinds of animals. Do not plant your field with two kinds of seed. Do not wear clothing woven of two kinds of materials. Additionally, not all of the Ten Commandments are absolute moral laws. Clearly, sabbath-keeping is not. It is included in this initial set of laws because it is the sign of the covenant. Just as circumcision is the sign of the Abrahamic Covenant, so keeping the Sabbath recognizes the true God of creation as Yahweh, the God of Israel (Ex. 31:12–17). It derives not from God's nature but from his celebration of his creative work as good. Paul, therefore, put the issue of keeping one day sacred in the category of things that each believer could determine on the basis of his own conscience (Rom. 14:5–8). No one is to judge another believer by his diet or his observance of sabbaths or other holy days (Col. 2:16–17). Many Christians observe the Sabbath in principle by resting on one day in seven, but not on the seventh day. This, of course, would not have been acceptable procedure for an Israelite, and evidence that the New Testament equates the first day of the week with the Sabbath is difficult to come by. So even though the Decalogue is the central instruction of Yahweh for Israel, it does not include all the absolute moral truths found in the Law, and neither are all its commands unchanging moral rules. Nevertheless, it is at the very first of the Law because it summarizes the major concerns of the whole of the Law.

If we were to choose one word to summarize these Ten Commandments, it would be faithfulness. First, faithfulness to God. No other gods. No idols. No misuse of his Name in oathtaking. Keeping the Sabbath is a sign of commitment to his rule over you. Faithfulness in relationship to others is the focus of the remaining commands. Parents deserve honor in the family. Faithfulness to your community of neighbors involves not lying, not committing adultery, not stealing, and certainly not murdering. It even involves faithfulness in your motivation. You should not mentally steal your neighbor's wife or anything else that is his. These commandments give the heart of the rest of the decrees, statutes, and ordinances that make up the national legislation. But wait . . . could we run a country with these laws?

The Book of the Covenant. To run a country you need more than stated principles.[15] Should stealing and murder be punished equally? Can coveting be punished at all? The next circle of laws is called the Book of the Covenant (Ex. 20:22–23:19). Here we find the specifics on obligations and punishments needed to implement a just society. It includes what we would call criminal and civil law, as well as detailing basic sabbaths and holy days to be observed by Yahweh's faithful nation. In these chapters the humane and just features of the Mosaic Covenant become clear.

The Tabernacle. The rest of the book of Exodus gives directions for the tabernacle or tent of meeting as the central worship place where Yahweh's presence with Israel was indicated (Ex. 25–40). It represents the unity of the nation around Yahweh who is Present.

Leviticus. The book of Leviticus is concerned about worship and holiness. But Israel's worship is not separate from the rest of life. To keep the

Figure 6.2
Model of the Tabernacle

Decalogue is worship—and these laws are included again in Leviticus (18:20; 19:1–16). The first part of the book continues the book of Exodus by dealing with worship at the tabernacle (Lev. 1–10). Worship is expressed by sacrifices and offerings (see figure 6.3 below) that provide the means for fellowship with God, forgiveness of sins, and expressions of thanksgiving and dedication to God (Lev. 1–7). Especially significant are the animal sacrifices. "The life of a creature is in the blood" (17:11, 14). Blood, representing life itself, is reserved for atonement (1:3–4; 3:2, 8; 4:22–35; 16:15–17). Life for life is the notion of atonement throughout the Bible. Even though these same animals are provided as food, their blood is not to be eaten (17:8–14).

Aaron and his sons are clothed, consecrated, and initiated as priests (Lev. 8–10). The people are overcome with joy and worship at Yahweh's acceptance of the first sacrifices with the presence of his glory and fire that consumed the sacrifice (Lev. 9:23–24). Another fire also comes, however, at the "unauthorized fire before the Lord, contrary to his command" offered by Aaron's sons, Nadab and Abihu (Lev. 10:1). This fire consumes the guilty pair and reminds in still another way that Yahweh is holy (Lev. 10:1). Being linked to a holy God is not a trifling matter!

The latter part of Leviticus deals with the totality of the life of the nation as holy (as "distinct" or "separate"). Physical conditions need to be met— the "clean and unclean" laws (Lev. 11–16)—to qualify one for worship in the tabernacle and for living among the community (see figure 6.4). This section closes with instructions for the yearly Day of Atonement (today's Yom

Figure 6.3
Sacrificial System

Name	Portion Burnt	Other Portions	Animals	Occasion or Reason	Reference in Lev.
Burnt Offering	all	none	male without blemish; animal according to wealth	propitiation for general sin demonstrates dedication	Ch. 1
Meal Offering or Tribute Offering	token portion	eaten by priest	unleavened cakes or grains, must be salted	general thankfulness for firstfruits	Ch. 2
Peace Offering a. Thank Offering b. Vow Offering c. Freewill Offering	fat portions	shared in fellowship meal by priest and offerer	male or female without blemish according to wealth; freewill: slight blemish allowed	fellowship a. for an unexpected blessing b. for deliverance when a vow was made on that condition c. for general thankfulness	Ch. 3 22:18–30
Sin Offering	fat portions	eaten by priest	priest or congregation: bull king: he-goat individual: she-goat	applies basically to situation where purification is needed	Ch. 4
Guilt Offering	fat portions	eaten by priest	ram without blemish	applies to situation where there has been desecration or de-sacrilization of something holy or where there is objective guilt	5:1–6:7

John H. Walton, *Chronological and Background Charts of the Old Testament* (Zondervan, 1978), 45.

Kippur), which pictured the removal of the nation's sins—by God's grace accepting a repentant people as his distinct (holy) people. The principle of substitution for sins is here firmly established—again, with sacrifice of life for atonement (16:15–34). A more detailed code than the Book of the Covenant follows. It includes civil, criminal, social, and festival regulations as part of being holy and worshiping a holy God (Lev. 17–25). This presentation of the Law is characterized by Leviticus 20:26—"You are to be holy to me because I, Yahweh, am holy, and I have set you apart from the nations to be my own." These laws would mark Israel out as Yahweh's distinct people. Blessings of abundance and peace are predicted for a holy people, but warnings of disease, famine, and destruction are announced for a people who turn from listening to Yahweh to false worship and idols (Lev. 26). The book ends (Lev. 27) with a stress on dedication and holiness with rules for making and keeping vows that dedicate people or things to Yahweh.

Law and the book of Numbers. Just as Leviticus continues on the narrative that ends the book of Exodus (the Hebrew text begins with "And . . ."), so Numbers picks up the narrative following the book of Leviticus. All of the Law falls within the narrative framework of the Pentateuch. With the book of Numbers there are additional laws—mostly related to cleanness and purity in the camp

Figure 6.4
Clean and Unclean Animals

Classes	Clean	Unclean
Mammals	Two qualifications: 1. cloven hoofs 2. chewing of the cud Lev. 11:3–7; Deut. 14:6–8	Carnivores and those not meeting both "clean" qualifications
Birds	Those not specifically listed as forbidden	Birds of prey or scavengers Lev. 11:13–19; Deut. 14:11–20
Reptiles	None	All Lev. 11:29–30
Water animals	Two qualifications: 1. fins 2. scales Lev. 11:9–12; Deut. 14:9–10	Those not meeting both "clean" qualifications
Insects	Those in the grasshopper family Lev. 11:20–23	Winged quadrupeds

Basic reasons:
1. Hygiene – Many of the forbidden animals were carriers of disease.
2. Cultic – Some animals were considered unclean because of their association with pagan cults.

John H. Walton, *Chronological and Background Charts of the Old Testament* (Zondervan, 1978), 46.

of Israel (chaps. 5, 19); offerings, vows, and sacred celebrations (chaps. 6, 15, 28–30); and ceremonies of consecration or blessing (6:22–8:26).

There are not a lot of laws included in Numbers. But, in Numbers—a book that covers the journey from Mt. Sinai to the very edge of Palestine— the Israelites get to put the Law into sandal-leather. It's time to walk the life of faith—a faith which believes Yahweh's promise and follows Yahweh's precepts. It's time to move out from Sinai and enter the land of promise. The book is aptly named "Numbers" in English (following the Greek Old Testament or Septuagint) as it centers around two generations of Israelites—both of whom were numbered or mustered for the coming battle. The first census, or numbering, of military men takes place as part of the preparations for leaving Sinai (Num. 1–10). Each numbered tribe is given a location for encampment around the tabernacle and for marching in the moving camp of Israel. The Levite clans are also numbered and given their tabernacle job descriptions. The tabernacle is dedicated with offerings, and the Levites purified for their holy task. The timing of the move, starting at the Passover, reminds them of the great deliverance from Egypt by their incomparable God, Yahweh, as they begin this most important trek home. The luminescent cloud again guides the tribes and trumpet signals are ordered for facilitating an orderly march. And then they are off (Num. 10:11)!

Unfortunately, the time "in the wilderness" (the Hebrew title for the book) for this generation of God's army (Num. 11–25) was definitely off—off target. On the way to the New Eden, they duplicate the failure of the old Eden. The holy army becomes an unholy people. Complaining about God's care is commonplace—beginning with boredom over manna. Rebellion is frequent. Miriam and Aaron against Moses; the people against entering the land when they hear the report about fortified cities and strong peoples; Korah and Levites against Moses and Aaron as leaders. Is not the whole community holy and Yahweh with each of them? Fear rather than faith is the congenital response. Complaining rather than obedience is the common denominator. Rebellion against divinely established leadership with the charge that it violates equality before God is again the all-too-human reaction.

Yahweh provides in spite of their complaint. He judges the rebellious, defends Moses as his unique prophet and servant, and threatens to destroy the nation and to start over with Moses alone. The abused Moses acts as intercessor and appeals to Yahweh's self-announced nature of compassion and forgiveness and to Yahweh's reputation among the nations—a reputation that Israel's deliverance was designed to vindicate. Yahweh responds with forgiveness for the nation, but true to his self-declared identity ("slow to anger, abounding in love and forgiving sin and rebellion. Yet he does not leave the guilty unpunished" [14:18; cf. Ex. 34:6–7]) declares that not one of the offenders will personally enter the land. Apart from Caleb and Joshua, the two spies who brought the report of faith, all those counted in the first census will die in the desert.

The second census records those males twenty years of age and older who had not been a part of the earlier census (Num. 26).[16] This holy second generation is going to experience God's blessing of entering the land as they journey from Kadesh to the eastern edge of the land (20:14–36:13). They experience victory over kings who try to stop their passage. A foreign prophet-for-hire, Balaam, cannot curse Israel. After his jackass makes him feel like a donkey, Balaam utters only oracles of blessing upon the tribes of Jacob (Num. 23–24). But even this generation has problems. A pagan ritual sexual festival is the downfall of many of these Israelites, and they worship Baal rather than sticking to the pure worship of Yahweh. God is faithful in defending them against nations, but who can defend them against their own perfidy? Rather than starting all over once more, a plague removes offenders who

Figure 6.5

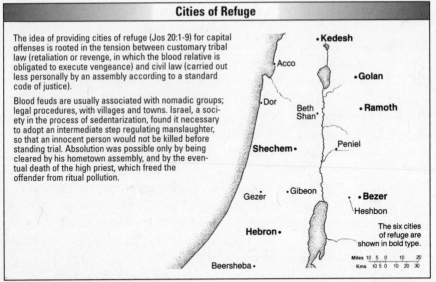

Cities of Refuge

The idea of providing cities of refuge (Jos 20:1-9) for capital offenses is rooted in the tension between customary tribal law (retaliation or revenge, in which the blood relative is obligated to execute vengeance) and civil law (carried out less personally by an assembly according to a standard code of justice).

Blood feuds are usually associated with nomadic groups; legal procedures, with villages and towns. Israel, a society in the process of sedentarization, found it necessary to adopt an intermediate step regulating manslaughter, so that an innocent person would not be killed before standing trial. Absolution was possible only by being cleared by his hometown assembly, and by the eventual death of the high priest, which freed the offender from ritual pollution.

Acco · Kedesh · Golan · Dor · Beth Shan · Ramoth · Shechem · Peniel · Gezer · Gibeon · Bezer Heshbon · Hebron · Beersheba

The six cities of refuge are shown in bold type.

Miles 10 5 0 10 20
Kms 10 5 0 10 20 30

From *The NIV Study Bible* (Zondervan, 1985) 241

are not qualified to accompany this generation into blessing. The remainder of the book deals with items of importance for this generation in the land (inheritance, Joshua's leadership, feasts, boundaries, levitical cities, cities of refuge). Thus God safely brings a holy people to the plains of Moab, ready at last to enter into the promised but yet unholy Land.

Kinds of Laws

We still have our questions about the Mosaic Law and the reasons for some of its commands. For instance, why not eat camels—or at least pigs? Why leave the corners of your field uncut? Does the same reason apply to leaving the corners of your hair and beard uncut? As we have suggested, many types and levels of laws make up a nation's legal code. Some are based on absolute morality and are unchangeable. Some are included for other reasons, yet still serve a useful function in a society. Does it matter if you drive on the right side of the road or the left? In moral principle, no. In practice, yes. Scholars have been disagreeing for centuries over the reasons for many of the Mosaic laws. I am going to wade in where no angel would dare wet his toe by suggesting a few possible reasons for some of them.

Faithfulness in relationships. We have seen this in the Decalogue and it carries through consistently, even in regard to foreigners (Lev. 19:33). Practical matters of justice, such as honest scales (Lev. 19:35–36), fit here as well. Poorer members of the community were not to be forgotten (19:9–10). The Law has a concern for social justice and integrity of personhood.

Figure 6.6
Feasts and Sacred Times

Name	Time	Purpose
Sabbath	Every 7th day	Day of rest
Passover	14th of 1st month (Abib) Mar-Apr	Remember Exodus deliverance
Unleavened Bread	15th–21st of 1st month Mar-Apr	Remember leaving Egypt in haste
Firstfruits	16th of 1st month (Abib) Mar-Apr	Recognize Yahweh as provider of harvest
Weeks (Pentecost)	6th of 3rd month (Sivan) May-Jun	Thanks for harvest/ firstfruits
Trumpets	1st of 7th month (Tishri) Sept-Oct	Assembly and sacrifice
Day of Atonement (cf. Lev. 16)	10th of 7th month (Tishri) Sept-Oct	Atonement to cleanse the nation
Tabernacles or Booths	15–22nd of 7th month (Tishri) plus 23rd as sacred assembly Sept-Oct	Harvest gathered festival/booths remind of wilderness provision
Sabbath Year (Lev. 25:1–7)	Every 7th year	Land lies fallow; year of rest
Year of Jubilee (Lev. 25:8–55)	Every 50th year following 7 Sabbath years	Freedom of debt – servants/return of land

Respect for blood as representing life given by Yahweh, the Creator. The blood of an animal must not be eaten (Lev. 17:10–12). Any animal hunted and killed must have its blood drained out and covered with soil (17:13–14). Human blood must be atoned for. Blood shed by murder must be accounted for by the blood of the murderer.[17]

Avoidance of false worship patterns. Of course, the nations around also practiced sacrifice. Sacrifice precedes the Law and the sacrificial practices of the false religions are likely twisted memories of earlier truth. Pagan temples even had an inner and outer sanctuary, much like Israel's. How then is Israel's worship different? Of course, the prime difference is that it was worship of Yahweh. The truth of who Yahweh is—the faithful, pure, forgiving, and just Creator—recasts the whole approach and attitude of worship. Israel's worship avoided sexual immorality and replaced the notion of attempting to convince capricious gods to provide the regularity of season with a faithful Creator. Condemned are soothsaying, mediums, tattoos and cuts, sexual rituals, child sacrifice, and even the cutting of the corners of the beard and hair (Lev. 19:26–31).[18]

Recognition that the earth is the Lord's. The sabbath year of rest for the land as well as the return of land to families every fifty years recognizes that the Israelites are stewards of his land. Land is not owned absolutely (Lev. 25:1–24).[19]

Reflecting Yahweh as Creator. This theme is represented not only in land laws but also in the bringing of the firstfruits of harvest and in dedication of the first year of produce from trees. It is represented even in purely symbolic ways. Seeds, animals, and clothing materials are not to be mixed, undoubtedly to reflect in the Israelite's daily life the distinctness of kinds that Yahweh created (Lev. 19:19). Even the Israelite's fields and his dress proclaimed: "Yahweh is the true Creator God." Perhaps some laws proclaiming certain abnormalities (such as skin infections) as unclean were intended to teach that abnormality does not represent Yahweh's original creation.[20] Certainly some of the laws of uncleanness were to protect the community as well (Lev. 15:1–15). Most significantly, the keeping of the seventh day as a Sabbath of rest declares that Israel's God, Yahweh, is Elohim, the true Creator God "for in six days the LORD [Yahweh] made the heavens and the earth, the sea, and all that is in them, but he rested on the seventh day" (Ex. 20:11). Yahweh, the God in covenant with Israel, is more than a local deity. He, in fact, is the one true God.

Though these laws seem complicated to us and impossible to live under, they actually served a positive purpose. By keeping them, Israel would demonstrate her distinctness. The beneficial standards as well as the rich symbolic meaning would continue to communicate her privilege as God's treasured possession (Deut. 4:6–8). Our concentrating on a mass of individual commands misses the true stress on the relationship with God. The key has always been: "If you love Me, you will obey what I command" (John 14:15).

THE NEW TESTAMENT AND LAW-KEEPING

Jesus and the Law

In the Old Testament, the people never seemed able to keep the Law's most basic requirements. The golden calf routine in one form or another was as regular as rain in Oregon. How is it, then, that when we come to the New Testament we run into a crowd that seems to have taken their law-keeping more scrupulously than Texans take their football? That's good news, isn't it? No, it's more bad news. Jesus' concern with the nit-picking law-keepers often identified as belonging to the Pharisees' denomination is not that they applied the Law stringently. In fact, he commends their care in tithing even the smallest pieces of produce (Matt. 23:23). His problem with them is that while they exercise great care in parceling produce, they overlook the main thrust. They're like good neighbors in an upstanding community who keep up their yards, have well-behaved kids, have great family loyalty . . ., but make their income from owning brothels across town. Or, to use some of our Lord's own picturesque language, they "strain out a gnat but swallow a camel"—neither one a clean animal in Leviticus! Or again, they are "like whitewashed tombs," looking good, but inside are dead men's bones—more uncleanness (Matt. 23:24, 27).

Jesus himself is more concerned with people's needs than keeping himself clean. Becoming unclean could happen in any person's daily routine, but certain types of uncleanness, though not sin, could put you out of circulation and certainly out of the tabernacle or temple area for a while. The woman approaching Jesus who for years has been without relief from a hemorrhage is unclean (see Lev. 15:25–30). She certainly has her nerve grabbing the edge of his robe and so rendering him unclean—without even warning him! No doubt the crowd figures she is in for a tongue-lashing. But Jesus is more impressed with the faith that brought her to dare such a scandal. He pronounces her whole. No longer constantly unclean and unable to go to the temple, she is healed (Mark 5:25–34). Jesus doesn't avoid contact with the dead either. He crashes funeral parties. This must have given the nitpickers pause: Is a man unclean when he touches a dead body that becomes alive again (Luke 7:11–16; Num. 19:11–13)?

They aren't confused, however, about his sabbath-keeping. Here is no debate over mere uncleanness. Nor is it a question about traditions. Here is the very sign of the Mosaic Covenant being transgressed by Jesus on many occasions—or so it seems to them. He and his disciples violate the Sabbath by harvesting grain and "threshing it" between their palms as they pass through a field (Luke 6:1–5).[21] Even more energy is expended when Jesus heals a man on the Sabbath. And if that isn't enough, Jesus even tells him to carry his bedroll home (John 5:5–8). Jesus lets them know he keeps the Sabbath, but not the way they do. He keeps it the way the priests kept it and the way God kept it. He does good on the Sabbath—not work for economic gain. They, too, allow exceptions for the Sabbath, but these relate only to animal needs, not human needs (Matt. 12:11–12). Jesus accuses them of not really understanding the Sabbath command. It was made for man's benefit (Mark 2:27). It got a man away from his economic concerns, saved him from being a workaholic, saved his household and servants from abuse, and turned his mind toward the Creator who originated the Sabbath. Because the Pharisees don't understand the Law, they misapply it. They have turned it into outward observance. In a particularly scathing denunciation of the state of Jewish legalism, Jesus points out that fashionably current teaching allows a man to commit mental adultery, deceive his neighbor by the use of misleading oaths, end his commitment to his wife with a piece of paper, get even for any wrongs he suffered, and hate everyone but his friends. The Pharisees have used the Law to allow for their own weaknesses (Matt. 5:17–48). Yet the point of the Law, as stated in Leviticus again and again, is to reflect Yahweh, their God. "Be perfect, therefore, as your heavenly Father is perfect" (Matt. 5:48) is the match for "Be holy, because I am holy" (Lev. 11:44–45; 19:2; 20:26). The Law, God's gift to Israel, had been turned into a way of gaining points with God. Like all human attempts at earning righteousness, the righteous standard of God must be scaled down so people could believe they qualify.

Paul and the Law

Paul takes up where Jesus left off. The legalists are a constant migraine for Paul. They dog his footsteps and collar his converts. It is not enough to believe in Jesus, they preach; you must be circumcised and keep the Law. What makes these false teachers particularly pesky is that their case looked good to new believers. After all, these teachers can declare "The Bible says," point to Old Testament verses, and command, "Be circumcised," "Don't eat pork," "Keep the sabbaths and new moons." In response, Paul has some pretty rough things to say. If you go that route, he says, you better be ready to keep everything perfectly, because "the man who does these things will live by them" (Gal. 3:12; Rom. 10:5; Lev. 18:5). He says the Law didn't solve sin; it increased it. He says Abraham didn't achieve God's blessing by Law, but by faith (Gal. 3:6–7, 10–12).

The tragedy is that Christians by and large believe the legalists correct in their view of the Law. The Law, they say, was a way of earning credit with God. The Law was an impossible bill of goods that God laid on Israel. Before the Law men lived by faith, but afterward they had to operate by rules. All the Law could do was arouse sin. Did God do that to his people? No! And Paul did not say God had. You see, we have been reading the Law as the legalizers were using it, and in the very way that Paul attacked. Imagine sitting in an airport lobby and the child next to you shows you a drawing he has found in a book. He has it upside down, but he thinks he is looking at it accurately. He has spotted what looks like a dog in the picture. He says, "Look, a puppy." Your response might be (assuming you wanted to teach him rather than simply humor him), "If that's a puppy, why are these trees hanging upside down?" The child turns back to his mother and says, "Look at the funny trees this nice man showed me." The church has been saying,

"Look at the funny Law this nice apostle showed us." The Law was not a rotten deal for the Israelites. It was the best possible life for God's people in that time and place. It was not a way of becoming God's people; it was the way to reflect and proclaim the true God, Yahweh. Did Paul say it was a rotten deal? No, Paul said if the legalizers are right it was a rotten deal. If you look at the picture their way, you will have to keep every last shred of it to be accepted before God. If you look at it their way, something is out of line because Abraham was counted righteous without doing all those things. God accounted to Abraham what he never achieved on his own—remember all those slips?—on the basis of faith. Paul said, "The Law is just and right and good, but if I'm supposed to keep it for righteousness I'm not going to make it." The Law cannot accomplish that because of the weakness of human flesh. Does that mean the Law was bad? Only if that was what the Law was trying to accomplish. The Law was so good and holy that Paul concedes: "If a law had been given that could impart life, then righteousness would certainly have come by the law" (Gal. 3:21).

But such a law was never given. No, what the Law could not do and was not designed to do, God did by sending his Son. Atonement by grace has always been the key, and those who read the Law right knew it all along (Gal. 2:15–16).[22]

The Law's Function

But Paul did make statements about the Law that reflect his own views. The Law is "holy, righteous, and good" (Rom. 7:12). The Law was our tutor to bring us to Christ (Gal. 3:23–4:7). The Law was added to the promise (Abrahamic Covenant) "because of transgressions until the Seed to whom the promise referred had come" (Gal. 3:19). The Law was not opposed to the promises of God (Gal. 3:21). The Mosaic Covenant was good, but it had a temporary function. It did not change God's way of working or make his promise based on works. It was a positive program for a time when things needed to be spelled out, when safeguards were needed to protect Israel from falling easily into Canaanite practices. The Law was like a disciplinarian in charge of your training as a minor. That is a good thing. You need to learn that discipline, those manners, that lesson. When you are older and are disciplined and understand the reasons for manners and lessons, you don't place yourself under the old rules, good as they were. You operate out of your full understanding. To continue going to bed at nine o'clock every night because that was your parents' rule will keep you in good health, but some things are worth staying up later for. No set of rules will be long enough to cover them, but a mature adult will know what they are. A mature adult will also understand why he had a nine o'clock rule as a child, and will continue to take care of his health even though he is no longer under such a rule.[23]

The Law As Scripture

So we are not "under the Law" as our operating covenant with God. Paul was opposed to any of his Gentile converts subjecting themselves to the Law either by circumcision or symbolic observances (Gal. 4:10–11; 5:2–3). Why? Because it denies the Gospel. It not only signals belief that works are needed to be acceptable to God (5:4) but also denies that Gentiles are on a par with Jews in the body of Christ (3:26–29). But Paul is not opposed to using the Law for instruction. It was from his pen that 2 Timothy 3:16–17 flowed, affirming that all Scripture, because it is inspired by God, is to be used for teaching. As a converted Pharisee, Paul was certainly aware that the Mosaic Law made up a good portion of those Scriptures and that all of them from Exodus on advocated obedience to the Law. Paul doesn't use the Law as a code that the believer is under (covenant), and certainly not as a way of gaining points with God (legalism), but as a source for insight into God's view of life (instruction). The Law is a revelation of God; and if we understand the reasons for the various laws, we can learn the righteous principles being taught. Paul is not inconsistent when he opposes the Judaizers' use of the Law in Galatians 3:10–12 and then quotes the Law himself, citing Deuteronomy 21:23 to show the meaning of Christ's death for us: "Cursed is everyone that hangs on a tree." Nor is he violating his own principles when he quotes Deuteronomy 25:4 to show that ministers should be paid (1 Cor. 9:9), or when he uses Leviticus 25:39–42 to conclude that the Lord's redeemed servants should avoid becoming slaves to men (1 Cor. 7:21–23). Paul's teaching on vengeance comes from the Law (Rom. 12:19; Lev. 19:18; Deut. 32:35). And Paul does not hesitate to remind his converts that honoring parents is a duty that was a special concern of the Law (Eph. 6:1–3; Ex. 20:12).

The Old Testament, including the Law, was the Bible of the New Testament Church. It was not disposed of as a modern tossable—used once and discarded. Nor was it treated as a museum piece for historic interest only. It was still Scripture. And though everything in it was no longer directly applicable, it still could instruct when used with full understanding of its place and purpose.[24]

THE FULFILLMENT OF THE LAW

At the same time Jesus denied any wish to abolish the Law or the Prophets, he also predicted their fulfillment (Matt. 5:17–18). The most minute part of the Law would not pass away "until everything is accomplished." Jesus himself brings the Law to fulfillment in a number of ways. First, he fulfills the sacrificial system. The sacrifices ordained by the Law could not take away sins

(Heb. 10:3), they had to be continually repeated (Heb. 7:27), and they were offered by imperfect and finite priests (7:23–28). They were part of a temporary covenant (8:13) that was a picture of the ultimate fulfillment, but they were unable to bring about forgiveness of sins (9:9–10; 10:1–3). For this reason the book of Hebrews calls the New Covenant a "better" and "superior" covenant (8:6). Jesus' death is a sacrifice (life for life) in which he bore our sins, so that we might be accepted as God's holy people because of his righteousness—"the righteous for the unrighteous" (1 Peter 2:24–25; 3:18). The first or Mosaic Covenant thus becomes "obsolete" (Heb. 8:13) and applied only "until the time of the new order" (9:1).[25]

Second, Jesus fulfills the righteousness of the Law. Paul declares the whole world guilty before God—the Jew with the Law and the Gentile without it. Some Gentiles were even able to live as righteously as their Jewish neighbors who had God's Law. (Substitute non-Christian and Christian and check your own neighborhood.) The bottom line on earning righteousness is: "No one will be declared righteous in his sight by observing the law; rather, through the law we become conscious of sin" (Rom. 3:20). Paul, however, denies that he is nullifying the Law. He insists that he is upholding or establishing it (3:31). The righteousness of the Law is not established by keeping it for merit before God. That is doomed to failure. The righteousness of the Law is established by receiving the gift of righteousness by faith in Christ (Rom. 9:30–33). Christ is the end of the Law (Rom. 10:4)—not only because he inaugurated a new covenant to replace it, but because he achieved its righteous standard for all who believe. Christ satisfies the righteous demands of the Law. It is in him that we "become the righteousness of God" (2 Cor. 5:21).[26]

Our focus is not the keeping of the Law as a merit system, but Jesus Christ himself. Our response is based on gratitude for what God has done in Christ. We love because he first loved us (1 John 4:19). We forgive, because we are forgiven (Eph. 4:32). We walk worthily because we have been graciously given a special calling (Eph. 4:1). We honor God with our body because we, like ancient Israel, are bought with a price (1 Cor. 6:19–20). No, the Law is not a white elephant. But then, don't feature it as a centerpiece either. Only Jesus deserves that spot!

SUGGESTED SCRIPTURE READING:

Exodus 20:1–20 and 21:12–22:3
Matthew 5:17–48
Galatians 3:21–4:7

For Interaction and Discussion:

1. If the Law is good, should a believer be under it today? Do you think it is valid to distinguish between being "under the Law" and recognizing the Law as Scripture? How would this affect our use of the Law today?

2. How does a comparison between the laws of Israel and those of her neighbors help us to understand the thrust of the Mosaic Law? What areas of the Mosaic Law might people today question as fair?

3. Do you agree that we can't legislate morality, or does most legislation reflect moral judgments? Why is there no distinction between religious and civil law in the Mosaic Law?

4. Was the Mosaic Law intended to motivate by works or by grace? Compare this to New Testament motivation for obeying God.

5. Why is the Presence of Yahweh important to the Law and Israel? In what ways does Yahweh's Presence raise the issue of responsibility as well as grace? Is this true with all spiritual privileges?

6. What is the primary emphasis of the Ten Commandments? How does Jesus' own teaching about the Law agree with this emphasis? How did many of the Pharisees violate this emphasis by emphasizing the letter of the Law? What are some correct examples of external rules that receive more emphasis than spiritual relationships?

7. How is the Law designed to be a proclamation of Israel's Yahweh as the true God? In what ways are believers today to be a proclamation of the God of the Bible?

8. How does Jesus' approach to the Sabbath differ from that of the Pharisees? What benefits did the Sabbath law bring to man? What other examples show Jesus' rejection of works-religion as an approach to God? What religions today are works-religions? In what ways has Christianity itself fallen into the trap of works to earn righteousness before God?

9. How do Christians sometimes misunderstand the apostle Paul's view of the Law? Is it the Law Paul rejects, or legalism? What is the Law useful for today?

10. In what ways is the New Covenant a "better covenant" than the old Mosaic Covenant? How has the Law been fulfilled?

11. How is the righteousness of the Law upheld and fulfilled? How can a person who fails to keep the Law achieve righteousness?

For Further Reading:

K. A. Kitchen. *The Bible in Its World*. Downers Grove, Ill.: InterVarsity, 1977, 79–85. See for covenant form.

G. J. Wenham. *The Book of Leviticus*. NICOT. Grand Rapids: Eerdmans, 1979. Scholarly commentary.

R. K. Harrison. *Leviticus*. TOTC. Downers Grove, Ill.: InterVarsity, 1980. Scholarly commentary for English reader.

Ronald M. Hals. *Grace and Faith in the Old Testament*. Minneapolis: Augsburg, 1980.

Christopher J. H. Wright. *An Eye for An Eye*. Downers Grove, Ill.: InterVarsity, 1983, 174–82. Ethical questions with the Law.

Douglas J. Moo. "'Law,' 'Works of the Law,' and Legalism in Paul." *WTJ*, 45 (1983): 73–100.

Shalom M. Paul. *Studies in the Book of the Covenant in the Light of Cuneiform and Biblical Law*. Leiden: Brill, 1970.

Notes and Comments:

[1]Charles C. Ryrie, *The Grace of God* (Chicago: Moody, 1963), 34. As this citation shows, not all dispensationalists viewed the Law as a burden—a view usually ascribed to C. I. Scofield. Ronald M. Hals, *Grace and Faith in the Old Testament* (Minneapolis: Augsburg, 1980) is an excellent work from a Lutheran reassessing the place of grace under the Law. Cf. Kenneth L. Barker, "False Dichotomies between the Testaments," *JETS*, 25 (1982): 3–16.

[2]Apparently Egypt, with its divine king, was an exception to this statement that nations need laws and so did not have a law code.

[3]George E. Mendenhall, "Covenant Forms in Israelite Tradition," *The Biblical Archaeologist*, 17 (1954): 50–76, was the first to discover this parallel. A good general introduction to the parallels and dating can be found in K. A. Kitchen, *The Bible in Its World* (Downers Grove, Ill.: InterVarsity, 1977), 79–85. Shalom M. Paul, *Studies in the Book of the Covenant in the Light of Cuneiform and Biblical Law* (Leiden: Brill, 1970), 32–33, maintains that the Decalogue is not the text of a covenant—that a more personal relationship is sustained between God and Israel than that of king to vassal. However, he does accept Deuteronomy as a good example of the treaty pattern.

[4]We will take up the full format of Hittite treaties in Deuteronomy (chap. 7).

[5]For "kingdom of priests" as a people who would act as priests for the world, see Paul, *Studies*, 30, 32, and the other studies cited there.

[6]Allowing other compensation to the family of the murder victim rather than capital punishment is found in the Middle Assyrian Laws (hereafter, MAL), A10 and B2, also the Hittite Laws (hereafter, HL), #1–5, *ANET*, 180–81, 185, 189. See Paul, *Studies*, 61–62, 69, where he notes that requiring capital punishment for the death of a slave is "without precedent in all other ancient Near Eastern collections."

[7]Passages in Exodus on capital punishment for human life are in chapter 21, verses 12, 14, 15, and 20. Verse 20 calls for proper vengeance for the slave, that is, the penalty of v. 12. Cf. Paul, *Studies*, 69–70.

[8]The equation of "equal justice for all" and "an eye for an eye" is that of W. F. Albright in *History, Archaeology, and Christian Humanism* (New York: McGraw-Hill,

1964), 74. Albright observes that the application of this model seen in Israel's laws (that is, the rich receiving the same punishments as the poor) has not yet been reached in modern society.

[9]HL 116, 210, 230, in *ANET*, 170–76.

[10]In the situations described in Exodus 21:28–31 and 22–24, no vicarious punishment was allowed in the case of sons and daughters. Though the Bible often recognizes that divine punishment comes on a family or a nation as a result of sin, its Law does not allow human judges to penalize other members of the family *instead of* the one committing the crime.

[11]The application of "an eye for an eye" in a nonliteral fashion (freedom for the slave, rather than requiring loss of the master's eye or tooth) shows that the principle of equal justice is in view—not an exacting literalness demanding the same injury. In all other law systems the slave was treated as property, and damage to a slave was an economic loss to the master. Of course, slavery's very existence in the Mosaic Law bothers us. A number of factors should be remembered, however: (1) Slavery as regulated by the Law was more humane than our own country's practice just over a century ago. (2) Specifically for that time and place, the Law's provisions were righteous. It limited fallen society and encouraged improvement. Divorce, for example, was regulated by the Law, though never viewed as the ideal. (3) The slave was given legal rights in Israel, the same legal rights as those of a hired man. (4) Temporary bond service to pay off debts was a fairer way of dealing with unpaid obligations than debtor prisons and perhaps contained more justice than declaring bankruptcy. (5) Runaway slaves were set free (Deut. 23:15–16; cf. Ex. 20:10; 12:44; Lev. 25:35–55; Deut. 15:12–18; 16:11–14). For a helpful discussion of the relationship of the Law to polygamy, divorce, and slavery, cf. Christopher J. H. Wright, *An Eye for An Eye* (Downers Grove, Ill.: InterVarsity, 1983), 174–82.

[12]HL 12, *ANET*, 166.

[13]Laws of Eshnunna 13, *ANET*, 162.

[14]MAL 15, *ANET*, 181. There is only one case of bodily mutilation as a penalty in the Mosaic Law: Deuteronomy 25:11–12. Compare MAL A8, *ANET*, 181.

[15]Note the distinction between apodictic (stated principles or prohibitions, but no penalties) and casuistic or case-laws usually in the form: "If a man does such-and-such, then he shall (make restitution, be put to death, etc.)."

[16]One of the main problems for the book of Numbers is the numbers! They seem too high for the ancient world and a trip through the desert. Why would there be any fear of taking Canaan and the powerful people there if they had these kind of numbers? Various solutions have been suggested. (1) Of course, the first solution is to accept the numbers literally in the same way we would read numbers today. These numbers are consistent throughout the Pentateuch (Ex. 12:37; 38:26; Num. 2:46; 26:51), about 600,000 men twenty years old and older. Such a number suggests a total population over two million. In that case we have a supernatural movement through the Red Sea and across the desert. No problem for Yahweh, of course, yet still we may wonder at why there would be any worry about the conquering the smaller cities of Canaan with this size people, a size equivalent to estimates for all

of Egypt. The numbers are theoretically possible in terms of maximum reproduction rates. But other internal questions arise. If there are 22,273 firstborn sons (Num. 3:43), then given normal odds there were over 40,000 mothers in Israel, a figure far too low for the stated total population. Cf. the full discussion by Sarna, *Exploring Exodus*, 94–102. (2) Another solution is to understand the Hebrew word for "thousand" to represent a clan-unit rather than a full 1000 people. Such references as Judges 6:15; Numbers 1:16; 10:4; Joshua 22:14, 21, 30 support such a usage. See George E. Mendenhall, "The Census Lists of Numbers 1 and 26," *JBL*, 77, 1 (1958): 52–66, who takes the word to refer to military units in distinction from Sir Flindars Petrie who took it to refer to tent-units; and J. W. Wenham, *TB*, 18 (1967): 19–53, who suggests a different pointing to the Hebrew word, changing the meaning to "chieftains," or "fully-armed soldier," or "officer" (and also has a nice discussion of the multiple ways in which OT numbers could be affected in transmission). He primarily sees these as special troops. However, Budd argues that all such views are weakened by the Hebrew text's never using the plural when referring to such groups, if that is what they are. Cf. Philip J. Budd, *Numbers*, WBC (Waco, Tex.: Word, 1984), 8. (3) Sarna proposes a new option. He sees the numbers as the larger, ideal numbers of the Davidic-Solomonic period of kingdom read back into the narrative. "From the perspective of the biblical narrator, the time span involved in the Exodus events is therefore not restricted to the forty years of wilderness wandering, but encompasses the period from Moses to Solomon. This is the Exodus era" (101). He sees this as legitimate due to corporate identity (all later Israel sees themselves as part of the Exodus) and his contention that the biblical view of the era and chronology extends from the Exodus to Solomon (1 Kings 6:1). This would not be a satisfactory solution for most conservatives who, without documentary evidence to the contrary, would not want to question the authenticity of the account as a pre-Solomonic product. (3) A fourth solution is offered by Ronald B. Allen, "Numbers," *EBC*, 2:688–91, who suggests "a rhetorical exaggeration by a factor of ten" (689), leaving an army of 60,000 and a total population of 250–300,000. Allen argues that "the numbers of the census are real figures," consistent and coherent, yet deliberately magnified by a factor of ten to celebrate Yahweh's greatness. The rhetorical use is also a "prophetic symbol" of the nation yet to come. In this way, Allen somewhat matches Sarna's view without recourse to a later reading back. He does not indicate why ten would be chosen as the factor to use. It simply is the figure that works admirably with the numbers that are given with the exception of Numbers 3:43— a number (22,273) when divided by 10 for the literal number would leave 0.3 of a firstborn son. Here Allen suggests that we have a literal number of total firstborn— our best clue to the actual size of the nation—compared to a symbolic number of Levites (22,000–22,200) (729–30). Another problem is this relatively small number compared to the other tribes (727–28).

[17]The provision in a case of accidental death that the man not leave the city of refuge until the death of the high priest also supports the notion that blood must be shed for blood. For unsolved murders a special ritual also involving atonement with

blood was necessary to keep that failure of justice from counting against the community (Deut. 21:1–9).

[18]G. J. Wenham, *The Book of Leviticus*, NICOT (Grand Rapids: Eerdmans, 1979), 223, points out that the uncleanness through sexual contact meant that no sex would take place in connection with the tabernacle as well as in holy wars. This insulates against Canaanite orgiastic practices as well as the evils of ravishing women in warfare (cf. Judg. 5:30).

[19]Walter Brueggemann, *The Land* (Philadelphia: Fortress, 1977) and C. J. H. Wright, *An Eye for an Eye*, have shown the importance of the land as a feature of Israel's ethics.

[20]G. J. Wenham, *The Book of Leviticus*, and R. K. Harrison, *Leviticus*, TOTC (Downers Grove, Ill.: InterVarsity, 1980), provide two excellent conservative commentaries on Leviticus. They take differing views on the laws of cleanness. Harrison prefers to see them as largely related to health. Wenham, following Douglas, sees more theological concerns involved. Cf. Gordon J. Wenham, "The Theology of Unclean Food," *EQ*, 53 (1981): 6–15; and Jacob Milgrom, "The Biblical Diet Laws as an Ethical System," *Int.*, 17 (1963): 288–301.

[21]See *The Mishna*, Shabbat 7.2.21.

[22]A great deal of current discussion concerns Paul's use of the term *Law*. Some believe Paul often uses it to mean "Jewish legalism" as well as for the Mosaic Law. Cf. C. E. B. Cranfield, "St. Paul and the Law," *Scottish Journal of Theology*, 17 (1964): 51; C. F. D. Moule, "Obligation in the Ethics of Paul," *Christian History and Interpretation: Studies Presented to John Knox*, eds. W. R. Farmer, et al. (Cambridge: Cambridge Univ., 1967), 392–93; Daniel P. Fuller, *Gospel and Law*, who cites the previous two, 86–88. Douglas J. Moo in a thorough study entitled "'Law,' 'Works of the Law,' and Legalism in Paul," *WTJ*, 45 (1983): 73–100, has argued that "law" (*nomos*) does not mean "legalism" in any passage of Paul and that the expression "works of the Law" is not equivalent to legalism either, as Fuller maintained. He sees the main distinction in Paul as between whether Paul is viewing the Law as a covenant in the progressive history of salvation or whether he is using it for the Mosaic body of commands. Moo may be right in questioning whether *nomos* is ever used technically to mean legalism. Both the Judaizers and Paul, of course, have reference to the Mosaic commands when they speak of Law. It is the different use of the Law, not the meaning of the word, that makes one context speak of the (Mosaic) Law as Paul's opponents understood it and another that makes it the (Mosaic) Law as really intended by God. No matter who wins the linguistic argument, we shall still have to recognize with Calvin that when arguing against Judaizers "to refute their error [Paul] was sometimes compelled to take the bare law in a narrow sense." *Institutes*, 2.7.2; cf. 2.11.7, cited in Moo, 85.

[23]Here I agree with Moo, "'Law,' 'Works of the Law,' and Legalism in Paul," 80–82, that some of these statements in Galatians are Paul's own view of the Law, not those of his opponents. The distinction drawn by Paul involves seeing the positive but temporary function of the Law as the Mosaic Covenant. Paul clearly does not see himself as operating under the Mosaic Covenant or Law (1 Cor. 9:20–21). I

believe both distinctions are necessary. Paul sometimes speaks of Law as it is used by his opponents and sometimes as a covenant God gave, but which believers are no longer under. Fuller's treatment, *Gospel and Law,* stresses so strongly the continuum between Law and Gospel that it is difficult to see why we are not refraining from pork or at least keeping the seventh day. We are left believing that the believer today is to do all that is commanded in Scripture (110). Cf. Douglas J. Moo, "Review of Gospel and Law," *Trinity Journal,* 3 (1982): 99–103.

[24]C. J. H. Wright, *An Eye for An Eye,* 148–73 and 187–96, seems to be advocating the use of the Law in a similar way. The tentativeness of some of his examples combined with his care to avoid oversimplistic, direct applications show that the use of the Law in this way will not be an easy hermeneutical exercise. But then, this is true for the application of any OT passage—for example, Joshua 1:1–9. The whole of OT Scripture needs to be read in light of the progress of revelation and redemptive history. Yet it is still Scripture.

[25]The strong contrasts in Hebrews between the covenant that is passing away and the new covenant makes it difficult to accept W. C. Kaiser, Jr.'s thesis that the new covenant is simply the old covenant "renewed."

[26]For a summary of views on Romans 10:4, see C. E. B. Cranfield, *A Critical and Exegetical Commentary on the Epistle to the Romans,* ICC (Edinburgh: T. & T. Clark, 1979), 515–20. See also the view of Felix Bluckiger, detailed by Wright, *An Eye for an Eye,* 69–81. I appreciate Robert Brinsmead's emphasis in "Jesus and the Law," *Verdict,* 4 (Oct., 1981): 5–30. The NT focus of ethics is on the word of Christ, just as the OT Law centers its ethics on gratitude around the Exodus salvation. In my judgment, however, Brinsmead in his justified reaction against Sabbatarianism as a holdover of the Mosaic Covenant has now neglected the use of the OT for instruction in righteousness and greatly underplayed Paul's use of the Law as Scripture.

chapter seven

LIVING THE LIFE: THE CHALLENGE OF DEUTERONOMY

Back in the sixties when antiwar sentiment was in full bloom, there arose a bumper sticker that announced in clear terms another opinion. It read, "AMERICA: LOVE IT OR LEAVE IT." The book of Deuteronomy introduces us to a far different cultural situation. The children of Israel, a landless people, find themselves standing at the border of the land God had promised to Abraham centuries before. They are entering a land, not leaving it. Taking the land is their top priority. Talk about losing it seems premature at best. And yet Moses, the man of God, delivers a warning about dangers that will ultimately bring God's judgment and the loss of the Promised Land.[1] Moses shows little concern over the battles ahead with the nations already occupying Canaan. Yahweh is adequate for that. Moses' concern, rather, is over the battle within Israel herself.

Love and Land—these are the concerns of Deuteronomy. The commands and statutes of the Law as recorded in Exodus and Leviticus may have seemed to the Israelite like so many parts and pieces. In Deuteronomy, Moses pulls the whole apparatus together into a sermon—a sermon that becomes the nation's handbook on land. How should Israel operate in the land? In its way, Moses' handbook is the opposite of that bumper sticker. The modern slogan calls for dedication to a country and asks those who fail to meet that level of dedication to depart. But Moses declares that the one who loves the Promised Land will lose it.[2] Patriotic commitment to a land or even to nationhood is not adequate. Only full commitment to Yahweh as the one true God will assure his full blessing in the land.

THE HANDBOOK IN OUTLINE

The book of Deuteronomy reflects the pattern of ancient vassal covenant treaties, as we noted previously.[3] The title and preamble come first

(Deut. 1:1–5). A course in History 101 follows—not for the purpose of learning names and dates but to remind Israel of the benefits the King has provided to the people (Deut. 1:6–3:29). Yahweh has cared for them even though they were not always faithful.

> Yahweh your God has blessed you in all the work of your hands. He has watched over your journey through this vast desert. These forty years Yahweh your God has been with you, and you have not lacked anything (2:7).[4]

Included in these benefits are the recent victories over Sihon and Og, kings of Heshbon and Bashan.

After the historical review, Deuteronomy records the basic stipulations of the treaty. These are found in two sets: chapters 5–11, and 12–26. Each set becomes more detailed. Chapters 5–11 highlight the major concerns—those central obligations and attitudes important to relationship with Yahweh. Chapters 12–26, sometimes called the Deuteronomic law code, take up the specifics and details of how to live in the land in a way that is consistent with their identity as Yahweh's people.[5]

Critical to treaties of the time was a litany of blessings and curses (chaps. 27–28). Blessings come for obedience to the covenant. Curses come as a result of disobedience. Such is Moses' concern about Israel that he gives a final exhortation (chaps. 29–30). Arrangements are then made for regular public reading and storing of the covenant (chap. 31). The Lord's concern about Israel is so great that Moses is commanded to provide a song (chap. 32) to remind Israel of God's faithfulness and their own tendency to rebel. For rebellion is what is predicted from these people (31:29). Moses, the superb prophet (34:10–12), then gives his farewell blessing, views the Promised Land from Mount Nebo, and finishes his course (chaps. 33–34).

Of course, Deuteronomy is not the covenant itself. It is largely an exhortation that reflects the covenant pattern with additional materials at the end. As an exhortation and also a literary work, it has a broader, creative balance to it as well. Christianson has pointed out this balanced symmetry of the book itself as follows:[6]

A—THE OUTER FRAME: A Look Backward (Deut. 1–3)

B—THE INNER FRAME: The Great Peroration (Deut. 4–11)

C—THE CENTRAL CORE: Covenant Stipulations (Deut. 12–26)

B'—THE INNER FRAME: The Covenant Ceremony (Deut. 27–30)

A'—THE OUTER FRAME: A Look Forward (Deut. 31–34)

THE CONCERNS OF DEUTERONOMY

Love and Covenant

It should no more surprise us that Moses' exhortations reflect a covenant pattern than to discover that Mother's Day cards often contain an acrostic poem that spells M-O-T-H-E-R. The very heart of Israel's relationship to Yahweh is one of covenant. The unique contribution of Deuteronomy is Moses' summary of that covenant in terms of one word: *love*. Yahweh has loved them (4:37–38; 7:7–9; 10:14–15) and he chose their fathers, Abraham, Isaac, and Jacob, to receive a promise of blessing. This choice was not made on the basis of achievement or greatness but simply because of Yahweh's love.

The commitment of Israel to Yahweh also may be summarized by that one word, *love*. Because Yahweh, the God of Israel, is the one true God, God's people are to pursue total commitment.[7]

> Hear, O Israel: Yahweh our God, Yahweh is one. Love Yahweh your God with all your heart and with all your soul and with all your strength (6:4–5).

The passage is clear. The type of love we are talking about is not a gushy, surface emotion—but a total involvement that demands complete commitment. Such commitment must begin in the heart—the true inner center of thinking and motives. It must engage the desires and appetites of the life ("soul") and involve all of one's exuberance (strength) in putting that devotion into action.[8]

Unlike modern situational ideas of love, this love for Yahweh is demonstrated by observing his laws. It is joined regularly with phrases like "fearing the LORD," "walking in his ways," and "obeying his commands" (10:12; 11:1, 13, 22; 30:16, 20). But unlike legalistic ideas of obedience, Moses stresses the need for a true inner commitment and devotion to Yahweh. Outer observance is not enough. Even circumcision must go deeper than the skin. It must cut into the heart (Deut. 10:16). This covenant of love brings Israel into relationship with Yahweh. Yahweh himself is their life. It is he they must choose and love (Deut. 30:15–20).

Love and Yahweh's Uniqueness

Having a relationship with Yahweh is a unique privilege. The Israelites thought it a bit too unique on occasion. When Yahweh demonstrated his majesty by thunder and lightning, trumpet and smoke at Sinai, he taught them a special fear and awe (Deut. 4:35–36; 10–12; cf. Ex. 20:18–21)—so much so that they wanted no more of it! They were not to think of Yahweh as just another god—

like the gods of the nations around them. No, Yahweh owns the whole earth (Deut. 10:14).[9] The uniqueness of Yahweh calls for specific response:

- Because Yahweh has no outer form, making images to worship him is forbidden (4:15–20).
- Because Yahweh is the only true God, they must commit themselves totally to him (6:4–12; 4:32–40).
- Because Yahweh is a jealous God, they must avoid worshiping other gods alongside Yahweh (6:13–15; 5:7–9). Yahweh will not be worshiped as one of many.
- Because Yahweh is a God who speaks and answers prayer, Israel has the opportunity to be unique among the nations in wisdom, understanding, and greatness (4:5–8).
- Yahweh fights uniquely for Israel; so when confronting her enemies, Israel must destroy not only the people but also the images of their gods (7:1–6, 21–26).[10]

Among the blessings of Moses at the end of the book is a special comment on the uniqueness of Israel's God:

There is no one like the God of Jeshurun,
    who rides on the heavens to help you
    and on the clouds in his majesty.
The eternal God is your refuge,
    and underneath are the everlasting arms.
He will drive out your enemy before you,
    saying, "Destroy him!" (33:26–27).

Only two verses later the comparison is made with Israel:

Blessed are you, O Israel!
    Who is like you,
    a people saved by Yahweh?

Because Yahweh is unique, Israel, like no other people, could be unique. Indeed, "Their rock is not like our Rock, as even our enemies concede" (32:31).

I will proclaim the name of Yahweh.
    Oh, praise the greatness of our God!
He is the Rock, his works are perfect,
    and all his ways are just.
A faithful God who does no wrong,
    upright and just is he (32:3–4).[11]

Love and Remembering

If a mutual love relationship with Yahweh is the engine that powers the response of obedience, then memory is the fuel. As Blair points out,[12] both Old and New Testaments motivate by two mental activities: hope and memory—focusing on God's promise for the future and remembering God's activities in the past. Israel is about to enter the land and experience another phase of fulfillment of God's promise to Abraham. But if they forget the past, the dynamic for love will be lost . . . and so eventually will the land.

What past events should stir and keep alive their love and commitment?

- God's love for and covenant with Abraham, Isaac, and Jacob and the Lord's choice of them to be his nation (4:37; 7:7–8; 9:5; 10:14–15). This choice, Moses stresses, was not because of their righteousness nor any greatness they possessed. It was purely by grace.
- Their slavery in Egypt and God's deliverance from it (1:30; 4:20, 34, 37; 5:6, 15; 6:12, 20–25; 7:8–11, 18–19). The deliverance from Egypt was convincing proof of his love for them as well as the basis for their gratitude (7:8–11; 4:20, 34; 6:12). It also supported laws that called for kindness to others in need (24:17–18; 10:19; 15:12–15). The ritual of Passover and the Feast of Weeks were specifically designed to put memory on their annual calendar (16:1–12). Their past situation warned against self-confidence, yet gave assurance that God will give them victory in the future (8:12–14; 7:18–19; 20:1).
- God's gift of superior laws by which they could be the marvel of the nations (4:5–14, 23).
- The experiences and lessons of the wilderness (1:31; 2:7, 36; 3:3; 8:2–5, 15–18; 9:7, 23; 11:5–7; 24:9). God was teaching them in the wilderness. He taught them the need for total trust and dependence on him for their needs. They learned their own weaknesses and tendencies to rebel.

Be assured the idea here is not the old adage, "Those who will not learn from history are condemned to repeat it." It is more than that. Israel must identify with this history, realize God's initiative in coming into relationship with her, and then choose life (Deut. 30:19–20).

This generation has experienced these great events of deliverance (11:1–7). But what of their children? How would a love relationship with God continue? Must their children return to Egypt and be delivered so that they, too, can know that Yahweh, the true God, is their God?

The importance of memory to love is such that Moses underscores the absolute necessity for teaching the nation's children about Israel's unique history as God's people. Following the central command of Deuteronomy 6:4–5 are these words:

> These commandments that I give you today are to be upon your hearts. Impress them on your children. Talk about them when you sit at home and when you walk along the road, when you lie down and where you get up. Tie them as symbols on your hands and bind them on your foreheads. Write them on the doorframes of your houses and on your gates.

This is total integration of truth to life! Teaching children to remember God's work for his people was not limited to a Sunday school, nor to a few minutes of "quality time." The child's question about the meaning of the commands is to be answered by recalling God's deliverance (6:20–25). Both the law and the experiences of the past must be communicated faithfully to future generations if the land is to be continually enjoyed (4:9–10; 31:9–13).

When their children were growing up, a family I know made a "Memory Board" in their home, on which the family displayed items showing how God had helped them in the past. This helps to make the truth live. Deuteronomy has even more than this in mind. It wants us to recognize that we were involved in God's deliverances, though witnessed only by former generations. Our memory board should include a cross and an empty tomb. For in these actions he delivered us as well!

Love and Repentance

But Moses did not expect Israel to succeed in keeping these commands out of a heart of love. He had too much experience with them for that. After all, he even blamed his own failure to obey on their rebelliousness (1:37). "Stiff-necked" is the term that fits these people. "You have been rebellious against Yahweh ever since I have known you" says it all (9:24). Or in even stronger terms,

> Your eyes have seen all that Yahweh did in Egypt to Pharaoh, to all his officials and to all his land. With your own eyes you saw those great trials, those miraculous signs and great wonders. But to this day Yahweh has not given you a mind that understands or eyes that see or ears that hear (29:2–4).

Moses anticipates their rebellion, but Yahweh predicts it. The results of their disobedience are announced ahead of time, acting as red flags to warn that the nation is headed for disaster. Rebellion will introduce, in increasing intensity, plagues, famine, defeat in war, and captivity (28:15–68). This litany of doom is given not to dishearten them but to warn them and to make them understand the extent of Yahweh's love and commitment.

Even when they are in captivity, Yahweh will have compassion on them and return them to the land when they turn with all their heart to him (30:1–10). What a God! They would fail, but he will not. What a way to love!

Love and Land

"There's only one thing that lasts—land." From Scarlett O'Hara to your local real estate broker, so many say it. It's pure paganism and idolatry. The land is Yahweh's. He is its creator and owner. Man lives on it as a steward to oversee and enjoy. "To Yahweh your God belong the heavens, even the highest heavens, the earth and everything in it" (10:14). But man turns gift into god just as he worships the creature rather than the Creator. He fails in that elemental recognition of God—thankfulness. Israel is about to "inherit" the land as a gift and stewardship from Yahweh (4:21; 12:9; 15:4; 19:10).[13] This land is their inheritance because Yahweh promised it to their forefathers: Abraham, Isaac, and Jacob (1:8; 8:1; 11:9; 26:5). Israel's attitude toward her possession of this land is to be shaped by three truths:[14]

- The land was given as an act of sheer grace (1:25).
- It remains with Israel only as long as they are faithful (11:16–17).
- It is not given because of any prior faithfulness (9:6).

In fact, land presents a new danger that the period in the desert did not. Moses outlines this danger in the central address on major issues and concerns (Deut. 5–11). Following his exhortation on love (chap. 6) and his warning of the danger of mixing with the Canaanite nations (chap. 7), Moses sees the primary danger of land (chap. 8)—the danger of self-sufficiency. In the desert, Moses says, God taught you that he was the provider:

> He humbled you, causing you to hunger and then feeding you with manna, which neither you nor your fathers had known, to teach you that man does not live on bread alone but on every word that comes from the mouth of Yahweh (8:3).

Over the years we have heard many comments on "man shall not live by bread alone." Advertisers want you to pile on meat from their deli. Well-meaning preachers suggest that you need not only physical food, but spiritual food as well. Yet Moses' point is not the absence of a well-rounded diet, physical or spiritual. The point is that Israel stayed alive in the desert *because God said they would live*. When he spoke, they got food. When he decided they would be hungry, they were hungry. All of life is determined by Yahweh's word.

Now they are going into a "good land"[15] that Yahweh has provided according to his word. Yet because Yahweh's provision in the land is not as obvious a gift as it was in the desert, the temptation to draw a faulty conclusion is there:

> You may say to yourself, "My power and the strength of my hands have produced this wealth for me." But remember Yahweh your God, for it is he who gives you the ability to produce wealth, and so confirms his covenant, which he swore to your forefathers, as it is today (8:17–18).

And how must Israel acknowledge that they live by Yahweh's word? By keeping his word, walking in his ways, and fearing him (8:6).

Another bumper sticker surfacing in the sixties repeated a toast by nineteenth-century naval hero Stephen Decatur: MY COUNTRY, RIGHT OR WRONG. To slap one of these on the back of an oxcart in ancient Israel would have been an announcement of rebellion against God. The land is a gift to be held in righteousness, or not at all. Injustice and moral pollution threaten the nation's life in the land (Deut. 16:20; 25:15; 18:9–13).[16] Commitment to land leads to paganism. Commitment to Yahweh means enjoying his land.

COMPLETION OF LOVE AND LAND

Completion of Love

In a verbal sparring match with the various theological fraternities of his day, Jesus answered each loaded question with a dynamite reply. The noise was still reverberating from such current issues as the church-state debate and the possibility of resurrection, when one scholar threw up a question important only to eggheads in the classroom: "Of all the commandments, which is the most important?" (Mark 12:28). Jesus gives him the only nonexplosive answer in the bundle. First place goes to Deuteronomy 6:4–5, says Jesus:

> Hear, O Israel, the Lord our God, the Lord is one. Love the Lord your God with all your heart and with all your soul and with all your mind and with all your strength (Mark 12:29–30).

Then, lest anyone misunderstand the unity of this primary command with the other commands, Jesus names the runner-up: "Love your neighbor as yourself" (Lev. 19:18). This command is not from Deuteronomy but nonetheless summarizes the spirit of the laws of Deuteronomy that are modeled after the loving care of God himself (Deut. 10:17–19). Not willing to enter a debate that falsely sets these two at odds with one another, Jesus ties them together. The second, though second, follows from the first. This not-so-theoretical answer by Jesus concerning the heart of the Law brings the only discernable agreement of the afternoon. In fact, the expert not only agrees, but also adds his own footnote (he is a teacher!). The footnote, though not novel—the prophets had said as much—must have earned him some raised eyebrows in those sacred temple precincts: "To love him with all your heart, with all your understanding and with all your strength, and to love your neighbor as yourself is more important than all burnt offerings and sacrifices" (Mark 12:33).

Here stands a man who is beginning to perceive the significance of the Law. The Torah of Moses was *instruction in knowing God*. Its center is relationship, not ritual. Its ritual is educational, not magical or manipulative. Its purpose was to picture relational truth and enrich memory, not promote a form of buying off God. God was not interested in bribes (Deut. 10:17). Pagans brought offerings to their deities to encourage divine generosity. Yahweh received thanksgiving offerings from his children for whatever had already been received.[17]

This relational truth of Deuteronomy is not passé. Though there are no certain quotations of Deuteronomy in James 1 and 2,[18] it is interesting to note how much these chapters reflect the central issues of Deuteronomy.

- It is to those who love him that God will give the crown of life (1:12). Every "good and perfect gift" comes from the Father of creation who chose us ("twelve tribes," 1:1) as a kind of firstfruits (1:17–18).
- The man who will be blessed is he who not only hears the perfect law, but also does it (1:25).
- Genuine religion is to look after widows and orphans and to keep pure from the world (1:27).
- It is those who are poor that God has chosen to inherit the kingdom promised to those who love him (2:5).

These parallels with Deuteronomy indicate the continuing relevance of these ancient concerns of God. Was the church at Jerusalem thinking Deuteronomy when it made sure there were no needy persons in its midst (Acts 4:34; Deut. 15:4–11)?[19] Caring Israelites, Deuteronomy said, should make the difference. Though there will always be poor people because of circumstances, the poor should be relieved by those enjoying God's blessing (15:4–11). The promised blessing of abundance on the nation as a whole did not guarantee the physical success of every Israelite. The abundant blessing is corporate, and, therefore, must be shared.

Did not Paul teach the same in 2 Corinthians 8:13–14 and 9:6–11? Those who blithely quote Philippians 4:19—"And my God shall supply all your needs"—should consider not only that this promise was given because they responded to Paul's need, but also whether the "you" in "your needs" is corporate. The church as a body may well have supply enough for all its needy. Just as they had responded to Paul's need, God through his people would supply their need. Even in the Old Testament God did not evenly distribute either physical or spiritual blessing. He looks for us to be the distributors—distributors of love.

When the gifts have served their purpose of building up one another in love, when there is no more hunger, no more suffering or tears, when all the instruction of Moses and teaching of Christ and the Apostles is swallowed up into perfect knowledge of God, one thing remains supreme—love.

Completion of Torah: Moses and Jesus

As the book of Deuteronomy closes, it throws a bouquet in Moses' direction:

> Since then no prophet has risen in Israel like Moses, whom the LORD knew face to face, who did all those miraculous signs and wonders the LORD sent him to do in Egypt—to Pharaoh and to all his officials and to his whole land. For no one has ever shown the mighty power or performed the awesome deeds that Moses did in the sight of all Israel (34:10–12).

Moses was the prophet *par excellence*. Long after this comment, Judaism still believed that none had arisen greater than Moses. Yahweh had given Torah (law, instruction) through Moses.

Of course a replacement had been promised (18:14–22). And though the language is singular, the testing of prophets in the context clearly indicates that the raising up of a prophet could be expected regularly. The danger involved is well illustrated today—self-proclaimed "prophets" who are only regularly successful at predicting the sunrise, yet continue to claim to be speaking God's instruction. One church in my locale actually has used the King James Version of 1 Corinthians 13:8 ("Where there be prophecies, they shall fail") to explain why their "prophets" regularly miss the mark.

Duly warned about false or presumptuous prophets, Israel looked for its true and faithful prophets; but it judged that none matched Moses. Elijah was first runner-up. Later another Elijah is predicted to announce the arrival of Yahweh and his day of refining and repentance (Mal. 3:1–4; 4:1–6), but the people still looked for the prophet to equal Moses. They asked John the Baptist, "Are you the Prophet?" (John 1:21). After seeing Jesus multiply the loaves and fishes, reminiscent of provision in the desert, they remarked: "Surely this is the Prophet who is to come into the world" (John 6:14). Following his other miracles and after hearing his teaching, some concluded: "Surely this man is the Prophet" (John 7:40).

But this same Gospel clears up the uncertainty:

For the law was given through Moses; grace and truth came through Jesus Christ. No one [including Moses] has ever seen God, but God the only Son, who is at the Father's side, has made him known (John 1:17–18).

Moses, "the servant of God," cannot compete with "the only Son." Moses, who spoke with God directly, had not seen him fully. Yet the Son, who was in the beginning with God and was God, has truly revealed the Father. He is the Word—the revelation—of God. Jesus may say, "Anyone who has seen me has seen the Father" (John 14:9).

When the disciples witnessed that extraordinary meeting of Jesus with Moses and Elijah (Matt. 17:1–5), the cloud of glory once more appeared and the voice of God spoke: "This is my Son, whom I love; with him I am well pleased. Listen to him!" No need for Moses to stay. The God of Moses has sent his Son. "Listen to him!" (Matt. 17:5; Deut. 18:15).

Completion of Land: "Inheriting the Earth"

David in Psalm 37 urges fellow Israelites not to worry about evil men who seem to be getting ahead in the land. To those fellow Israelites who always find themselves at the mercy of an unprincipled Philistine used-cart dealer he advises:

Trust in the LORD and do good;
　　dwell in the land and enjoy safe pasture.
Delight yourself in the LORD
　　and he will give you the desires of your heart (37:3–4).

He counsels them not to worry, but to wait; not to strike out in anger, but to watch for God to finally put things right.

A little while, and the wicked will be no more;
　　though you look for them, they will not be found.
But the meek will inherit the land
　　and enjoy great peace (37:10–11).

Perhaps you recognize that last verse as a New Testament passage. Jesus placed it in the middle of his list of blessings or beatitudes (Matt. 5:5). He was speaking to his disciples to encourage them. Even more so than in David's time, those committed to faithfulness to God had fallen on hard times. Pagan Rome held sway over David's Jerusalem. All was not right. Many Israelites, like the father of John the Baptist, looked for God

> to rescue us from the hand of our enemies,
>> and to enable us to serve him without fear
>> in holiness and righteousness before him all our days
>>> (Luke 1:74–75).

Yet the righteous person committed to God does not grab for all he can get. He yearns after the righteous order that God had promised in the land. Jesus says, "He will get it."[20] These descriptions in Matthew 5 are not of different people—one who is poor in spirit, one who is gentle, one who is pure in heart—but are various descriptions from the Old Testament for the righteous person committed to Yahweh. They look ahead to the final installation of peace on earth. Those who are afflicted and brokenhearted—poor in spirit—will receive news of freedom from captivity (Isa. 61:1). Those who mourn will be comforted because the long exile is over (Isa. 61:1–2; 40:1–2). Those who hunger and thirst for what really counts will find it (Isa. 55:1–7).

Is there a new world coming? Yes, there is. In fact, its life is already available. Those who have put their trust in Jesus as God's deliverer already have "eternal life" (John 10:28; 3:36). They are members of the kingdom (Col. 1:13). They await the return of Christ to see the full implementation of his deliverance, which has come not just for Israel but for the whole world.[21] "Christ was sacrificed once to take away the sins of many people; and he will appear a second time, not to bear sin but to bring salvation to those who are waiting for him" (Heb. 9:28).

But Until Then?

We purchased our first house while I was still in seminary. It was a good buy. It put our rent money to use, and in the expanding housing market of the early seventies it sold quickly when we were ready to move on. Moving into that house in Irving, Texas, gave us a sense of permanence. We had a place of our own. That purchase, however, also brought into jarring perspective several Scriptures.

> By faith he [Abraham] made his home in the promised land like
> a stranger in a foreign country; he lived in tents, as did Isaac and Jacob,
> who were heirs with him of the same promise. For he was looking for-
> ward to the city with foundations, whose architect and builder is God
> (Heb. 11:9–10).

Here was a man who never lived in a city with foundations and walls, but in tents. Here was a man whose accommodations showed his faith. He wasn't taking. He was waiting. The testimony of Hebrews 11:13–14 is significant:

> All these people were still living by faith when they died. They did not
> receive the things promised; they only saw them and welcomed them

from a distance. And they admitted that they were aliens and strangers on earth. People who say such things show that they are looking for a country of their own.

The New Testament sees believers today as in a similar position to the patriarchs. It is a better position (Heb. 11:40) because Christ has come and provided redemption, the forgiveness of sins. We have seen the time of fulfillment begin. But we are aliens and pilgrims, for we have "an inheritance that can never perish, spoil or fade—kept in heaven" while we await "the coming of the salvation that is ready to be revealed in the last time" (1 Peter 1:4–5). We are "aliens and strangers in the world" (2:11). Our position is more like Abraham and Israel in the desert than it is like Israel in the land. We are citizens of a kingdom that has not yet been revealed in its fullness.

In 1 Peter 2:11–3:12 instructions are given on how to live life as an alien. It involves real down-to-earth options. Nothing esoteric here. As C. S. Lewis once observed, it is precisely those who are heavenly minded who are the most earthly good:

> If you read history you will find that the Christians who did most for the present world were just those who thought the most of the next. . . . It is since Christians have largely ceased to think of the other world that they have become so ineffective in this. Aim at Heaven and you will get earth "thrown in"; aim at earth and you will get neither.[22]

The principle for believers today is: Use the things of this world, but avoid being entangled in them, because "this world in its present form is passing away" (1 Cor. 7:31). We may not be limited to living in tents, but our lifestyle should reflect our faith. The choice: Will we be part of the Now Generation . . . or will we live for the future Kingdom?

SUGGESTED SCRIPTURE READING:

Deuteronomy 1–8
Mark 12:28–34
Matthew 5:1–16

For Interaction and Discussion:

1. Why is loving the land such a danger? Who owned the land? What questions does this raise about possessions?

2. How does the covenant form of Deuteronomy help to emphasize God's love and grace in his making Israel a nation? How is the idea of love (for God or from God) in Deuteronomy different from either romantic or situational ideas of love?

3. Why is Yahweh's uniqueness important? Is Christ's uniqueness equally important? How does the comparison of Jesus and Moses stress Christ's uniqueness? What makes him greater than Moses?

4. Why is memory important to faith? Can historic events be part of our understanding of who we are? Would Valley Forge, Gettysburg, and Pearl Harbor be part of the "memory" of an American? What events need to be part of your "memory"?

5. What lessons on parenting are found in Deuteronomy? How can Deuteronomy 6:4–5 be practiced in fast-paced, modern society?

6. What sins cause the loss of the land? How do these sins stack up in our culture? Do you think such sins justify a surgical removal of whole nations?

7. What marks the difference between pagan offerings and offerings to Israel's God? How does this relate to bargaining with God?

8. How does a believer live as an "alien and pilgrim"? How should his outlook toward the future relate to his life at present?

For Further Reading:

Meredith G. Kline. *Treaty of the Great King*. Grand Rapids: Eerdmans, 1963.

Kenneth A. Kitchen. *The Bible in Its World*. Downers Grove, Ill.: InterVarsity, 1977, 79–85.

Walter Brueggemann. *The Land*. Philadelphia: Fortress, 1977.

Edward P. Blair. "An Appeal to Remembrance." *Int*, 15 (1961): 41–47.

Patrick D. Miller, Jr. "The Gift of God: The Deuteronomic Theology of the Land." *Int*, 23 (1969): 451–60.

L. E. Toombs. "Love and Justice in Deuteronomy." *Int*, 19 (1965): 399–411.

John D. W. Watts. "The Deuteronomic Theology." *R&E*, 74 (1977): 321–36.

Notes and Comments:

[1]Deuteronomy, taken at face value, contains addresses of Moses to the second generation of Israelites out of Egypt at the border of the land. Most nonconservative scholars, impressed by the reoccurrence of Deuteronomy's theology in the former prophets (Joshua–2 Kings), have suggested a later date, either shortly after the fall of Samaria or shortly before or after the exile of Judah. For a summary of these views see R. K. Harrison, *Introduction to the Old Testament*, 637–53. It should be noted that most of these attempts to date Deuteronomy as the work of a later author involve a theory of a "pious fraud." Cf. Gerhard von Rad, *Deuteronomy: A Commentary* (Philadelphia: Westminster, 1966), 28. Though the theology of Deuteronomy extends its influence through the former prophets, it is, as Walter Kaiser points out (*Toward an Old Testament Theology*, 122), entirely another matter to assign it to an author at the end of this period. What is so difficult about recognizing this theology as having been the original base for the "school" of thinking that followed and later evaluated Israel's history in the former prophets? It is as if Adam Smith had to be

invented after his economic school developed. Did Marxists invent Marx or did the philosophy come first? As Harrison points out, the work of Kline on Deuteronomy (see note 3 below) has provided significant historical support for the earlier dating of Deuteronomy.

[2]Deuteronomy 8 is devoted to the danger of land. The possibilities of land as a temptation for Israel to focus on the gift rather than the covenant is spelled out by Walter Brueggemann, *The Land*, 53–54.

[3]Deuteronomy follows the pattern of the Hittite treaties of the fourteenth and thirteenth centuries B.C. This pattern is discussed by K. A. Kitchen in *The Bible in Its World*, 79–85. Kitchen cautions that none of the biblical accounts (Exodus, Leviticus, Deuteronomy, Joshua 24) are the actual treaties themselves, but narratives about them. We should, therefore, expect some differences. The student should also consult Meredith G. Kline, *Treaty of the Great King* (Grand Rapids: Eerdmans, 1963), for his more extensive treatment of Deuteronomy. Compare also Kitchen's earlier work, *Ancient Orient and Old Testament* (Chicago: InterVarsity, 1966), 90–102.

[4]Unless otherwise indicated citations are from the NIV with "Yahweh" inserted for "the LORD."

[5]Attempts to discover a pattern or organization for the detailed laws of chapters 12–26 have been many. Kaiser, *Toward Old Testament Ethics*, 129–31, has followed Stephan Kaufman, ("The Structure of the Deuteronomic Law," *Maarav* 1, 2 [1978–79], 105–58), with the view that this group of laws is organized to follow the order of the Ten Commandments. Each block of laws reflects or applies in some way the central concern or principle of each successive command. Cf. Andrew H. Hill and John H. Walton, *A Survey of the Old Testament*, 145–48, who have followed Walton's modification of Kaufman's work, add chapters 6–11 and identifying them with the first commandment. Alternately, McBride, *Int*, 41 (1987): 239–44, has suggested "a remarkably coherent five-part structure" for Deuteronomy 12–26, chiastically arranged.

[6]Christensen points out that in each of these chiastic pairs, the outer frame and the inner frame may be read as a single document. The outer frame (Deut. 1–3 and 31–34) have Joshua as a common element. The inner frame are "joined together by the reference to blessings and curses connected with a cultic ceremony on Mount Gerizim and Mount Ebal (Deut. 11:26–32 and 27:1–14), which are mentioned only in these two contexts." Duane L. Christensen, *Deuteronomy 1–11*, WBC (Waco, Tex.: Word, 1991), xl–xli.

[7]On the meaning of love in the Old Testament, see Larry L. Walker, "'Love' in the Old Testament: Some Lexical Observations," *Current Issues in Biblical and Patristic Interpretation*, ed. Gerald F. Hawthorne (Grand Rapids: Eerdmans), 277–88. Walker lists examples where love is found in contexts of treaties to indicate faithfulness and loyalty. Cf. W. Moran, "The Ancient Near Eastern Background of the Love of God in Deuteronomy," *CBQ*, 25 (1963): 77–87. L. E. Toombs has pointed out the third aspect of love in Deuteronomy—i.e., justice (10:19)—in "Love and Justice in Deuteronomy," *Int*, 19 (1965): 399–411. J. A. Thompson's analysis of distinctive vocabulary of Deuteronomy has shown the dominance of covenant loyalty as a theme. Cf. *Deuteronomy* (Downers Grove, Ill.: InterVarsity, 1974), 30–35.

[8]The words heart, soul, and strength—especially the first two—often are misunderstood because the Hebrew words carry different connotations than our English counterparts. Biblically, heart is not to be contrasted with mind. In fact, in the Old Testament it is often translated as "mind." The heart represents the true inner person—his thinking, motives, plans, and feelings. Wolff observes: "In by far the greatest number of cases it is the intellectual, rational functions that are ascribed to the heart—i.e., precisely what we ascribe to the head and, more exactly, to the brain" (Hans Walter Wolff, *Anthropology of the Old Testament*, 46). The word *soul* also is subject to misunderstanding. Too often the Greek idea of "soul" is applied to the Old Testament as if it were referring to the immaterial part of man, as is the tendency of our English word. In the Old Testament the word has in view the physical life of the person, the person as an individual, or the particular passions and appetites of the person. It is, therefore, often translated as "life" or "self." McBride sees these terms as concentric in Deuteronomy 6:5 (*TDOT*, 9:617–37; cited in *TWOT*, 1:487). For a comparison of OT and NT usage, see D. M. Lake, "Soul," *ZPEB*, 5:496–98. The word translated as "strength" looks at abundance or excess, so I have used the word *exuberance*.

[9]Because Yahweh owns all the earth, he may disestablish the Canaanites when his justice demands it and give the land to Israel. Neither action involves giving up his own claim to ultimate ownership of the whole earth. Marvin E. Tate, in an otherwise very helpful article on Deuteronomy's theology, has misread the book on this point. Following von Rad, he concludes: "It [the land) could not have been Israel's without Yahweh's taking it away from other people—for it did not originally belong to either Israel or Yahweh" (*R&E*, 61 [1964]: 315). He neglects Deuteronomy 10:14. Kaiser, *Toward an Old Testament Theology*, 125–26, answers von Rad. John D. W. Watts, "The Deuteronomic Theology," *R&E*, 74 (1977): 328, puts it succinctly: "The foundation of all that Deuteronomy teaches about the land is the understanding that it belongs to Yahweh. He made it. He cares for it by sending rain. And now he is in process of throwing the latest tenants out to make room for his chosen people."

[10]The issue of Yahweh's wars and *herem*, total destruction and dedication to Yahweh, will be discussed in the next chapter.

[11]See Michael L. Goldberg, "The Story of Moral: Gift or Bribes in Deuteronomy?" *Int*, 38 (1984): 15–25, for further aspects of uniqueness in the laws themselves.

[12]Edward P. Blair, "An Appeal to Remembrance," *Int*, 15 (1961): 41–47. This excellent article details the importance of memory to the dynamics of Deuteronomy in a way I could only partially reflect in this overview. Cf. Brueggemann, *The Land*, 54–55.

[13]Other references in Deuteronomy designating the land as an inheritance include 4:38; 12:10; 20:16; 21:23; 24:4; 25:19; and 26:1.

[14]This is Walter Brueggemann's summary of the theology of land in "The Kerygma of the Deuteronomistic Historian," *Int*, 22 (1968): 395. Cf. Brueggemann, *The Land*, 53–59, on the danger of land to the memory of Yahweh's gift and covenant.

[15]The use of "good" in covenants indicating covenant faithfulness also adds a covenantal flavor to the expression "good land." Cf. Brueggemann, "The Kerygma of the Deuteronomistic Historian," 387–402.

[16]Patrick D. Miller, Jr., "The Gift of God: The Deuteronomic Theology of the Land," *Int*, 23 (1969): 459–60, shows the distinctive emphasis on land even in the more detailed stipulations of chapters 12–27: "A large number of the laws in the legal corpus of Deuteronomy are specifically associated with the land and Israel's existence on it: the year of release (15:1ff); judicial procedure (16:18–20); law of kingship (17:14ff); law against abominable practices (18:9ff); cities of refuge (19:1ff); not removing a landmark (19:14); expiation for an unknown murder (21:1ff); law against leaving a hanged man's body on a tree (21:22 ff); just weights and measures (25:13–16); divorce law (24:1–4). Introductory or motive clauses relative to land appear in all these laws. In some cases disobedience of the law brings defilement or guilt upon the land itself (21:23; 24:4). In other cases long life and blessing are motivations for obedience."

[17]See Goldberg, "The Story of Moral," 22.

[18]James (in James 2:8–11) does quote the Law three times: Leviticus 19:18, and two commandments of the ten that could be from either Exodus 20 or Deuteronomy 5. It is clear that James is thinking of Law in these chapters.

[19]This parallel was suggested by L. E. Toombs, "Love and Justice," 399–411.

[20]Brueggemann notes W. D. Davies' belief that Psalm 37:11 is spiritualized in the NT, but comments that this conclusion must be reached "only with a troubled conscience" (*The Land*, 183, n. 36). His own treatment of land in the NT is filled with misgivings about divorcing the promise from land (167–83). M. H. Woodstra, *The Book of Joshua* (Grand Rapids: Eerdmans, 1981), 18, 35, seems to believe Matthew 5:5's use of Psalm 37:11 proves a widening of the land promise in the NT because of the change from "the land" to "the earth." He fails to note, however, that the LXX already had translated "land" as "earth" without apparently intending to announce something new. As Matthew's wording follows the LXX text here, too much should not be made of any supposed widening of meaning.

[21]Verses that relate to Israel's deliverance include Romans 11:26–27, Acts 3:19–21, and Luke 1:32–33. Blessing on the whole world is anticipated in Luke 2:30–32 and Isaiah 42:1–6 and 49:6.

[22]C. S. Lewis, *Mere Christianity* (New York: Macmillan, 1952), 104.

Part Three

Joshua – 2 Kings

STRUGGLE
FOR
CONSISTENCY

chapter eight

LIVING BY FAITH
(Joshua, Judges, and Ruth)

"Tibet—a land of contrasts." So reads the travel guide. If travel guides and documentaries are any indication, *most* countries on earth are lands of contrast. One thinks of our own purple mountain majesties and amber waves of grain.

The next biblical books also are lands of contrast. Both Joshua and Judges chronicle Israel's history in the land prior to the monarchies of Saul and David—but no two books could be so different.

Joshua is upbeat and joyful.

Judges is discouraging and depressing.

Joshua faces difficulties and solves them.

Judges encounters difficulties and compounds them.

In Joshua the leader is faithful.

In Judges the leaders are increasingly inconsistent.

Both books, however, operate on the same principles. These principles begin by recognizing Yahweh as exclusive Sovereign. Everything else follows predictably from there. It's all in the guidebook already provided by Moses. Are you ready for the travelogue?

THE STRATEGY OF THE BOOK OF JOSHUA

The book of Joshua is laid out according to the strategy of Israel's military campaigns. Joshua's first military goal was to establish Israel in Canaan by taking the whole land, breaking the back of the opposition, and eliminating major political centers. The list of conquered kings and cities in Joshua 12 marks the completion of this effort.

The rest of the book takes up phase two. Having achieved control over Canaan, the land is divided and territory given to each tribe. It is the duty of each tribe to remove the smaller pockets of resistance and finally settle the entire area. This distinctive strategy is key to understanding the book. Without recognizing this two-stage program, many of the book's statements seem contradictory. For instance, the land is said to have been totally taken by Joshua (11:23), yet the Lord may say to Joshua: "There are still very large areas of land to be taken over" (13:1). In Joshua 21:44 we read, "The LORD handed all their enemies over to them," yet in 23:5 Joshua relays to Israel this promise concerning the conquered nations: "God himself will drive them out of your way."

The major campaigns of the book's first half also show a distinctive pattern. Jericho and Ai in the center of the land are taken first (chaps. 6–8). Israel then faces a military confederacy made up of kings to the south. This warfare is triggered by the sly and desperate Gibeonites, who against all odds find a way of changing sides, but then are attacked by their former confederates. With spectacular divine aid, Joshua defeats this southern coalition (chaps. 9–10). Finally, the great city of Hazor in the north attempts to establish an alliance capable of stopping Israel. The destruction of this formidable force brings to an end any effective military opposition within the land (chap. 11).

Spliced in between these campaigns is the renewal of the covenant at Mount Ebal (8:30–35), as commanded by Moses (Deut. 27). This ceremony reconfirms their commitment to Yahweh as King. The one giving them the land is the God they will follow and obey.

One other feature of the first half of Joshua also is critical: Like a daughter's marriage, there is almost as much importance given to preparation as to execution (no pun intended!). The first five chapters of the book are all preparation. As we shall see, however, they are not incidental. They are vital for communicating the true significance of God's activities.

UNDERSTANDING JOSHUA AND JUDGES

God Acting to Accomplish His Plan

As we said earlier, God announced his plan of reversal with Abraham. Beginning with the Exodus, God actively moved to fulfill those promises. He delivered Israel from Egypt. He made her into a great nation. He brought her through the desert, providing for and protecting her. Her recent military victories over Sihon and Og on the east side of the Jordan gave concrete assurance of God's ability.

Were it not for the sheer fear of it, the Israelites on the border of Canaan would feel like kids on Christmas Eve alive with anticipation, unable to sleep, gloriously expectant. Israel is about to possess the land promised to Abraham, Isaac, and Jacob (Josh. 1:6).

Now the God of Israel no longer works slowly behind the scenes, as in the days of slavery in Egypt. For Joshua and Israel he is gloriously public in fulfilling his promise. In this book the Jordan dries up, perfectly timed to the

Figure 8.1
Map of the Land of the Twelve Tribes

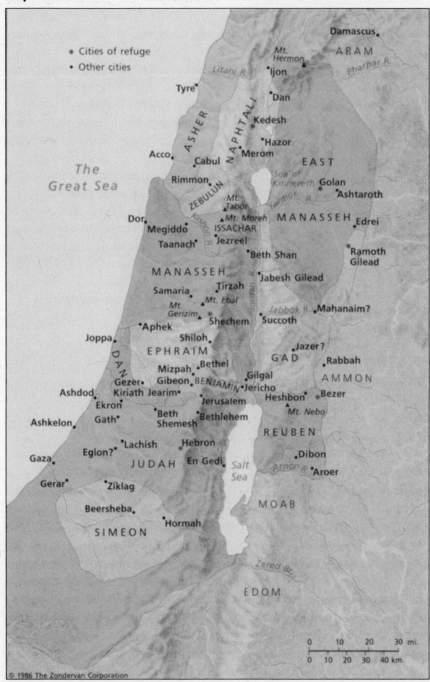

From *The NIV Study Bible* (Zondervan, 1985), map 4 of color maps.

entrance of the ark-bearing priests into the stream. The walls of Jericho fall in unison with the blast of trumpets and shouts of the people, after they ceremoniously circle the city for a week (Josh. 6). The southern confederation of Amorites is defeated when God sends hailstones and answers Joshua's prayer for extended light (Josh. 10).[1]

These events prove to this first generation of landed Israelites that they are Yahweh's people. They now have their own "Red Sea" experience. Their deliverance *and* their land have been provided by God.

They are further prepared by a series of ceremonies as soon as they enter the land. Circumcision is the first. It would certainly be better military strategy to circumcise all the men while the Jordan still separated them from Jericho. Ask Shechem (Gen. 34). But this ceremony is performed *inside* the land (Josh. 5:1–9). This generation had not been circumcised during its travels in the wilderness. A hint at the reason is given in 5:9—"Today I have rolled away the reproach of Egypt from you." The first generation was faithless in wanting to go back to Egypt, but this generation starts now with a clean slate. Circumcision shows that they recognize the covenant with Abraham (Gen. 17:14). If they are to be Yahweh's people, they must be circumcised.

Second, they observe Passover (5:10). The conquest was timed to parallel the Exodus. *What an anniversary celebration!* Just as Israel had been delivered from Egypt, so God would give her the land.

The next preparation may be labeled a non-event. They sample the produce of the land, and the manna stops (5:12). Remember the lesson of the manna in Deuteronomy 8? Manna in the wilderness was evidence that God was their provider. The provision of food through the more "natural" processes of the land is to be taken as no less a divine blessing. "I Did It My Way" must never enter the Israelite hymnbook.

The observances do not stop there. The first battle itself is a ceremony. For *seven* days *seven* priests march around the city, blowing trumpets, carrying the ark of the covenant. On the *seventh* day they circle Jericho no less than *seven* times. Enough sevens for you? If you ask the average Bible reader the significance of seven, he will tell you it is the number of completion. But such abstract notions fail to see the concrete significance of the text.

How many days are in a week? Where did the Bible first introduce us to the seventh day? The seventh day was the Sabbath to be kept as a mark of the Mosaic Covenant (Ex. 31:14–17; 20:8–11). It was the day the true God of creation, having finished that work, rested (Gen. 2:3). Israel's sabbath observance, therefore, declared her the nation of the true Creator God. The numbers here are not mystical but practical. Taking Jericho is a sacred activity, showing who is God of all the earth.

Jericho is also the *firstfruits* of the land. Just as the first of the crop was Yahweh's, so the first of the cities—with all its livestock and plunder—is his also. Later God allows Israel to keep plundered goods and cattle (Josh. 8:2).[2]

Yahweh acts in history to achieve his purpose. At each new step in his program, he miraculously vindicates his message so its significance is not lost (cf. Heb. 2:1–4).[3] Yahweh could have promised Israel the land, ferried her across the Jordan, and had her attack Jericho by normal military strategy. But this might have left a garbled message about the conquest. "Weren't those Jews lucky?" would have been as plausible an opinion as "Yahweh is God of all the earth."

Moses' Instruction Revisited

If the concerns Moses emphasized on the border of the land were important then, they are doubly important now. Like a good piano sonata there has been a change in movement, but major themes keep appearing.[4]

Land and Rest. As in Deuteronomy, the land is an "inheritance" (Josh. 11:23; 23:4–5) given to them by Yahweh (Josh. 1:3–5; 23:16). This partially fulfills the promise to Abraham, Isaac, and Jacob (Josh. 1:6). If Israel obeys, the result will be "rest" (Josh. 21:44–45; 23:1). But if she is unfaithful, God will destroy her from "this good land he has given" (23:15–16).

Memory. While experiences of previous generations were to be passed on as reminders of God's faithfulness, this generation has its own experience worthy of a special memorial—the crossing of the Jordan on dry ground. Twelve stones are set up to commemorate the event.[5] If the Israelites are to be continuing landholders, they must be continuing teachers. There is a better way to learn than by hard experience—*learning by godly heritage.*[6] By communicating both positive and negative lessons, each succeeding generation will see that the fear of the Lord is truly the beginning of wisdom. Walking in God's well-defined ways avoids a lot of heartache.

Covenant Obedience. The book of Joshua is upbeat. Judges is downbeat. This major difference is due to one man, Joshua, who complies with God's instruction to "be careful to obey all the law my servant Moses gave you" (Josh. 1:7). Consistently throughout the book, Joshua shows himself a man of obedience.

The Law of Moses becomes Joshua's constant meditation. One caution here: Meditation in Scripture must not be confused with altered mental states so popular today. Joshua is not trying to sit on the ceiling and pretend he's a golf ball. Meditation for Joshua means a thoughtful study and review of God's instruction so he can put it into practice at the proper time (Josh. 1:8).

Joshua 1:1–9, repeating much of what was recorded in Deuteronomy, anticipates the flow of the book. God's chosen leader, Joshua, gives close attention to the Law (meditates), keeps it totally (turns neither to the right nor to the left), and secures the land promised to Israel (good success).[7]

The inspired penman plants a green flag of obedience over and over in the text as he marks how Joshua obeys the Law of Moses (4:10; 8:31, 33; 11:12, 15, 18–20, 23; 14:2, 5, 6–14; 17:4; 20:2–7; 21:1–3, 8). Even in "small matters" where the writer does not remind us—such as not allowing a body to hang on a tree overnight (Josh. 10:26; Deut. 21:23)—Joshua is obedient.

Two clear cases of disobedience mar the book of Joshua: the sin of Achan (chap. 7), who takes booty from Jericho that the Lord had claimed as exclusively his; and making a treaty with the deceitful Gibeonites (chap. 9). The first is neither Joshua's sin nor the rest of Israel's, though it threatens their success. The second sin is inadvertent, though it could have been avoided with more care (9:14). In neither case is the sin allowed to continue and become a pattern.

To Joshua, covenant obedience focused on loving the Lord, just as it did with Moses:[8]

> But be very careful to keep the commandment and the law that Moses the servant of the LORD gave you: to love the LORD your God, to walk in all his ways, to obey his commands, to hold fast to him and to serve him with all your heart and all your soul (Josh. 22:5).

Rebellion and Land. Joshua, like Moses, reminds his people that they are still under the threat of cursing should they depart from the Lord (Josh. 23:14–16). They have been blessed under Joshua. In spite of possessing the land, they could call down God's wrath upon themselves.

> If you violate the covenant of the LORD your God, which he commanded you, and go and serve other gods and bow down to them, the LORD's anger will burn against you, and you will quickly perish from the good land he has given you (23:16).

Joshua also warns them about their tendency to rebelliousness.[9]

> You are not able to serve the LORD. He is a holy God; he is a jealous God. He will not forgive your rebellion and your sins. If you forsake the LORD and serve foreign gods, he will turn and bring disaster on you and make an end of you, after he has been good to you (Josh. 24:19).

It is not complexity of commands that will trip them; their own tendency to idolatry will bring down on them Yahweh's jealousy.

Yahweh Is a Warrior

The notion that God fights for Israel is not original with the book of Joshua. The Exodus itself demonstrated that Yahweh was Israel's military deliverer. Faced with Pharaoh's forces, the people were told, "Yahweh will fight for you; you need only to be still" (Ex. 14:14). The "Song of the Sea" celebrated the victory (15:3):

> Yahweh is a warrior;
> Yahweh is his name.

In Deuteronomy we saw that Yahweh's uniqueness included fighting for Israel. This fighting meant absolute victory and destruction of Yahweh's enemies:

> See now that I myself am He!
> There is no god besides me.
> I put to death and I bring to life,
> I have wounded and I will heal,
> and no one can deliver from my hand.
> I lift my hand to heaven and declare:
> As surely as I live forever,
> when I sharpen my flashing sword
> and my hand grasps it in judgment,
> I will take vengeance on my adversaries
> and repay those who hate me.
> I will make my arrows drunk with blood,
> while my sword devours flesh:
> the blood of the slain and the captives,
> the heads of the enemy leaders (Deut. 32:39–42).

It is Yahweh who will drive out the enemy, encouraging Israel with the shout, "Destroy him!" (Deut. 33:27).

Not only does Deuteronomy assure Israel that Yahweh will fight for her and drive out her enemies, it gives specific instructions on how to wage war:

- The priest initiates the war by reminding them that Yahweh fights for them. This clearly shows the war's sacred character (20:2–4).[10]
- Cities outside the land need not be entirely destroyed, but attacks on cities inside the land require destruction of all life (20:10–18). This practice is known as the "ban" or *herem*. To put a city under the ban was to devote its occupants to Yahweh for destruction. It is often translated "completely destroyed" or "devoted" (Deut. 20:17; 2:34; 7:2; Josh. 6:17; 8:26).[11]

- The military camp is to maintain a state of holiness (Deut. 23:9–14), as defined in Leviticus.
- They are specifically to show no pity to inhabitants of the land (Deut. 7:1–2). These wars cannot be explained as cases where man's sinful violence is used by God to accomplish his purpose.[12] God believes they will not want to fully carry out his directions. He warns against pity.

Why does God insist on total destruction or *herem*? Because he doesn't want his favorites to share the land with anyone? No. His "favorite," Abraham, never possessed the land because the inhabitants had not yet reached a level of depravity that required their removal (Gen. 15:16). God is not partial. When Israel reaches the same level of immorality, he will treat them in exactly the same way (Lev. 18:24–28).

So this war of total destruction is first of all a final judgment of God against these nations. God has always reserved this right of judgment. Those who object to it here would object, no doubt, to the Flood (Gen. 6–7) and to the destruction of Sodom and Gomorrah (Gen. 19). This judgment on the Canaanites continues the theme of God as Moral Governor of the universe.[13]

Yet isn't this situation in Joshua different in that human beings rather than the elements of nature are the agents of destruction? No doubt this is true. But rulers of state are also required to carry out God's moral laws and punish evildoers (Rom. 13:4). So David, as God's king, promises to eliminate evildoers in his kingdom (Ps. 101:8).

Like a child sent to get his own paddle, Israel, by being the instrument of God's moral judgment on the Canaanite nations, is graphically taught its need to obey Yahweh, who indeed is God of the whole earth. And God takes his duties seriously! Israel is warned that failure to remove this cancer of wickedness would eventually bring her own infection and judgment (Deut. 7:1–6; 20:18).

But now let us move from theory to practice. The book of Joshua keys its notion of success to this practice of *herem*. Jericho (6:17, 21), Ai (8:1–2, 26–27), the kings and cities of the southern region (10:25–40), and Hazor and its allies (11:8–14) all receive this radical judgment. Joshua's obedience prompts Yahweh to fight for Israel (10:40–42). And it *is* Yahweh who fights. Before the warfare begins, in a scene reminiscent of Moses at the burning bush, Joshua comes face-to-face with the commander of the army of Yahweh (5:13–15). *He* will bring victory—not the puny army of Joshua.

At Jericho, Israel is warned that if she does not practice *herem*, she herself will be *herem*—under God's judgment (6:18). At Ai she fights without Yahweh's help because Achan failed to observe the ban. Thirty-six men perish . . . and Joshua is absolutely devastated (Josh. 7). Why? Is thirty-six a high number of men to lose in battle? It apparently is in Yahweh's wars. We search in vain for other casualties.

Another violation of the ban occurs in Joshua 9. The Gibeonites deceive Israel into thinking they are from a distant country. A treaty is made, but three days later the truth is discovered. Caught by their own negligence (9:14), Israel has already violated the ban by making such a treaty in the Lord's name. Instead, they put the Gibeonites into service to the Levites—"devoting" them to the Lord as nearly as they now can.[14]

Rahab also stands as an exception to the ban. The spies, rightly or wrongly, buy their own protection with a promise of safety for this woman who believes "Yahweh your God is God in heaven above and on the earth below" (2:11–14). Joshua honors this agreement (Josh. 6:17). Like the Canaanite woman who believed strongly enough to press past Jesus' initial refusal (Matt. 15:21–28), Rahab stands as a memorial to a faith not often found in Israel. Could Jesus refuse mercy to such a person when Rahab herself is found in his own family tree (Matt. 1:5)?

Israel under Joshua stands as a memorial to obedience (Josh. 24:31). Because of that commitment to Yahweh, Joshua is able to say at the end of his life, "No one has been able to withstand you. One of you routs a thousand, because the LORD your God fights for you, just as he promised" (23:9–10).

The tragedy of the rest of Israel's history is that no other generation matches this one.

Deterioration of Commitment in Judges

If the book of Joshua is a flowing stream, fresh and invigorating with direction and power, then in Judges the river turns sluggish and muddy, its polluted water ultimately spiraling down a storm drain.

Judges teaches the same principles that Joshua did. But it teaches them as "lessons from the woodshed." Rather than the thrill of victory, the generations living in the time of the judges experience all too often the agony of defeat.

The book starts at the close of Joshua's era, giving a brief but telling overview of progress in taking the land (1:1–2:5). Close to Joshua's own time, there is success.[15] Judah succeeds initially (1:1–18), but later is unable to drive out those who live on the plains and possess chariots (1:19). She practices *herem* (1:8, 17), but does she practice it consistently (1:6–7)? Defeats begin to alternate with victories. Bethel is taken and put to the sword (1:22–25), but the tribe of Manasseh is unsuccessful (1:27). When Israel becomes strong she makes slaves of the Canaanites rather than eliminating them (1:28–36). Economics have taken on a higher priority than obedience!

The divine messenger announces the climax to all this "partial obedience" in 2:1–5. Like the proverbial rose, disobedience by any other name smells the same—especially to God. Because Israel has made treaties with the people of the land, God will not remove these nations. Israel will face the result of her sin by daily facing temptation to false worship.

Having given us the bad news, the writer begins again at Joshua's time (2:6–9) and gives us *more* bad news. His concern this time, and through the bulk of the book (chaps. 2–16), is to trace in detail the period of the judges and the reasons for Israel's failure to make any progress at fully taking the land.

The writer's theme is not subtle. He announces it clearly (2:10–3:4), then illustrates it with stories of judges and oppressors. To put it bluntly, Israel begins to worship other gods. Oh, they retain Yahweh as one among many; but to the Lord this is the same as forsaking him. The first commandment required worship of Yahweh *alone*.

Their unfaithfulness means that Yahweh will not fight for them. In fact, they are under the curse announced by Moses (Judg. 2:15; Deut. 28:25). Even when Yahweh provides judges to deliver them, disobedience grows worse following each judge's death (2:18–19).

The conclusion here is the same as in the introductory overview. The Lord will not remove the pagan nations from Canaan because of Israel's disobedience. Now every future generation will have the opportunity to prove whether it will obey as Joshua did (2:20–23), giving exclusive allegiance to Yahweh and obeying him in warfare (3:1–4). Judges 2:23 even hints that Joshua's generation was not allowed to take the full country so that more than one generation would have to be faithful before the land would be totally occupied.[16]

The repetitive and sinfully boring cycle of the book of Judges may be summarized as follows:

SIN: Disobedience to the first commandment by Israel.

SERVITUDE: The nation loses its freedom to its enemies.

SUPPLICATION: Israel cries to Yahweh for deliverance.

SALVATION: Israel is delivered and enjoys temporary peace.[17]

It is not simply that Israel's history goes nowhere. It goes downhill (2:19).

Note the character of the judges themselves. The first is Othniel (3:7–11). He delivers Israel from an outside oppressor. His history is brief, but all we know about him is positive (1:12–14). From there we move to Ehud, who is brave but who certainly does not go about war in the normal way (3:12–30).

Deborah provides a positive note (chapter 4), but her military commander, Barak, is hesitant to act without her continual support. For his hesitancy, though the Lord gives a mighty victory, Barak is deprived of the honor of capturing the opposing general, Sisera.

The chapters on Gideon illustrate more the Lord's mercy and patience than the quality of the leader (Judg. 6–8). Gideon needs sign after sign. His "fleeces" clearly test God's patience. These do not "discover" God's will but rather are given to encourage a man weak in faith. Under God's careful nurturing, Gideon is finally able to lead a force of only three hundred men in destroying the Midianites, demonstrating how Yahweh desired to fight for Israel.

Deterioration sets in again after Gideon (8:33–10:10). By this time the Lord announces he is tired of delivering Israel only to be forsaken afterward. He will no longer deliver them (10:11–14). The Israelites repent and get rid of their idols (10:15–16).

The last full accounts of judges are those of Jephthah in the east and Samson in the west. Jephthah is not chosen directly by the Lord as earlier judges were. Instead, with no promise of deliverance, the leaders of Israel ask Jephthah to be their military commander against the Ammonites (11:4–6). He wants to be recognized as judge if he is victorious (11:7–11). The Lord finally comes to Israel's aid by empowering Jephthah. His history ends, however, with the loss of his daughter and civil war with Ephraim.[18] While Jephthah delivers east of the Jordan, Samson became judge in the west (chaps. 13–16).[19] The writer gives more space to Samson than to any other judge. He was chosen to be judge before birth, so his beginnings rival those of Samuel, Jeremiah, and John the Baptist. Certainly much should be expected from this man. But he is woefully disappointing. He regularly disregards the law, intermarries with the Philistines, and uses his delivering power to carry out acts of incidental vengeance.

God can move his "judge" to action only by stirring him up with personal disappointments in dealings with Philistines. And Samson never does deliver Israel. His last act is still one of personal revenge (16:28) in which God does not deliver even him! The final estimate that "he killed many more when he died than while he lived" is a sad commentary on his life. Even sadder is the fact that his earlier capture brought praise to Dagon that should have been Yahweh's: "Our god has delivered our enemy into our hands" (Judg. 16:24).

Why spend so much time on Samson's failure? Because he climaxes the message of Judges. His life matches that of the nation itself. Samson, like Israel, had a special calling but deserted it to pursue his own desires. His power, though great and bestowed by Yahweh, did not deliver because his life was marked by unfaithfulness to Yahweh and intermarriage with the nations of the land.[20]

Figure 8.2
Chronology of the Judges

Oppressor	King	Years	Estimated Dates B.C.	Reference (All Judges)	Judge	Tribe	Years	Place of Battle
Mesopotamia	Cushan-rishathaim	8	1385–1377	3:8				
			1377–1337	3:9–11	Othniel	Judah	40	
Moabites	Eglon	18	1337–1319	3:12–14				
			1319–1239	3:15–30	Ehud	Benjamin	80	Jericho
Philistines				3:31				
			1260–1250	3:31	Shamgar		10	
Canaanites	Jabin	20	1259–1239	4:2–3				
			1239–1199	4:4–5:31	Deborah	Ephraim	40	Esdraelon
Midianites	Oreb, Zeeb, Zebah, Zalmunna	7	1199–1192	6:1–6				
			1192–1152	6:7–8:35	Gideon	Manasseh	40	Hill of Moreh
Civil War of Abimelech			1152–1149	9	killed at Thebez			
			1149–1126	10:1–2	Tola	Issachar	23	
			1126–1104	10:3–6	Jair	Gilead	22	
Ammonites		18	1104–1086	10:7–9				
			1086–1080	10:10–12:7	Jephthah	Gilead	6	Transjordan
			1080–1072	12:8–10	Ibzan	Judah	8	
			1072–1062	12:11–12	Elon	Zebulun	10	
			1062–1055	12:13–15	Abdon	Ephraim	7	
Philistines		40	1115–1075	13:1				
			1075–1055	13:2–16:31	Samson	Dan	20	

John H. Walton, *Chronological and Background Charts of the Old Testament* (Zondervan, 1978), 48.

In an appendix to the book (chaps. 17–21), our writer gives another sample of the failure of the period. With two complex stories he illustrates the religious and civil confusion that results from ignoring and disobeying the Law. Rather than following the Law, "everyone did what was right in his own eyes" (17:6; 21:25 NASB).[21] The book of Judges concludes in total contrast to the beginning of Joshua. Joshua meditated on the Law, kept it, and had good success. Israel under the judges was inconsistent and ignorant in her practice of God's word—even in the most basic matters. Judges illustrates the futility and frustration caused by a lack of total commitment.[22]

Relief in Ruth

On a totally different note, among the poetic books in the last section of the Hebrew Old Testament (but belonging to this time period and included here by English and Greek Old Testament texts), is the short book of Ruth. It is not only a heartwarming story, but a literary jewel.[23] Whereas Judges shows the spiraling downhill thrust of the overall period in Israel's history, with Ruth we encounter a story of life when common people are in harmony with Yahweh and alert to his grace.

Of course, it did not start out that way. The story is set in the time "when Judges ruled" (1:1) and there are other hints that things are not well. The land is experiencing famine (1:1), perhaps reflecting God's judgment during this period (cf. Lev. 26:3–5, 18–20). Under the impact of famine, Elimelech and Naomi leave their inheritance and move their family to neighboring Moab, where they become resident aliens. The two sons marry Moabite women. Now, marriage with Moabites was not forbidden. But Moabites, though related to Israel through Lot (Gen. 19:36–37), were not allowed entrance into the assembly of Yahweh because of their attempts to stop Israel's passage to the land (Deut. 23:3–6). Finally, things do not go well for this family outside of the land. "Blessing" is not their middle name. In quick succession the first part of the story yields tragedy after tragedy for Naomi. First, famine; then loss of her husband; then after ten years, both sons die.[24] Two Moabite widows and the widowed mother, Naomi, are all that is left—so much for their name and future.

The theme of grace and redemption in the story begins with the decision of the Moabitess, Ruth, who refuses to leave Naomi totally desolate, but chooses Naomi, Naomi's people, and Naomi's God (1:16–17). Ruth, the foreigner, by taking refuge under the wings of Yahweh and showing great kindness to Naomi, becomes the vehicle of Yahweh's blessing (1:11–12).

Purposefully, the story contrasts end and beginning. The book opens in the time when judges ruled and ends with David the king. It opens with names of a failed genealogy and ends with an famous genealogy. It opens with Elim-elech ("My God is King") and ends with David, God's appointed king. A son and line is impossible, says Naomi at the beginning (1:11–13). There are no more brothers for them to marry to save the family line (cf. levirate marriage in Deut. 25:5–6). Yet, the story ends with a son for Naomi (4:13, 16), a kinsman-husband for Ruth, and a continued line for Elimelech (4:10). Naomi becomes "empty" and her situation is not "pleasant" but "bitter," she tells the women of Bethlehem as she arrives back (1:21). By the end she is full again, and the women praise Yahweh for the birth of the son (4:13–17).

Though she begins as a Moabitess and is officially identified as one in the legal proceedings (4:10), the blessing of the elders and other legal wit-nesses at the gate carry the reader back to the patriarchal narratives of Gen-esis. Yahweh is called upon to make Ruth like Rachel and Leah, the mothers of all Israel (4:11). Boaz's family is to be like that of the tribal forefather, Perez, "whom Tamar bore to Judah" (4:12). These benedictions anticipate the final end to the story—an end that makes the line famous through King David. Like these mothers of nation and tribe, Ruth, a Moabitess widow, gains stature in Israel. Especially significant is Tamar, a Canaanite who through questionable methods diligently sought a levirate marriage to carry on the line of Judah's first son (Gen. 38). If her line could be blessed so as to produce their own tribe, God could surely bless this faithful, converted Moabitess! Though the original blessers could not have foreseen it, the writer knows the fulfillment of these benedictions in the choice of King David as king of all Israel (Ruth 4:17, 18–22). Even our writer did not live to see a larger fulfillment of blessing (cf. Matt. 1:5–16).

It is important to note that as far as Naomi is concerned, Yahweh is in charge of all of these circumstances, even though they are bitter (1:13, 21). And it is Yahweh who turns it around at the end (4:11, 12, 13, 14). *A pri-mary theme of the book is God's control of life's events.* The writer and partici-pants assume that he is in charge of both the pleasant times as well as the "misfortune" (1:6). All of it comes through his hand—even fallen events in a fallen world. But because it is Yahweh, this book alerts us to anticipate an outcome that may involve unexpected and creative opportunities for love and grace. Even while experiencing bitter pain, Naomi is certain of who is the cosmic Sovereign. It is he who empties, and it is he who fills. For our writer, even more, God is working out his purposes—often unknown to us—but important in his plans for his King and kingdom.

A second theme is redemption. The word group involved is used over twenty times in our small book. The redemption activity as prescribed by the Law reflects how God himself works. In Ruth it is carried out in a way that goes beyond the letter of the Law to the spirit of the Law, imitating Yahweh.[25] Another word that reinforces this in the book is the word *hesed*. This is the word for God's covenantal love—a loyal, committed love. In our book, it is used for Yahweh, Boaz, and Ruth. It would not be badly translated as "grace" in this context. God is seen at work as one who surprises us by his gracious, steadfast love and brings restoration and redemption out of the pain and death that mark the human landscape. The history of Israel is enhanced by this story that reminds them that their God, Yahweh, is at work even at the darkest times to fulfill his promises beginning with those who do not count in the halls of greatness.

ON THE WAY: COMPLETION OF WAR AND REST

Entering into Rest

The concept of rest summarizes the goal of Joshua, as Israel—faithful to the covenant—inherits the land, occupies it, and lives in blessing under Yahweh. The land is the same land as promised to Abraham (Josh. 1:6).

This idea of rest is borrowed by the writer to the Hebrews as he exhorts his readers to follow Jesus. Jesus is greater than Moses and has become the author of our eternal salvation. Jesus will bring us into the glory God first planned for man by overcoming the barrier to that glory—death, the penalty for sin (Heb. 2:9–10; 3:1–6).

But the writer fears that some of his readers, though they have heard the Good News, will not be allowed to enter God's rest because of their rebellion (Heb. 3:15; quoting Ps. 95). They may become like those who died in the desert, having sinful, unbelieving hearts (Heb. 3:16–19). For hearing the message is not enough—it must be accepted by faith (4:1–2).

The author of Hebrews, like John Bunyan in his *Pilgrim's Progress*, sees believers as pilgrims on the way to rest. Those who truly believe will successfully make it through the pilgrimage and enter that rest (4:3). But there is an apparent difficulty. Psalm 95 tells about the failure of the first generation under Moses and calls on Israel in David's time to "kneel before the LORD our Maker" so they may experience God's rest. Why is David offering the possibility of rest if Joshua has already given them rest? The answer of Hebrews: "If Joshua had given them rest, God would not have spoken later about another day. There remains, then, a Sabbath-rest for the people of God" (4:8–9).[26]

Earlier, the writer of Hebrews pointed out that God put everything under man, yet man never achieved perfect rule on earth. This rule awaits its fulfillment in Jesus (Heb. 2:5–9). Now the writer points out that in spite of the success and "rest" of Joshua's generation, rest was never fully achieved—as our own study of Joshua shows. Actually, other temporary or partial experiences of rest occur later than Joshua (2 Sam. 7:1; 1 Kings 5:4), yet the full and continuous experience (2 Sam. 7:10–11) of the promise to Abraham was never accomplished.[27] That promised, undisturbed blessing of being Yahweh's people and enjoying Yahweh's rest is still a future, ultimate goal (Heb. 4:11).[28]

We look for a heavenly country as did the patriarchs (Heb. 11:15–16). Our promise brings us to Mount Zion, the heavenly Jerusalem, the city of the living God—where God is present along with myriads of angels and the spirits of righteous men awaiting resurrection. Jesus, who has made it all possible, is also there (12:22–24).

Abraham looked forward to this city "whose architect and builder is God" (11:10). And where was Abraham expecting this city? Hebrews 11:9 identifies the "promised land" as the very area he was tenting in![29] That Abraham was looking for a "heavenly country" does not mean he expected it to be extraplanetary! Hebrews 6:4 indicates some have tasted "the heavenly gift," but this gift is not *in* heaven. It is *from* heaven.[30] The Jews often used the word "heaven" to refer to God. To receive a heavenly city or a heavenly country is equivalent to saying its "architect and builder is God" (11:10). It has been prepared by God (11:16).

This already-prepared city will be a part of the New Creation, the new "heaven and earth" (Rev. 21:1–2).[31] With its coming, "rest" will be finally achieved in all its dimensions—for such rest was never possible apart from fellowship with God and loving him with all the heart, soul, and strength. This new cosmos will be characterized by righteousness (2 Peter 3:13). But the most important thing about this new city, country, and final rest is that we will finally have "come to God" . . . and "to Jesus" (Heb. 12:23–24). "The dwelling of God is with men" (Rev. 21:3).

Jesus Is a Warrior

The completion of rest is achieved in the same way—though on a wider scale—as Yahweh commanded Joshua. Because of its "holy war," Joshua has not been a popular book:

> Many can remember how Joshua the warrior used to figure as a hero-saint in sermons and in Bible stories for the young. The present writer recalls a picture in a Bible for children portraying the general equipped with Greek helmet and a combination Greek and Roman suit of armor, kneeling before the Prince of the Lord's host in front of a very Roman-looking Jericho. That seemed quite as it should be! Today, however, Joshua presents a problem. . . . The present writer holds entirely with those who reject the War-God concept. To his mind God is not, and

never was, what Joshua thought Him to be. He never led an armed force into Canaan, and He leads no armed force today.[32]

We can agree entirely with those who do not believe any nation on earth today is justified in taking territory and eliminating its inhabitants on the basis of a special call of God. Neither is the church today called to rule any physical land. The Christian college group that walked all around the campus of a secular university had, I hope, something else in mind besides walls falling down.

The New Testament, however, does predict a time of future warfare and judgment at the return of Christ. Just as God brought judgment in the Flood, and to Sodom and Gomorrah, and in ancient Canaan, so also has he promised judgment in the future. Judgment, too, must have its fulfillment.

The scene of Revelation 19:11–16 graphically portrays Jesus engaged in Holy War at his return.

> I saw heaven standing open and there before me was a white horse, whose rider is called Faithful and True. With justice he judges and makes war. His eyes are like blazing fire, and on his head are many crowns. He has a name written on him that no one but he himself knows. He is dressed in a robe dipped in blood, and his name is the Word of God. The armies of heaven were following him, riding on white horses and dressed in fine linen, white and clean. Out of his mouth comes a sharp sword with which to strike down the nations. "He will rule them with an iron scepter." He treads the winepress of the fury of the wrath of God Almighty. On his robe and on his thigh he has this name written: KING OF KINGS AND LORD OF LORDS.

In the battle that follows, all the troops of the kings of the earth "were killed with the sword that came out of the mouth of the rider on the horse" (19:21).

This is just what was requested by the martyrs who earlier called out to God: "How long, Sovereign Lord, holy and true, until you judge the inhabitants of the earth and avenge our blood?" (Rev. 6:10). Is it right for saints in God's presence to call for vengeance? Isn't this kind of vengeance an Old Testament concept that Jesus rejected in teaching us to love our enemies?

Not in the least. The New Testament teaches, like the Old, that vengeance belongs to God alone, and that we must "leave room for God's wrath" (Rom. 12:19; Deut. 32:35). We are not to avenge ourselves. But God is just and holy in his judgments (Rev. 16:5–7). He is the Avenger.

> God is just: He will pay back trouble to those who trouble you and give relief to you who are troubled, and to us as well. This will happen when the Lord Jesus is revealed from heaven in blazing fire with his powerful angels. He will punish those who do not know God and do not obey

the gospel of our Lord Jesus. They will be punished with everlasting destruction and shut out from the presence of the Lord and from the majesty of his power on the day he comes to be glorified in his holy people and to be marveled at among all those who have believed (2 Thess. 1:6–10).

Then Christ will rule. *Then* there will be rest. What a land of contrast!

SUGGESTED SCRIPTURE READING:

Joshua 1:1–9
Judges 2:8–3:5
Hebrews 3:16–4:11; 11:8–16; 12:22–29

For Interaction and Discussion:

1. What are each of the two parts of Joshua about? Why may the Lord have wanted each tribe to take its own territory? Were they successful?

2. What areas of disobedience characterize Judges, but not Joshua? In your estimation, how much of our own spiritual failure is due to direct disobedience, how much to difficult circumstances and trials, and how much to confusion over the will of God?

3. Do you think the failure during the period of the judges could have been avoided if God would have provided more supernatural occurrences, such as the Jordan River crossing or the collapse of Jericho?

4. How does Samson's judgeship illustrate the failure of being only half-committed to God? Why does a life like this fail to bring honor to God?

5. How is the true Creator God celebrated and honored in the taking of Jericho?

6. What is the meaning of *meditation* in Scripture (as in Joshua 1:8)? What is the goal of meditation? How is the goal achieved?

7. How does the idea of "Yahweh Is a Warrior" tie in to divine justice? How will this idea of divine judgment have its fulfillment?

8. What does "rest" mean? Why is the need for peace and rest a commonly felt need among us? How is this need met by Jesus? How is rest related to fellowship with God? Is this true on a personal level as well?

For Further Reading:

Gordon J. Wenham. "The Deuteronomic Theology of the Book of Joshua." *JBL*, 90 (1971): 140–48. Themes that bind Deuteronomy and Joshua together.

Robert L. Hubbard, Jr. *The Book of Ruth.* NICOT. Grand Rapids: Eerdmans, 1988. Excellent commentary.

D. F. Rauber. "The Book of Ruth." *Literary Interpretations of Biblical Narrative*, ed. Kenneth R. R. Gros Lewis. Nashville: Abingdon, 1974, 163–76.

Arthur E. Cundall. *Judges*. TOTC. Downer's Grove, Ill.: InterVarsity, 1968. Fine academic commentary for the English reader.

Trent Butler. *Joshua*. WBC 6. Waco, Tex.: Word, 1983. Academic with fine discussion of themes.

Walter C. Kaiser, Jr. "The Promise Theme and the Theology of Rest." *BSac*, 130 (1973): 135–50.

Notes and Comments:

[1]Among the debates about the history of Joshua, surely none stands out more than the account of "Joshua's Long Day." An extensive number of theories have been developed to explain it in scientific terms. Cf. the list by John J. Davis and John C. Whitcomb, *The History of Israel* (Grand Rapids: Baker, 1969–71), 66–70. No objection should be brought against this miracle because the text uses phenomenological language (the language of appearance rather than the language of scientific explanation). Such language is the normal language of observation, such as is used today for "sunrise" and "sunset."

Another problem associated with the southern campaign is the chronology of Joshua 10. In 10:15 he returns to the camp at Gilgal, but the next verses show him in hot pursuit of the fleeing kings. At the chapter's end, Joshua returns to Gilgal (10:43). This is likely another example of the Hebrew literary pattern of a summary account followed by a more detailed one (see Gen. 1 and 2). The return to Gilgal then is the same return in both verses. The events of 10:16–42 fit between verses 14 and 15.

[2]I have distinguished the practice of *herem* at Jericho from the rest of the towns by understanding that Jericho was the exception. M. H. Woodstra, *The Book of Joshua*, 113, sees various degrees of *herem*. He understands this most rigorous application of *herem* at Jericho to have been for purposes of example. There is a problem, however, with understanding the original intent of Deuteronomy 20 in terms of livestock and plunder. I discuss this further in note 11 below.

[3]The activity of God in history is an important biblical theme, going under the German term *Heilsgeschichte*. See Graeme Goldsworthy, *Gospel and The Kingdom* (Exeter: Paternoster, 1981) for a use of it as the Bible's central theme. Any use of God's acts as a replacement for God's words, as others have done, is an unbiblical dichotomy. Both God's words and his acts in history function as revelation of himself and his program.

[4]Trent C. Butler has summarized the Deuteronomic themes in Joshua under four headings: the land, leadership, law, and the Lord. He also suggests that the structure of Joshua is marked out by Deuteronomic emphases. Cf. *Joshua*, WBC 7 (Waco, Tex.: Word, 1983), xxiv-xxv. Gordon J. Wenham, "The Deuteronomic Theology of the Book of Joshua," *JBL*, 90 (1971): 140–48, sees five themes that bind Deuteronomy and Joshua together: "The holy war of conquest, the distribution of the land, the unity of all Israel, Joshua as the successor of Moses, and the covenant" (141).

[5]NIV translates 4:9 so that there is only one memorial. NASB and NRSV have two—one in the middle of the Jordan and the one at the camp, which God commanded for teaching purposes.

[6]Terence E. Fretheim, *Deuteronomic History* (Nashville: Abingdon, 1983), 80, adds to what we have said about the place of memory in Israel by pointing out that Israel's worship was designed to actualize past events so "the worshipers understand themselves to be involved in these events. . . . This gives the people historical depth so they may see that it has always been Yahweh, and no other god, who has enabled their history."

[7]Carl Graesser, Jr., "The Message of the Deuteronomic Historian," *CTM*, 39 (1968): 542–51, indicates that "more than 50 percent of the speech to Joshua (1:2–9) can be reproduced from verses in Deuteronomy." Cf. Deuteronomy 5:31; 11:24; 11:26; 31:23; 5:32; 31:6. Cf. Butler and Wenham (note 4 above) as well as Walter C. Kaiser, Jr., *Toward an Old Testament Theology*, 122–23.

[8]Regarding the need for covenant obedience, Fretheim, *Deuteronomic History*, 78, quite rightly points out that Joshua 24 emphasizes "one clear point: the future of the community in the land is finally determined by whether it worships Yahweh alone, or turns to the worship of other gods." Again, the problem with Israel is not that they were sloppy in following all the details of the Law, but that they failed in the most basic commitment.

[9]Though we are treating the theology of Joshua, the fact that Joshua 24 assumes the covenant pattern we saw earlier in Deuteronomy should not be overlooked. Cf. K. A. Kitchen, *The Bible in Its World*, 79–84.

[10]Peter C. Craigie, *The Problem of War in the Old Testament* (Grand Rapids: Eerdmans, 1978), 48–50, notes that the expression "holy war" is not a biblical one and objects to it with the statement: "While war was religious by association, it was no more a cultic and holy act than was sheep shearing." In the light of the priestly activities surrounding the initiation of war (cf. Peter C. Craigie, *The Book of Deuteronomy*, NICOT [Grand Rapids: Eerdmans, 1976], 271, n. 5), the comparison seems extreme. As Craigie notes, the biblical expression is equally forceful: "Wars of Yahweh."

[11]*Herem* was followed outside Israel, as the Moabite Stone of a later period (c. 830 B.C.) shows. Cf. *ANET*, 320.

The instructions of Deuteronomy 20:16–18 indicate that the Israelites are to destroy "all that breathes" when practicing *herem*. Robert Polzin, *Moses and the Deuteronomist* (New York: Seabury, 1980), 114–15, understands Deuteronomy 20 to include the destruction of animals and so sees a modification of the law in the case of Ai. He sees (122–23) the same fluctuation between a rigorous interpretation of the law during the southern campaign and at Hazor—where "all who breathed" (Josh. 10:40; 11:11) are destroyed—and the other northern cities where "all who breathed" is understood to require killing people but to allow cattle to be taken (11:14–15). Polzin is arguing a thesis that Joshua and Judges are giving new hermeneutical applications of Deuteronomic law.

It is true that "all that breathes" applied literally would include animals, yet the term is not always used as widely as that, and depending on the context may refer to human beings alone (Josh. 11:13–14; Ps. 150:6). Deuteronomy 20 at once defines the objects of destruction in the land by the national identifications and warns that to fail to destroy everyone that breathes would invite learning from them detestable ways. The writer clearly has people in mind at this point. Cf. Keil and Delitzsch, *The Pentateuch*, 3:403.

The fact that Deuteronomy's practice of *herem* did not include animals (Deut. 2:34–35; 3:6–7) weakens Polzin's thesis. The understanding of Joshua 11:14–15— that Israel was fulfilling the command to put to death "all that breathed" even when they were keeping livestock need not be a new understanding of Deuteronomy 20, but one intended in Deuteronomy itself. That leaves Jericho as the only clear case where livestock were put to death. This is likely for other reasons, as indicated in note 2 above. Woodstra, as indicated, has simply taken the view that there were various levels of *herem*. Later, under specific command of Samuel, Saul was to destroy Amalek, including the livestock (1 Sam. 15:2–3).

[12]The explanation that *herem* was God's use of sinful human agents and the fallen institutions of society to accomplish his purposes is a favorite explanation for those who do not wish to reject the God of Joshua outright. Cf. G. Ernest Wright and Reginald H. Fuller, "God's Gift of a Land," *Perspectives on Old Testament Literature*, ed. Woodrow Ohlsen (New York: Harcourt Brace Jovanovich, 1978), 99–101. Fretheim in *Deuteronomic History*, 69–75, after listing views which try to avoid the reality of the destruction, settles for a similar view, though with much more qualification.

[13]All three destructions—the Flood, Sodom and Gomorrah, and the Canaanites—involved judgment that came upon the *whole community* (men, women, and children). In each case the unity of the family and nation is accepted. All Israel came under the ban when Achan disobeyed. If they as a nation did not want to accept responsibility for that sin, then they must remove the guilty party from their society. If an individual does not want to suffer God's judgment on a society gone bad, she (as Rahab) must renounce and leave the society. A society is viewed as a unit. What it allows is its responsibility. There are other aspects to what has been called *corporate solidarity* or *corporate personality* in the Bible. See Kaiser, *Toward an Old Testament Theology*, 67–70. Cf. Sarna, *Understanding Genesis*, 124, on the guilt of the Amorites and God's absolute justice.

[14]This inadvertent but negligent sin of allowing the Gibeonites to live does not seem to have received further punishment. They dare not further sin by violating an oath taken in Yahweh's name, though to our way of thinking and practice, a commitment gained by deceit would be contestable.

[15]It is difficult to date Judges 1. Verse one begins "after the death of Joshua," yet some of the material (1:10–15) repeats material given in Joshua (15:14–19). Arthur E. Cundall, *Judges*, TOTC (Downers Grove, Ill.: InterVarsity, 1968), 51, suggests that the phrase is a title to the whole book and that 1:1b–2:5 serve as an introduction to the time after the death of Joshua (that is, the period of the judges) by giving background material from the book of Joshua. But Joshua 15:14–19 clearly occurs at a later time than the gathering to dispense the land.

[16]The observation that the Lord may not have given total control of the land to Joshua's generation—even though they were obedient—but waited for at least two generations to be obedient is that of R. Polzin, 152.

[17]I do not know who originally suggested this more alliterated outline of the cycle. The cycle itself is noted by nearly every writer. The usual weakness with the presentation of the cycle in this alliterated form is in the first step: SIN. The cycle in Judges is not built around sin in general, but around that most basic sin: the violation of the first commandment. It is also possible that the cry to God does not always mark a full repentance. In Judges 6 the response to their cry is the prophetic announcement of the problem: worship of the gods of the Amorites. God's speech in 10:11–14 and their response suggests that they may not always have put aside their idolatry before previous deliverances.

[18]Robert C. Boling, *The Anchor Bible: Judges* (Garden City, N.Y.: Doubleday, 1969), 210, 214, suggests that Jephthah was the most exemplary judge since Othniel. This is hard to justify. It is more likely that in Jephthah and especially Samson we reach a low point.

Of course, Jephthah's vow is a perennial problem. Did he commit child sacrifice, clearly unacceptable to the Law? Or did his daughter become devoted to the Lord's service? Or, was an animal sacrifice made to redeem her as was the case with every firstborn male? See Keil and Delitzsch, *Commentaries on the Old Testament: Joshua, Judges, Ruth* (Grand Rapids: Eerdmans, n.d.), 388–92, who conclude that the grammar supports actual sacrifice, but the historical situation of Israel's laws makes this unacceptable. Davis and Whitcomb, *The History of Israel*, 124–28, summarize the views and conclude that this type of legal confusion, given Jephthah's background, is very possible and in line with the period of confusion of the judges. Cf. Cundall, 147–49.

[19]The observation at 10:7 of dual oppressors, the Ammonites and the Philistines, followed by the judgeships of Jephthah against the Ammonites and Samson against the Philistines suggest that these judgeships overlapped. Jephthah served in Gilead and Samson served in the west where the tribes of Dan and Judah lived next to the Philistines on the coastal plain. Cf. the chronology in Davis and Whitcomb, *The History of Israel*, 16.

[20]Keil and Delitzsch, 101, are responsible for the insights concerning the significance of Samson and his importance for the theme of the book, although they have taken a more positive stance concerning his contributions as a judge than I have.

[21]It is interesting that the phrase "everyone did that which was right in his own eyes" occurs in Deuteronomy for the practice of religious activities outside the land. Clearly, in Judges we are talking about more than a lack of strictness in how and where to worship, but the extreme of false worship. It should be noted as well that the phrase "in those days there was no king in Israel" (17:6; 18:1; 19:1; 21:25) is given as an explanation to the reader as to how things could get this far out of line. Of course, a king who worshiped falsely could get things even farther out of line, but our readers lived during the early monarchy where Saul and David both worked to correct the problem of false worship and pagan practices.

[22]In spite of the emphasis on futility, there is in the actual numbers of Judges an emphasis on the grace and mercy of God. In a time of such consistent disobedience the periods of rest far exceed the periods of oppression. "The fourteen judges were an overplus of grace for the five lapses into idolatry," Charles C. Ryrie, *The Grace of God*, 35.

[23]The literary genius of the book of Ruth is discussed and illustrated well in D. F. Rauber, "The Book of Ruth," *Literary Interpretations of Biblical Narratives*, ed. Kenneth R. R. Gros Louis (Nashville: Abingdon, 1974), 163–76.

[24]Ibid., 165. According to Rauber the theme of emptiness/fullness is initiated by these four pictures: famine with its contrast of plenty; widowhood with its contrast of fullness in the complete and harmonious family on the social level—which is completed with finality with the death of the sons.

[25]The law provided for a kinsman-redeemer to buy back the property of a relative (Lev. 25:23–28) and to buy a relative out of debt-slavery (Lev. 25:39–43, 47–55). The law also provided for levirate marriage (Deut. 25:5–10). In the case of a widow who had not had a son, a brother would marry her and the first son produced would carry on the line of the dead brother. But, nothing is said in the Law about a wider kinsman carrying out that function. Cf. Robert L. Hubbard, Jr., *The Book of Ruth*, NICOT (Grand Rapids: Eerdmans, 1988), 48–63, 236–52, for a complete discussion of the issues and options. Hubbard decides that this is not a combination levirate and redemption situation, but an application of the notion of kinsman-redeemer to this situation. One needs to recognize that the Law did not cover all cases. Part of the function of elders and judges would be to see that the fairness exhibited by the Law's decisions and principles were reached in any given complicated case. Boaz's insistence on marrying Ruth as part of the kinsman-redeemer's function may well have had the force of a moral obligation even though not strictly required by the Law.

[26]It is common to interpret this as a totally different kind of rest here than Joshua provided. But the writer does not say that. Neither does Psalm 95 which he is quoting. Rather, he argues that Joshua did not give them rest and this is proven by the fact that Psalm 95 says Israel does not yet have it.

[27]2 Samuel 7:8–11 still reads as open to fulfillment.

[28]See Stanley D. Toussaint, "The Eschatology of the Warning Passages in the Book of Hebrews," *Grace Theological Journal* (Spring 1982): 71–72, for reasons why the "rest" is not present spiritual rest.

[29]See Walter C. Kaiser, Jr., "The Promise Theme and the Theology of Rest," *BSac*, 130 (1973): 135–50, who finds 11:9 to state the promise of the land as Abraham's.

[30]The uses of "heavenly" in Hebrews are 3:1, heavenly calling; 6:4, heavenly gift; 8:5, copy of the heavenly things (plural); 9:23, copies of things in the heavens (plural); 9:23, heavenly things themselves (plural); 11:16, heavenly country; and 12:22, heavenly Jerusalem. See BAGD, which also indicates the variety of uses and the notion of source, 305–6.

[31]Anthony A. Hoekema, *The Bible and the Future* (Grand Rapids: Eerdmans, 1979), represents a form of amillennialism that also sees the fulfillment of the Old

Testament promises on the new earth rather than in "heaven." Thus, for him the fulfillment to Abraham also takes place on earth (278–79). Toussaint, "Eschatology," 72–74, and Kaiser, "Promise Theme," 142–46, see the use of Psalm 95 in the context of other enthronement psalms—all millennial and conclude that the "rest" must be millennial.

[32]Fleming James, "Some Thoughts on Joshua's Religion," *Perspectives on Old Testament Literature,* ed. Woodrow Ohlsen (New York: Harcourt Brace Jovanovich, 1978), 98.

chapter nine

MODIFICATION TO MONARCHY

(Samuel)
A King from Among Your Own Brothers

It's being the last employee hired when the economy begins to slide.

It's motoring along a lonely stretch of road at night when the car starts to sputter.

It's discovering you're wearing your pajamas to church (a recurring dream I had as a youngster).

It's trying to steer with a vise-grip on the steering hub.

It's *insecurity*.

Helen Keller said about security, "It is mostly a superstition. Security does not exist in nature, nor do the children of men as a whole experience it. . . . Life is either a daring adventure or nothing."

We all like to hear rags-to-riches stories. But what we enjoy most is the "to riches" part. Vulnerability, like chicken pox, is given a wide berth. The children of Israel felt vulnerable. As disjointed tribes they faced raiding parties from outside the land and settled, skilled enemies from within. The Philistines were better organized and better equipped than Israel.[1] The system of judges had been tried and found wanting. Or more accurately, as G. K. Chesterton once said about the Christian ideal, it was "found difficult, and left untried."[2] Israel had operated under a pure theocracy on a national level. God directly intervened to raise up leaders for the whole nation when necessary.

The book of Samuel (1 and 2 Samuel to us) is about the move to monarchy—the change to kingship. Surprises are in store, however. No one ever invented a system of security apart from God. Even God can't. But then, he knows better than to try.

SCOPING OUT SAMUEL

The book of Samuel is a repository of favorite Bible stories: the tale of Samuel's birth, the account of the Philistines' trouble when they capture the ark, the heroism and true friendship of Jonathan, and certainly the defeat of Goliath by the "boy" David. Often, however, these favorites have been torn from their surroundings. Treated as individual snapshots without regard to the total landscape, their larger significance often is missed.

After Judges we need a break. With an even dozen judges, it was hard to keep the players straight without a scorecard. In Samuel there are only three main participants: Samuel, Saul, and David. But don't dispense with the scorecard just yet—there are a number of lesser players who have a lot to do with the final outcome.

The Barren Woman—1 Samuel 1–2

One of these participants is a barren woman, and with her the story opens. Here is a woman emotionally in rags. Though her husband loves her, he has taken another wife—no doubt because she has given him no children. Her rival mocks her, much as Hagar did Sarah. To put it in a word, Hannah feels *vulnerable*.

But this is just the kind of case in which God has shown his power in the past. He has produced a whole nation from a barren womb—in fact, from a whole succession of them (Gen. 11:30; 25:21; 29:31). Hannah's distress leads her to cry to the Lord and dedicate her offspring to exclusive service to him. This response—the response the Lord wanted from the whole nation—leads to the birth of the last judge: Samuel.

Hannah's experience and her prayer (2:1–10) exalt the Lord as the one who

> raises the poor from the dust
> and lifts the needy from the ash heap;
> he seats them with princes
> and has them inherit a throne of honor (2:8).

The unique Lord of Israel is security. He is the Rock of safety. *"There is no Rock like our God"* (2:2).

Samuel, Prophet and Judge—1 Samuel 3–7

After that quick introduction to the Lord's ability to deliver, we are returned to the shocking reality of Israel's dismal state. This is nowhere more obvious than in the very center of Israel's worship of Yahweh—the tabernacle. Under current priest Eli and his boys, Samuel at the Lord's tent joins a situation that could not be more disgusting. Eli's sons violate the rules of sacrifice to satisfy their own tastes, threaten violence against faithful worshipers, and introduce Canaanite sexual abominations (2:12–17, 22–25).

In the midst of this loathsome disobedience, God raises his leader from infancy to manhood, marking Samuel's progress against the continuing failure of Eli's sons (2:11, 18–21, 26; 3:1–21). We all are familiar with the story of Samuel sleeping in the tabernacle, hearing the voice of the Lord, and three times rousing Eli to ask what he wanted before finally being told to answer the Lord the next time. It is a dynamic and positive story for children, though I have since forgotten what direct relevance it could have for them. No doubt, children are told that here was a good boy who did what he was told. Perhaps they are advised to consider that voices they hear might be from the Lord! Or, more likely: "Listen to God." But I fear that often the real significance of the event is missed.

This is not an incidental story but the beginning of a great career. This is Samuel's first experience as a prophet of God. The fact that all of Samuel's words came true—remember the test for a true prophet—prompted Israel to recognize again that here was a prophet in their midst (3:19–21; cf. 3:1).

Not only is Samuel a prophet, but he becomes a judge. The capture of the ark and its history in Philistine territory (chaps. 4–6) show that God does not need Israel to vindicate himself as the true God. Rather, *they need him*. With Eli and his sons dead, deliverance from the Philistines may begin. Samuel in his role as judge achieves one of those mighty deliverances in which Yahweh himself fights for Israel (chap. 7).

But now Samuel's final and most famous task begins—to take Israel into its monarchy. Samuel is God's kingmaker (chaps. 8–12). Not that Samuel likes the job. He considers the elders' request for a king a personal slap in the face; worse than that, so does Yahweh (8:6–8; 12:13–19). Yet the idea of a king in Israel isn't new: Jacob predicted the rising of the king's ruling scepter in the tribe of Judah (Gen. 49:10), regulations for the king were given in Moses' handbook (Deut. 17:14–20), and Hannah's prayer spoke of Yahweh strengthening his king (1 Sam. 2:10).

The people, however, request a king in a desire for visible security. They have no hope that Samuel's sons will follow as faithful judges (8:1–3), and they don't want to wait until the next invasion for a deliverer to arise. Better to have a permanent king who will fight their battles (8:19–20). Their failure to completely trust Yahweh for safety will mean higher taxes to support a defense complex, a costly central bureaucracy, and a draft to establish a standing army (8:10–18). What a price to pay for lack of faith!

Yet it is not an absolute evil, though these people ask out of evil motives. Yahweh will give them their king, and that king is Saul (1 Sam. 9–

11). Saul seeks out the prophet to help him find his father's donkeys and ends up with the throne.

Saul As King

Saul is privately anointed, then publicly proclaimed by the Lord's direction. Like the judges before him, he is empowered by the Spirit of God to deliver from an oppressor (1 Sam. 11). This initial victory leads to complete acceptance of Saul as king.

Saul is a successful king. He defeats Israel's enemies, freeing them from outside oppression (14:47–48). He worships Yahweh, not idols (14:35; 15:31), and expels mediums and spiritists from Israel (28:3). David praises him for having brought economic prosperity as well (2 Sam. 1:24). But our book is interested not so much in King Saul's general success as in why he and his line were removed from kingship. So 1 Samuel 13–15 focuses on two particular failures:

- not following instructions to wait for Samuel to offer a pre-battle sacrifice;[3]
- and not carrying out *herem* against the Amalekites as commanded by the Lord through Samuel.

Both these failures show that Saul has a mistaken notion of kingship—one that Yahweh will not bear. The notion: that like other ancient kings, Israel's king would be an absolute monarch—that his rule would be law.

No, Israel already has a law given by God, not developed by the king. Also, Yahweh speaks through prophets. That word is higher than the king. Moses specifically warned about the king's considering himself above the Law (Deut. 17:18–20). Rather, like Joshua, the king was to be a student of the Law that he might obey it. Torah is higher than king. Prophet is higher than king. Both are Yahweh's instruction.[4]

For Saul's first disobedience to Samuel's instruction, Saul loses the right to pass on the kingship to his sons (13:13–14). At his second failure to carry out orders, he loses his own right to the throne (15:26).[5]

David As King

Because Saul no longer is God's choice for king, Samuel immediately anoints David (16:1–13). Not only that, the Spirit who empowers the king comes upon David and leaves Saul (16:13–14).

King Without a Throne: 1 Samuel 16–31. David, though unknown publicly as king, begins to carry out his task. Why the story of David and Goliath? For David, like Saul and the judges before him, divine appointment is proven by a great delivery. *That* is what the story of David and Goliath is all about. It is about faith—but the faith of Israel's new and unknown king, rather than a little boy who has enough faith to go around killing giants like an Old Testament Jack-and-the-Beanstalk.

The old king, no longer empowered by God, is not leading his nation into battle and expecting great deliverances. He is huddling in his tent, trying to figure out a way to answer the challenge of Goliath. He is willing to try even a strapping youth (not a little boy) who rejects the tall Saul's armor, not because it is too big but because he is not used to it.

David wins his initial victory as king, but no one recognizes its full significance. David's continuing success, however, alerts Saul to the truth (18:5–8). When David does not die in battle against great odds, Saul tries to kill David directly. The rest of 1 Samuel finds Saul chasing David around the wilderness of Judah. It is a time for David to learn security in the midst of vulnerability (Ps. 4:8). Saul becomes increasingly unstable as he tries to fight against the word of judgment through Samuel.[6]

Figure 9.1

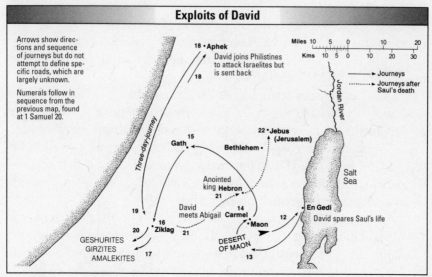

David as the Model King: 2 Samuel 1–10. After Saul's death, David is quickly anointed king over Judah. Saul's surviving son reigns over the rest of the tribes, but the real power behind his throne is his general, Abner. David conducts this struggle without animosity. He laments the deaths of Saul and Jonathan (2 Sam. 1). He congratulates the men of Jabesh Gilead who rescued Saul's body from further dishonor (2:4–7). He punishes the murderers of Saul's son who thought David would reward them (chap. 4). The one blot on his record is the death of Abner who was visiting to arrange terms of peace (3:12–37).

When Jimmy Carter was president, the press loved to call his contingent of advisers "The Georgia Mafia" because of the number of former associates he brought to Washington from his home state. The writer of 2 Samuel clearly explains that a "Bethlehem Mafia" surrounds David. Most readers miss it, however, because they don't recognize the names.

For instance, who is Zeruiah (2:18)? No, Zeruiah is not a man's name, but the name of David's sister (1 Chron. 2:13–16). The three "sons of Zeruiah" are David's nephews. Joab is one of these. He has fought for David in the wilderness and has become David's general. Though totally loyal to David (and to himself—we are never sure in which order), Joab with his brother are a challenge for the king throughout the book. The king often sees them as thorns in his royal side (3:39; 16:10; 19:22). Joab's murder of Abner incenses David. He calls a curse on Joab's house and personally mourns the death. Somehow he is able to avoid a "Davidgate" crisis as the rest of Israel recognizes that Abner's death was Joab's personal vendetta and did not involve the king.[7]

After being anointed king over all Israel, David scores immediate successes against Israel's enemies. He conquers the secure Jebusites at Jerusalem and whips the Philistines, who take their best shot at nipping this rising monarch before he blooms (5:6–25).

David establishes Jerusalem as his capital and moves the ark of the covenant there. His desire to build a permanent temple for the Lord is refused, but he receives a promise that more than compensates for the immediate disappointment (chap. 7). Yahweh gives David more military successes (8:1–14; 10:1–19), and David does what is "just and right for all his people" (8:15). This includes even the house of Saul and Jonathan, as David seeks to show kindness to their remaining heir (chapter 9).

A Sword in David's House: 2 Samuel 11–20. The inspired account of David's faithfulness and the blessing of God comes to a screeching standstill in chapter 11. The story of David's reign now turns on the noisy hinge of David's monstrous sin. Ask any pagan about King David and the immediate association will be "Bathsheba." Though David establishes a rule of justice unexcelled in future generations, his name will live in infamy for this startling succession of sins against Yahweh.

Nothing is held back from us in this chapter. God's record is honest. David's sin was not a sudden slip, but a conscious decision. He saw her bathing—an innocent enough accident, given the geography of Jerusalem and the height of the king's palace. But he inquires. He sends for her. He

Figure 9.2
Kingdoms of Saul, David, and Solomon

From *The NIV Study Bible* (Zondervan, 1985), map 5 of color maps.

sleeps with her. Here David has taken to himself the rights of an absolute monarch and violated the Law. He has coveted another man's wife and committed adultery with her (Ex. 20:14, 17; Deut. 5:18, 21).

In time she informs David that she is pregnant. A practical problem develops. Her husband, Uriah, has been out fighting David's wars and will know the baby is not his. David develops a series of plans to cover his sin.

Plan #1: Call Uriah home from battle. He will sleep with his wife. When the baby comes, he will believe it is a bit premature. This plan fails because Uriah's sense of duty puts David's to shame. Uriah will not play when his comrades are still in the field.

Plan #2: Get him drunk. Uriah's sense of duty will be lowered, and he will go home. Failure again: Even when drunk he is more honorable than David.

Plan #3: Have him die in battle. Then David will marry Bathsheba and not be discovered. This plot is successful only because it depends on Uriah's honor: He carries his own death message to the front and never takes a peek. David's nephew Joab can be counted on to keep the secret.

There it is—the raw power of the typical ancient king whose word is law.[8] "But the thing David had done displeased Yahweh" (2 Sam. 11:27). God's verdict is short and stunning.

God sends the prophet Nathan to the king to arouse that deep sense of justice that in David had been derailed. In the case of a rich man stealing a poor man's only lamb so the rich man wouldn't have to cut into his own reserves, David sees the issue clearly. He bursts out with the self-condemning verdict, "The man who did this deserves to die!" This fierce indignation evaporates when he learns *he* is the rich man. Had David lived in the twentieth century his rationalization no doubt would be, "We couldn't help ourselves. God wants us to be happy, doesn't he?" But he acknowledges his guilt.

God decides not to kill David, but the sword will now interrupt the peace of his house. The sacredness of his own marriages will be violated. His sin was secret. His penalty will be public (2 Sam. 12:7–12).[9]

The sword touches the rest of David's reign (chaps. 13–20). The happy blessedness of rule is gone. With this sin David has lost all control over his own family—for what can he say to his sons when their lusts run rampant? Amnon wants his half-sister Tamar and gives in to his lust. Absalom, brother of Tamar, takes revenge by killing Amnon. Absalom's desire for revenge probably is heightened by the fact that Amnon is firstborn. Absalom has his eye on the throne and sees himself as next in line. Not willing to wait, he attempts a coup against his father. He is initially successful, but a civil war ensues in which Absalom loses his life. As David grieves over Absalom, he wishes instead that his own life had been demanded for his sin:

O, my son Absalom! My son, my son Absalom! If only I had died instead of you—O Absalom, my son, my son! (18:33).

Final Matters: 2 Samuel 21–24. To round out David's reign, other events and records are added at the story's end.[10] Two psalms are included here, both celebrating Yahweh as the Rock, much as Hannah did at the beginning. The king learns that his strength is not in his standing army (chapter 22) but in Yahweh the deliverer.

The second of these psalms (23:1–7) constitutes David's last words. It focuses on two truths: the beauty of a righteous reign, and the promise of God to David for a continuing dynasty. There are the pillars of Israel's kingship.

THE CONCERNS OF SAMUEL

The Nature of Kingship

The people were premature in demanding a king. Their motives had been evil. But the choice of Saul was God's opportunity to make the main point right at the beginning. Israel's king was a subregent: a ruler under God. Yahweh is Israel's king and always had been (1 Sam. 12:12). The human ruler was, in fact, no more than a permanent judge over all Israel. Like the judge, the king was directly selected by God and was vindicated by victory over Israel's oppressors. The king was, therefore, not an absolute monarch. He was subject to Yahweh's word. No matter how great the pressure, no matter how fine the rationalization (and Saul makes us feel sorry for him on both counts), kingship demanded obedience.

By making clear with the very first king that this principle was not to be qualified or compromised, Yahweh etched into Israel's history a lesson for all future kings. They are implementers of law, not originators. Creativity is not a virtue when used to twist Torah. The king is to be a student of Scripture with a love for its God-intended instruction. He is not to become a loophole hunter who finds arguments to justify his own desires.[11]

Do not feel too bad about Saul. When he does not submit to God's judgment, he reaffirms the rightness of God's sentence. What should he have done as rejected king? Resign and return to his farm. He had lost his office, but he could still be right before God and live as any other Israelite. The real injury to Saul was self-inflicted. He tried to hold on to what was no longer his.

David, too, like Joshua, must study God's Law in order to apply it. Moving the ark on a new cart (2 Sam. 6), though considered proper in Philistine culture (1 Sam. 6:7), was not the way Yahweh had instructed. The Levites were to carry the ark with poles inserted in the rings on its side (Ex. 25:10–16). Even Levites who touched the ark would die (Num. 4:15). David had clearly learned his error before moving the ark again (2 Sam. 6:12–15).

David's sins against Uriah and Bathsheba were also sins against Yahweh.[12] These were certainly no less sins than those of Saul. David's sins were more than personal violations of the Law; they were the use of the kingship itself to stand above the Law. So why was David's line not removed from office? The only possible answer is 2 Samuel 7:8–16—the Davidic Covenant.

The Davidic Covenant

Clearly 2 Samuel 7 is the charter that plots the future of kingship for Israel. The Abrahamic Covenant plotted the future of God's program to ultimately bless the world. Through one man, Abraham, all the world's nations would be blessed (Gen. 12:3). This blessing would come through his descendants who were to receive the land of Canaan (Gen. 17:7–8). These descendants became a nation at Mount Sinai under the Mosaic Covenant. Now, within this nation, David's line is fixed as the line of rulers.

The scene of 2 Samuel 7 finds David desiring to establish a central worship place at Jerusalem by building a permanent temple to replace the movable tent of worship. Yahweh responds that he has never implied that he wants such a "house." Rather than allow David to assist him, he will assist David. He will establish David's "house" as the perpetual ruling line over Israel. This guarantee is based not on the presence of a temple, but on the promise of Yahweh himself.

The promise includes:

- David's name made great (7:9).
- An undisturbed place for Israel and rest from enemies (7:10–11).
- The establishing of David's line as rulers over his kingdom forever (7:16; 22:51; Ps. 89:28–29).
- A special Father-son relationship between Yahweh and the king (2 Sam. 7:14; "You are my Son," Ps. 2:7; "my firstborn," 89:27).
- Sin would bring punishment (2 Sam. 7:14), but no removal of the line of kingship as in Saul's case (7:15; Ps. 89:30–33).

As in the other covenants, enjoyment of the promise is conditioned upon obedience, but the promise itself is eternal (cf. 2 Sam. 23:5).[13]

The Uniqueness of Yahweh

David's response (7:18–29) revives the theme of Yahweh's uniqueness. Yahweh has been unique as Israel's delivering God (7:22–24). David has known this from the past. But now he can only exclaim,[14]

Who am I, O Sovereign LORD, and what is my family, that you have brought me this far? . . . Is this your usual way of dealing with man, O Sovereign LORD? (7:18–19).

Yahweh is unique in his gracious promises. By his grace he already has established Israel as his people (7:24). Now by his grace he is establishing the Davidic line.

But this has been the proclamation from the beginning of Samuel. Hannah recognized this sovereign action of Yahweh:

> The LORD brings death and makes alive;
>   he brings down to the grave and raises up.
> The LORD sends poverty and wealth;
>   he humbles and he exalts.
> He raises the poor from the dust
>   and lifts the needy from the ash heap;
> he seats them with princes
>   and has them inherit a throne of honor. . . .
> It is not by strength that one prevails;
>   those who oppose the LORD will be shattered (1 Sam. 2:6–10).

Samuel was raised up from a barren womb. David, though the youngest of Jesse's sons, was chosen king. But the real shock comes in 2 Samuel 12:24–25 with the second son, Solomon, born to David and Bathsheba:

> The LORD loved him; and because the LORD loved him, he sent word through Nathan the prophet to name him Jedidiah [loved by Yahweh].

Solomon would be the son to follow David on the throne and build the temple for the Lord.[15] Yahweh is a God of grace.

Students often ask, "What would have happened had Saul not disobeyed? How would the King have then come from Judah (Gen. 49:10) if God had continued Saul's kingdom forever (1 Sam. 13:13)?" Questions like these, which try to understand God's ability to control history using even the sinful choices of men, are beyond human understanding.

At any rate, I have a more interesting question. What would have happened had David not sinned with Bathsheba? Would there have been no Solomon? And further, how could God choose Solomon—the product of a marriage which never should have been—over other sons?

> The LORD is compassionate and gracious,
>   slow to anger, abounding in love.
> He will not always accuse,
>   nor will he harbor his anger forever;

he does not treat us as our sins deserve
> or repay us according to our iniquities.
For as high as the heavens are above the earth,
> so great is his love for those who fear him;
as far as the east is from the west,
> so far has he removed our transgressions from us
> > (Psalm 103:8–12).

COMPLETION OF KINGSHIP

The Promise Continued

Psalm 2 vividly captures the Davidic promise in action. The psalm begins by picturing rebellion against Yahweh and his anointed ruler or "messiah." What reaction is there to this rebellion? Yahweh derisively laughs and gives his answer: He names his king, the one he has installed on Mount Zion in Jerusalem (2:4–6). This Davidic king in Zion now speaks: "He [Yahweh] said to me, 'You are my Son; today I have become your Father' " (2:7). Here the language of 2 Samuel 7 is used. David and his line have been installed as Yahweh's kings. And how is this significant? At the king's request, Yahweh will give victory in putting down attacking nations. Ultimately Israel will possess "the ends of the earth" as nation after nation rebels against Yahweh's rule and is defeated (2:8–9).

The kings of the earth must not kick against God's ordained order. With wise insight, they must submit to Yahweh and his king, before it is too late (2:10–12). If God's intention of universal rule for his anointed king is not clear enough from Psalm 2, then Psalm 72 should solve the matter.

> He will rule from sea to sea
> > and from the River to the ends of the earth.
> The desert tribes will bow before him
> > and his enemies will lick the dust.
> The kings of Tarshish and of distant shores
> > will bring tribute to him;
> the kings of Sheba and Seba
> > will present him gifts.
> All kings will bow down to him
> > and all nations will serve him (72:8–11).

Even when Yahweh's chastening hand came as promised upon sinful Davidic kings, and even when Israel went into exile, *the promise itself held firm*. In David's line "rascals there may be, but the blessing would never be revoked from the family."[16]

> This is what the LORD says: "If I have not established my covenant with day and night and the fixed laws of heaven and earth, then I will reject the descendants of Jacob and David my servant and will not choose one of his sons to rule over the descendants of Abraham, Isaac and Jacob. For I will restore their fortunes and have compassion on them" (Jer. 33:25–26).

New Testament Completion

Christians often read the New Testament as if its Old Testament quotations about Christ are referring *only* to him. This frequently is not the case. For instance, when we read Hebrews 1:5 and see 2 Samuel 7:14 quoted, we might assume that "I will be his Father and he will be my Son" was a direct quotation about Jesus. Students are quite surprised the first time they read the very next phrase in 2 Samuel 7: "When he does wrong, I will punish him with the rod of men." Could this passage be speaking of the perfect Son of God?

As often as not, the New Testament quotations reflect the *completion* of God's promises in Christ. Christ is predicted throughout the Scriptures (Luke 24:27), but he is not necessarily *directly* predicted in all the Scriptures. Nor is he hidden there in some mystical or allegorical way. All of these lines of promise and great themes of the Old Testament ultimately meet in Christ. If it was true for the Roman Empire that "all roads lead to Rome," it is also true for Scripture that "no matter how many promises God has made, they are 'Yes' [fulfilled] in Christ" (2 Cor. 1:20).

How is the promise to David and the theme of kingship fulfilled in Christ? On this the New Testament is very clear. Check out these facts:

- Jesus was born in the line of David (Matt. 1:1–17; Luke 2:4; Rom. 1:3).
- He rode into Jerusalem in the predicted manner, and accepted the acclamations of those who saw him as the son of David who would save them and introduce the coming kingdom (Mark 11:2–10; cf. Ps. 118:25–26; Zech. 9:9).
- On the cross he experienced the same persecution from which David asked God to deliver him. Both David and Jesus were apparently forsaken by God into their enemies' hands (Matt. 27:46; Ps. 22:1), were mocked for believing God would deliver them (Matt. 27:43; Ps. 22:8), were physically pinned down by their enemies (Matt. 27:35; Ps. 22:16), had lots cast for their clothing (Matt. 27:35; Ps. 22:18),

were thirsty and received sour wine to drink (Matt. 27:48; Ps. 22:15; 69:21), and were delivered (Matt. 28:6; Ps. 22:22–24). Could these parallel circumstances happen just by chance, or is God trying to tell us something?

- His resurrection from the dead fulfilled Psalm 2:7—"You are my Son; today I have become your Father" (Acts 13:32–33). For though Jesus was always the Son of God in his divine nature, here we are speaking of the announcement by Yahweh concerning his rule as David's heir. The resurrection was God's public announcement of his King.
- His ascension to heaven marked the beginning of a period predicted in Psalm 110:1—"Sit at my right hand until I make your enemies a footstool for your feet" (Acts 2:32–36). In the Resurrection and Ascension, God has exalted Jesus to the position of Lord and Christ (Messiah, Anointed King—Acts 2:36 and 5:31; Heb. 1:3–13).
- His reign over the nations on earth—when he "will rule them with an iron scepter" (Ps. 2:9)—is yet future. It will be implemented at his return to earth (Rev. 19:15; 12:5).

Like a well-synchronized multiprojector slide presentation, each phase clicks off. And so the hope of Israel for a Davidic king to give them what was promised is "Yes" in Christ Jesus. His rule not only will be over those of physical Israel who put their trust in him but will extend from sea to sea and to the ends of the earth. Security is to be found in The King, after all!

"Amen. Come, Lord Jesus."

Suggested Scripture Reading:

1 Samuel 1–2, 13–17
2 Samuel 5–7, 11–12
Psalm 2
Acts 2:29–41

For Interaction and Discussion:

1. What was it about the "pure theocracy" of the judges that made the Israelites feel vulnerable? On the other hand, what advantages did this government have for the people? How do "security" and "faith" relate in the Bible?

2. What is the story of David and Goliath really about? Is the passage teaching that belief will slay any "giant" or difficulty? Can you think of opposite examples?

3. Why is it important for the biblical writer to show that the Word of God was higher than the king's word in Israel? Why did Saul end up in such

a pitiful spiritual and psychological condition after being rejected as king? How would these principles relate to human response to God today?

4. Identify some poor decisions of David in the first part of 2 Samuel. If David is not perfect in his judgment, why is he so blessed? Why is the sin with Bathsheba such a disastrous sin if David has made mistakes before, yet continued to be blessed?

5. What effect did David's sin with Bathsheba have on his family? How does the Bible's frankness about failure affect you as a reader?

6. What promise kept David's line from losing the kingship? How does this promise meet its ultimate fulfillment? How does God mark out Jesus so that no one can miss the fact that he is the promised King? How will those who are wise respond to the King?

For Further Reading:

William J. Dumbrell. *The Faith of Israel*. Grand Rapids: Baker, 1988, 75–84. Brief but solid coverage of the theology of Samuel.

Carl J. Laney, Jr. *1 and 2 Samuel*. Chicago: Moody, 1982. Brief commentary that nicely covers the crucial issues of the narrative for the English reader.

Joyce G. Baldwin. *1 and 2 Samuel*. TOTC. Downers Grove, Ill.: InterVarsity, 1988. Commentary on Hebrew text for English reader.

Walter C. Kaiser, Jr. *Toward an Old Testament Theology*. Grand Rapids: Zondervan, 1991, 143–64. Full discussion of the Davidic Covenant.

Terence E. Fretheim. *Deuteronomic History*. Nashville: Abingdon, 1983, 108–21. Academic discussion of Davidic Covenant.

Notes and Comments:

[1]When the book of Samuel opens, the Israelites are largely subject to the Philistines. The Philistines had transplanted themselves from southwest Asia Minor, settling in Crete and along the Mediterranean coast of Canaan. They formed five city-states: Ashdod, Ashkelon, Ekron, Gath, and Gaza. Though each city was under its own ruler, together they formed a united front (cf. 1 Sam. 5:11; 6:4). They integrated with the local Canaanite population and were especially skilled in warfare and the use of iron. Cf. F. F. Bruce, *Israel and the Nations* (Grand Rapids: Eerdmans, 1963), 21–27. The Philistines, in fact, had kept the skill of ironworking to themselves, attempting to enforce a monopoly even in agricultural tools so as to control the ability to make weapons (1 Sam. 13:19–22). As a result, Saul's army was drastically short of modern weaponry.

[2]Gilbert K. Chesterton, *What's Wrong with the World* (New York: Dodd, Mead & Co., 1922), 48.

[3]The exact nature of Saul's first sin is debated. Some take it as a violation of the priesthood by offering a sacrifice himself. Cf. John Bright, *A History of Israel*, 192;

and G. L. Carr, "'ola," *TWOT*, 2:667. Others see it as a violation of Samuel's instruction to wait for him. It was at least that.

It seems to me that the words "offered a sacrifice" are too quickly understood to mean the priest's function. The offerer, too, "offers a sacrifice" even though a priest is there to carry out the duties of his office. Since we know that a priest was present among Saul's men (1 Sam. 14:2–3; cf. 13:15), and Samuel himself was not a priest but a Levite only (1 Chron. 6:33–38), normal usage assumes the meaning to be that Saul offered the sacrifice to begin the battle by providing the sacrificial animal, killing and preparing it (the worshiper's responsibility, Lev. 1), and having the priest put it on the altar. Since the same words are used for both David's and Solomon's offering of sacrifices to Yahweh (2 Sam. 24:24; 1 Kings 3:3–4), it is stretching the vocabulary too much to insist on intrusion into the priest's office for Saul.

Samuel's rebuke and a comparison with 1 Samuel 10:8 yields only the conclusion that Saul failed to wait for Samuel to come to initiate the campaign with the sacrifice. It is this command that he failed to keep. Cf. C. F. Keil and F. Delitzsch, *Biblical Commentary on the Books of Samuel* (Grand Rapids: Eerdmanns, n.d.), 128–29.

[4]The Israelite function of king may be contrasted with that of the other kings. For instance, in the prologue of the Code of Hammurabi, King Hammurabi says he was commissioned by Marduk to guide the people, and he offers his set of laws as his fulfillment of that function (*ANET*, 164–65). Later in biblical history we experience the "Laws of the Medes and Persians," which were to be unchanged once the monarch had decreed them.

[5]Keil and Delitzsch, *Biblical Commentary on the Books of Samuel*, 129, also point out this distinction between the penalties announced for Saul's first and second sins of disobedience. This solves any supposed problems of duplication, cf. R. K. Harrison, *Introduction to the Old Testament*, 702.

[6]There are several issues raised in the latter part of 1 Samuel worthy of discussion. Among these are David's honoring Saul's office so that he will not kill him. His conscience bothered him even in the matter of cutting off a corner of Saul's robe (24:4–5). Only Yahweh has the right to take Saul's life, either in battle or by natural death (26:8–11). To take Saul's life would have placed David in the same position as any other usurper of a throne. The tradition of assassination would not be introduced into Israel's history by David.

Another problem is David's becoming a mercenary under the Philistine king, Achish of Gath (1 Sam. 27). Was this right? David's thought and motive for his move (27:1)—a thought which even Saul in his saner moments knows is untrue (26:25; 24:20)—shows that David's move was not based on faith in God's promise.

While under Achish, the account continues to inform us that David is carrying out his responsibilities as king. Rather than attacking Israel and her allies, David carries out raids against the enemies of Israel (1 Sam. 27:8–12). He completely eliminates these villages—not for any reasons of *herem* but to keep the report of his activities from Achish. Prior to this, David had delivered Keilah from the Philistines (1 Sam. 23), even though they were not committed to him.

[7]Joab's killing of Abner is totally outside of the Law. Joab is taking vengeance on Abner for the death of his brother, Asahel (2 Sam. 2:18–23). But Joab had no right of revenge, because Asahel's death was in warfare. Even if it were in peacetime, Abner would have been considered only defending himself under the circumstances. But, in addition to all this, Joab does his misdeed in the very gates of Hebron—one of the cities of refuge—at the very place where Abner's case should be heard. David knows Abner's death was unjustified homicide as indicated by the curse he calls on Joab (3:29–30). Joab should have been executed.

[8]Attempts to shift some of the blame to Bathsheba tempting David go beyond the statements of the narrative and seem designed to lessen the character of the sin here. It is likely that Bathsheba assumed the right of the king to do what he wanted.

[9]Nathan's rebuke of David includes the statement from the Lord: "I delivered you from the hand of Saul. I gave your master's house to you, and your master's wives into your arms." This has raised the question as to whether David took Saul's wives. I'm sure David could find his own wives (and did!) without the older women who belonged to Saul. The statement is more a reflection of a cultural practice that occurs a number of times in Samuel and Kings. To take a former king's wives was one way of indicating a claim to kingship. So, Ishbosheth in 2 Samuel 3:7 is upset when Abner takes one of Saul's concubines. Also, in the fulfillment of the judgment of 12:11, Absalom will take David's concubines publicly to certify his claim to the throne (16:21–22). Additionally, in 1 Kings 2:13–25 Solomon rightly interprets his brother Adonijah's request for Abishag as another plot to take the throne. In 2 Samuel 11:8, therefore, we simply have another way of saying that David was given the throne rights that had belonged to Saul. There is no evidence that he actually took Saul's wives, though we may speculate that he might have sequestered them to make sure that no one else did either!

[10]Brevard S. Childs observes that the appendix to the book (2 Sam. 21–24) has an important function in focusing on the book's important issues. Cf. *Introduction to the Old Testament As Scripture* (Philadelphia: Fortress, 1979), 273–77. Each supplemental item, though too cumbersome to insert in the narrative, adds a needed perspective to a theme of the book. The first story in the appendix helps explain David's innocence in the near demise of Saul's house, though he had promised earlier not to carry out the normal practice of eliminating the previous king's line (1 Sam. 24:21; 20:14–15). As we noted in the main discussion, the two psalms in the middle of the appendix bring us back to the major themes of Yahweh as the true Rock of Israel, the propriety of righteous rule, and the Davidic Covenant. Surrounding these are the exploits of David's loyal troops: Especially noteworthy is the inclusion among the Thirty Mighty Men—last so we cannot miss it—of Uriah the Hittite. The last incident (2 Sam. 24) provides the background to the site of the temple as the place where God's mercy was again shown.

[11]Walter Brueggemann, *The Land*, 71–89, stresses the danger of kingship for seeking self-security. Seeking to hold the land by alliances and military might rather than by attention to Torah and covenantal memory would ultimately lose the land.

[12]The statement of David in 2 Samuel 12:13: "I have sinned against Yahweh" has its equivalent in Psalm 51:4: "Against you, you only, have I sinned and done what is evil in your sight." I would suggest that the contrast is not one between Uriah and Yahweh but between Yahweh and other gods. David has sinned against Yahweh and against no other god. His faithlessness has been to Yahweh's covenant, whereas other kings under other gods were allowed such absolute power over their citizens.

[13]See Terence E. Fretheim, *Deuteronomic History*, 108–21; Walter C. Kaiser, Jr., *Toward an Old Testament Theology*, 156–57, for more complete discussions of the unconditional nature of the Davidic Covenant. Kaiser also has a list of linguistic parallels that show the continuity of this covenant with previous ones (153).

[14]The last sentence in 2 Samuel 7:19 is difficult to translate. See discussions in Keil and Delitzsch, *Biblical Commentary on the Books of Samuel*, 350–51; S. Goldman, *Samuel*, Soncino Books of the Bible (Soncino, 1949), 229; and Kaiser, *Toward an Old Testament Theology*, 154–55. Because of the parallel in 1 Chronicles 17:17 it seems best to stick with the context of amazed gratitude rather than a statement of new information.

[15]The statement of Yahweh's love for Solomon is the only hint in Samuel of who the next king will be. The notion of God's loving often includes the idea of his choosing (cf. Deut. 4:37; 7:7–8; Neh. 13:26; Ps. 78:68; Mal. 1:2). First Chronicles 22:9 indicates that God's choice of Solomon was told to David.

[16]Kaiser, *Toward an Old Testament Theology*, 157.

chapter ten

NATION HEADING FOR JUDGMENT
(Kings) Theology of Kings

The repetition is deafening. Over and over the Scriptures announce the diagnosis. Like a skillful surgeon doing an exploratory operation, the divinely inspired author dissects the near-corpse of Israel to find the cause of her fatal malady. Again and again, as he examines each organ, he discovers a spreading cancer.

The body politic of Israel is not doomed because of a minor slip in dietary regulations or other miscellaneous commands. Nor is the root problem to be found in unwise economic theory or insufficient military capacity. No, the root cause is moral and religious. Israel sinned. And her sin is not slight, but basic. As the author-prophet looks at Israel's kings, he announces his diagnosis with boring regularity:

> He committed all the sins his father had done before him; his heart was not fully devoted to the LORD his God, as the heart of David his forefather had been (1 Kings 15:3).

> He walked in all the ways of Jeroboam son of Nebat and in his sin, which he caused Israel to commit, so that they provoked the LORD, the God of Israel, to anger by their worthless idols (1 Kings 16:26).

> He did evil in the eyes of the LORD, because he walked in the ways of his father and mother and in the ways of Jeroboam son of Nebat, who caused Israel to sin (1 Kings 22:52).

> He did not turn away from the sins of Jeroboam, which he had caused Israel to commit (2 Kings 10:31).

> He did evil in the eyes of the LORD, just as his fathers had done (2 Kings 23:37).

The Downward Track to Judgment

In an unexpected place the downward track to judgment begins. The seeds of destruction take root in the soil of blessing, during the reign of Solomon, that illustrious son of David. The author of Kings highlights for us the glory of Israel during Solomon's reign. And glorious it is! After Solomon secures his throne against the double treachery of Adonijah (1 Kings 1–2), he offers no less than a thousand burnt offerings to Yahweh at Gibeon (1 Kings 3:4). Yahweh appears to him on that occasion and offers to Solomon whatever he wishes. The scene is the closest the Bible gets to a genie-out-of-the-bottle opportunity, and Solomon is equal to the occasion. Therein lies the greatness of his reign.

Having enough insight already to see the seriousness of his responsibility as king, Solomon asks for more wisdom. He asks for it not simply to be the wisest man on earth, but so that he could fairly judge his people (3:9), as illustrated in the case that follows about the two harlots (3:16–28). *That is what is so pleasing to God.* Solomon doesn't ask for himself at all, but for others' benefit—those for whom he is responsible as the shepherd of Israel.

King Solomon lifts Israel to its peak of fame—only in music and battle is David more famous. Truly the golden age of Israel has arrived (10:14, 21). At the center of his kingly accomplishments is the building of the temple of Yahweh in Jerusalem. Solomon's majestic prayer at the dedication of that sanctuary acknowledges Israel's mission to spread belief in Yahweh. Solomon calls on God to accept this sanctuary as a house where prayers are answered and mercy is granted (8:22–61). As a result, God again appears to Solomon (9:1–9). He accepts the temple as his own but warns that obedience is still required to receive his blessing. He will not save Israel from judgment just because his temple is here. This warning has prophetic significance, for those in Jeremiah's day will say "The Temple, The Temple," and place their hope in the faulty notion that God would never destroy it.

Ultimately, all this blessing becomes a mere foil for disappointment. Solomon's marriages with foreign women lead to his spiritual downfall. By allowing them to go to the "shrine of their choice" to worship, Solomon introduces false worship on Israelite soil. The women finally are able to turn him from his view of God's uniqueness (8:60) to worshiping other gods along with Yahweh (11:4–8). For this defection, God takes the ten northern tribes from Solomon and gives them to one of his servants, Jeroboam, the son of Nebat.[1]

A RATING SCALE FOR KINGS

For the military, college football, and top tunes, it's *rankings.*
For students, restaurants, and eggs, it's *grading.*

Figure 10.1

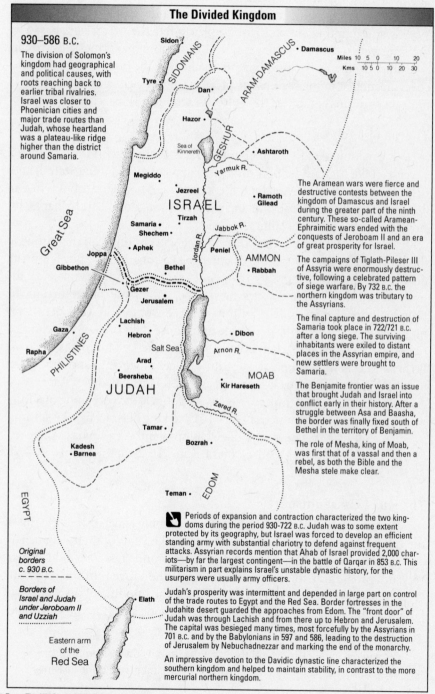

The Divided Kingdom

930–586 B.C.

The division of Solomon's kingdom had geographical and political causes, with roots reaching back to earlier tribal rivalries. Israel was closer to Phoenician cities and major trade routes than Judah, whose heartland was a plateau-like ridge higher than the district around Samaria.

Sidon

Damascus

SIDONIANS

ARAM-DAMASCUS

Miles 10 5 0 10 20
Kms 10 5 0 10 20 30

Tyre

Dan

GESHUR

Hazor

Sea of Kinnereth

Ashtaroth

Megiddo

Yarmuk R.

Jezreel

Ramoth Gilead

ISRAEL

Tirzah

Jabbok R.

Samaria
Shechem

Jordan R.

Aphek

Peniel

AMMON

Joppa

Gibbethon

Bethel

Rabbah

Great Sea

Gezer

Jerusalem

Lachish

Gaza

Hebron

Dibon

PHILISTINES

Salt Sea

Arnon R.

Rapha

Arad

Beersheba

Kir Hareseth

MOAB

JUDAH

Zered R.

Tamar

Bozrah

Kadesh Barnea

Teman

EDOM

EGYPT

Original borders c. 930 B.C.

Borders of Israel and Judah under Jeroboam II and Uzziah

Elath

Eastern arm of the
Red Sea

The Aramean wars were fierce and destructive contests between the kingdom of Damascus and Israel during the greater part of the ninth century. These so-called Aramean-Ephraimitic wars ended with the conquests of Jeroboam II and an era of great prosperity for Israel.

The campaigns of Tiglath-Pileser III of Assyria were enormously destructive, following a celebrated pattern of siege warfare. By 732 B.C. the northern kingdom was tributary to the Assyrians.

The final capture and destruction of Samaria took place in 722/721 B.C. after a long siege. The surviving inhabitants were exiled to distant places in the Assyrian empire, and new settlers were brought to Samaria.

The Benjamite frontier was an issue that brought Judah and Israel into conflict early in their history. After a struggle between Asa and Baasha, the border was finally fixed south of Bethel in the territory of Benjamin.

The role of Mesha, king of Moab, was first that of a vassal and then a rebel, as both the Bible and the Mesha stele make clear.

Periods of expansion and contraction characterized the two kingdoms during the period 930-722 B.C. Judah was to some extent protected by its geography, but Israel was forced to develop an efficient standing army with substantial chariotry to defend against frequent attacks. Assyrian records mention that Ahab of Israel provided 2,000 chariots—by far the largest contingent—in the battle of Qarqar in 853 B.C. This militarism in part explains Israel's unstable dynastic history, for the usurpers were usually army officers.

Judah's prosperity was intermittent and depended in large part on control of the trade routes to Egypt and the Red Sea. Border fortresses in the Judahite desert guarded the approaches from Edom. The "front door" of Judah was through Lachish and from there up to Hebron and Jerusalem. The capital was besieged many times, most forcefully by the Assyrians in 701 B.C. and by the Babylonians in 597 and 586, leading to the destruction of Jerusalem by Nebuchadnezzar and marking the end of the monarchy.

An impressive devotion to the Davidic dynastic line characterized the southern kingdom and helped to maintain stability, in contrast to the more mercurial northern kingdom.

From *The NIV Study Bible* (Zondervan, 1985), 495.

For TV programs, movies, and automobile tires, it's *ratings*.

It's hard to imagine modern life without our "scale from one to ten." Weekly and monthly tabloids ask couples to rate their marriages based on their answers to twenty or fewer questions. Entire magazines exist to rate consumer products. But these are not the first. In the book of Kings we discover an ancient rating scale as the prophet-author evaluates Israel's rulers.[2] Four types of sins emerge as the pulse of each reign is measured.

The Sin of Jeroboam

Every king of the ten northern tribes is charged with the "sin of Jeroboam." Like a greasy-spoon diner that repeatedly fails the state health inspection for the same violation, the kings of the northern tribes refuse to reverse this policy of Jeroboam and save their kingdoms. And what is this sin that meant a rating of failure?

Jeroboam has God's word that his line will continue on the throne in the north under one condition: obedience (1 Kings 11:38). But Jeroboam believes in good politics more than God's promise, and reasons away the promise out of fear that the northern tribes might want to return to the Davidic king. He concludes that if his people worship in Jerusalem, they might have a nostalgic desire to return to those days of glory as a unified nation. So as far as Jeroboam is concerned, unified worship has to go. At Bethel and Dan he sets up two substitute places of worship and introduces images to represent Yahweh—golden calves, no less. Shades of Aaron!

But Jeroboam's attempt to save his kingdom is the very thing that loses it, and judgment is announced (14:7–16). No king of Israel has the spiritual sense to eliminate this unacceptable worship—and every dynasty after Jeroboam meets its doom because of it (1 Kings 16:2–3; 2 Kings 10:30–31; 15:8–12).

The Sin of Canaanitism

Solomon's idolatry is the initial step in turning Israel toward the sins of the Canaanites, who had been expelled from the land for their debauchery and idolatry. His son Rehoboam, who had an Ammonitess for a mother, cancels any progress made since the period of the judges. In his reign, the Canaanite sins committed by Judah include the building of high places of false worship with sacred pillars and Asherim poles, and reintroduction of male prostitutes as part of worship.

> Judah did evil in the eyes of the LORD. By the sins they committed they stirred up his jealous anger more than their fathers had done (1 Kings 14:22).

Later kings not guilty of this false worship are said to be "like David" (1 Kings 15:11–14; 2 Kings 18:3; 22:2; cf. 1 Kings 15:5).[3]

The Sin of Ahab

Also deserving a negative rating is the sin of Ahab. Ahab follows his father, Omri, to Israel's throne after the fall of Jeroboam's line. His father is generally more well-known than he in ancient Near Eastern history; but in the Bible, Ahab is the more prominent.[4] The reason is infamous.

> He not only considered it trivial to commit the sins of Jeroboam son of Nebat, but he also married Jezebel daughter of Ethbaal king of the Sidonians, and began to serve Baal and worship him. He set up an altar for Baal in the temple of Baal that he built in Samaria (1 Kings 16:31–32).

Don't miss the full significance of this action. If other kings allowed images to represent the Lord and even allowed false worship, Ahab was first to introduce another god as Israel's official deity. Will Yahweh be robbed of his inheritance? Will he be displaced by Baal under the strong-willed pressure of Jezebel on her wimp of a husband, King Ahab?

Figure 10.2
The Cylinder of Sennacherib

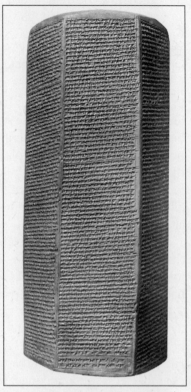

The Assyrian king's record of his campaign against Judah and Jerusalem. He claims to have shut up Hezekiah "like a bird in a cage," indirectly confirming the biblical account that he did not take Jerusalem.
Courtesy of the Oriental Institute of Chicago

Worship at High Places

One final sin is noted by the inspired writer: the failure to limit sacrifice to the temple in Jerusalem. This is not a disabling sin. A king could commit this sin and still be labeled "good" by our writer-guide. But an approved king might find a postscript on his reign: "The high places, however, were not removed, and the people continued to offer sacrifices and burn incense there." This is the postscript for Jehoshaphat (1 Kings 22:43) and for Asa (1 Kings 15:9–14).

At first glance, it might seem that these men allow the worship of other gods at high places. But Asa had removed Canaanite worship and idols (1 Kings 15:12–13). These were high places on which *Yahweh* was worshiped! Note carefully our writer's observation on Solomon in the early part of his reign: "Solomon loved the LORD, walking in the statutes of his father David, except he sacrificed and burned incense on the high places. And the king went to Gibeon to sacrifice there, for that was the great high place; Solomon offered a thousand burnt offerings on that altar" (1 Kings 3:3–4 NASB).

Sacrifice to Yahweh at other than the tabernacle or temple was common following the overrunning of the tabernacle at Shiloh (1 Sam. 4; 7:6, 9, 17; 9:12–13; 10:8). God's desire, expressed in the Law, was that one central location be used for sacrifice (Deut. 12:1–14).[5] His acceptance of the temple made it clear that all sacrifice and incense was to be offered at Jerusalem (1 Kings 9:3; 8:10–11).

Every king of Judah who receives a "good" rating has that rating qualified by his failure to limit sacrifice to Jerusalem—until we come to Hezekiah. This is what the writer says of him:

Figure 10.3
The Stela of Shalmaneser III

The stela of Shalmaneser III, containing twenty panels in sequence, all depict tribute being brought to the king. The second panel mentions the tribute paid by "Jehu, Son of Omri."
(Copyright British Museum)

> Hezekiah trusted in the LORD, the God of Israel. There was no one like him among all the kings of Judah, either before him or after him. He held fast to the LORD and did not cease to follow him; he kept the commands the LORD had given Moses. And the LORD was with him; he was successful in whatever he undertook (2 Kings 18:5–7).

Hezekiah rates first among the kings in trusting God. Therefore he is not satisfied to eliminate Canaanite idolatry. Halfway obedience is not his style.

Only one other king has as good a rating: Josiah (2 Kings 23:25). But Manasseh, Josiah's grandfather, reigned so long and committed so many abominations that God already has determined to send Judah into exile to Babylon (2 Kings 23:26). When Josiah finds the book of the Law in the temple, the exclusive worship of Yahweh becomes national policy. The idols occupying the temple are destroyed. False worship is rooted out of the land along with Canaanite practices. Josiah even goes to Bethel and destroys the high place set up there by Jeroboam (2 Kings 23:15–16).

What is the key to rating a king? For this too we may go back to the reign of Solomon. This king, who so pleased God by asking for wisdom, had written, "The fear of the LORD is the beginning of wisdom" (Prov. 9:10). Or we could look at Solomon's prayer and dedication of the temple. There we find showcased the view of God that pervades the book of Kings. The God of Israel is unique when compared with the "gods" of other nations (1 Kings 8:23). In fact, there is no one else (8:60). And Israel's mission is to be a testimony of Yahweh (8:43, 60). Israel's temple should be a house of prayer for all people (8:41–43).

But because Yahweh is a unique God, Israel must be a unique people. Unlike Josiah, the good king who came too late, Israel did not love Yahweh with all its heart and all its soul and all its might (Deut. 6:5; 2 Kings 23:25).[6]

And what of the temple of Solomon, which was to be the central worship place? "I will reject Jerusalem, the city I chose, and this temple, about which I said, 'There shall my Name be'" (2 Kings 23:27). A sad final commentary on such an illustrious and glorious beginning!

Final Ratings

The author of Kings has given us a spiritual assessment of each ruler of both the northern (also called Israel and Ephraim) and the southern (also called Judah) kingdoms. Like a rating scale in a tour guidebook, he has carefully graded each reign. If a king has avoided all the pitfalls above, he receives what we might call a four-star rating. This is the highest possible. Only two kings receive it: Hezekiah and Josiah.

None of the nineteen northern kings repent of the sin of Jeroboam. Bethel becomes the primary sanctuary in the north and images are worshiped there. Jehu, that military man so violent that Elisha commands his messenger to flee as soon as he has anointed him king, is given a reward of five generations on the throne because he eliminated the sin of Ahab (official Baalism) from Israel. But because Jehu's zeal for Yahweh does not extend to eliminating the false image worship at Bethel, he is not given the seal of divine approval.

Eight kings of the southern kingdom (Judah) receive some commendation:

- Asa removes the false high places and demotes his idolatrous grandmother (1 Kings 15:11–15).
- Jehoshaphat follows his father Asa's example in freeing the land from idolatry, yet like his father does not limit sacrifice to Jerusalem (1 King 22:43).
- Joash, the boy king, is faithful as long as he is under the tutorship of the priest Jehoiada (2 Kings 12:1–3; 2 Chron. 24:2, 17–25).
- Amaziah "did what was right . . . but not as his father David had done" (2 Kings 14:3). This indicates a failure during his reign to stay completely free from idolatry (cf. 2 Chron. 25:14).
- Azariah, also called Uzziah,

Figure 10.4
The Babylonian Chronicles

A portion of the Babylonian Chronicles which describes the capture and exile of King Jehoiachin and his being exiled to Babylon around 600 B.C.
(Copyright British Museum)

and his son Jotham are rated as good, though Uzziah is stricken with leprosy as a judgment for trying to be his own priest and burn incense (2 Kings 15:1–5, 32–35; 2 Chron. 26:16–21).

Finally come Hezekiah and Josiah, who are more faithful than all the kings before them. On the other side of the coin are those kings who give the body of Israel its greatest case of ptomaine poisoning. Clearly King Manasseh deserves his "most-wicked" rating. The list of his sins is foul and sickening. Among them:

- He introduces child sacrifice, killing even his own son.
- He uses the temple for false worship and idols.
- He practices astrology.
- He consults mediums and spiritists.

Our author declares the "Midnight Reign of Manasseh"[7] as the seal of Judah's doom. She will be exiled. Even Josiah's fine rule cannot reverse the impact of his grandfather's wickedness.

His sons, Jehoahaz (Shallum) and Jehoiakim (Eliakim), then failed to carry on their father's heritage and Josiah's grandson, Jehoiachin, was taken to Babylon by Nebuchadnezzar. Nebuchadnezzar placed another son of Josiah, Zedekiah (Mattaniah), on the throne. His rebellion in 588 B.C. touched off Nebuchadnezzar's final campaign against Jerusalem that led to its destruction in 586 B.C.

In the northern kingdom, Ahab and his sons are viewed as a profound threat to Israel. They not only continue the sin of Jeroboam, but they introduce Baal worship from Phoenicia as the official religion. This threat and the importance of eliminating it make the reigns of Ahab and his sons significant as the setting for the ministry of Elijah and Elisha, prophets of Yahweh.

THE SIGNIFICANCE OF ELIJAH AND ELISHA
The Contest with Baal

Among all the drama surrounding the Old Testament prophets, one event is certain to capture the imagination of both children and adults: the contest on Mount Carmel between Yahweh's prophet Elijah and the prophets of Baal (1 Kings 18). The backdrop is the reign of Ahab and his foreign queen, Jezebel. Under her painted thumb, Ahab not only allows her to worship Baal on Israelite soil—as Solomon had done with his foreign wives—but also cannot resist her desire to enthrone Baal as the official sovereign god of Israel. For disobedience to the Mosaic Covenant, Ahab's territory already is suffering from lack of rain. This judgment of drought was outlined in Deuteronomy 28:23–24. Elijah announces it (1 Kings 17:1) so there can be no doubt about its purpose as a judgment from Yahweh.

The contest on Carmel, suggested by Elijah, will test whether Yahweh or Baal is to be God of Israel (1 Kings 18:20–46). Whose God can light his own sacrifice? A pitiful scene follows. The prophets of Baal gyrate, wail, and cut themselves in ultimate devotion. Elijah taunts them with scornful sarcasm. Perhaps their god has stepped out for the moment. Perhaps he is hunting. He is such a difficult fellow to get hold of! He seems unavailable for the moment.[8]

But the contest is unfair! Elijah makes it so. An old, disused altar to Yahweh is rebuilt using twelve stones to represent the nation Yahweh formed. Twelve jugs of water are poured over the sacrifice to make it nearly impossible to light.

With only one climactic call to Yahweh the contest is won. It's over. As King Ahab watches, the prophets of Baal are executed as false prophets and the people declare, "The LORD, he is God." Elijah intercedes for the land and awaits the rain. Then, tasting the thrill of this victory for his God, he outraces Ahab to Jezreel to witness the final scene of the elimination of Baal in

Israel. Ahab will announce to Jezebel the result of the contest. The kingdom will be secured again for Yahweh.

But it doesn't turn out to be that simple. Not until many more years and one prophet later will Baalism be eradicated from Israel's royal court.

Though most Bible students recognize the theme of Elijah's victory on Carmel, it remained for Leah Bronner in her study of Canaanite Baal epics discovered at Ugarit to demonstrate that nearly everything Elijah and Elisha did was devoted to showing that Yahweh was stronger than Baal.[9] Note each of the following teachings about Baal and how it was clearly disproven in the actions of Elijah and Elisha:

Figure 10.5

Teaching about Baal	Action of Elijah & Elisha
Baal controls the rain (he "rides upon the clouds").	Rain stops and starts at Elijah's word.
Baal is the god of fertility and vegetation.	Israel suffers famine due to lack of rain, yet Elijah and Elisha are able to provide increased oil and grain.
Baal has power over fire and lightning.	Yahweh, not Baal, lights his sacrifice; Elijah calls down fire on the king's troops (2 Kings 1:10–12), and a chariot with horses of fire precedes his departure by whirlwind (2 Kings 2:11).
Baal controls life, including power over barrenness, sickness, and death.	A son is provided to a barren woman, healings take place, and resurrections occur.

Baal is disproven. If only Israel—all twelve tribes—would learn to follow Yahweh, the Most High God. Why will you die, O Israel, when the truth is clearly before you? Why do you leave the God who has chosen you and is able to care for you? Why do you forsake Yahweh, the God Who Is Present to fulfill his promises, for gods who are unavailable?

Violation of Covenant Law

The worship of Baal was, of course, a violation of the Mosaic Covenant (Deut. 5:6–10; 6:4–5). When Yahweh is not recognized as sovereign, there will be additional violations of his justice. Other gods do not provide righteous laws. Other nations' kings make laws and are the law. This was not to be with Israel. Yahweh is the only absolute ruler. Even the human king in Israel is subject to his Law.

Nowhere else is this difference between Israel and the surrounding nations better illustrated than in the reign of Ahab. The story of Naboth's vineyard is not given simply to entertain and excite. Dramatic though it is, it is more important as a demonstration of the level to which Israel had fallen under Ahab and Jezebel. First Kings 21 narrates the incident.

Ahab wants Naboth's property because it would make a good vegetable garden near his palace. Naboth, completely within his rights under the covenant, refuses to sell since this property had been allotted to his ancestors and handed down according to the Law. Ahab, wimp that he is, heads for home, dejected.

Jezebel marvels that there is a problem. Certainly kings get what they want, don't they? That's how eminent domain works back home in Phoenicia! Using the power of the throne, Jezebel arranges for Naboth's unjust death and secures the property for Ahab. Ahab goes down to take possession and lay out his vegetable plot, only to meet disappointment again. The plot is occupied by the persistent prophet. Elijah declares that it will be the king's inheritance that is destroyed! Ahab's line will be exterminated. No males will survive Yahweh's judgment.

Care for the Faithful

With covenant justice taking a backseat, the ministry of the prophets to those in trouble becomes critical. God's care is shown through these prophets' concern for the needs of the faithful. A jar of oil is multiplied for a woman to redeem her sons from slavery (2 Kings 4:1–7). A barren woman is provided a son (4:8–37). A poisoned stew is rendered harmless (4:38–41). Food is multiplied to feed a crowd (4:42–44).

THEMES FOR THE EXILE

But what have these major emphases of Kings to do with the book's purpose? Is this book just a chronicle of God's power, mighty in his prophets yet unable to change the course of the nation? Both Israel and Judah are carried off into captivity. Did God fail? Is it all over? After Elijah fails to see Baal worship exterminated by the Mount Carmel victory, is his disappointment the whole story? "Take my life; I am no better than my ancestors" (1 Kings 19:4). "Nothing is going to change," he seems to say.[10]

For the discerning reader in captivity, the book of Kings provides answers full of meaning and hope, answers based squarely on the Mosaic Covenant and its significance.

The Land

We have already seen the importance of the land of Canaan as part of God's promise. Deuteronomy clearly outlined the conditions for any generation enjoying the blessing of that land. Kings also is a book about land . . . about being expelled from the land.

Most nations believed being expelled from their land meant their god was weaker than the god of the conquering nation. But the exiles from Israel are to learn exactly the opposite. It is not that Marduk of Babylon is more powerful than Yahweh, but that Yahweh himself is driving out his people, just as he promised. The covenant has been violated and the land has been polluted. Yahweh is a God of promise. He promised to bring them in, but he also promised to take them out if they befouled the land as the nations before them did (Lev. 18:24–28). He is keeping his promise.

Yahweh Is Sovereign

Yahweh showed he was more powerful than Baal and that he could sovereignly destroy Baalism in Israel even when the majority had not repented. The discerning reader will learn that Yahweh is in sovereign control even in exile.

Some Israelites thought their security was in the temple (Jer. 7:4–8). Some found their security in the very Law they were breaking (Jer. 8:8–9). But, like Habakkuk, the nation must learn that "The righteous will live by his faith" (Hab. 2:4). Only faith in Yahweh is adequate. The ruins of temple, Jerusalem, and land prove it (Hab. 3:16–19). *The God of Elijah still lives.*

Yahweh Is Gracious

After reading the book of Kings, the thoughtful Israelite could not question Yahweh's justice in punishing Israel. In fact, he might wonder why it had not come earlier—especially if he had also read Deuteronomy. The predicted judgments of Deuteronomy had come time and time again. There was lack of rain, famine, destruction by invaders, lack of peace. Prophetic announcements had warned of apostasy. Exile to Assyria for Israel (722 B.C.) and to Babylon for Judah (606–586 B.C.) came after prolonged patience. Like an overanxious mother watching both the door and the clock, God waited and waited before declaring the situation hopeless.

But even in exile there is hope. Hints of God's continuing commitment appear like beacons throughout the book. Solomon's prayer dedicating the temple asks God to hear them even in exile (1 Kings 8:46–52). God leaves a tribe for the Davidic ruler because of his promise to David that there would be a lamp in Jerusalem (1 Kings 11:12–13, 36; 2 Kings 8:19). Will he let that lamp go out forever? The final scene of the book is the release of King Jehoiachin from prison. Could God still be at work?

The Need for Repentance

Our author is no mere academician writing a multivolume treatise on the fall of an empire, like Gibbon's on Rome. He writes to achieve a *response*. He selects those events which show what has gone on in Israel's history so that his readers-in-exile may understand what their hope is—and also what their responsibility is.

The nation in exile, reading this history, can have no doubt concerning the cause of their calamity. Neither can they have any doubt concerning their only hope. Solomon's request, coming at the peak of God's blessing, clearly states the hope of Yahweh's people when they sin:

> If they have a change of heart in the land where they are held captive, and repent and plead with you in the land of their conquerors and say, "We have sinned, we have done wrong, we have acted wickedly"; and if they turn back to you with all their heart and soul in the land of their enemies who took them captive, and pray to you toward the land you gave their fathers, toward the city you have chosen and the temple I have built for your Name; then from heaven, your dwelling place, hear their prayer and their plea, and uphold their cause. And forgive your people, who have sinned against you; forgive all the offenses they have committed against you, and cause their conquerors to show them mercy (1 Kings 8:47–50).

It is when they turn with "all their heart and with all their soul" that God may have compassion and return them to the land (cf. 1 Kings 8:33–34). The people must turn back to the standards laid out by Moses (Deut. 6:4–5). Repentance is their hope.[11]

Josiah provides the model of how one should act when under God's judgment:

> Neither before nor after Josiah was there a king like him who turned to the LORD as he did—with all his heart and with all his soul and with all his strength, in accordance with all the law of Moses (2 Kings 23:25).

This noble king's decision to "follow the LORD, and keep his commands, regulations and decrees with all his heart and all his soul" (23:3) reminds the Israelite of the way back prescribed by the Law:

> When you and your children return to the LORD your God and obey him with all your heart and with all your soul according to everything I command you today, then the LORD your God will restore [return] your fortunes and have compassion on you and gather you again from all the nations where he scattered you (Deut. 30:2–3).

NEW TESTAMENT COMPLETION

Mistaken Identity?

No doubt it's happened to you. A child grasps the leg of your slacks as you are shopping and begins to come with you. How to minimize the shock when he discovers that you are not "Daddy" or "Mommy"? As we open the pages of the New Testament, the Jewish people were not searching for a parent, but they were expecting Elijah.

It should not surprise us, then, that when John the Baptist preached repentance in preparation for the Kingdom, questions about his identity were raised. The last prophet of the Old Testament, Malachi, had predicted a future Elijah who would rebuke the Israelites for their disobedience. This is like saying, "You will have another, final warning before judgment." The ministry of this coming Elijah? "He will turn the hearts of the fathers to their children, and the hearts of the children to their fathers; or else I will come and strike the land with a curse" (Mal. 4:6).

Israel must repent and return to the true faith of Abraham, Isaac, and Jacob, or the land will again come under God's judgment. For though some have returned to the land from captivity, the kingdom of David has not been restored. They are ruled by Gentile kings.

John rejects the idea that he is Elijah (John 1:21). Indeed, Jesus affirms that the predicted Elijah had not yet come (Matt. 17:11). Yet in the same breath he adds, "But I tell you, Elijah has already come, and they did not recognize him, but have done to him everything they wished" (17:12). They can experience Elijah's ministry by accepting the message of John the Baptist and repenting. But the officials of Israel—like the house of Ahab—will not repent. Once more it will be necessary to say to Jerusalem: "Your house is left to you desolate" (Matt. 23:37–39).

A Greater Identity

If John the Baptist is not Elijah, is Jesus? Some think so (Matt. 16:14). Certainly there are reasons for thinking he is. Notice the similarities in ministry and miracles between Jesus and Elijah and his successor, Elisha—resurrections, provisions of food, and control over natural forces.

The Gospel of Luke particularly is interested in a comparison between Elijah, Elisha, and Jesus. Luke includes the prediction that John the Baptist comes "in the spirit and power of Elijah" (Luke 1:17), but he focuses most on works and sayings of Jesus that compare to those of Elijah and Elisha:[12]

- Jesus ruffles the feathers of those in his hometown synagogue, pointing out that Elijah went to a Phoenician widow's house rather than to a Jewish home, and that Elisha healed a Syrian leper, Naaman, though Israel had its full share of lepers. The synagogue is angered by this scarcely veiled suggestion that Israel was in a state of unbelief similar to that in Elijah and Elisha's day (Luke 4:25–30).

- He resurrects a young man and gives him back to his widowed mother, as well as another child who is dead before he arrives (Luke 7:11–16; 1 Kings 17:17–24; 2 Kings 4:1–37).
- He feeds a multitude and has twelve baskets left (Luke 9:12–17; 2 Kings 4:42–44).
- Moses and Elijah talk with Jesus on the mountain following his announcement that some standing there would not see death (Elijah's experience) before seeing the kingdom (Luke 9:27–31).
- Jesus' disciples, enthusiastic about the dramatic aspects of Elijah's ministry, want Jesus to allow them to call fire down from heaven on an inhospitable Samaritan village (Luke 9:54; 2 Kings 1:10–12).
- Jesus refuses to allow a potential disciple to join him if he must go and say good-bye to his parents. And then, using the very imagery of Elisha's plow, he declares: "No one who puts his hand to the plow and looks back is fit for service in the kingdom of God" (Luke 9:61–62; 1 Kings 19:19–21).

Seeing only a nice set of parallels, however, would be to miss the point. Jesus is not just another great prophet like Elijah: He is greater than Elijah and Elisha. A second trip through these passages is in order.

- In Luke 4 Jesus announces himself not as Elijah but as the Servant of Yahweh who was to come (4:17–21).
- In the cases of resurrection, Jesus does not pray for resurrection as Elijah and Elisha did but commands it.
- Elisha's multiplication of food fed about one hundred men. Jesus feeds five thousand.
- On the mountain with Moses and Elijah, Jesus is identified as the chosen Son whose instruction should be followed.
- Finally, if you want to follow Jesus but desire to go back to say good-bye to your parents, you receive not a mild rebuke—as did Elisha—but a removal of the opportunity. Those who do not immediately snatch the opportunity to follow Jesus have no true perception of who he is. Jesus is Elijah. He is the Son. Those who follow him have true insight given from the Father (Luke 10:21). Theirs is the highest privilege:

Blessed are the eyes that see what you see. For I tell you that many prophets and kings wanted to see what you see but did not see it, and to hear what you hear but did not hear it (Luke 10:23–24).

Like the kings of old, many today try all kinds of nostrums to gain security: an improved economic theory, a more highly skilled military, survivalistic practices. But there is a more basic yardstick that determines human events . . . and ultimate destiny.

SUGGESTED SCRIPTURE READING:

1 Kings 1–3; 8:1–9:9; 11:1–13; 18:20–46
2 King 1–2, 9, 18–19, 22
Luke 9

For Interaction and Discussion:

1. Why is Solomon's request for wisdom so pleasing to God? What kinds of requests would be similar today?

2. How did Solomon's reign start Israel down the track to judgment? How was Jeroboam's sin similar? How can "good politics" (substitute "economics," "business," and so forth) get in the way of obedience? What makes this temptation so formidable?

3. Why is the sin of Ahab a more serious threat than other sins of monarchs? How do the ministries of the prophets Elijah and Elisha relate to this threat?

4. Who are the two best kings and what makes their reigns distinct? What is the key to rating a king? Are any of these ratings relevant for today's world?

5. How does Yahweh show himself as the only true God in the book of Kings?

6. Could an Israelite know why his nation failed? What is the remedy to failure? How is this pointed out in this "history" book?

7. How is Jesus shown to be a greater person than Elijah? What greater response is required? What greater benefits are given?

For Further Reading:

Edwin R. Thiele. *A Chronology of the Hebrew Kings.* Grand Rapids: Zondervan, 1977. Practical treatment of the issues of chronology in the book of Kings.

William J. Dumbrell. *The Faith of Israel.* Grand Rapids: Baker, 1988, 85–93. Treatment of the theology of Kings.

Donald J. Wiseman. *1 and 2 Kings*. TOTC. Downers Grove, Ill.: InterVarsity, 1993. Commentary for the English reader.

Leah Bronner. *The Stories of Elijah and Elisha*. Leiden: E. J. Brill, 1968, 50–122. Academic study of Baal epics as background for the prophetic activities of Elijah and Elisha.

Notes and Comments:

[1]Idolatry was not Solomon's only sin as king. He also sinned in multiplying horses and wives and accumulating wealth (Deut. 17:14–17). It is clear also that a growing economic burden fell upon the people, which becomes an immediate cause of the break following Solomon's death (1 Kings 12:4–19).

[2]For years the chronology of the kings of Israel and Judah was a puzzle to scholars, many concluding that the writer was a poor historian. The work of E. R. Thiele, *The Mysterious Numbers of the Hebrew Kings*, rev. ed. (Grand Rapids: Zondervan, 1983) has changed all that. By discovering and following the practices of the time for counting king's reigns (differing calendars, differing ways of counting partial years, co-reigns), Thiele found that the years for reigns given in Kings fit together perfectly, leaving only one unsolved case. A popular summary of Thiele is available under the title, *A Chronology of the Hebrew Kings* (Grand Rapids: Zondervan, 1977). Thiele's one unresolved case has been resolved, using the same methods, by K. A. Kitchen and T. C. Mitchell in the *New Bible Dictionary* (Grand Rapids: Eerdmans, 1962), 192–93.

[3]Some have attempted to make David's sin with Bathsheba the turning point for Israel's history. As we have seen in Samuel, it was the turning point for David's own reign. The historian-theologian of Kings is aware of David's sin with Bathsheba (1 Kings 15:5), nevertheless he uses David as the model of obedience and traces the slide of the nation from the failure of Solomon in accommodating false worship.

[4]Omri's fame is indicated by the Assyrian records that refer to Israel as the "House of Omri" (*ANET*, 280, 284, 285). Jehu, the destroyer of Omri's house, is even referred to as the son of Omri on the Black Obelisk of Shalmaneser III (*ANET*, 281).

[5]Walter C. Kaiser, Jr., *Toward an Old Testament Theology*, 130–33, and G. J. Wenham, "Deuteronomy and the Central Sanctuary," *TB*, 22:103–8, suggest that Deuteronomy does not require a limitation of one central site for sacrifices. It is not clear how this view avoids putting the book of Kings into conflict with Deuteronomy. The most straightforward understanding of Deuteronomy 12 is the same as the apparent position taken by the writer of Kings—sacrificial worship was to be limited to the central sanctuary, wherever it happened to be located. For the writer of Kings, its location is no longer in doubt.

[6]It is apparent from the book of Jeremiah that Josiah's reign, though turning official policy and formal practice back to true worship of Yahweh, did not change the heart of the people generally.

[7]I believe this colorful expression that handily summarizes this longest and darkest reign in Judah was originated by Howard G. Hendricks.

[8]For a literal translation of Elijah's mockery, toned down by most versions, read the text in *The Living Bible* (Wheaton: Tyndale, 1971).

[9]Leah Bronner, *The Stories of Elijah and Elisha* (Leiden: E. J. Brill, 1968), 50–122. Bronner also suggests that Elijah's ascension may have been an answer to Baal as the "Rider of the Clouds" (123–27), and that the two prophets' parting the Jordan River may be an answer to Baal's power over the waters (127–38). This last miracle, however, has other possible motivation than as an answer to Baal worship. It copies the Exodus and entrance into the land. It, therefore, validates the two prophets as the spokesmen of Yahweh, who brought Israel out of Egypt and into Canaan—i.e., the God to whom the nation owes its very existence.

[10]Elijah is often portrayed as discouraged and irrational in facing Jezebel's threat after Mount Carmel. He wants to die, yet he flees for his life! Ronald B. Allen, "Elijah, the Broken Prophet," *JETS*, 22 (1979): 193–202, has provided a better explanation. Elijah thought that his ministry had failed and that Israel would never turn from her rejection of prophets. He did, therefore, want to die, but not at Jezebel's hands. That would be an opportunity for Baal to claim victory over Yahweh. Therefore, he escaped to Judah and wanted God to take his life there.

[11]Carl Graesser, Jr., "The Message of the Deuteronomic Historian," *CTM*, 39 (1968): 542–51, has identified the themes of repentance and hope and also the central focus of Kings on worship practices.

[12]I. Howard Marshall, *Luke: Historian and Theologian* (Grand Rapids: Zondervan, 1970), 126, 147, and *Commentary on Luke*, NICOT (Grand Rapids: Eerdmans, 1978), 178, 188–89, 276, 283, 286, 388, 412, has recognized the occurrence of the Elijah comparison in many of these passages. Cf. Charles P. Baylis, "The Elijah-Elisha Motif in Luke 7–10," unpublished Th.M. thesis, Dallas Theological Seminary, Dallas, Tex., April 1985.

Figure 10.6

KINGS OF ISRAEL AND JUDAH

This chart depicts the reigns of the kings of Israel and Judah from Jeroboam of Israel and Rehoboam of Judah until the fall of Jerusalem. As best can be determined, the dates reflect the official reign of each king and not any years of his co-regency with another king. The center column is divided into increments of twenty years; the outside columns give the passages in 1 and 2 Kings and 2 Chronicles where the reign of each king is described. By using this chart, you can see at a glance both the length of each reign and the kings in Israel and Judah who were contemporaries. The final column depicts when the major prophets lived and ministered.

PASSAGES	KINGS OF ISRAEL	DATE B.C	KINGS OF JUDAH	PASSAGES		PROPHETS
I Kings				I Kings	2 Chron.	
12:25 –14:20	JEROBOAM I	930	REHOBOAM	12:1-24; 14:21-31	10:1 –12:16	
			ABIJAH	15:1-8	13:1-14:1	
15:25-31	NADAB	910	ASA	15:9-24	14:2 –16:14	
15:32 –16:7	BAASHA					
		890				
16:8-14	ELAH					
16:15-22	ZIMRI, TIBNI/OMRI					
16:23-28	OMRI					
16:29 –22:40	AHAB					Elijah
		870	JEHOSHAPHAT	22:41-50	17:1–21:3	
2 Kings						
1:1-18	AHAZIAH					
3:1–8:15	JORAM	850				Elisha

KINGS OF ISRAEL AND JUDAH

PASSAGES 2 Kings	KINGS OF ISRAEL	DATE B.C	KINGS OF JUDAH	PASSAGES		PROPHETS
				2 Kings	2 Chron.	Elisha (cont.)
		850	JEHORAM	8:16-24	21:4-20	
9:30 –10:36	JEHU		AHAZIAH	8:25-29	22:1-9	
			ATHALIAH	11:1-21	22:10 –23:21	
			JOASH	12:1-21	24:1-27	
		830				
13:1-9	JEHOAHAZ	810				
13:10-25	JEHOASH		AMAZIAH	14:1-22	25:1-28	
		790				
14:23-29	JEROBOAM II					Jonah
			AZARIAH (UZZIAH)	15:1-7	26:1-23	
		770				Amos
						Hosea
15:8-15	ZECHARIAH, SHALLUM					
15:16-22	MENAHEM	750				

KINGS OF ISRAEL AND JUDAH

PASSAGES 2 Kings	KINGS OF ISRAEL	DATE B.C	KINGS OF JUDAH	PASSAGES 2 Kings	2 Chron.	PROPHETS
		750				Hosea (cont.)
15:23-26	PEKAHIAH					
15:27-31	PEKAH		JOTHAM	15:32-38	27:1-8	Isaiah Micah
17:1-6	HOSHEA	730	AHAZ	16:1-20	28:1-27	
	FALL OF SAMARIA	722				
			HEZEKIAH	18:1 −20:21	29:1 −32:33	
		710				
		690				
			MANASSEH	21:1-18	33:1-20	
		670				
		650				

KINGS OF ISRAEL AND JUDAH

PASSAGES	KINGS OF ISRAEL	DATE B.C	KINGS OF JUDAH	PASSAGES		PROPHETS
				2 Kings	2 Chron.	
		650				
			AMON	21:19-26	33:21-25	Zephaniah
			JOSIAH	22:1 −23:30	34:1 −35:27	Nahum
		630				Jeremiah
		610	JEHOAHAZ	23:31-33	36:1-4	Habakkuk
			JEHOIAKIM	23:36 −24:7	36:5-8	Daniel
			JEHOIACHIN	24:8-17	36:9-10	Ezekiel
			ZEDEKIAH	24:18 −25:21	36:11-21	
		590				
		586	FALL OF JERUSALEM	25:8-17	36:15-19	
		570				
		550				

Part Four

LIFE
IN THE
LAND

chapter eleven

PRAISE AND PETITION
(The Psalms)
Worship the King

As I write this, the United States celebrates the twenty-fifth anniversary of the Apollo 11 moon landing. In the words of Neil Armstrong, stepping onto the lunar surface was "One small step for man, one giant leap for mankind." Yes, the occasion was marked by poetry! Poetry is the medium for our greatest moments. If it's worth talking about, if it's worth writing about, if it's momentous or romantic, then there's a good chance it will end up in poetry. Three thousand years ago, another writer expressed himself in poetry about space:

> The heavens declare the glory of God;
> > the skies proclaim the work of his hands (Ps. 19:1).

Like moderns, the psalmist also was awestruck by the view of the heavens:

> When I consider your heavens,
> > the work of your fingers,
> the moon and the stars,
> > which you have set in place,
> what is man that you are mindful of him,
> > the son of man that you care for him? (Ps. 8:3–4).

The vast spectrum of the heavens makes us feel insignificant—always has. But, even more amazing: the Creator of it all has concern for mankind. Humans have value, not because the earth is the center of the universe; not because our planet predominates space; but because the Creator cares for us. It was the Creator who provided this habitable space in all the vastness of the universe for us—the same Creator who is responsible for space and galaxies!

Such thoughts and such poetry are the stuff of the Psalter . . . and more! The Psalms express the praise, petition, struggles, emotion, celebration, worship, and the wisdom of Israel in relation to her Creator and Redeemer. Many of these struggles, feelings, and thoughts are the same as we experience. Our technology may have advanced, but the longings of our hearts and our humanity is no different. And, best of all, we can still relate to our Creator and Redeemer in many of the same ways. No wonder, of all the books of the Bible, people still turn to the Psalms to find encouragement, express their fears and anxieties, and find faith for today.

FEATURES OF THE PSALMS

Before the astronauts could experience the exhilaration of a moon walk, there was a lot of technical work to be accomplished. In much the same way a better understanding of how psalms work will help us to appreciate them better, read them more accurately, and find them even more profitable in our lives.

The Title and Titles

Our English Bibles title the book, "Psalms" and contain 150 psalms.[1] The words *Psalms* and *Psalter* come from the Greek Septuagint (hereafter abbreviated LXX) and mean "a song accompanied by stringed instruments." The traditional Hebrew title (*tehellim*), however, means "Praises." Though all psalms are not praise psalms—many are prayers—virtually every psalm contains an element of praise.

Individual psalms also have titles that appear as superscriptions (often in italics or smaller print in English translations though the Hebrew Bible treats them as part of the text). These often contain an ascription of authorship (e.g., "of David") as well as a term that classifies the type of song it is: a *mizmor* (song with stringed instruments), *miktam* (proverb, parable), *shur* (song), and so forth. The precise meanings of many of these ancient terms are not at all clear to us today. Some are musical terms and instruments (e.g., flute, gittith, and so forth). There are also fourteen historical notes in the superscriptions relating those psalms to David's experiences (e.g., "When he fled from his son Absalom," Ps. 3).

The Layout

Think of the Psalms as you would think of a hymnbook and you will quickly catch on to a number of factors about the shape of the book of Psalms. First of all, the hymns in your hymnbook do not all come from the time that the hymnbook is published. Many date from several hundred years before. Our English hymnbooks include such hymns as "Jesus, Thou Joy of Loving Hearts" by Bernard of Clairvaux, "And Can It Be" by Charles Wesley, and multiple hymns by Isaac Watts. The first comes from the twelfth century and the latter two from the eighteenth. Just so, the Psalms begin as personal experience and response to God. Later these became shared expressions of worship in the hymnbook of ancient Israel.[2]

The oldest psalm in the psalter may be Psalm 90, which is ascribed to Moses. A song as old is found in the book of Exodus where the "Song of the Sea" is a worship celebration for Yahweh's deliverance (Ex. 15). The latest psalms come from the Babylonian exile and beyond (e.g., Pss. 137; 102:16–22). The bulk of the psalms, however, are credited to David (73 psalms). And, many that have no indication of authorship may belong to David as well (for instance, Pss. 2 and 95; cf. Acts 4:25–26; Heb. 4:7–8).[3] No wonder David is called "the sweet psalmist of Israel" (2 Sam. 23:1). His songs are found in the narrative of Samuel (2 Sam. 1:17–27; 3:33–34; 23:2–7). And, his original reputation was in music, not warfare (1 Sam. 16:15–23)! His joy, apparently, was worship (Ps. 27:4–6). He organized temple singers and musicians (1 Chron. 6:31–32; 15:16, 27; 25:1–31; 2 Chron. 29:25–26). For these and other authors, check the chart of authors and books (figure 11.1).

Figure 11.1
Authors and Psalms

Author	List of Psalms	Total
David	3–9, 11–32, 34–41, 51–65, 68–70, 86, 101, 103, 108–110, 122–123, 131, 133, 138–145	73
Solomon	72, 127	2
Asaph	50, 73–83	12
Sons of Korah	42, 44–49, 84–85, 87–88	11
Moses	90	1
Heman	88	1
Ethan	89	1
Anonymous	1–2, 10, 33, 43, 66–67, 71, 91–100, 102, 104–107, 111–121, 124–126, 128–130, 132, 134–137, 146–150	50

Actually, we should think of the Psalms not as one hymnbook but as five books or scrolls of collected prayers and praises by different authors. You will see these divisions indicated in your Bible before Psalms 1, 42, 73, 90, and 107. Each book ends with a verse or two of doxology, and the final book ends with a full psalm of doxology ("Praise the Lord!"). In fact, the last five psalms are all doxologies—perhaps to finish off all five books appropriately! Psalms 1 and 2 form an introduction to the whole Psalter. Psalm 1 clarifies the appropriate life of the righteous who comes to worship Yahweh—those who meditate constantly on the Law of Yahweh. This ties the worship of Israel to the Mosaic Covenant of God's instruction. Worship involves living the life, not just ritual or emotion! Psalm 2 ties the Psalter into the Davidic Covenant. Worship looks to God's ultimate rule and blessing for the world through his king on Zion.

It is difficult to discover an overall plan for the five-book division. Some suggest that it was intended to match the five books of the Pentateuch. If so, the match is only formal—the psalms in each book do not reflect the theme for each parallel book of the Pentateuch. More likely, the books reflect times of completing collection or filling a scroll. The Davidic psalms are the latest in Books I and IV. Book V clearly contains some psalms written after the Exile and so were not fully complete until the time of the second temple (515 B.C. and later). Like the proverbs that were collected at different times, collecting the psalms took place during several stages, most likely in the reigns of David, Solomon, Jehoshaphat, Hezekiah, and after the Exile. Evidence of earlier smaller collections is still found in the larger "Books"—such as the note at the end of Book II: "the prayers of David son of Jesse" (72:20) and the "Songs of Ascent" (120–134) in Book IV.[4]

The Poetry of the Psalms

As we have noted, the Psalms are poetry. They are often included in what have been called the "books of Poetry": Psalms, Proverbs, Ecclesiastes, Song of Songs, Ruth, Esther, and Lamentations. A look through any modern translation of the Old Testament, however, will reveal vast sections of poetry in the prophetic books as well. Our remarks then about poetry in the Psalms apply to Hebrew poetry in general.

Because of the nature of Hebrew poetry, modern readers often misinterpret the psalms. For instance, take Psalm 23:1–3a:

> The LORD is my shepherd, I shall not be in want.
>> He makes me lie down in green pastures,
> he leads me beside quiet waters,
>> he restores my soul.

Some try to make each element of this verse something distinct. Lying down in green pastures is taken to mean something quite different and contrasted with the experience of being led "beside quiet waters" and having a restored "soul." Rather, what we have here is one of the most important features of Hebrew poetry: *Parallelism.* The poet repeats his basic idea in different words. So then, the basic idea is that the LORD, like a shepherd, takes care of David's needs. His needs will be met. This idea is repeated in the metaphors appropriate to the notion of care for a sheep: green pastures, quiet waters, a restored "soul." To try to make much out of the differences between pastures and waters would be to distract from the real point. These are just different modes of being physically cared for—all the needs of the sheep. And, "restored soul!" (as the word "soul" in Hebrew is often used) looks at the physical life. Just as the life of the sheep is restored through provision, so the life of the psalmist is cared for by the Shepherd.

Parallelism, even the *synonymous parallelism* we have seen, is not simply straight repetition—spare us the boredom of repeating everything twice! The second (and often a third) line in the verse, though not changing the idea, adds color and substance to the first:

> Blessed is the man
>> who does not walk in the counsel of the wicked
>> or stand in the way of sinners
>> or sit in the seat of mockers (1:1).

Again, much should not be made of the differences between sitting, walking, and standing. Together they include everyplace that we could decide to be. "Wicked," "sinners," and "mockers" also make up one crowd—not three, but the various words give dimension and depth to the total picture.

Other types of parallelism include *antithetical parallelism,* which achieves the total picture by stating the contrasting side of the truth.

> For the LORD watches over the way of the righteous,
> but the way of the wicked will perish (1:6).

Parallelism can involve the full previous line or only one part of the previous line. Another variation that adds interest is to change the order in the second line:

> But his delight is in the law of the LORD,
> and on his law he meditates day and night (1:3).

Notice the reverse ordering. The law of Yahweh is the last element in the first line but comes first ("his law") in the second. The "delight" of the first line is matched in the second line by the last element: the fact that he meditates on it day and night. It is his delight! This mirror-imaging reversal of order is called *chiasm.*

Emblematic parallelism is a more specific form of synonymous parallelism which notes that one line may speak literally and the next give an emblem or symbol. Psalm 23:1 not only involves synonymous parallelism, but more specifically, it is *emblematic parallelism*. The lines following "I shall not want" use emblems or metaphors (green pastures, still waters) to repeat and picture the literal idea of the first line. This would be true as well for the well-known beginning of Psalm 42:

> As the deer pants for streams of water,
> so my soul pants for you, O God.

Here the emblematic line is the first, and the literal synonymous line (though the verb "pants" is retained) is the second.

Often the two lines do not have any repetitions of thought or idea:

> I have installed my King
> on Zion, my holy hill (2:6).

When the lines are only parallel in form—really just continuing the sentence, as above—it is called *formal parallelism*.

Recognizing these varieties of parallelism will help any reader understand and enjoy the psalms even more. I highly recommend that you practice immediately. Many of the above examples have been taken from the first two psalms. Read through these psalms in a modern translation and identify the parallelism in each verse. Do not be discouraged if you cannot identify the specific type of parallelism for every verse. Some lines defy categories due to the creativity of the writer. The exercise will raise your awareness and enjoyment of each psalm.

In addition to parallelism as a feature of the psalms, there is also *rhythm*. Ancient Hebrew poetry does not have specific meter or "feet." Aren't you thankful that you won't have to count them? So far, the rhythm pattern of the Psalms has defied analysis, but it is there! It can be sensed in reading. It is mostly a balanced line, but because it is not exacting, the writer again has room for more creativity. These two features (parallelism and rhythm) are the dominant elements of Hebrew poetry. Thank God that both of them come across well in translation. It's almost providential! If rhyme were the dominant feature, translators would have headaches, and the result would never closely match the original. Lesser features of Hebrew poetry like assonance, alliteration, and wordplay do tend to get lost, but these are less important to meaning. We leave these for the commentators to point out to us. There is always employment for good commentators!

As poetry, the Psalms include a good deal of imagery, metaphor, simile, and other figures of speech, including hyperbole. A few psalms (25, 34, 37, 111, 112, 119, 145) are acrostic (alphabetical). Some translations will indicate this by putting the Hebrew letter in the margin. You might turn in your English Bible to Psalm 119, which is usually marked with a Hebrew letter at the head of every eight verses, each of which begins with that letter.

Types of Psalms

Perhaps only geologists could get really excited about the barren lunar landscape, but centuries of saints have mined the landscape of the Psalms. For geologists, familiarity with types of rocks helps to observe and understand new landscapes. For Psalms it is helpful to recognize different types of psalms. Some of these types reflect settings, others content, and still others involve the order and pattern of a psalm.

Penitential psalms—Those psalms in which the psalmist confesses sin and seeks to be restored to divine favor (Pss. 6, 32, 51, 102, 130, 143).

Hallel psalms—"Praise the Lord" is an essential feature of this set of psalms (Pss. 113–118).

Songs of ascent—This group of psalms, so labeled in the superscription, seem to have been written for the occasion of "going up" (ascent) to Jerusalem at one or more of the yearly festivals (120–34). Psalm 121 takes a feature of Jerusalem ("I lift up my eyes to the hills") as a reminder that it is Yahweh who "watches over Israel" and is their help. Psalm 122 progresses from the joy of being asked to journey up to the temple, to the arrival at Jerusalem's gates (v. 2), to the admiration of Jerusalem as the place of the temple and of Davidic justice (vv. 3–5). Prayer for Jerusalem's peace is then urged because it is so important to worship (vv. 7–9). Psalm 125 draws still another lesson from Mt. Zion (cf. 125:3).

Wisdom psalms—these psalms are contemplative about life and involve some of the same elements as we will see in the book of Proverbs: two ways; the fear of the Lord; blessing; righteous versus wicked (Pss. 1, 37, 49, 73, 111–112, 127, 128). Psalm 1 is a prime example of wisdom as it looks at the type of life for the saint in the Psalms. First comes what to avoid: the counsel and comradeship of the wicked (vv. 1–3), which is contrasted antithetically to the positive approach: delight and meditation in the Law of Yahweh. Imagery follows: a healthy, fruitful life (tree, v. 3) reinforces the point of blessedness. The back half of the psalm (vv. 4–6) contrasts the wicked with the blessed person. It starts with imagery: the wicked are like chaff which lacks stability and disappears. This is stated literally in verse 5 (mirroring v. 2) as not having a place in the righteous assembly. The final summary (v. 6) enforces the contrast of the psalm with antithetical parallelism:

> For the LORD watches over the way of the righteous,
> but the way of the wicked will perish.

This beautifully designed yet simple wisdom psalm sets the tone for the whole psalter, suggesting the main issue for the one who wishes to worship Yahweh.

Unlike Psalm 1, Psalm 73 as a wisdom psalm raises a problem that Psalm 1 in its simplicity did not tackle: the success of the wicked. The freedom from concerns and the lavish prosperity of an unscrupulous neighbor almost caused our psalmist (Asaph) to stumble. Living a righteous life without cutting corners did not seem to be getting him anywhere (v. 2–14). He is glad, however, that he did not express his doubts about God's goodness in words and stumble others (v. 15). His time of doubt was temporary. It was cured by a visit to the temple where he had a vision of the final end of the wicked (vv. 16–17). He realizes that the wicked are like a bad dream—a nightmare that seems so real, but then is gone (v. 20)! Asaph regrets his bitterness about outward circumstances, because it reduced him to life as an animal—only looking at present feeding and instincts (vv. 21–22)! There is so much more to life in relationship to God (vv. 23–28). God will guide him with his counsel into glory—even after his heart and flesh fail! Now he is satisfied in being near God in worship and trusting God as his refuge (v. 28). This brings us full circle to the theme of the first verse—a theme Asaph was able to affirm only after his experience: "Surely God is good to Israel, to those who are pure in heart."

Messianic psalms—those which anticipate the ideal anointed King. *Messiah* means "anointed" in Hebrew. Thus, the "anointed" in Psalm 2 is the king on Zion (2:2, 6) who repeats Yahweh's decree—a decree that gives him the right to rule as the Son on the day of his ascension to the Davidic throne (2:7, cf. the similar language of the Davidic Covenant in 2 Sam. 7:14). The nations who rebel will be defeated (2:8–9). Wisdom suggests they should submit to the rule of Yahweh and his king (2:10–12).

Only one or two psalms speak exclusively of the final Davidic king (110 and possibly 2). Others speak of the Davidic promise generally (Ps. 89) or David's experiences as king (Ps. 22) which the final king might also experience. Most psalms are labelled "Messianic" by looking backward from the New Testament as it quotes events that reoccurred for Jesus. The fulfillment of these psalms will be treated further in the next section.

Imprecatory psalms—these psalms or parts of psalms call upon God to judge the enemies (35:4–8; 58:6–9; 69:22–28; 109:6–20; 137; 140:9–11). Many have trouble accepting that these psalms are in Scripture at all, and a close reading demonstrates why. It is hard to imagine a saint praying for teeth to be kicked in or for children to be dashed against a rock (Ps. 137:8–9). However, a few qualifying observations are appropriate:

1. We must dismiss objections that come from a presupposition that judgment is never appropriate. The vengeance of God (justice) is

not just an Old Testament concept. It is also found in the New Testament (Rom. 13:1–3).

2. To read these psalms as personal vengeance is erroneous. Personal vengeance is condemned in the Old Testament, just as it is in the New. In fact, its condemnation in Romans 12:17–21 is made up of several Old Testament quotations (Prov. 3:4 LXX; Lev. 19:18; Deut. 32:35; Prov. 25:21–22). Calling for God to bring just punishment is not personal vengeance but is turning all vengeance over to the Lord.

3. Normally, the king is the speaker and the vengeance desired is a call for justice on the enemies who have attacked the king and nation. The call is for victory in a just war, not for personal vengeance.

4. The expressions that offend us are typically either metaphorical (the teeth is in the mouths of lions, 58:6) or simply reflects the realities of ancient warfare. Our modern societies, even with television that shows us otherwise, want to pretend that the choice of warfare does not involve horrors, gross mutilation, and death. Jesus' description of the fall of Jerusalem (Luke 19:44) is typical of ancient warfare and resembles the awful prayer for equal justice in Psalm 137:9—a prayer that does not advocate what is described but does call for their oppressors to experience the warfare they so enjoyed. Warfare was often less severe than ours.

5. In the present age, the Christian church is called upon to be suffering servants and dispensers of Christ's compassion and grace during this time of God's patience, though still recognizing the legitimacy of governmental vengeance (justice) on evildoers for society's good.

6. There will come a day when final justice will be rendered, and it will not be pretty (Rev. 18:8; 19:17–21; cf. Zech. 14:12). The imprecatory psalms, then, are not appropriate prayers of New Testament believers, except as we cry for God to bring to a conclusion the present age (cf. Rev. 6:9–10).[5]

Lament or complaint psalms—such psalms find the writer, usually the king, in a jam. Pinned down by his enemies, and with defeat seeming imminent, he is crying to God for help. This prayer may rival the foxhole prayer, except that the petitioner has not necessarily been neglectful of God in the past. Such prayers often contain many or all of the following elements:[6]

1. A call to God for help. A very direct cry often including a short summary of his problem and request.
2. The difficulty expressed (lament). The psalmist expresses not only his difficulty but his feelings, fears, anxieties, and frustration. He is very open and direct with God.
3. Confession of trust in God. In spite of the difficulties and frustrations expressed, the psalmist is counting on God for deliverance and expresses that confidence and trust.
4. The petition for deliverance.
5. A vow of praise or statement of praise. This is the praise that the petitioner anticipates he will give to the congregation when he praises God for his deliverance.

A look at Psalm 3 shows how recognizing these elements can help in reading a psalm. First comes the cry for help (vv. 1–2). A short summary of the problem is included: Enemies have arisen who conclude that God has given up on David and will not deliver him. The confession of trust comes in verse 3. It contrasts with the situation. David believes Yahweh protects him and gives him victory. With this confidence he is able to put down any fears and sleep well. The petition for deliverance from the opposing army begins in verse 7. Verse 8 is the statement of praise that he gives as an anticipation of what he will be able to proclaim to the congregation in praise of God.

In addition, the following psalms are examples of the lament psalm (4–7, 12, 13, 22, 26, 28, 54–57, 88). Some might be surprised to learn the Psalm 22 is a lament with the usual categories (some elements are repeated twice)—including the call for help (22:1—"My God, my God, why have you forsaken me?") that Jesus cried out as he was crucified (Matt. 27:46). Does this then mean that God had actually forsaken Jesus? Or was it, as in the original psalm, the beginning of a prayer for deliverance and rescue that would be answered? In that case, perhaps we should read the end of the psalm to see how it would turn out (cf. 22:22 ff.)!

Declarative praise or thanksgiving psalms—if the lament psalm promised praise to God for deliverance, we should expect psalms that carry out that promise. These are the declarative praise or thanksgiving psalms. They spell out the deliverance God brought and give full credit and praise to God for answering the prayer. The short praise at the end of the lament psalm is hardly enough! It was just a summary or vow ("I will praise . . ."). The real thing has several elements:

1. A call to praise ("I will praise Yahweh because . . .").
2. A short summary of the praise, similar to what would have been found at the end of the lament.

3. A review of God's deliverance from the problem. Often threefold: ("I cried . . . He heard . . . He delivered me.").

4. The praise declared. The praise for the specific deliverance is expressed.

5. Praise to God for his qualities. The deliverance brings praise to God for what he is always like, not just this deliverance.

6. Instruction. The opportunity is sometimes taken to instruct the congregation in principles that were learned from this experience.

Again, remember that this is not a straitjacket. The writer could create variation by combining categories, leaving out others, or repeating some. Examples include Psalms 18, 30, 32, 34, 107, 116, 138. Follow along now in Psalm 34 as we check the pattern.

Psalm 34 begins with a superscription that takes us back to David's behavior when he acted like he was crazy, slobbering on his beard, before Achish (cf. 1 Sam. 21:10–15). As one who sports a beard (very biblical), I can agree that anyone who will slobber on his beard is surely crazy! It seems that David had been praying during his slobbering. Now he gives praise for his deliverance from this tricky situation. All the credit goes, not to the acting job, but to Yahweh. (1) Verses 1–3 mark the call to praise. Notice the "I wills." The mention of the "humble" in the call gives a clue about the theme. (2) The review of God's deliverance comes next. Notice the threefold: "I sought . . . He answered . . . He delivered." In this psalm David alternates report (vv. 4, 6) with the principle learned (vv. 5, 7): God protects and delivers. (3) The next section could be viewed as praise to God for what he is always like: He is good—a protector and provider (vv. 8–10). Or, it might be the start of instruction ("Taste and see . . ."). (4) But instruction begins in full force in v. 11: "Come, my children, listen to me; I will teach you the fear of the LORD. . . ." The instruction argues for control of the mouth, avoiding evil, and pursuing peace. These qualities set you up for deliverance by God. Even though a righteous person may endure many afflictions, ultimate and complete deliverance is the kind Yahweh works, not the judgment that awaits the wicked.

The example of the Old Testament about praise is clear. When prayer was answered, Yahweh must receive the glory. Private thanks to God was not enough. It must be told. Yahweh is to be magnified by the praises of his people. His name is glorified through testimony about his deeds for his people.

The hymn or descriptive praise psalm—a second type of praise psalm also occurs. Praising God for what he is like and always does is something we have seen as a small part of the descriptive praise psalm. It is not surprising that whole psalms are devoted to direct praise of God's person. The categories here, as we might expect, are broader and more open to variety.

1. A call to praise. Like declarative praise, a call to praise begins, often with a hint the nature of the praise.
2. The cause for praise. This often takes the form of a summary of the reasons to praise Yahweh, followed by examples that support the reasons. Often the dual aspects of God's greatness and grace are represented both in the summary and the examples.
3. Conclusion. Often the psalm concludes with a renewed call to praise, but it can end in prayer or an exhortation.

For examples of this type of psalm see Psalms 103, 113, 117, 135, 146, 147.

THEOLOGY OF THE PSALMS

Out of twenty-four lunar walkers, only a few claim to have a changed approach to life because of the experience. Yet, innumerable saints and sinners through centuries of time have been uplifted, consoled, inspired, and radically changed by reading and meditating on the Psalms. Much of this is due to the depth of human emotion and travail that these psalms contain—fears, hopes, frustrations, and joys—all vividly expressed. This human frustration with pain, suffering, injustice, and opposition resonates with our own deepest experiences. But such experiences can be interpreted a number of ways. The Psalms do not merely plumb human experience; they reflect a certain perspective and worldview as well. What outlook do the Psalms affirm?

Life Is Conducted in Relation to the Creator, Who Is Also King

As moderns, the notions of "creator" and "king" do not carry with them the full significance that they have in the Old Testament. We think of a creator, if we accept the notion at all, as the originator—nothing more. To modern man of Western civilization, there is no necessary connection between creation and current rule or authority. The Creator has little to do with life today. And, as far as kingship goes, where it still exists it has been relegated to a purely titular and ceremonial function. Further, kingship is out-of-date. We now vote on our leaders and we will vote for our own Creator as well. Anyone may vote for him as their king if they wish, but for moderns he lacks any divine right to rule. It follows that these central concepts of the Psalms are hard to grasp and are often reduced in significance by the modern reader. But, time may prove that the ancient model of kingship is a better model for God's relation to the creation—past, present, and future—than prime minister, president, or supreme court justice.

The God of the Psalms is the Creator, and that means he is in total control. Not only is this the focus for psalms that center on creation itself (e.g., Pss. 8, 19), but it pervades the prayers and praise of the Psalms. Yahweh is the Creator, and as Creator is the King over creation and all nations (9:7; 10:16; 47:1–9; 93:1–2). This King is enthroned in the heavens, even while his king reigns on Mount Zion in Jerusalem (2:4, 7; 33:13, 14). As King, Yahweh rules and judges from on high (5:7, 8). He actively governs world events (33:6–17) and from his lofty perspective the Creator-King examines both the motives and thinking of men (5:8; 11:4). Not only is he the Creator of the world, he is the Creator of Israel and Regent of the nation (95:3–7). So it is not strange to find a psalm that begins with the heavens declaring God's glory as the sun makes its circuit, and finishes with the perfection of the Law that the Creator gave to instruct Israel in his ways (Ps. 19).

God Is Also the Redeemer

It follows that as the Creator has created and entered into covenant with Israel, as King and God, he declares victories for Jacob. He is frequently pictured as a Rock, Fortress, and Deliverer (18:1–2; 62:1–2, 6). Here *rock* is not a building metaphor. The best place to hide or defend was to find refuge in the rocks that could serve as a natural fortress against attack. Yet the classic deliverance is the deliverance of Israel through the sea on dry ground (66:3–7; 74:12–13). This event is not merely an ancient incident but the assurance of God's commitment to his people and the measure of what God could do now. The psalmist expects the King to deliver, to support the poor and the needy, and to correct injusice by judging the wicked (140:11–12). Moreover, it is Yahweh

> who forgives all your sins
>> and heals all your diseases,
> who redeems your life from the pit
>> and crowns you with love and compassion,
> who satisfies your desires with good things
>> so that your youth is renewed like the eagle's (103:3–5).

Yet, the Psalms show that deliverance is often slow. God seems to put off deliverance until things have gone so far—farther than seems fair to the praying saint who counts on his God, but sees little result (cf. Ps. 10:1; 22:1; 28:1). Farther even than seems good for God's own reputation among the nations as other peoples wonder: "Where is their God?" (79:9–10).

The Presence of God

Deliverance, however, speaks of Presence—as in the book of Exodus where the theme of Yahweh's Presence dominates the deliverance from Pharaoh and Egypt. The book of Exodus ended with the tabernacle, the place of Yahweh's dwelling among his people. Just so, the Psalms celebrate the miracle of Yahweh's Presence with the nation. Though Yahweh is enthroned above the heavens, he is also enthroned and dwells in Jerusalem (Pss. 9:11; 74:2; 99:1). The pilgrims who go up to Jerusalem long for the place of Yahweh's Presence (84:2, 7). The one who has been driven away from the temple pants for God like the deer for fresh water. He is downcast because he cannot join the procession to go and meet with God (42:1–5). The City of God is just that because of "the holy place where the Most High dwells" (46:4, 5). For the same reason, Zion is a "holy hill" (15:1). Here the power and glory of God may be seen in the sanctuary (63:2). This is not an ecstatic, mystical, or magical experience. Rather, it was a real encounter with the Presence of Yahweh, much as the glory of Yahweh originally filled the tabernacle (Ex. 40:34–35). No wonder there was such excitement and joy at anticipating the opportunity to go up to Jerusalem (Ps. 122:1). Such demonstration of the Glory or Presence was lost at the time of the Babylonian exile, and those who built the second temple after the return from exile looked forward to a return of this Presence with hope—a return anticipated when Messiah should come.[7]

The Life of Faith

The frustration that God is often slow in delivering his people is a frustration that many people experience in the difficulties of life. Such trials cannot be soothed by the truism that it will all work out in the end. Such existential struggles involve the exercise of faith in a crucible where things don't always go smoothly even with a strong and loving God (Pss. 13:1–2; 62:12). Of course, the wisdom books of Job and Ecclesiastes give perspective on this problem and the wisdom psalms also teach a life of faith and fear of Yahweh. But the lament psalms provide us with a model of practical trust—to express confidence in God even when life seems to have caved in and God seems not to hear our prayers. The lament psalms allow full expression of distress alongside a confession of continued trust in Yahweh. They affirm frustration, real pain, and deep disappointment in life without associating such honest turmoil with a lack of faith—no plastic "supersaint" model here! The believer has the opportunity to believe God "in the dark," not just in the bright times, and to promise him praise when the answer does come. God is God and he will answer in his time and way—and, perhaps not the answer for which we prayed! But we are human, and as God's creatures he does not chasten us for voicing our real complaint (to be distinguished from complaining!) or expressing openly *to him* our deep pain and struggle. The King will hear our complaints. And, one way or another, our faith in him will be vindicated.

The Covenants

The Covenants of Israel form the backdrop for the interaction of the Psalms. The Abrahamic Covenant is the basis for the choice of this nation and their creation as a people (Pss. 105 and 106). The Mosaic Covenant is the Law in which the psalmist delights and which the king will uphold (101). But the strongest connection of the Psalms is with the Davidic Covenant. Most psalms reflect the experience of the Davidic king. It was he who was chosen to act for God. It was he who, having been promised victory, wrestled with the frustration of enemies who seemed to have the upper hand. If he sinned in his function as king, he could expect defeat (cf. 2 Sam. 7:14–16; Ps. 51), and so often there is a statement of innocence and a call for justice against the oppressors (17:1–5; 59:3–5; 35:22–27). The king acted for the nation, and so Psalms at times shift between "I" and "we" as praise for deliverance is given. Following the Exile, when no Davidic king sat on the throne, the psalms of David became more than historic remembrances of a more glorious past. They became expressions of hope for the future as Israel looked for the promised ideal Davidic king from Yahweh.[8]

THE FULFILLMENT OF THE PSALMS

The New Testament quotes the Psalms directly at least ninety-six times with perhaps two hundred more clear allusions.[9] Many of these are events of the Psalms that happen to Jesus. Yet, how embarrassing! When we look back at the Old Testament these are not direct predictions about Jesus but experiences of David and Israel. What are we to say? Didn't the New Testament writers know that these events happened hundreds of years before Jesus appeared on the scene? Of course they did. So what are they telling us when they report these events as Jesus' experience?

Just imagine yourself a disciple of Jesus and a Jew familiar with worship from the Psalms. You walk with him down those dusty roads and listen to him teach, see him heal, watch him provide for the humble of the land. And then, you see something happen that happened to David. And, then another . . . and another. Is Jesus intentionally doing things that David did? But many of the things that happen—especially while hanging on a Roman cross—could not possibly be prearranged or self-fulfilled by his own design. The question on the minds of many people as Jesus fulfilled his mission was: Who is this?

"Who is this? He commands even the wind and the water, and they obey him" (Luke 8:25).

The whole city was stirred and asked, "Who is this?" (Matt 21:10).

"Who is this fellow that speaks blasphemy?" (Luke 5:21).

"Who is this who even forgives sins?" (Luke 7:49).

"Who then is this I hear such things about?" (Luke 9:9).

How better could God give the answer than to repeat events from the life of David? The picture of who Jesus is begins to be clear as the final duplicate events complete the puzzle. In fact, at times David used hyperbole to describe his experience—he probably was not literally pierced or pinned down by his enemies (Ps. 22:16–17). Yet for Jesus, these things are experienced literally.[10] If Jesus is the ideal Davidic king, what clearer clues could be given than a pattern of repeated events? You say, how about a voice from heaven? Well, of course, that happens too (Matt. 3:18)! Jesus' identity is not left as a vague guess for those faithful Israelites who know their hymnal! The intuitive powers of a Sherlock Holmes are not required.

But there is one psalm in which David does not speak of his experiences but speaks of another king whom he calls "Lord."

> Of David. A psalm.
> The LORD says to my Lord:
> "Sit at my right hand
> until I make your enemies
> a footstool for your feet" (Ps. 110:1).

Here the speaker looks at the subjugation of the enemies of the Davidic king (110:1–3), yet the king is not David himself because David is the speaker ("my" in the first line). In addition, the psalm sees the king also conferred with priesthood. This priesthood is not that of the Aaronic line but an ancient line that preceded that of Aaron—the priesthood of that pre-Israelite king of Salem, Melchizedek (110:4; cf. Gen. 14:18–20). The psalm ends with worldwide victory of the doubly anointed king-priest (110:5–7).

It is this psalm that Jesus used to probe the thinking of the religious leaders:

> Jesus asked them, "What do you think about the Christ? Whose son is he?"
> "The son of David," they replied.

He said to them, "How is it then that David, speaking by the Spirit, calls him 'Lord' . . . ? If then David calls him 'Lord,' how can he be his son?"

The answer must be that the ideal son of David, the Christ or Messiah, is greater than David—the King to whom David himself would ultimately bow.

This psalm provides the kernel prophecy central to Jesus' whole mission as presented by the writer of the book of Hebrews. Jesus, as the Davidic King (Heb. 1:5 which connects 2 Sam. 7:14—the Davidic Covenant—with Ps. 2; and Heb. 1:13, which adds Ps. 110:1) and final Son is the representative of humanity who suffered death "so that by the grace of God he might taste death for everyone" (2:9). This Son is not only the representative King, but, like Aaron, was appointed by God as high priest so that he might deal with the sinfulness of humanity.

> *The One who said to him:*
> "You are my son,
> Today I have begotten you";
> *[conferring kingship]*
>
> *So he also says in another place:*
> "You are a priest forever
> according to the order of Melchizedek"
> *[conferring priesthood]* (Heb. 5:5–6, *my translation*).[11]

The first quote (Ps. 2:7) has identified him as king. The second (Ps. 110:4) adds the office of high priest. This priesthood of the Messiah differs from the Aaronic priesthood of the Law in that Jesus is a permanent priest, his sacrifice is final and does not need repetition, he lives on and so is able to intercede in the very presence of God for us (Heb. 7:11–28).

Just as David was a less than perfect model of the final King, so Aaron and the tabernacle were an incomplete model of the final Priest and sacrifice (Heb. 8:1–6; 10:1–14). At the present time, Psalm 110 says, Jesus is sitting at the right hand of Yahweh, awaiting the time when his enemies will be put under his feet (Heb. 8:1; 10:12). Then "he will appear a second time, not to bear sin, but to bring salvation to those who are waiting for him" (9:28).

Just as the writer of Hebrews recognizes Christ's priesthood and kingship introduced at Jesus' first advent as well as his present intercession as he waits in exalted position at the right hand of Yahweh, so he recognizes that the time when he will fully reign is yet to come "when his enemies will be put under his feet." Thus, "he will appear a second time, not to bear sin [accomplished the first time], but to bring salvation to those who are waiting for him" (9:28).

The book of Revelation pictures this future event (19:13–16):

He is dressed in a robe dipped in blood, and his name is the Word of God. The armies of heaven were following him, riding on white horses and dressed in fine linen, white and clean. Out of his mouth comes a sharp sword with which to strike down the nations. "He will rule them with an iron scepter" [Ps. 2:9]. . . . On his robe and on his thigh he has this name written: KING OF KINGS AND LORD OF LORDS.

The King has come. The King will come to earth.

SUGGESTED SCRIPTURE READING:

Psalms 1, 2, 3, 19, 22, 23, 24, 27, 34, 73, 110, 146

For Interaction and Discussion:

1. What are the features of Hebrew poetry? How does it help to be alert to these features?

2. How does thinking about the Psalms as five hymnbooks help to distinguish between the issue of each psalm's message and its collection? How important is it to us to know how the collection was made and ordered?

3. What important notions about giving praise to God can be learned from the Psalms?

4. What features are involved in prayer? Are there features that we cannot duplicate, or should we use these prayers as a pattern?

5. In what ways are imprecatory prayers a way to leave vengeance to God rather than taking personal revenge? Could one pray this type of prayer today? What attitudes might we develop if we did?

6. How could the historic prayers of David be relevant for people who come after David's time? For those after the Exile? For the New Testament? For believers today? How does David's kingship relate to the notion of Messiah and our work as his Church?

For Further Reading:

Ronald B. Allen. *And I Will Praise Him: A Guide to Personal Worship in the Psalms*. Nashville: Nelson, 1992. Most accessible and practical guide to types of psalms for the English reader.

C. Hassell Bullock. *An Introduction to the Old Testament Poetic Books*. Rev. ed. Chicago: Moody, 1988, 113–54. Helpful academic coverage of poetry, introductory matters, and issues for the English reader.

Derek Kidner. *Psalms 1–72*. TOTC. Downers Grove, Ill.: InterVarsity, 1973. Insightful on the meaning of the Hebrew text for the English reader.

Tremper Longman III. *How to Read the Psalms*. Downers Grove, Ill.: Inter-
  Varsity, 1988. A helpful literary introduction for the English reader.
Claus Westermann. *The Psalms: Structure, Content & Message*. Minneapolis:
  Augsburg, 1980. Readable treatment by one of the pioneer scholars of
  psalm types.
Bruce K. Waltke. "A Canonical Process Approach to the Psalms." *Tradition
  and Testament: Essays in Honor of Charles Lee Feinberg*. Eds. John S. and
  Paul D. Feinberg, Chicago: Moody, 1981, 14–16. Especially helpful in
  suggesting how historic psalms would be sung by later generations as
  hope for a future king.

Notes and Comments:

[1]The numbering of the Psalms differs in the Hebrew and Greek (LXX) Bibles
with the English following the Hebrew Masoretic Text. This can lead to some problems when using scholarly reference materials. In general, when the number of the
psalm is not the same, the Greek LXX is one lower than the Hebrew. Verse numbering can also be confusing. Because the Hebrew text counts any title as verse 1,
the verse numbers of psalms in the Hebrew text are one higher than the verse numbering in English and Greek Bibles in any psalm that has a title or superscription.

[2]Kidner corrects the frequent critical theory that sees the cultic setting as the original setting for the psalms, which only moved to life-experience later. The content of
the psalms themselves along with the titles suggest that the reverse was more often the
case: life-experience that then became incorporated into the worship of Israel. Derek
Kidner, *Psalms 1–72*, TOTC (Downers Grove, Ill.: InterVarsity, 1973), 17.

[3]This judgment about authorship takes the Hebrew preposition, *lamedth*, to
refer to authorship when connected with a personal name in the superscription
(e.g., "of David," cf. Ps. 4). Many scholars question two items: (1) Whether the
lamedth is a *lamedth* of authorship and (2) whether the titles belong with the
inspired text or were added at a significantly later date and have questionable historic value. The titles predate the LXX translation, and some of the terms used
were clearly archaic at the time of translation, as the translators had difficulty
understanding them. As to authorship, *lamedth* can mean other than authorship.
It is usually translated "for" in the expression "for the director of music" that
occurs alongside the designation "of David" in some psalms (e.g., Ps. 4). It is clear,
however, that the *lamedth* is the common way to designate authorship, especially
when attached to a personal name (cf. the extended title of Ps. 18). In addition,
the historic notes in many of these titles fit the understanding that authorship is
intended (Pss. 3, 7, 18, 34, 51, 52, 54, 56, 57, 59, 60, 63, 142). Of course, it can
be argued that these notes are later additions, but even if that were the case, they
affirm an understanding of the *lamedth* to mean authorship and predate the LXX
translation. For discussions of both sides of this issue cf. Willem A. VanGemeren,
"Psalms," *EBC*, 5:33–35; Peter C. Craigie, *Psalms 1–50*, WBC (Waco, Tex.: Word,
1983), 33–35; Derek Kidner, *Psalms 1–70*, 33–36.

[4]Cf. Payne, "Psalms," *ZPEB*, 4:929–932. Andrew E. Hill and John H. Walton, *A Survey of the Old Testament* (Grand Rapids: Zondervan, 1991), 278–81, have suggested a theory of editorship of the books of the psalter that follow a thematic-historical pattern as follows: Psalms 1–2—Introductory; Psalms 3–41—David's conflict with Saul; Book II—David's kingship; Book III—The Assyrian crisis; Book IV—Introspection, destruction of temple and exile; Book V to Ps. 145—Praise and reflection on the new era; Pss. 146–150—concluding praise. This arrangement seems to be important to them not simply for the history of compilation but also for understanding the theology of the psalms. Yet they also observe that the final two books may have assumed their current order near the first century B.C. If that is the case, does the order of the psalms have any real function in proclaiming the theology of the psalms, or are only the individual psalms themselves the locus for theology? Can the theology based on ordering that was not inspired be the focus of our concern? For a full academic discussion of views see Gerald H. Wilson, *The Editing of the Hebrew Psalter*, Society of Biblical Literature Dissertation Series, No. 76 (Atlanta: Scholars Press, 1985).

[5]For further reading on the imprecatory psalms see C. Hassell Bullock, *An Introduction to the Old Testament Poetic Books*, rev. ed. (Chicago: Moody, 1988), 139–41. Note especially his coverage of the New Testament usage of these psalms. Cf. Walter C. Kaiser, Jr., *Toward Old Testament Ethics* (Grand Rapids: Zondervan, 1991), 292–97.

[6]The Lament or Complaint Psalm as well as the following two types represent efforts to study the psalms' literary development. The present state of such studies and the treatment here owes much to Claus Westermann, *The Praise of God in the Psalms*, trans. Keith R. Crim (Richmond, Va.: John Knox, 1965). See also the more popularly written Claus Westermann, *The Psalms: Structure, Content & Message* (Minneapolis: Augsburg, 1980); and Ronald B. Allen, *And I Will Praise Him: A Guide to Personal Worship in the Psalms* (Nashville: Nelson, 1992).

[7]For much of the material of this paragraph I am indebted to Hans-Joachim Kraus's excellent and uplifting discussion of the presence of God, *Psalms 1–59*, trans. Hilton C. Oswald (Minneapolis: Augsburg, 1988), 68–72. Kraus does, however, promote the notion of a yearly reenactment or enthronement ceremony—a notion developed earlier by S. Mowinckel and others by reading the psalms in the light of Babylonian and Canaanite practice. To his credit, however, Kraus eliminates these foreign elements. He reconstructs by putting together bits and pieces of various psalms into a hypothetical ceremony and rejects any mythical or magical cultic practice. Cf. Kidner, *Psalms 1–72*, 9–15 for a review of the various theories and a thoughtful response. Kidner points out that Israel's approach was not reenactment, but remembrance. For example, the Passover, though celebrated yearly, never reenacted the central feature—the daubing of blood on the lintels and doorposts.

[8]Bruce K. Waltke, "A Canonical Process Approach to the Psalms," *Tradition and Testament: Essays in Honor of Charles Lee Feinberg*, ed. John S. and Paul D. Feinberg (Chicago: Moody, 1981), 14–16.

[9]Such a count of quotations of the Psalms in the New Testament, of course, varies, dependent on the extent of the quotation necessary to make a positive iden-

tification. My first figure is based on the texts included in Gleason L. Archer and G. C. Chirichigno, *Old Testament Quotations in the New Testament: A Complete Survey* (Chicago: Moody, 1983).

[10]Delitzsch's categories of fulfillment for messianic psalms reflect this kind of fulfillment and his treatment is still worth reading for the range of types of fulfillment. Cf. Franz Delitzsch, *Biblical Commentary on the Psalms*, 3 vols. (Grand Rapids: Eerdmans, 1952 [1867]), 1:64–71.

[11]The translation of Hebrews 5:5–6 is important for understanding the point of the writer of Hebrews. Mistakenly the author of Hebrews is read as if he thinks Psalm 2:7 conferred priesthood. The NIV fails to bring out the distinction the writer is making between the first and second quote. The result is that the reader of the NIV must conclude that Psalm 2 is cited as a text about the priesthood of Jesus—and Psalm 2 clearly does not refer to priesthood at all, only kingship! The NRSV and NASB translate 5:6 more literally ("just as . . . also") and so allow for distinguishing the second quote as progressing on to the new and added feature of priesthood—rather than both quotes supporting the same subject. With the first quote (Ps. 2:7) the writer is taking a backward look at his previous argument for kingship. Now he is adding to that the second text (Ps. 110:4) to show the priesthood of Messiah as well.

chapter twelve

PRUDENT LIVING
(Proverbs, Job, Ecclesiastes, Song of Songs)
Wisdom for Life

Every nation has its proverbs, maxims, parables, and other forms of wit and wisdom—ways to express the marrow of life with graphic intensity. These "pithy grabbers" are meant to bring home plain truth with the force of a sledgehammer. Common sense and not-so-common insight are wedded to practical instruction for life. Who does not smile at the double portrayal of laziness in Proverbs 26:14–15?

> As a door turns upon its hinges,
>   so a sluggard turns on his bed.
> The sluggard buries his hand in the dish;
>   he is too lazy to bring it back to his mouth.

Who does not recognize the practical insight in these snatches of life?

> A cheerful heart is good medicine,
>   but a crushed spirit dries up the bones (Prov. 17:22).

> Even a fool is thought wise if he keeps silent,
>   and discerning if he holds his tongue (Prov. 17:28).

> The last proverb may be the nicest way ever devised of saying, "Shut-up!"

> "Fish and visitors stink in three days."[1]

Yes, that is Benjamin Franklin, not the Bible. But Solomon had his finger on the same truth twenty-seven centuries earlier:

> Seldom set foot in your neighbor's house—
>   too much of you, and he will hate you (Prov. 25:17).

On the other hand, friendly letters or those with a check enclosed are always welcome.

> Like cold water to a weary soul
> is good news from a distant land (Prov. 25:25).

BIBLICAL WISDOM

But biblical wisdom isn't limited to helpful or witty observations about everyday life in the same mold as Ben Franklin or Erma Bombeck. Its net takes in a larger catch. Its purpose is not mere "observations on life" but how to live life. Along with the bits and pieces of getting along, making a living, and conducting oneself appropriately, are the weightier matters of commitment to God, good and evil, reward and punishment, and life's pitfalls.

The Torah Connection: The Fear of the Lord

To some, the books of wisdom (Proverbs, Ecclesiastes, Job), seem unrelated to the history of Israel and her faith in God. In Proverbs, sacrifice is mentioned fewer than a handful of times, the temple or tabernacle not at all, and references to Yahweh's covenant with Israel are nonexistent. Job and Ecclesiastes score about the same. How can the Old Testament include books about living life with so little teaching in matters so central to Israel's faith and history? The answer, like the sluggard's dish, is readily at hand. That it is not immediately recognized is due to the failure of modern readers to have dipped their hand into the dish of the Law. The central phrase, "The fear of Yahweh," is the umbilical cord that unites Proverbs to the nourishing Law.[2]

The importance of this phrase to the wisdom books is clear.[3] In an opening section, we learn that the Proverbs are

> "for attaining wisdom . . .
> discipline . . .
> understanding . . .
> prudence . . .
> knowledge . . .
> discretion."

And what is the first item—in fact, the absolute prerequisite—for this training?

> The fear of the Lord is the beginning of knowledge,
> but fools despise wisdom and discipline (1:7).

The phrase occurs no less than fourteen times in Proverbs, proclaiming the only approach for wise living.

Job, in the first chapter of that book of wisdom, is described by Yahweh as "blameless and upright, a man who fears God and shuns evil" (Job 1:8). This initial pitch by God opens up a long season for Job when Satan refuses to acknowledge the strike: "Does Job fear God for nothing?" he asks (1:9). The book not only vindicates Job and God but suggests there are reasons for life's circumstances that man cannot know. This lack of knowledge, however baffling, is no basis for unfaithfulness to God. The wise man will recognize that God is wiser than himself and will believe God has a purpose for even the difficulties of life. The Law says the same thing:

> The secret things belong to the LORD our God, but the things revealed belong to us and to our children forever, that we may follow all the words of this law (Deut. 29:29).

And Ecclesiastes, though different in tone, is no different in conclusion:

> Now all has been heard;
>   here is the conclusion of the matter:
> Fear God and keep his commandments,
>   for this is the whole duty of man (12:13).

This is not just his conclusion but a refrain scattered throughout the book. Added to all the emptiness and senselessness the Preacher finds in life is man's total inability to understand the meaning of all that happens to him. Yet the theme rings clear:

> In many dreams and in many words there is emptiness. Rather, fear God (Eccl. 5:7 NASB).

> Although a sinner does evil a hundred times and may lengthen his life, still I know that it will be well for those who fear God, who fear Him openly (Eccl. 8:12 NASB).

What is meant by "the fear of the LORD?" The concept is well developed in the Torah. It first occurs in Genesis 20:11. Abraham has passed off Sarah as his sister because he thought, "There is surely no fear of God in this place, and they will kill me because of my wife." Abraham thought they had no moral standards, so he lowered his to match. Later, Abraham's own commitment to God is vindicated when he is willing to obey God at the cost of his own son. "Now I know that you fear God" is the verdict (Gen. 22:12).

The idea is found most often in Deuteronomy, where it is coupled with other expressions like "walk in his ways," "keep his commands," "serve the

LORD," "love him," and "follow him" (4:10; 5:29; 6:13, 24; 8:6; 10:12, 20; 13:4; 17:19; 28:58; 31:12–13). How does a person fear the Lord?

> These are the commands, decrees and laws the LORD your God directed me to teach you to observe in the land … so that you, your children and their children after them may fear the LORD your God as long as you live by keeping all his decrees and commands that I give you (Deut. 6:1–2).

The "fear of the LORD" is not limited to a feeling of reverence and awe. *It is a commitment to the LORD by following his instruction.* It is a response of faithful obedience to the LORD by subjection to his revealed will. It would be impossible for the Israelite to fear the Lord without instruction in the Law (Deut. 31:12–13).[4]

Proverbs is not a popularized substitute for the Law—a kind of primer for those too negligent to learn Torah.[5] Rather, it is a supplement. As Kidner so graphically puts it, "There are details of character small enough to escape the mesh of the law and the broadsides of the prophets, and yet decisive in personal dealings. Proverbs moves in this realm."[6]

An example of this finer mesh that Proverbs supplies can be discovered by comparing it with the Law on the subject of adultery. The Law, of course, condemns it. The person who fears Yahweh will keep clear of it. Proverbs instructs the young man to do exactly that; but it also prepares him by practical description for the temptation that may come:

> Do not lust in your heart after her beauty
>   or let her captivate you with her eyes,
> For the prostitute reduces you to a loaf of bread,
>   and the adulteress preys upon your very life (6:25–26).

> The lips of an adulteress drip honey,
>   and her speech is smoother than oil;
> but in the end she is bitter as gall,
>   sharp as a double-edged sword (5:3–4).

Not only is the young man told to stay away from a woman like that, he is warned of practical consequences.

> A man who commits adultery lacks judgment;
>   whoever does so destroys himself.
> Blows and disgrace are his lot,
>   and his shame will never be wiped away;
> for jealousy arouses a husband's fury,
>   and he will show no mercy when he takes revenge.
> He will not accept any compensation;
>   he will refuse the bribe, however great it is (6:32–35).

Only fools turn in at that tempting call of folly:

> Stolen water is sweet;
>> food eaten in secret is delicious! (9:17).

Such men are ignorant of the consequences:

> Little do they know that the dead are there,
>> that her guests are in the depths of the grave (9:18).

Rather than the illicit, captivating theft of what is another man's, the ideal of marriage and its joys are fully and unashamedly recommended.

> May your fountain be blessed,
>> and may you rejoice in the wife of your youth.
> A loving doe, a graceful deer—
>> may her breasts satisfy you always,
>> may you ever be captivated by her love (5:18–20).

This combination of the Mosaic Torah, graphically supplemented by the *torah* (instruction) of the wise parent,[7] is designed to fully implement the fear of the Lord.

> To fear the Lord is to hate evil (8:13).

> The fear of the Lord adds length to life (10:27).

> He who fears the Lord has a secure fortress,
>> and for his children it will be a refuge (14:26).

> The fear of the Lord is a fountain of life (14:27).

> Better a little with the fear of the Lord than
>> great wealth with turmoil (15:16).

> The fear of the Lord teaches a man wisdom (15:33).

> Through the fear of the Lord a man avoids evil (16:6).

> The fear of the Lord—that is wisdom, and to
>> shun evil is understanding (Job 28:28).

The Creation Connection

But Proverbs goes beyond putting feet to the commands of the Law. It also develops the truth of creation. Genesis 1–2 taught the creation of an orderly and beautiful world. Proverbs teaches the creation of an orderly and beautiful life. If Yahweh is Creator, man must learn to live in harmony with the order that the Creator ordained.[8] This is wisdom indeed!

We might be surprised to read this description of the man celebrated as wiser than all others of the East: "He described plant life, from the cedar of Lebanon to the hyssop that grows out of walls. He also taught about animals and birds, reptiles and fish" (1 Kings 4:33). Solomon would have enjoyed some of my children's favorite questions when they were younger: "Dad, why did God create slugs?" followed quickly by "Why mosquitoes?" "Why flies?" I quickly gulp down the temptation to ask, "Why questioning kids?" The answer is too obvious: "To keep parents on their toes."

There are proverbs that deal with planting and reaping, with diligence, with the poor as God's creatures. Lessons of wisdom are borrowed from the ant and badgers. Ancient wisdom does not distinguish between the sacred and the secular, the scientific and the moral. It is all the wisdom of God. A skilled craftsman is wise because he has learned his trade well. A man is wise when he has learned to live skillfully according to God's order. Wisdom was the "craftsman" at the Creator's side when he created the world, and the discerning man will live in harmony with it (Prov. 8:22–36). We neglect such wisdom at our own risk.

The proverbs warn of attitudes and actions that cause a man to literally destroy himself. "Envy rots the bones"(14:30). Pride brings disgrace (11:2). "Food gained by fraud tastes sweet to a man, but he ends up with a mouth full of gravel" (20:17). "The evil deeds of a wicked man ensnare him" (5:22).

The belief that Yahweh created an orderly world joins the fear of the Lord as a major emphasis of wisdom teaching. Yahweh is Creator and is still in charge of the world. It is man's duty to live in harmony with Yahweh's rule as Creator. Wisdom was Yahweh's possession at the creation, and it is by wisdom that creation took place (8:22–31).[9] It is man's duty to discover this wisdom and to operate according to it (8:32–36).

> Blessed is the man who listens to me,
>> watching daily at my doors, waiting at my doorway.
> For whoever finds me finds life
>> and receives favor from the LORD (8:34–35).

The Life Connection

Reduced to essentials, most truths are marvelously simple. Proverbs recognizes this. When all the scrambling is over, it comes down to *life or death*. There are only two tracks. Track one is the way of the wise, the way of the righteous, the way of prosperity, the way of life. Track two is the way of the fool, the wicked, poverty, and death.

Wait a minute! Isn't that oversimplistic? Doesn't Solomon know, as Job did, that some wicked enjoy prosperity? Doesn't he know that some righteous are poor? Doesn't he know that some good men die young, and evil men die old?

I just had a look at the obituary column of our local paper. There were the requisite number of deaths of older people. Then there were deaths of younger men. One death was from a motorcycle accident when the driver lost control of his vehicle. A second man flipped a car on an empty freeway at 3 A.M. A third young man died from an apparent overdose of sleeping pills; his wife had been drunk and in a car wreck the night before. A fourth was stabbed by a friend, drugs being the apparent motivator. Finally, a young lady died after an extended illness. Notice anything? All but one of these younger deaths, possibly two, were due to disregard of wisdom in the conduct of life. They took the track of death, and they got there early.

When we lived in Texas—and it's not much different in Oregon—there was still a vestige of the old frontier shoot-'em-up approach in and around bars in the early hours of the morning. The TV news carried the inevitable results the next day. In other words, you have a better chance of living if you are in bed at what my mother used to call "a decent hour." It seems that even on the purely physical plane, a person who follows these principles is likely to live a longer and "better" life.

Sure, Proverbs knows there is no mechanical guarantee about these formulas. Some good people die young. You and I both could name some. The righteous have their setbacks (Prov. 24:16). The wicked often do so well that the righteous are tempted toward envy (24:1–2; 23:17; 3:31). But as our own folk wisdom recognizes, those people are "living on borrowed time." They are swimming against the tide. The odds will catch up with them.

It is not merely odds that will catch up with them. It is Yahweh himself, who oversees his creation. He brings vengeance on those who violate his people who live in harmony with him (Prov. 16:5; 17:5; 29:26). He assures of judgment and of retribution. It is Yahweh who is to be trusted. And though Proverbs concentrates on present life, true life is not limited to the here and now. Just as some people experience death even while yet alive, so life is more than mere existence. The life entered now through submission to Yahweh does not end at death. Death and the grave are for those who live in the realm of folly. For the righteous—and for no one else—there is a future (12:28).[10] Apart from God's revelation, can we prove that this divine order exists? Reading obituaries helps, but we also have to recognize (as the book of Ecclesiastes does) that if we want absolute proof—and perfect sense—in this world, we are not going to find it.

Ecclesiastes does more than point out that "life isn't a bowl of cherries." If you want everything in life to make sense, says the Preacher, forget it. As earth dwellers, we don't have heaven's perspective—and we cannot have it. For us, "the creation was subjected to frustration [futility, vanity, meaninglessness]" until it is fully redeemed by God (Rom. 8:20–21).

If Proverbs encourages us to live positively in the light of divine revelation, Ecclesiastes warns us against requiring full explanations. From the human vantage point, time and chance happen to us all (Eccl. 9:11).

But one rule also applies to all. It stands unchanged throughout the wisdom books:

Fear God and keep his commandments,
for this is the whole duty of man.
For God will bring every deed into judgment, including every
hidden thing,
whether it is good or evil (Eccl. 12:13–14).

THE BOOKS OF BIBLICAL WISDOM

Though the wisdom books—Job, Proverbs, Ecclesiastes, Song of Songs—all communicate something of biblical wisdom as presented above, they are far from being mere duplicates of one another. There are some profound differences in emphasis.

Proverbs

The book of Proverbs is optimistic and pragmatic. As we have seen, it presents advice based on the fear of the Lord and God's creative order. If you follow these teachings, says Proverbs, you can expect blessing, prosperity, wisdom, and life. If you fall into the traps that living offers (sexual license, greed, pride, laziness, failure to respect one's parents, bad companions, lying, and more), then you can expect poverty, disappointment, failure, and other aspects of death.

Most of the proverbs are ascribed to Solomon (1:1; 10:1; 25:1), who could have used a little more skill in living in key areas of his own life (1 Kings 11). Some of Solomon's proverbs were copied and collected by King Hezekiah's men centuries later (25:1). In addition there are proverbs by King Lemuel (31:1–9) and Agur (chap. 30). Two "Sayings of the Wise" occur (22:17–24:22; 24:23–34). The first of these contains parallels to the Wisdom of Amen-em-opet from Egypt. The inspired collector of Proverbs did not mind borrowing wisdom from wherever he found it. King Lemuel may also be a foreign king.[11] The difference: the biblical proverbs understand Yahweh as producing the truths involved. Practical wisdom is to be accepted no matter who said it first. Yet, the fear of Yahweh is still the ultimate moral base for all wisdom. Proverbs, then, is didactic wisdom—teaching directly how to do it.

Ecclesiastes

The writer of Ecclesiastes identifies himself as the "Teacher" or "Preacher" (*Qohelet* in Hebrew). The self-identification that appears beyond the title suggests Solomon as the Teacher (1:1, 12, 16; 2:4–9), yet unlike most titles his name is not directly stated.[12] Our English title, *Ecclesiastes*, comes from the Greek word for *teacher*. The book of Ecclesiastes is the other side of the coin from the book of Proverbs. So much so, that some have suggested that the bulk of the book is inferior and represents Solomon's folly as he wrote in an unrepentant and carnal condition. Such a view is unnecessary and, in fact, contradicts the final verdict that pronounces the Teacher wise and his teaching good (12:9–14). Yet, the contrast with Proverbs is still there. Proverbs is positive, whereas Ecclesiastes has a pessimistic tone to it. Proverbs tells us that wise living, righteousness, and diligence all work. Ecclesiastes points out that all too frequently they don't work. There is a futility and frustration to life as we view it on the earthly level. It is too hard to figure out (8:16–17; 7:14). And not only hard to figure, but like a giant horse pill, life is sometimes difficult to swallow. A man accumulates wealth, but is never able to enjoy it—a stranger enjoys it instead (6:1–2). Man comes into the world with nothing and leaves with nothing. In between he experiences "great frustration, affliction and anger" (5:16–17). A righteous person may get what a wicked person deserves and vice versa (8:24). These things are meaningless, grievous evils to our author (6:2, 12; 8:24). Life does not always go as it should. Nonetheless, says the Preacher, live your life with enjoyment of those good pleasures that are God's gift while you can: enjoy your work; enjoy your wife; enjoy your food (5:12, 18; 8:15; 9:7–9).[13] Is this sarcasm or is this stark reality?

Proverbs and Ecclesiastes do not really contradict. Just as Proverbs really knows that things do not always go well, Qohelet would tell us that we can't expect to make sense of everything as if this were a perfect, unfallen world. Yet there are things to enjoy as we live a life moderated by the knowledge of future judgment and directed by the fear of Yahweh and his commands (11:7–9; 12:13–14). In the end, Ecclesiastes corrects an improper reading of Proverbs. We are to practice justice, diligence, loyalty, and integrity because they are right, not because they always profit or always work out for our benefit. Even today outrageous health and wealth blessings are promised to believers by false qohelets—especially if a donation is forthcoming! They need to read our Teacher. The realities of God's commands and future judgment incorporate a perspective not limited to experiences "under the sun" (1:14) and are to guide our behavior beyond the incompleteness of fallen human experience.

Job

The book of Job is anonymous. The setting for the story fits the patriarchal era. Job himself is a non-Israelite who, like the patriarchs, performed priestly functions for his family (1:5). The land of Uz (1:1) is elsewhere identified with the area of Edom, east of the Jordan River (Lam. 4:21; cf. Gen 36:28). Though the setting is patriarchal and non-Israelite, the writer of our book is an Israelite. The name, Yahweh, occurs frequently in this book, but not in the discussions between Job and his friends—with one exception (12:9). Otherwise, Yahweh is mentioned only in the prologue of heavenly background (about which Job knew nothing throughout his suffering) and in the final sections where the Almighty is identified when he engages in dialogue and rewards Job. That God was truly known and worshiped by non-Israelites in the period before the Exodus is evident from the examples of Jethro, Moses father-in-law, who was a priest of Midian and Melchizedek, the king-priest of Salem (Ex. 3:1; Gen. 14:18–20). Suggestions for identifying the Israelite author have run the gamut from Moses to Solomon and beyond the Exile.

Like Ecclesiastes, Job is a wisdom book that ponders the problem areas of life. Ecclesiastes asks, Why do things not always go well for those who live carefully? The author of Job ponders a similar problem: Why do the righteous suffer? In fact, why do good people suffer under a good, all-powerful God? Finally, the onus is put on humanity: Is there anyone who will worship God for who he is, rather than for what God gives? This is Satan's charge in the prologue that forms a background to the discussion of the book (1:1–2:10; cf. 1:9–11). So, an issue that might initially seem to put God on trial—why should people suffer if God is good and powerful—is turned on its head. While the man Job wrestles with whether God is fair, mankind is also on trial as to their motives in serving God. Do people just serve God for what they can get? Will God be served during periods of undeserved, seemingly meaningless, suffering? Or is God served only when he resembles Santa Claus? Is man a fair-weather friend to God?

Three friends arrive and sit in silence for a full week (2:11–13). Job finally speaks, lamenting the day of his birth (chap. 3). This is followed by three rounds of accusation by friends Eliphaz, Bildad, and Zophar—each speaker followed by Job's answer (chaps. 3–14; 15–21; 22–31). The friends insist that Job must be a sinner, because God is righteous. Job must be experiencing retributive justice. Each friend tends to have less to say each round with Zophar saying nothing in the third round. Job is rarely outdone—even in speech length. He argues that, though he is a sinner, he has done nothing deserving of this great suffering. He believes he will be vindicated—even if it must be after death (19:25–27). A younger man, Elihu, frustrated by the failure of the earlier three to convince Job, and angry with Job for defending himself rather than God, enters the fray with arguments for defending God's silence, God's motive (chastening), and God's justice (chaps. 32–37). Elihu makes some good points about suffering and man's attitude before God, but he still does not touch upon the real reason that Job is suffering.

God does speak (chaps. 38–42:6)! And Job's answers now become exceedingly short! Further, God does not explain the reason that Job has suffered. Instead, he quizzes Job about the mysteries of creation. If Job gets such a low score in the mysteries of natural science, how can he think to correct the Creator? Job is quiet, humbled, and repentant: "Surely I spoke of things I did not understand, things too wonderful for me to know" (42:4). Yet Job is vindicated before his friends (42:7–9) and, as he has demonstrated integrity in serving God, God is free to bless Job doubly without the prospect of further accusation that Job only serves God out of self-interest (42:10–17).

The book of Job adds profoundly to our understanding of suffering. Reward for good behavior and punishment for sins do not correspond one-to-one with our experience of pleasure or pain in this life. From one perspective, we may never know why a particular experience of pain or suffering occurs. From another perspective, the author has added one more reason that such suffering does occur: There is a wider conflict in which humans play an important part. Our part is to operate in the fear of Yahweh, even when we do not understand the reason. Our part is to be loyal worshipers of God. In this we may well vindicate God and man against the Adversary.

The Song of Songs

All four wisdom books focus on creation. Unlike the other three, the Song of Songs or "Best Song" focuses on one aspect of the creation. Because of this, it is sometimes questioned whether it is truly a wisdom book and even whether it should be in Scripture at all.

What aspect of the Creation is the focus of human thoughts, activity, art, and even merchandizing more than the love of man for woman and vice versa? This feature that formed the climax to the original creation (Gen. 2) deserves a book of its own—a book that goes beyond instruction about rights and wrongs, blessings and dangers (like Proverbs). Why not a book that focuses on the joy and delight of committed, exclusive love.[14] That book is the Best Song, ascribed to Solomon.[15]

Unfortunately, beyond the insight that this is a story of love, interpreters through the centuries have agreed on little else about the arrangement and plan of the book. Some ancient and modern interpreters, both Jewish and Christian, have suggested that the book is an allegory or type of God's love for Israel or Christ's love for the church. Yet, the book gives no suggestion of any hidden meanings—apart from some metaphorical terms for physical intimacy!

Figure 12.1
Some Current Views of the Song of Songs

	W. J. Dumbrell	G. Lloyd Carr	Dennis Kinlaw	J. S. Deere/ C. Glickman	Andrew Hill & John Walton
Author	No objection to Solomon	Solomon's time or shortly after	Solomon (?) – A Royal wedding	Solomon	Dedicated to Solomon satirically
Theme	Idealized human love as pictured in Eden	Mutual longing and surrender	The human love that reflects divine love	Extolling human love and marriage	Power & fidelity of genuine love
Development of Book	No plot, but a literary unity. Interweaving of themes and imagery – especially garden theme and the preeminence of love.	Two persons (Shulamite & shepherd – not Solomon). No plot. Literary development. A chiastic arrangement as follows: A. 1:2–2:7 Anticipation B. 2:8–3:5 Found/ lost/found C. 3:6–5:1 Consummation B'. 5:2–8:4 Lost/found A'. 8:5–14 Affirmation	Two persons (Shulamite & king) with progress of relationship: Title, 1:1 Courtship, 1:2–3:5 Bridal Procession, 3:6–11 Wedding, 4:1–5:1 Life of Love, 5:2–8:7 Conclusion, 8:8–14	Two persons (Shulamite & Solomon); logical progression from courtship (1:2–3:5) to wedding & wedding night (3:6–5:1); marriage problems & resolution (5:2–8:4); the nature & power of love (8:5–7) & epilogue (8:8–14).	Ancient lyrical ballad with 3 persons & plot: The maiden is at Solomon's court but desires her shepherd lover. She rejects Solomon's proposals and is reunited with her northern shepherd.

Though the Song can be compared in language to other ancient Near Eastern love poems, its closest parallel in imagery and ideas are found in Proverbs.

> Drink water from your own cistern,
>> running water from your own well.
> Should your springs overflow in the streets,
>> your streams of water in the public squares?
> Let them be yours alone,
>> never to be shared with strangers.
> May your fountain be blessed,
>> and may you rejoice in the wife of your youth.
> A loving doe, a graceful deer—
>> may her breasts satisfy you always,
>> may you ever be captivated by her love (Prov. 5:15–19).

Here is the essence of the Song! The imagery of fountain, garden, and graceful wildlife (cf. 4:5, 12–16; 5:1; 6:2–3; 8:14). The captivation with the beauty of each other (5:10–16; 7:1–9). The unhesitating enjoyment of the eyes, neck, lips, hair, and breasts (4:1–7; 7:1–9). Of course, the images are not what we might choose to describe physical beauty: defense towers, flocks of black goats coming down mountain slopes, and fawns (cf. 4:1, 4; 7:2–3, 8)! A few years ago a sketch circulated of this Shulamite beauty— reconstructed by taking the descriptions in the Song literally. What a long neck! What a grotesque combination!

Most recent interpreters have seen the Song as lyric poetry—love poems tied together by recurring images, participants, and themes. These poems form a unity, but what kind of a unity? Do they form a sequence for a plot? If so, is it a plot involving two main characters (the Shulamite maiden and a lover [Solomon or a shepherd] or three main characters [add a shepherd-lover who wins out over Solomon]). The Hebrew distinguishes a masculine and feminine speaker (see NIV "Beloved"—her; "Lover"—him), but if there are two masculine figures other clues will have to distinguish them. Other scholars see a progression of poems but no story line or plot. The progression is in terms of ideas about genuine love. Many see no progression, simply repeated themes. (See figure 12.1 and the notes for a comparison of viewpoints.)[16]

What themes does this book invoke concerning human love? Understood as wisdom literature, the book is not simply contributing love poems but a closer look at the way creation was made to operate in this select but important area of human experience. The elements in the Song contribute to an understanding and appreciation for the depth of this intense and dominate relationship. *Presence/absence* is a theme. The desire for the presence of the beloved is a mark of the intense interpersonal relationship of love (3:1–4). A dream of missing the lover and being beaten in the streets while searching for him emphasizes again the desire for the presence of the one loved and the fact that absence itself heightens the sense of the desire for the partner (5:2–7). *Physical attraction* for each other is another theme (4:1–7; 5:10–16; 6:4–9; 7:1–9). Unlike the growing tendency in our culture to treat sex as recreation and to use physical beauty as the total standard for value of the (especially female) person, for our biblical lovers the body is never falsely separated from the whole person. Admiration of the body is a natural and wholesome expression of admiration for and commitment to the total person. The beloved's beauty may not be recognized by all (1:6), but he or she is beautiful because she is loved. The imagery of a garden, both for the setting as well as for the lovers themselves, suggests another emphasis: the ideal setting and *experience of one-fleshness between male and female* that was Eden.[17] But perhaps the strongest and most dominant theme is the *exclusiveness of love*—"My lover is mine and I am his" (2:16; 6:3)—a theme which yields the climactic poetry near the end:

> Place me like a seal over your heart,
>   like a seal on your arm;
> for love is as strong as death,
>   its jealousy unyielding as the grave.
> It burns like blazing fire,
>   like the very flame of the LORD.
> Many waters cannot quench love;
>   rivers cannot wash it away.
> If one were to give
>   all the wealth of his house for love
>   it would be utterly scorned (8:6–7).

WISDOM FULFILLED

Jesus and Proverbs

Jesus' sayings and parables about the essence of life have lost none of their punch, though delivered almost two millennia ago. Consider these:

> Blessed are the poor in spirit,
>   for theirs is the kingdom of heaven (Matt. 5:3).
> Where your treasure is, there your heart
>   will be also (Luke 12:34).

> Which of you, if his son asks for bread,
>> will give him a stone? (Matt. 7:9).
> A man's life does not consist in the abundance
>> of his possessions (Luke 12:15).
> Neither do men pour new wine into
>> old wineskins (Matt. 9:17).
> If a blind man leads a blind man,
>> both will fall into a pit (Matt. 15:14).

Such simple observations on life cut through to issues that continue to confront us. Are we living for this life or the next? Is God really good? Are the concerns for food and clothing ultimate concerns, or distractions? Is the landscape dotted with counterfeits who lead ignorant men to destruction?

Like Proverbs, Jesus teaches trust in the Creator God. "Solomon in all his splendor" could not match the natural dress of the lilies (Matt. 6:28–29). For Jesus, like Solomon's Proverbs, there are only two tracks: life or death. One path is worn wide by the multitude who take it. The other path has become narrow and hidden so that few find and follow it (Matt. 7:13–14).

The Wise King

The name Solomon became known not only for royal splendor and proverbs but stood also for the idea of the wise king—in spite of his failures in old age. It was Solomon who knew enough to ask for wisdom to judge God's people rightly.

Yet Solomon did fail. He failed in the very fear of the Lord that he knew wisdom required. He first permitted, then catered, to idolatry. He also took full advantage of his kingly position to surround himself with all the trappings of empire—in spite of the warnings of Deuteronomy (17:16–20).

God dumped Rehoboam, Solomon's son, from ruling over all Israel because of Solomon's idolatry. The people rejected him because of oppressive taxation. Solomon, they said, had "put a heavy yoke on us, but now lighten the harsh labor and the heavy yoke he put on us" (1 Kings 12:4). Rehoboam promised them more of the same. Exit ten tribes.

Such was the wisdom of Solomon. Renowned but inconsistent. Dazzling but short-lived. Remarkable for its life-insight. Profoundly puzzling in its demise. Like a fourth of July rocket it lit up the sky but soon disappeared in smoke and vapor.

Yet Isaiah predicts a future king in David's line who would be perfect in his wise rule:

The Spirit of the LORD will rest on him—
> the Spirit of wisdom and of understanding,
> the Spirit of counsel and of power,
> the Spirit of knowledge and of the fear of the LORD
and he will delight in the fear of the LORD (Isa. 11:2–3).

The King with these qualities will provide Israel with a ruler who will do what no king has managed to date—bring perfect justice and peace (Isa. 11:3–9).[18]

Like a child trained to hear the summons to come home, the words of Jesus in Matthew 11:28–30 must have raised the head of many a Jewish listener:

> Come to me, all you who are weary and burdened, and I will give you rest. Take my yoke upon you and learn from me, for I am gentle and humble in heart, and you will find rest for your souls. For my yoke is easy and my burden is light.

No burden of oppressive kingship here. Jesus' rule would liberate.

Jesus not only claims a wisdom for ruling that Solomon could not match, but asserts his exclusive rights to the franchise:

> All things have been committed to me by my Father. No one knows the Son except the Father, and no one knows the Father except the Son and those to whom the Son chooses to reveal him (Matt. 11:27).

His followers, pictured as "little children" compared to those considered "wise and learned" (11:25), receive his invitation to "find rest for your souls" (11:29).

Again, the Jewish listener would not miss the reference to Jeremiah 6:16 (emphasis added):

> Stand at the crossroads and look; ask for the ancient paths, ask where the good way is, and walk in it, and *you will find rest for your souls*. But you said, "We will not walk in it."

The Israelites of Jeremiah's time were rejecting God's way, though they offered sacrifices. God was not impressed.

> What do I care about incense from Sheba
> > or sweet calamus from a distant land?
> Your burnt offerings are not acceptable;
> > your sacrifices do not please me (Jer. 6:20).

In spite of experiencing the judgment of exile that Jeremiah proclaimed, nothing has changed. Israel had lapsed back into mere external and outward worship. Jesus, like Jeremiah, calls them back to the wisdom of the good way—the ancient path of true relationship to Yahweh. One greater than Solomon has come (Matt. 12:42) with wisdom and relief. Because he is "gentle and humble in heart" (Matt. 11:29), he will rule his people in the fear of the Lord without arrogance and rebellion. Will they reject the wise King?[19]

The Worthy Lamb

When the announced wise King becomes a sacrificial lamb upon a Roman cross, the hopes of those expecting relief and rest seemed dashed. How can rule be reconciled with sacrificial death?

A scene in Revelation 4–5 brings the two themes together in dramatic clarity. Called up into heaven to see the future, the apostle John finds himself viewing God's throne room. Almighty God, surrounded by groups of creatures, is worshiped as the Holy and Sovereign Creator (4:1–11). But before John's eyes a drama develops that interrupts this praise and brings activity in heaven to a halt. The Almighty holds the scroll of destiny, but no one in all creation is found who is worthy to approach the throne and open this scroll that will unravel the scenes necessary to bring history to its climax. John is visibly shaken and weeps at this setback but is told someone has been found who is worthy.

> The Lion of the tribe of Judah, the Root of David, has triumphed. He is able to open the scroll and its seven seals (5:5).

But when John looks, he sees no glorious, triumphant King. He sees a Lamb that looks as if it had been recently sacrificed! This lowly, bloody Lamb is permitted to take the scroll. The creatures closest to the throne begin a new song, soon to be joined in chorus by a myriad of angels:

> Worthy is the Lamb, who was slain,
> to receive power and wealth
> and wisdom and strength
> and honor and glory and praise! (5:12).

The message is clear. Jesus triumphed in crucifixion—as a sacrificial lamb. God's plan may proceed toward its grand climax because he died. The Lamb who was slain is worthy to reign to receive the power and wealth and wisdom of office.

And with your blood you purchased men for God from every tribe and language and people and nation. You have made them to be a kingdom and priests to serve our God, and they will reign on the earth (5:9–10).

Jesus Is Wisdom

It is no wonder Paul identifies Christ crucified as God's power and wisdom (1 Cor. 1:18–31). In contrast to the best that human wisdom can do, Jesus is God's plan for human redemption. This plan looks like foolishness to earthbound philosophers. How can man comprehend a plan so based on love and servitude that his own deliverance and restoration is achieved by the death of the very "Lord of glory" (2:8)? How foolish to give up position to serve! How foolish to serve than be served!

But how redemptive!

The foolishness of God is wiser than man's wisdom, and the weakness of God is stronger than man's strength (1 Cor. 1:25).

Worthy is the Lamb who is "our righteousness, holiness, and redemption" (1 Cor. 1:30). His death and resurrection have cleared the track that leads to life. He "has destroyed death and has brought life and immortality to light through the gospel" (2 Tim. 1:10).

The Way of Wisdom is complete.

SUGGESTED SCRIPTURE READING:

Proverbs 1, 5, 16
Ecclesiastes 1, 12
Job 1, 38, 40, 42
Song of Songs 1, 8
Matthew 11:25–30
Revelation 5

For Interaction and Discussion:

1. How do biblical proverbs compare with our own proverbs? How are they similar? What makes them different?

2. Is the wise person the one with all the answers? What lesson about life does the book of Job teach? How does this relate to wisdom?

3. In what way is the message of Ecclesiastes similar to that of Job? What does each wisdom book add to a holistic understanding of life? What instances can you think of where the message of one book would be more relevant than the others?

4. What is the fear of the Lord? What other ideas are similar to it? How does it relate to the Law?

5. What does Proverbs advise about sex and marriage? Is Proverbs prudish or true to life? What correctives does the Song of Songs hold for today's reader about love?

6. Why are wisdom and creation connected? Is belief in a Creator necessary to have an assurance of an order and meaning to life?

7. What is the way of life and the way of death in Proverbs? Is Proverbs too optimistic in its description of the life of the righteous person? Is Ecclesiastes pessimistic or realistic?

8. Why are temporary setbacks not finally important to the writer of Proverbs? How does this come through in Jesus' teaching?

9. How does the scene in Revelation 4–5 tie Jesus' sacrificial death into his rule as the wise and worthy king? How does the route of sacrifice differ from conventional, earthly wisdom? Is it necessary to true wisdom?

For Further Reading:

C. Hassel Bullock. *An Introduction to the Old Testament Poetic Books*. Rev. ed. Chicago: Moody, 1988, 53–110, 146–234. A fine conservative introduction to these books.

William J. Dumbrell. *The Faith of Israel*. Grand Rapids: Baker, 1988, 207–51. Themes and literary development of these books.

Frank E. Gaebelein, ed. *The Expositor's Bible Commentary*. Vol. 5. Grand Rapids: Zondervan, 1991, 883–1244. This commentary for the pastor and English reader is conservative and scholarly.

Derek Kidner. *Proverbs*. TOTC. Downers Grove, Ill.: InterVarsity, 1977. Succinct scholarly commentary on the Hebrew text for English readers.

Bruce K. Waltke. "The Book of Proverbs and Old Testament Theology." *BSac*, 136 (1979): 302–17. Fine discussion of thematic links of Proverbs with the earlier theology of the Old Testament.

J. Stafford Wright. "Interpretation of Ecclesiastes." *Classical Evangelical Essays*. Ed. Walter C. Kaiser, Jr. Grand Rapids: Baker, 1972, 133–50. A classic article on the movement and purpose of Ecclesiastes.

Notes and Comments:

[1]Benjamin Franklin, *Poor Richard's Alamanack*, January 1736, ed. Benjamin E. Smith (New York: The Century Co., 1899), 79.

[2]B. K. Waltke, "The Book of Proverbs and Old Testament Theology," *BSac*, 136 (October, 1979): 302–17. Waltke, in fact, finds ten lines of agreement between the outlook of Proverbs and that of Deuteronomy and the prophets. Moshe Weinfeld, "Wisdom Substrata in Deuteronomy and Deuteronomic Literature," *Deuteronomy*

and the Deuteronomic School (Oxford: Clarendon Press, 1972), 244–74, listed extensive parallels between the instruction of Deuteronomy and Proverbs. A partial list is cited by Walter C. Kaiser, *Toward an Old Testament Theology*, 167.

[3]J. Kenneth Kuntz, "The Canonical Wisdom Psalms of Ancient Israel—Their Rhetorical, Thematic, and Formal Dimensions," *Rhetorical Criticism: Essays in Honor of James Muilenburg* (Pittsburgh: The Pickwick Press, 1974), 211–15. Kuntz lists four thematic elements present in wisdom psalms. These include: (1) the fear of Yahweh and veneration of the Torah; (2) the contrasting lifestyles of the righteous and the wicked; (3) the reality and inevitability of retribution; and (4) miscellaneous counsels pertaining to everyday life.

[4]See Kaiser, *Toward an Old Testament Theology*, 168–70.

[5]Gerhard von Rad, *Wisdom in Israel* (Nashville: Abingdon, 1972), 26, makes the startling suggestion that memorized proverbs were "of greater importance for the decisions of daily life and thus for orientation in the thick of everyday activity than, for example, the ten commandments which were pronounced over the cultic assembly only rarely on great festivals."

[6]Derek Kidner, *Proverbs* (Downers Grove, Ill.: InterVarsity, 1977), 13.

[7]The debate over taking "Son" as an indication of parental instruction or as a term used by a teacher continues.

[8]For discussion of the concept of a created order and its relationship to the Egyptian concept of *Ma'at*, see Bruce K. Waltke, "The Book of Proverbs and Ancient Wisdom Literature," *BSac*, 136 (July 1979): 232–34; and G. von Rad, *Wisdom in Israel*, 72. Roland E. Murphy, "Wisdom—Thesis and Hypothesis," *Israelite Wisdom: Theological and Literary Essays in Honor of Samuel Terrien*, eds. J. G. Gammie, W. A. Brueggemann, W. L. Humphreys, and J. M. Ward (New York: Union Theological Seminary, 1978), 35–36, objects to the notion of a created "order" because of the Israelite view that the Lord is the primary cause of everything. If, indeed, an order was proposed as independent of Yahweh's direct involvement—a kind of deistic watchmaker's universe, then we could agree with Murphy. We do not think, however, that the notion of a regular order and Yahweh's direct involvement should be seen as alternatives. There is order, but it is directly ordered and upheld by Yahweh.

[9]The translation of Proverbs 8:22 is difficult. In this personification, is wisdom "possessed," "created," or "begotten" before the creation of the world? See Kidner, *Proverbs*, 78–81, who summarizes recent discussion and concludes that wisdom is here a personification as in the following 9:1–18 and "possessed" is the best translation to indicate that wisdom "comes forth from Him [God]."

[10]See C. Hassell Bullock, *An Introduction to the Old Testament Poetic Books*, rev. ed. (Chicago: Moody, 1988), 59–63, for a summary of recent scholarship on the doctrine of a future life in wisdom literature. Cf. Waltke, *The Book of Proverbs and Old Testament Theology*, 314–15.

[11]For the issue of the priority of Amen-em-opet or the Hebrew proverbs and the issue of non-Israelite contributions, including Agur and Lemuel, refer to discussion in Bullock, *Poetic Books*, 163–65, 174–76.

[12]Ibid., 183–87. Bullock concludes that personification (not pseudonymity) is possible for the portrayal of Solomon in Ecclesiastes 1—i.e., the writer wanted to make a point by an intentional and obvious personification of one who had and tried it all but didn't achieve happiness. Pseudonymity is to write under the false pretext of someone else's name. Personification is to use a literary device that would be recognized as just that—not a claim to authorship. However, personification in a title is exceptional.

[13]For a more complete overview of Ecclesiastes see J. Stafford Wright, "The Interpretation of Ecclesiastes," *Classical Evangelical Essays*, ed. Walter C. Kaiser, Jr., (Grand Rapids: Baker, 1972), 133–50, originally published in *EQ*, 18 (1946): 18–34. For a more painstaking literary analysis which arrives at much the same conclusion see Addison G. Wright, "The Riddle of the Sphinx: The Structure of the Book of Qoheleth," *CBQ*, 30 (1968): 313–34: reprinted in *Studies in Ancient Israelite Wisdom*, ed. James L. Crenshaw (New York: KTAV, 1976), 245–66.

[14]The Hebrew preposition *lamedth* attached to a name (such as Solomon) in the title is the normal way to ascribe authorship, as in the Psalms. However, others suggest that it sometimes can mean "about," "dedicated to," and "for." Cf. the discussion in Bullock, *Poetic Books*, 220–23. As Brevard S. Childs, *Introduction to the Old Testament*, 573–75, observes, ascribing the Song to Solomon also has the effect of categorizing it as wisdom literature.

[15]Many writers have noted the appropriateness of a whole book on human marital love as a fitting practical emphasis based on the theology of Genesis 2. Cf. Roland E. Murphy, *The Song of Songs*, Hermenia (Minneapolis: Fortress, 1990), 100–105; Walter C. Kaiser, Jr., *Toward Old Testament Ethics*, 192–95.

[16]As the chart (Figure 12.1) of some current views on the Song of Songs shows, there is little agreement on the development of notions or events in the Song—even though most agree on the themes. Bibliography for those cited is as follows: William J. Dumbrell, *The Faith of Israel* (Grand Rapids: Baker, 1988), 234–39; G. Lloyd Carr, *The Song of Solomon*, TOTC (Downers Grove, Ill.: InterVarsity, 1984); Dennis F. Kinlaw, "Song of Songs," *EBC* (Grand Rapids: Zondervan, 1991), 5:1201–44; Jack S. Deere, "Song of Songs," *The Bible Knowledge Commentary* (Wheaton: Victor, 1985), 1009–25; S. Craig Glickman, *A Song for Lovers* (Downers Grove, Ill.: InterVarsity, 1976); Andrew E. Hill and John H. Walton, *A Survey of the Old Testament*, 299–306.

George A. F. Knight, *Revelation of God: The Song of Songs and Jonah,* International Theological Commentary (Grand Rapids: Eerdmans, 1988), also sees no story line or plot, but an ordering of the poems to present a progressive message about love. Brevard S. Childs, *Introduction to the Old Testament*, 569–79, holds a view closest to Dumbrell, but seems to see less integration of the poems than most listed here. C. Hassell Bullock, *Poetic Books*, 224–34, takes a three-person view, as Hill and Walton, who follow Bullock with adaptations.

[17]Dumbrell, *The Faith of Israel*, 237–38, suggests and develops the idea of the garden paralleling Eden with its "one-flesh" ideal, whereas the negative motifs in the book are threats of our real world to the ideal of the original garden.

[18]The connection between wisdom and royal wisdom is developed by Norman W. Porteous in "Royal Wisdom," *Wisdom in Israel and in the Ancient Near East*, ed. M. Noth and D. Winton Thomas, *Supplements to Vetus Testamentum* (Leiden: E. J. Brill, 1969), 3:247–61.

[19]Porteous, "Royal Wisdom," 3:258–61. Porteous concludes that Matthew 11 identifies the royal Messiah as the wisdom of God. Sirach 6:24–31 also identifies wisdom as a yoke that gives rest. Cf. James M. Ward, "The Servant's Knowledge in Isaiah 40–55," *Israelite Wisdom: Theological and Literary Essays in Honor of Samuel Terrien* (New York: Union Theological Seminary, 1978), 121–36.

chapter thirteen

THE PROPHETS OF THE DIVIDED KINGDOM

Messages of Judgment and Hope

We live in strange times. Carl Sagan, popular scientist-philosopher, proclaims that science has defeated religion and now must provide culture with the unifying goals provided by religion in the past.[1] In spite of this confident proclamation about the demise of religion, we are witnessing the revival of ancient superstitions: the rise of "neo-paganism," worship of the goddess, popularity of astrologers, spiritists, and "psychic advice networks." All compete and prosper in a world that still looks for some advantage and control by insight into the unknown and the beyond.

People want control, power, affirmation, and advantage over the uncertainties of life whether by newer scientific religion or older, darker efforts at prognostication. Ancient kings also wanted control. And, like most political leaders—and most of us—they did not want to hear bad news. Result: The prosperity of false prophets who were in tune with their times. They understood that economics and politically desirable results are the backbone of relevant (or at least profitable) social ethics.

Real prophets of the true and living God had no such advantage. God's prophets often suffered because they would not adjust God's Word or pander to leaders for prominence, position, or plush rewards. Isaiah, tradition tells us, was sawed in two. Jeremiah spent time in the bottom of a cistern. Micaiah ended up in prison. Elijah ran for his life. Perhaps prophets of Yahweh lacked the proper marketing strategy for their century.

PROPHETS AND PROPHECY

The Prophetic Books

The second of the three sections in the Hebrew Bible (see Fig. 0.1) is called "The Prophets" (*Nebi'im*). It includes four books of prophetic history called the *former prophets* (Joshua, Judges, Samuel, and Kings) and four scrolls of *latter prophets* (Isaiah, Jeremiah, Ezekiel, and The Twelve). Our English Bibles do not follow the Hebrew ordering. Instead we follow the Greek (LXX) version in which the latter prophets plus Daniel and Lamentations are the last section of the Old Testament (Isaiah to Malachi). Be assured, however, that it is all the same Bible. In addition, Isaiah, Jeremiah, and Ezekiel along with Daniel are often called "the major prophets" and The Twelve prophetic books (Hosea to Malachi) "minor prophets." This, however, only refers to the size of the books, not the stature of the prophets!

In order to better match the prophets to their timing in the book of Kings, our own coverage will follow neither of the above orders. Rather, in the next two chapters we will treat each prophet according to his time of ministry to better see each one in the ongoing history of Israel as overviewed already in the book of Kings.

The Message of the Prophets

Both the Hebrew order and the content of these prophets' messages affirms *the Law as the foundation* for their message. Their job description involves calling kings and people back to the Law and covenants. They are not simply predictors, they challenge living that has gone astray.

While prophets would give short-term predictions, called "signs," to verify their calling as God's messengers (cf. 1 Sam. 2:34; Isa. 7:10), their messages often contain a longer view down the tunnel of history. Note the following features: (1) *Connection*. Rarely is a prediction given that is detached from present events. The predictive element is there to spotlight God's ultimate plan and so to influence present conduct by awareness of ultimate concerns. (2) *Telescoping*. A long-term prediction is often fulfilled in several stages in the future, even though the prophecy seems to read as a single event. To the prophetic eye, the future is telescoped into one picture. This has been graphically illustrated by several mountain peaks off in the distance. In prophetic oracles those higher and more distant peaks seem to be a continuation of the first peak. In fact, they are. They deal with the same theme coming to pass in the future. As part of the same mountain range time gaps simply are not revealed. (3) *Dating*. Futuristic prophecies ought to be thought of more as the unveiling of the promise of the future and God's plan than as detailing a chronology of events. Definite events are included, but chronology is often disregarded for a topic on aspects of completion of God's plan and promise. Date-setting is always a dangerous proposition when it comes to interpreting biblical prophecy. (4) *Nearly contradictory themes*. Cataclysmic judgment is frequently followed by hope. The warning of severe judgment by itself would lead to pessimism among the faithful. Ultimate hope is not "pie in the sky" but a necessary encouragement to faith in God and the ultimate success of his plan.

Functioning As Prophets

Does a prophet find a street corner, stand on a soapbox, and start speaking? Moses, of course, was the prototype prophet. By virtue of his prophetic call, he was to lead Israel to the Promised Land (Ex. 3–4). He delivered God's Word to Pharaoh and the Law or Torah to the newly created nation of Israel.

Deborah is another example of a prophet who led Israel as a judge (Judg. 4–5). National leadership by prophets changed with Samuel. Like Deborah, Samuel was also a judge—the last one. When Samuel anointed Saul as king, the office of judge came to an end. With Samuel's anointing of David and the announcement of the Davidic Covenant by the prophet Nathan, David's line became the source for national leaders—not the prophets. Samuel's function following Saul's anointing shows the new role for prophets. They are divine counselors to the kings, who are to follow their instruction. Saul's failure to follow the prophetic word led to his removal from kingship and no further guidance from Samuel (1 Sam. 13–15).[2] This function is sometimes called a *court prophet*. Most prophets after Samuel were court prophets—when they were allowed to be! Some, like Elijah and Elisha, were not welcome in the court of disobedient Ahab. Others, like Nathan and Gad, were trusted counselors at David's court. At times, then, a message in the prophetic books addresses the king as the implementer of national policy and justice. At other times messages are directly addressed to the people as a challenge to their lifestyle or an encouragement of their faith.[3]

JONAH—RELUCTANT PROPHET OF YAHWEH'S COMPASSION

Our earliest prophetic book is unique. The book of Jonah is a narrative about a series of events in the life of this prophet. Jonah's ministry belongs alongside that of Amos and Hosea in the eighth century B.C., during the reign of Jeroboam II (793–753). Jonah's only other prophecy is recorded in 2 Kings 14:25 where he predicts the full restoration of the borders of Israel.

Some have questioned the historical reliability of the narrative, preferring to read it as historical fiction, parable, or allegory with a theological point. No doubt, a theological point is being made—something true of all biblical narrative—but this does not signal that the events are nonhistorical. Of course, those who cannot accept the supernatural must declare the book less than historical. Being swallowed by a great fish does have the ring of a fable to it, but like other biblical miracles it has a significant purpose and rationale and is narrated without fascination or sensation. It is not for mere astonishment. Furthermore, the account itself recognizes its exceptional character. It was a fish that the Lord had "provided" or "appointed." Those who need their miracles on a more moderate scale have less problem with God growing a vine at just the right time and place to shade Jonah's temporary hut (4:5–8). Yet, how is this more difficult for God? Both involve only timing and control of animal or plant life. And, though this narrative is unique among the Twelve, it is similar to the stories of the prophetic ministries of Elijah and Elisha in the former prophets.

Literary Flow

The book is composed in a balanced manner. It divides neatly in half, corresponding to Jonah's two calls and responses (see outline below). Each half also divides into two parts—the last half paralleling the first.

Figure 13.1

Jonah's First Call (chs. 1–2)	Jonah's Second Call (chs. 3–4)
Jonah's flight (ch. 1)	Jonah's obedience (ch. 3)
God's deliverance (ch. 2)	God's deliverance (ch. 4)

For a narrative so creatively crafted, significant differences arise among interpreters over the point of the story. Virtually all agree that whatever the major point, it must line up with the abrupt ending of the book. Jonah finishes with a rhetorical question from the Lord: "You have been concerned about this vine. . . . Should I not be concerned about that great city?" (4:10–11). Also crucial is Jonah's anger. He says he is angry because he knew all along that Yahweh was a gracious and compassionate God . . . "a God who relents from sending calamity." And he requests his life be ended (4:1–3). Multiple suggestions have been made as to why Jonah is angry and what point God is making with his rhetorical question.

An older and widely held view understands Jonah's anger to arise from his concern that God would relent on the predicted judgment and then Jonah would be viewed as a false prophet. Thus, he was angry with God's compassion.[4] More recently Jonah has been pictured as a narrow nationalist, representing the nation Israel after the Exile, who had developed an exclusivistic theology that limited God's grace to Israel. The notion that Jonah was written to combat post-exilic narrowness, however, overshoots the evidence, as Dumbrell points out.[5] It is appropriate, however, to recognize the emphasis on God's compassion beyond the borders of Israel in our book. First, there is the irony of Gentile sailors who in fear first cry to their own gods, then hear about Jonah's God, Yahweh, who is the Creator, and fear even more (1:10). Finally, through Jonah's admission, they end up praying to Yahweh and when the sea grows calm, fearing him, and offering sacrifice and making vows to him (1:16).[6] Jonah himself knows God as compassionate. He applies to Nineveh terms found in God's own self-description at the Exodus when he had compassion for Israel, though they deserved to be eliminated as a nation (4:2; Ex. 33:19). Jonah has no narrow nationalist theology. He knows God is likely to be compassionate. Jonah does not want compassion for Assyria in particular—the ruthless nation that has invaded Israel in the prior reign of Joash and the biggest threat to Israel in his century. And in that regard, Jonah proved accurate. Whatever level of repentance Assyria demonstrated, there is no historic evidence that it was long-lasting. And, it is Assyria who leveled Israel within a generation.

Jonah, then, is angry because God's sovereign mercy does not line up with his idea of how and when it should be exercised. The Assyrians deserve punishment, not compassion. The irony of the story is that Jonah's own disobedience in the first half of the book did not really deserve God's deliverance either. Yet Jonah expected his own deliverance, as his thanksgiving psalm shows (2:1–9).[7] Neither did the angry prophet deserve the vine that God provided to shade him under his inadequate shelter. As Jonah did not create the vine in which he rejoiced, Yahweh had more reason to be concerned about the people of Nineveh whom he created. How is it that God's people sometimes feel they deserve God's grace, but others have sinned too greatly?

Themes and Theology

Surely the book knows Yahweh as the true Creator (1:9), who is in full charge over the natural elements (1:4; 1:17; 2:3, 6, 10; 4:6, 7, 8), over peoples (3:10; 4:11), over his prophet (1:1, 17; 3:1–4), and over history (3:4, 10). Further, Yahweh is the living God who exercises, not only moral judgment but also grace and compassion—a compassion that no one truly deserves.

> Those who cling to worthless idols
>> forfeit the grace that could be theirs (2:8; cf. 4:2).

AMOS—PROPHET OF JUSTICE

> Let justice roll on like a river,
> Righteousness like a never-failing stream (6:24).

Amos, a mere shepherd-orchardist by trade, shows up at Bethel, the central shrine of the northern kingdom, Israel. Here he addresses a newly prosperous class under Jeroboam II (793–753 B.C.) who were sure that they had entered the millennium of God's blessing. Borders seemed secure; commerce boomed; religious rites were celebrated. Yet much of this golden age was marked by oppression (2:6–8). Yahweh, however, as a roaring lion from Zion, the legitimate place of worship, was ready to attack (1:1–2). Through Amos, the tree farmer from Judah, listen to him roar.

Flow of the Book

Oddly, the book opens, not with judgment on Israel but on her neighbors (chaps. 1–2). Though the circle of nations on Israel's borders are not in covenant with Yahweh, he is the sovereign Creator and calls them to account for atrocities against humanity. The circle of judgment ultimately closes in on Judah (2:4–5) and finally the pin drops: The longest charges are against Israel herself (2:6–16). Any earlier smugness of Amos' audience over the judgment on foreigners is wiped away as she is charged with violations of covenant law, including idolatry, cultic prostitution, and persecution of Nazarites and prophets. Not only do these leaders fail to live up to covenant justice, but they prevent others from the pursuit of God.

As one might expect, a full round of judgment oracles—this time aimed exclusively at Israel—follows (chaps. 3–6, see outline). Each oracle begins with "Hear this word." Two "Woe" oracles follow these judgment oracles, then a final oath of destruction. Each oracle tears away the mask of Israel's rationalizations. Israel's special calling does not exempt her but demands more severe judgment because she has failed to mediate world blessing (chap. 3). The prosperous "cows of Bashan" (4:1–13) push their husbands for luxuries at the price of oppressing the poor but think

Figure 13.2

Outline of Amos
I. Judgment on the Nations (chs. 1–2)
II. Judgment on Israel (chs. 3–6)
A. Three oracles of judgment
B. Two woes of exile
C. Final oath of destruction
III. Five Visions of Judgment (7:1–9:4)
A. Locust plague
B. Fire
C. Plumb line
[Amos defends his call and message]
D. Summer fruit
E. Smashing of temple pillars
IV. Two Final Messages (9:5–15)
A. Destruction of the sinful kingdom
B. Restoration of Davidic rule

their love of worship affirms their rightness with God. With irony the prophet mocks their worship: "Come to Bethel and sin." Oracle #3, a funeral dirge, anticipates the death of Virgin Israel for her injustices. Two judgment "Woes" finish the section. The popular notion that the current prosperity signals the golden age of "the Day of the LORD" is countered with the Woe that that Day would be a day of judgment and darkness for Israel. Look for exile beyond Damascus rather than for the coming kingdom (5:18–27). Woe to leaders who enjoy perks and amusements but make no effort to turn the nation or "grieve over the ruin of Joseph" (6:1–7). Yahweh's self-attesting oath guarantees the doom of Samaria (6:8–14).

Five picturesque visions form the backbone of the next set of prophecies (7:1–9:4). The judgments announced by the first two visions (locust and fire) are passed over when the prophet intercedes. But the vision of the plumb line and that of a basket of ripe summer fruit affirm that Israel is out of plumb morally and going rotten. Thus, the message is, "I will spare them no longer," and is coupled with three "In that day" pictures of the doom to come. In the final vision, the Lord himself stands by the altar at Bethel and commands that the pillars of the temple be smashed. In language that reflects Moses' final challenge (Deut. 30:11–14) to the Israelites to obey the Law because it was not out of reach (in heaven or beyond the sea), the Lord now indicates that even hiding in these distant places will not provide escape from judgment for the moral abuse of that very covenant.

The third plumb-line vision struck a raw nerve with its attack on the false sanctuaries and the house of Jeroboam. Amaziah, priest at Bethel, brought a charge of conspiracy to Jeroboam, the king, and returned with an edict for Amos to go home (7:10–17). Amos defends his prophetic call and for good measure adds a more specific prediction about the dire consequences for the priest's family when the nation falls.

The fifth vision of the Lord smashing the altar and destroying the worshipers is followed by the two final messages (9:5–15): one that celebrates Yahweh as the Almighty Creator who will destroy the "sinful kingdom"; another that predicts restoration of "David's fallen tent," return from exile, and blessing. Finally a note of hope! For the northern kingdom the Day of the LORD is nothing but darkness and destruction, but ultimately under a restored Davidic throne the whole nation will experience "that day" as a blessed future.

Themes and Theology

Amos pronounces a high theology of Yahweh as Creator. As we have seen earlier in Genesis, Yahweh, the God of Israel, is the Creator God and so is sovereign. In Amos this is seen prominently in the pronouncement of judgment on the surrounding nations for atrocities (1:3–2:3) and in the poetic doxologies or hymns (4:13; 5:8–9; 9:5–6). In these it is Yahweh, the Almighty God, who is to be recognized and honored. It is he who gave the

Law to Israel, and it is he who will judge for the social violations of covenant that mark the ruin of the Joseph tribes.

A second theme is the validity of Jerusalem/Zion as the place of worship and the Davidic kingship as the source of future hope. The house of Jeroboam and the false worship shrine at Bethel will be destroyed (7:9, 11; 4:4–5; 7:9; 9:1). It is from Zion, not Bethel, that Yahweh roars (1:2); and it is David's tent that will be restored (9:11). Those who say that the last message is contrary to the rest of the book by announcing hope, fail to realize that such hope is tied not to the future of the doomed northern kingdom but to the future of the Davidic throne.

The dominant theme of the book, however, is its insistence on moral obedience—covenant justice. The rich and politically strong had forsaken a commitment to the social justice of the Law in favor of their own power and luxury. They use God to affirm the status quo. The ease that comes from greed and violence is credited to Yahweh's blessing. How easy to claim God's approval for questionable choices. How easy to use the ritual and emotion of worship and think that God is pleased. But worship must extend to the scales of business, the quality of the product, and the fair treatment of others or it is nothing but empty ritual and self-affirming emotion.

HOSEA—GOD'S UNCONDITIONAL COVENANT LOVE

Who would want to be a prophet if it included the home life of Hosea? Yet, that is the point. Who would want to be God if it includes the pain that he must feel?

Hosea was commanded to take a "wife of harlotry." This situation forms the analogy developed in chapters 1–3. But was she already a harlot, or does this description anticipate her unfaithfulness during the marriage?[8] Either way, Hosea's wife, Gomer, had three children. The first son is named Jezreel (1:3–4). His name predicts the place of God's judgment on the northern kingdom of Israel (1:4–5). The next child, a daughter, is called Lo-Ruhamah ("not loved"). This also announces God's judgment on the northern kingdom. Yet, God will continue to show love to Judah and save them (1:4–7). The third child is called Lo-Ammi ("not my people") by which God announces the official dissolution of his covenant with Israel—"You are not my people, and I am not your God."

Figure 13.3

Outline of Hosea
I. Hosea's Marriage: Judgment and Restoration (chs. 1–3)
II. Catalog of Israel's Failures (chs. 4–13)
III. Final Call to Return for Blessing (ch. 14)

Oddly enough, following such an announcement, what immediately follows is an affirmation about Israel's future, in language reminiscent of the promise to Abraham: "Yet the Israelites will be like the sand on the seashore, which cannot be measured or counted. In the place where it was said to them, 'You are not my people,' they will be called 'sons of the living God'" (1:10–11). This restoration will be accompanied by a reuniting of Israel and Judah under one leader.

The fact that only the first child of Hosea is specifically noted as the prophet's own (1:3–4) appears to be significant. For in the oracle of chapter two, the children are tagged as "children of adultery" (2:4). Such a wife must be dishonored publicly, as will Israel by God. Yet, again, this oracle of dishonor is barely announced, when the announcement of future restoration of relationship is made:

> I will plant her for myself in the land;
>   I will show my love to the one I called 'Not my loved one.'
> I will say to those called 'Not my people,' 'You are my people';
>   and they will say, 'You are my God' (2:23).

Hosea acts out this restoration (chap. 3) by buying back his wife who must stay committed to him for "many days." This "many days" becomes a picture of Israel's intervening time before the blessing:

> For the Israelites will live many days without king or prince, without sacrifice or sacred stones, without ephod or idol. Afterward the Israelites will return and seek the LORD their God and David their king. They will come to the LORD and to his blessings in the last days (3:4–5).

Leaving the analogy of Hosea's marriage and the back-and-forth swing between judgment and restored relationship of chapters 1–3, the next section begins a running catalog of the failures of Israel (chaps. 4–13). Not surprisingly, these include: (1) idolatry and temple prostitution at the false shrines with ignorant priests (4:1–19; 8:11–13); (2) empty ritual, rather than full covenant-keeping ("For I desire mercy, not sacrifice; and acknowledgement of God rather than burnt offerings. Like Adam they have broken the covenant—they were unfaithful to me there," 6:6–7); (3) turning to Assyria for security rather than to repentance and dependence upon God for safety (5:13–15; 8:14). Notably, the prophet is concerned lest the wicked, idolatrous practices of Israel should affect Judah, who is already infected with injustice (4:15; 5:10).

Rather Israel must return to the Lord and fully acknowledge her sins (chap. 14).

> Take words with you
>> and return to the LORD.
> Say to him:
> "Forgive all our sins
> and receive us graciously,
>> that we may offer the fruit of our lips.
> Assyria cannot save us;
>> we will not mount war-horses.
> We will never again say 'Our gods'
>> to what our hands have made,
>> for in you the fatherless find compassion" (14:2–3).

It is then that the relationship can be fully restored:

> I will heal their waywardness
>> and love them freely,
>> for my anger has turned away from them (14:4).

Theme and Theology

This rhythm of God's initial love/Israel's unfaithfulness/judgment/call for repentance/full restoration that runs throughout the book yields its profound theme: *Yahweh is the gracious God of the Covenant.* Whether husband-wife, parent-child, or other analogy is used, Yahweh has given Israel tremendous privilege, calling, and covenant. And she has regularly turned aside. Yet the Lord God Almighty is totally faithful and committed to the good of his people! This high privilege of covenant blessing was the goal for which their forefather Jacob struggled. Where is the struggle and desire for covenant blessing now?

> In the womb he [Jacob] grasped his brother's heel;
>> as a man he struggled with God.
> He struggled with the angel and overcame him;
>> he wept and begged for his favor.
> He found him at Bethel
>> and talked with him there—
> the LORD God Almighty,
>> the LORD [Yahweh] is his name of renown!
> But you must return to your God;
>> maintain love and justice,
>> and wait for your God always (12:3–6).[9]

JOEL—THE DAY OF THE LORD

No one knows when Joel prophesied. He mentions no king but addresses his message to the elders. Only priests are mentioned in the book.

For some this suggests a post-exilic date (485–400 B.C.). For others, his early place in the Twelve, not at the end with the other post-exilic prophets, suggests the reign of the boy-king, Joash, when his uncle and high priest, Jehoiada, ruled (835 B.C.). Barring clear evidence, I have left Joel in its canonical order—a time that has itself recently been advocated convincingly.[10]

Movement and Message

Whatever Joel's timing, his message is clear. In line with the covenantal warning of Deuteronomy 28, Joel calls all members of society to take seriously the current locust plague (cf. Deut 28:38–42). Drunks mourn the loss of drink; priests mourn the lack of drink and grain offerings; farmers will not reap their harvest of grapes and grain (1:1–12). Such a plague could wipe out production for two years! The prophet calls elders and people to fast before Yahweh and cry out to him at the temple (1:13–18). A lament prayer is offered in 1:19–20.

But the existing locust plague is only a forerunner of an even greater impending disaster: The Day of the LORD is coming. This future invasion and judgment—described in terms of an almost surrealistic plague of locusts—is a dark and dreadful day of Yahweh's judgment on the people (2:1–11).[11] "Who can endure it" (2:12)? This impending eschatological judgment, however, can be averted "even now" if the people turn to Yahweh with real repentance and national fasting before Yahweh: "Rend your heart and not your garments" (2:13–17).

Figure 13.4

Outline of Joel
I. The Locust Plague (1:1–20)
A. The devastation mourned (1:1–12)
B. Fasting urged (1:13–18)
C. A lament prayer (1:19–20)
II. The Greater "Locust" Plague (2:1–27)
A. The Day of the Lord is near (2:1–11)
B. Call to repent (2:12–18)
C. Yahweh's answer: deliverance from both plagues (2:18–27)
III. Future Blessing on Israel (2:28–3:21)
A. The Spirit, astral phenomenon, and deliverance at the Day of the Lord (2:28–32)
B. Victory over the nations (3:1–16)
C. Physical blessing, forgiveness, and Presence (3:17–21)

Apparently the nation responded with repentance because the prophet announces Yahweh's compassion upon his people.[12] The invasion of the northern army has been avoided. And, the harvest that the initial locust plague had devoured will be restored (2:18–27). Such a restitution anticipates the future Day of the LORD for blessing (2:28–3:21) that includes: a future outpouring of the Spirit upon all of God's servants regardless of age, class, or gender; end-time astral phenomenon and deliverance for everyone who calls on Yahweh; victory over the nations in the "Valley of Yahweh's Judgment [Jehoshaphat]"; physical prosperity and abundance in the land; forgiveness for his people and the presence of Yahweh in Zion.

Themes and Theology

Joel is a master of succinct phrases that underscore his themes:

- "Rend your heart and not your garments" (2:13).
- "I will pour out my Spirit on all people" (2:28).
- "And everyone who calls on the name of the LORD will be saved" (2:32).
- "I will gather all nations and bring them into the Valley of Jehoshaphat [the LORD's Judgment]" (3:2).
- "Beat your plowshares into swords and your pruning hooks into spears" (3:10).
- "Multitudes, multitudes in the valley of decision! For the day of the LORD is near in the valley of decision" (3:14).
- "The LORD will roar from Zion and thunder from Jerusalem" (3:16).

And the book culminates with the most assuring phrase of all—Yahweh's Presence: "The LORD dwells in Zion!"

Joel raises the daunting specter of Israel herself as the one in need of *repentance* to avoid the wrath of *the Day of the LORD*. The Day of the LORD still will involve judgment on the opposing nations and the ultimate experience of kingdom rule of Yahweh from Zion. Yet everyone in Israel needs to be responsive to Yahweh's warnings to avoid experiencing the Day of the LORD as wrath. If responsive, all of society can experience what few have ever experienced— *direct revelation* by God's Spirit and ultimately the *very Presence of God*.

MICAH—PROPHET OF COVENANT JUSTICE

Micah, a native of Judah, prophesied in the last half of the eighth century during the reigns of Jotham, Ahaz, and Hezekiah (1:1). Assyria was the threatening invader, but the real enemy was the nation's own injustice. A native of Moresheth in the central Judean lowland, Micah lived in the eventual path of the destruction of Sennacherib V.

Flow and Arrangement

The first and final sections of Micah's prophecy summon people and nation to court for Yahweh's witness against them (1:2–2:11; 6:1–7:13; see outline). They have violated their covenant with Yahweh. Samaria is charged with idolatry and injustice, and her infection has spread to Judah as well. The

Figure 13.5

Outline of Micah
I. Prologue: The Word of the LORD (1:1)
II. Indictment of Samaria and Judah (1:2–2:13)
A. Yahweh comes to pronounce judgment (1:2–7)
B. Michah's call to mourning (1:8–16)
C. Woe to oppressors and prophets (2:1–11)
D. Promise of deliverance of a remnant by Yahweh (2:12–13)
III. Present leaders denounced; future greatness proclaimed (3:1–5:15)
A. Present transgression and disaster; future hope for temple and remnant (3:1–4:8)
B. Present agony and exile; future hope for Zion (4:9–13)
C. Present humiliation; future King for Israel (5:1–4)
D. Present Assyrian threat; future victory for Israel (5:5–15)
IV. Yahweh's case against the nation (6:1–7:13)
A. The indictment against Israel (6:1–16)
B. Israel's social decay and misery (7:1–6)
C. The prophet's hope (7:7)
D. Israel's future restoration (7:8–13)
V. Final prayer of worship (7:14–20)

injustices include seizing of lands, bribery of judges, violence, dishonest weights and scales, fraud and deceit. Farmers, small landowners, and poor peasants were dispossessed and cheated by merchants and power brokers. Yahweh's arrival to shake up the nation is announced by a spectacular quaking of mountains and valleys (1:3–4). As is typical in Micah, indictments are capped with messages of hope. Following the first indictment, there is hope for a gathered remnant who will be delivered directly by the Lord, their King, from the Assyrian judgment (2:12–13). This corresponds with what we know about the deliverance of Jerusalem from Sennacherib's siege in 701 B.C. (cf. Isa. 37:14–37; 2 Kings 19:20–36). And, following the final case against the nation, the faithful prophet places his ultimate hope in God as savior (7:7). Such hope will be vindicated in a future rebuilt city of God's justice (7:7–13).

The middle oracles of the book rebuke the leaders and their court prophets for their love of evil and abuse of power (3:1–5:15; see outline). In opposition to the well-rewarded prophets who pronounce peace and blessing upon injustices, Micah proclaims his own inspiration to speak for justice and with God's power (3:5–12). Their abuse will lead not to blessing, but to reducing the capital city of Jerusalem with its proud walls and populated houses into rubble and thickets.

As with the rest of Micah, this middle section alternates between judgment and hope in four rounds (see outline). Each capsule of hope adds a unique feature. Round one: The present will bring total destruction to Jerusalem, but a greater future is predicted: the temple mount as the world-wide center of instruction and Yahweh's gathering of a remnant (3:1–4:8). Round two: The present holds agony and exile to Babylon, but the future holds victory for Zion (4:9–13). Round three: Israel's present king will be humiliated and under siege, but in the future the original birthplace of David will yield a king whose origins are from ancient days.[13] He will shepherd the flock in security (5:1–4). Round four: Presently Assyria is a threat, but the future holds ultimate victory over all foes (5:5–15).

A final prayer of worship looks to God as that future Shepherd—a God who is unique in his pardoning of sin, his compassion, and his uncondi-tional love and faithfulness to his covenant with Abraham (7:14–20).

Themes and Theology

Far from containing contradictory themes of judgment versus deliver-ance, as some scholars argue, Micah provides a consistent alternating pat-tern between present judgment and future hope. Micah's theology centers around the covenants. In the present is *Israel's violation of covenantal law*. Micah's prescription "to act justly and to love mercy and to walk humbly with your God" (5:8) is not a new commandment, but summarizes the very essence of submitting to God's just decrees and so loving him with all one's heart, soul, and strength as the Mosaic Covenant proclaimed. For deliberate failure, Israel and Judah would feel the near-term judgment of the Assyrian invader—a judgment which would decimate the land and bring Jerusalem under siege. Yahweh will deliver the remnant in Jerusalem (2:12–13), but the judgment would mean exile immediately for many and a further exile to Babylon for the rest. *God's own mercy and faithfulness to the Abrahamic Covenant*, however, will mean a future for the nation, a future for Zion, a future Davidic King and final victory and peace.

ISAIAH—PROPHET OF THE HOLY ONE OF ISRAEL

Born in the eighth century B.C. and prophesying under four kings, Isa-iah has long been considered the prince of prophets. In fact, his access to kings suggests a noble birth. However that may be, the book of Isaiah addresses a wide range of audience—from King Uzziah (Azariah) of Judah to those beyond him experiencing the Babylonian captivity. As this exceeds the normal lifetime of several prophets, it has become commonplace to see at least two prophets—the original Isaiah and an anonymous prophet of post-exilic Judaism given the moniker Deutero- or Second Isaiah.

Such a designation does point to something very clear about the book: There are two very distinct halves written from different perspectives. The first half (Isa. 1–39) is largely filled with indictments of the nation for her sin and threatens the Assyrian invasion. The last half (Isa. 40–66) is often called the "Book of Consolation" and addresses people in exile in Babylon to challenge their faith and offer hope. In addition, chapters 36–39 provide a narrative transition that irreversibly links the two parts.

Flow of the Book

The first half of the book provides the context for the whole. It is laid out in intriguing fashion with the first twelve chapters forming the crucial base for the whole prophecy.

The mini-book. Isaiah 1–5 precedes the account of Isaiah's call in chapter six. Usually a prophet's call comes first. Why five chapters of material before the call? Two likely answers: (1) The first five chapters with their burning indictment of Israel, invitation to repentance, and visions of judgment and hope provide both an introduction and a mini-book of the essence of Isaiah's prophecy. This introduction concludes with the Song of the Vineyard—a stirring parable about God's disappointment in the nation. (2) The description of Israel's tragic condition gives clear meaning to the symbolism and significance of Isaiah's call. Israel is described as "a sinful nation . . . loaded with guilt" (1:4). She is compared to an ox and donkey, and comes in third (1:2)! Addressed as "Sodom" and "Gomorrah" (1:9–10), her sacrifices (as in Amos) and temple activities are no more meaningful to God than wearing out the temple floor (1:11–12). Her scarlet hands, bloodied by injustice, need cleansing (1:15–17). Judgment is inevitable (1:25–28), yet a future day of eschatological blessing for Jerusalem is still the hope of the world (2:1–5).

Vision and call. Isaiah 6 as Isaiah's call opens with a surreal vision of the Ultimate Ruler that makes even modern computerized cinematography seem like child's play. This vision uniquely defines the perspective and message of the book. First, it recognizes who is truly the King, the Lord seated on an exalted throne. The throne is positioned high above the temple—the designated place of worship of the King—and the train of his robe fills it. Yahweh, the powerful Ruler of the Armies of Heaven, is recognized as the true King, worthy of worship, by the seraphim. These angelic beings with three pairs of wings, surround him in his exalted form and recognize him as absolutely unique. So awesome is the King that two pairs of wings are needed to humbly cover their angelic faces and feet in the presence of such glory. Reduced in flight to one-third wing power, they speak of him as they hover: "Holy, holy, holy is the LORD Almighty; the whole earth is full of his glory." Immediately, in response, the doorposts and thresholds of the temple shake and the sanctuary is suddenly filled with the smoke of worship.

Next, in contrast to the superlatively Holy One, Isaiah and Israel are seen to be in abysmal shape. The vision of the King is self-condemning and suggests dire consequences. Professing unclean lips for himself and Israel, Isaiah is cleansed by Yahweh with a live coal from the altar. Forgiveness and atonement are possible with Yahweh.

Finally, Isaiah's mission is defined. After readily volunteering to be the Lord's messenger, Isaiah is handed a discouraging message and mission. His message will fall on deaf ears and callous hearts. It will only serve to harden them further. Such a difficult ministry begs for Isaiah's next question: "For how long, O Lord?" The unsettling answer: until the nation is ruined and in exile.

Case study. Isaiah 7–12 provides the reader with a case study of Israel's problem. It opens with Isaiah confronting the faithless King Ahaz of Judah. Isaiah, along with his prophetically named son, Shear-Jashub ("a remnant shall return") confronts a king haunted by fear. Judah is threatened by Israel ("Ephraem"), who has allied itself with Aram (Syria). Isaiah's message was intended to calm his fears. The two invaders are mere "smoldering stubs of firewood" whose kingdoms are soon to expire. But Ahaz, lacking faith, cannot accept good news—even though he is offered a sign, any sign, from as low as Sheol or as high as the heavens (7:10). Ahaz uses Scripture to reject the offer of a startling miracle with a pious-sounding answer: "I will not put the LORD to the test" (cf. Deut. 6:16; cf. Matt. 4:7). A frustrated Isaiah rebukes Ahaz for truly testing God's patience and announces that the LORD will choose the sign. Yahweh's sign: A virgin will become pregnant, produce a son, and call him Immanuel ("God with us"). By the time the son is old enough to tell right from wrong, the lands of the two dreaded kings will be laid waste.[14] This title, Immanuel, and its meaning ("God with us") is used throughout this oracle of Isaiah (8:8, 10) and ultimately leads us to a final Immanuel in 9:1–7. This final child, who is called by divine names ("Mighty God,"[15] "Everlasting Father"), brings the light of salvation to Israel first in Galilee and then on David's throne forever. The local sign of 7:14, then, however fulfilled in Isaiah's time,[16] was the acorn out of which grew the long-term prophecy of a Future Ruler who would be God with Us for salvation and an enduring kingdom of peace.

But Ahaz's faithlessness calls for chastening, and his own land will be laid waste—not by his feared foes of Israel and Aram, but by Assyria. Assyria as the rod of Yahweh's anger (10:5) will eliminate the two opponents, but also will deal Judah a devastating blow (8:6–8). The threat of the Assyrian plague invokes another ultimate eschatological prophecy of blessing—the prediction of a righteous and wise Davidic King whose reign will bring in ultimate peace and universal knowledge of Yahweh (chap. 11). Israel will then finally recognize the thrice Holy One of Israel as her true strength and delivering King. "Great is the Holy One of Israel among you" (12:6).

Nations and the future. Isaiah 13–27 introduce Isaiah's prophecies against the nations. Such prophecies encourage Israel by affirming God's justice as well as his ability to redeem them from the nations who oppress and carry them off into exile. An eschatological prophecy of God's judgment of the earth and final establishment of the worship of all the earth at Zion caps off the section (chaps. 24–27).

Judah and the future. Isaiah 28–35 switch to a series of "woes" that highlight the blindness and folly of Judah. Following the pattern of Isaiah 13–27 this section of judgment is also capped by an eschatological vision (chaps. 34–35, which pronounce final judgment on the nations and the thrilling prospect of restoration for the redeemed—"everlasting joy will crown their heads," 35:10).

From Assyria to Babylon. Isaiah 36–39 serve as a transition from the Assyrian period to the Babylonian. Switching to narrative, the amazing story of Jerusalem's deliverance from Sennacherib is related (chaps. 37–38). This concludes the Assyrian threat that dominated the first half of Isaiah. The next story about God's deliverance of Hezekiah from a fatal illness and the subsequent tour he gave to emissaries from Babylon opens the door to the rest of the book. This tour of the king's treasures becomes the occasion for Isaiah to prophesy that the Babylonians, not the Assyrians, will be the ones who will carry Jerusalem into exile. When Hezekiah hears that this will occur after his death, he comments: "The word of the LORD you have spoken is good." These transitional chapters conclude with his haunting words: "There will be peace and security in my lifetime."

Consolation and challenge. In Isaiah 40–66, the bullet of exile is certain, and looking down the line of history, Isaiah—just as he prophesied exile in prophecies of the first half of the book (5:13, 14:1–4)—now provides Judah with messages for exiles.[17] So begins the second half of the book of Isaiah, the "Book of Consolation."[18] And consolation comes quickly as the prophet announces God's message of comfort.

> Comfort, comfort my people,
>   says your God.
> Speak tenderly to Jerusalem,
>   and proclaim to her
> that her hard service has been completed,
>   that her sin has been paid for,

that she has received from the LORD's hand
   double for all her sins (40:1–2).

As pictured, exile is about over! Not only that, the exiles may look for a new and greater Exodus journey back to the land, led by God in a triumphal parade of his glory on a smooth highway. Humanity perishes, generation after generation—including Israel's oppressors—but God's Word and promise hold good (40:3–8)! Can they grasp it? Can they understand that God will come to Zion and tend his flock like a shepherd? Can they fathom that the great Creator of heavens and earth is greater than the nations, greater than their useless idols? Can they realize that Yahweh, the Holy One of Israel, has no equal; that their God is Creator and rules sovereignly over all that comes to pass? Or have they become discouraged over the passing of generations? Why do they complain, "My way is hidden from the LORD; my cause is disregarded by my God"? Those who still hope—those who wait for Yahweh to fulfill his Word—will see it happen. Even now he gives strength to the weary exile who waits, but someday, someday

They will soar on wings like eagles;
   they will run and not grow weary,
   they will walk and not be faint (40:31).

They will see it happen. Faith will become sight. They will walk that highway back to Zion.

But there is more to deal with than the *ultimate restoration of Zion* and return from exile. Isaiah weaves in other alternating themes. For one, Judah needs, not just consolation, but a *challenge to finally reject idolatry*. Idolatry is leading to exile, and a restored Israel must finally reject the gods and their demeaning worship. With scathing satire the prophet mocks the making of these useless vanities (44:12–20). In contrast to speechless idols, the Holy One of Israel (remember Isaiah's call?) predicts history and fulfills it! Even Cyrus, who has no knowledge of Yahweh, is announced by name in advance and does Yahweh's bidding on the pages of history. Cyrus is Yahweh's anointed king and conqueror for the task of delivering Israel, God's servant (44:26–28; cf. 48:3–6). Yahweh alone is Creator; there is no god besides him who declared long ago what happens today (45:18–22; cf. 55:11). His Word alone is good and will see its ultimate vindication in the eschatological future:

By myself I have sworn,
   my mouth has uttered in all integrity
   a word that will not be revoked:

> Before me every knee will bow;
>> by me every tongue will swear.
> They will say of me, "In the LORD alone
>> are righteousness and strength" (45:23–24).

Just as Yahweh as the true God alone fulfills his promise and brings to pass his predictions, so he has a plan for world redemption. This plan centers on his servant. *The servant theme* in these chapters is strategic for God's plan for Israel and the world. It started with Abraham as God's friend (41:8). God's promise to Abraham is Israel's and the world's hope. Because of her connection to Abraham as his offspring, Israel was called to be God's servant (41:8–14) and a light to the nations to illumine them concerning the true and living God (42:6–7). Unhappily, she herself has become blind, following other gods (42:19). Yet, Jacob is still his chosen servant. Yahweh will redeem her and give her new life by his Spirit (44:1–5, 21–22).

The servant, however, is not merely Israel. There is a future Servant who will restore Israel herself and finally succeed at being the light to the nations. The salvation of Yahweh will finally reach to all the earth, fulfilling the mission of the Abrahamic Covenant (49:6). This individual Servant is described in detail—his marred and startling appearance, his unlikely beginning, his rejection, his vicarious suffering (52:13–53:12). This Servant is not the whole nation, for "He was pierced for our transgressions, he was crushed for our iniquities" (53:5). Indeed, "We all, like sheep, have gone astray, each of us has turned to his own way; and the LORD has laid on him the iniquity of us all" (53:6). His death is a guilt offering, yet he will see his offspring and prolong his days! Again, the Servant's suffering cannot be Israel's suffering in the exile, because Israel there suffers for her own guilt (cf. 50:1). This final Servant, who arises in the line of servant Abraham and servant Israel, is undoubtedly to be equated with the Davidic King whom they await (55:3–4).[19]

Those sins for which the Servant suffers are detailed in chapters 57–60. Her idolatry "under every green tree" and her slaughter of children; her empty fasting; her injustice and neglect of the poor; her violence and iniquity—all bring God's wrath for a season. "In anger I struck you, in favor I will show you compassion" (60:10). Her ending glory will be greater than the darkness of her transgression. And, not finding anyone—no Cyrus—up to the task, *God himself will intervene as conqueror*—still another important theme:

> So his own arm worked salvation for him,
>> and his own righteousness sustained him.
> He put on righteousness as a breastplate,
>> and the helmet of salvation on his head;
> The Redeemer will come to Zion . . . (Isa. 59:16–20; cf. 63:1–6).

So far we have seen Yahweh the Conqueror, Cyrus the anointed deliverer, the Servant, the Davidic King. Who else? In Isaiah 61:1–4 another voice is heard. Is it the prophet? Or, is it the Servant? This one—reminiscent of the ideal Davidic King from earlier in Isaiah (cf. 11:1–5)—announces that God's Spirit is upon him and he is *anointed* to bring good news—the news of liberty and the restoration of Zion.

Ultimately, there is not only a new name for God's servants among Israel and a delivered Zion, but there is a new heavens and new earth in which the former troubles will not be remembered. Jerusalem will be a joy. Violence and destruction will cease, even among the animal kingdom (65:15–25). The people of Covenant will remain as long as the new heavens and earth; and all humanity shall come to worship the God of Jacob (66:18–24).

Summary of Themes

To sum up, the whole book of Isaiah may be viewed as a triangle of themes:[20]

Figure 13.6

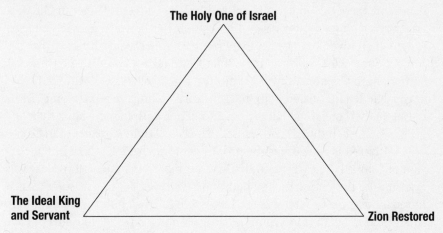

God as the heavenly King is transcendently the Holy One and the true Creator who will ultimately redeem Zion. The ideal Davidic King and/or Servant will suffer, then rule in justice, not only over Zion but over the whole earth. Nations will recognize Yahweh as the true God and come to Zion to worship. Thus Israel's national destiny will finally be fulfilled with world redemption and peace.

COMPLETION OF THE PROPHETS

On the way to Emmaus with two disciples, Jesus proclaimed that Moses and all the prophets spoke of him (Luke 24:27). As we examine the prophets, how did they speak of him? There are, of course, those highly direct passages that speak of a future and a Davidic King who will rule over Israel and the nations in peace and justice forever. These obviously anticipate one whom the Jewish people came to look for as "the Messiah." Passages like Micah 5:2 come to mind, where the future Davidic King is born, not in Jerusalem, the normal place of birth of all kings subsequent to David, but like the original David—in Bethlehem. This King would be a new David who would "shepherd his flock in the strength of the LORD" and whose "greatness will reach to the ends of the earth" bringing "peace" (Mic. 5:4–5). Hosea 3:4 likewise looks for a new David whom the people after "many days without king or prince . . . will come to the LORD their God and David their king. They will come trembling to the LORD and to his blessings in the last days" (Hos. 3:4–5). Isaiah 9 and Isaiah 11 must be mentioned here as well. Out of the stump of Jesse comes a future Branch who reigns in justice and bears divine titles. Such titles as "Everlasting Father" must surely have raised the eyebrows of the godly in Israel and Judah. The term *Father* in Old Testament thought could represent the relationship between Yahweh and the King—"I [Yahweh] will be his Father, and he [the Davidic King] will be my son" (2 Sam. 7:14). On the other hand, the term *Father* is often used as equivalent to Creator. Yahweh is thus the Father of creation and the Father of Israel in that he created both. In either case, calling the human king "Everlasting Father" suggests that we have someone with higher status than any human king, including David himself. The New David is greater than David.

Also in this category is the prophecy of Isaiah 52:13–53:12. The Servant of Yahweh is clearly an individual, yet represents the nation. Here was one (unlike the nation) who "had done no violence, nor was any deceit found in his mouth. Yet it was the LORD's will to crush him and cause him to suffer" and make his life "a guilt offering." Though "we all, like sheep, have gone astray, each of us has turned to his own way; and the LORD has laid on him the iniquity of us all." Can anyone read the whole of Isaiah 53 and fail to make the connection with the fulfillment in the son of David named Jesus of Nazareth? And how does this servant become a guilt offering and yet "prolong his days?" After his suffering, "he will see the light of life" and "justify many." Do not the details speak for themselves? And no one can claim that the prediction was made after the fact, as we possess copies of Isaiah that are actually older than the birth of Jesus of Nazareth. Who can avoid the connection made by the apostle Peter to Christ (1 Peter 3:21–25). "By his wounds you have been healed. For you were like sheep going astray, but now you have returned to the Shepherd and Overseer of your souls." Who would want to avoid this glorious message? God has sent his Servant, who has addressed the problem of sin and guilt. Redemption is provided!

Yet, the message goes deeper than that. For in the convergence of themes, we find that not only the servant theme is fulfilled in Jesus, we find that the anticipation of Yahweh himself as conqueror is understood to be fulfilled in Jesus. Just as the New David bears divine names, so *God coming himself to conquer* will be fulfilled in Jesus. It is significant that as Paul lists the Christian's battle armor in Ephesians 6:10–20 he combines the armor of the coming King and the armor of God as conqueror from the book of Isaiah. (By the way, Paul did not get the armor in Ephesians 6 from looking at a Roman soldier. The battle gear comes from Isaiah 11:5, 59:17, and 52:7.) Even though the final battle that Christ leads at his second coming is still future, Paul believes that Christians may already be suited in Christ's conquering armor to fight spiritual battles today for Christ as his people. The story of Christianity is the story that God himself found "no one to intercede" (Isa. 57:16) and so himself comes—"The Redeemer will come to Zion" (Isa. 57:20).

SUGGESTED SCRIPTURE READING:

Hosea 1–3
Joel 2:28–3:21
Amos 1–2; 9
Jonah 1–2
Micah 1; 5:1–4, 7
Isaiah 1–12; 40; 52–53; 57; 61

For Interaction and Discussion:

1. How does the prophetic notion of justice relate to notions of justice today? What types of injustice are particularly stressed in these prophetic books?

2. How does the notion of hope relate to the message of judgment? How can these both be true?

3. What examples do we have of "telescoping" of the final outcome in a way that associates it with the current times? What are the advantages and disadvantages of this feature of prophesy? How does this relate to the question of the imminency of the future kingdom of God?

4. What features of God does the title "The Holy One of Israel" suggest? How does this title relate to the future servant and restoration?

5. In what variety of ways is the Day of Yahweh pictured in the prophets? Why is it called "the Day of the LORD"?

6. What is the importance of covenant to the prophets? In what way is God's grace evident in these books?

For Further Reading:

C. Hassell Bullock. *An Introduction to the Old Testament Prophetic Books*. Chicago: Moody, 1986.

William J. Dumbrell. *The Faith of Israel*. Grand Rapids: Baker, 1988, 97–111, 141–73. Helpful summary of the theology of each book.

John R. Kohlenberger III. *Jonah and Nahum*. Chicago: Moody, 1984. Insightful treatment for the English reader.

Robert B. Chisholm, Jr. *Interpreting the Minor Prophets*. Grand Rapids, Zondervan, 1990. Serious treatment for the English student with literary insights.

Herbert W. Wolf. *Interpreting Isaiah: The Suffering and Glory of the Messiah*. Grand Rapids: Zondervan, 1985. Excellent compendium and commentary on Isaiah for the English student.

J. Alec Motyer. *The Prophecy of Isaiah: An Introduction and Commentary*. Downers Grove, Ill.: InterVarsity, 1993. Solid academic and readable treatment, especially for discussion of themes.

Thomas Edward McComiskey, ed. *The Minor Prophets*. 2 vols. Grand Rapids: Baker, 1992. Solid academic commentary by evangelical scholars on The Twelve.

Duane A. Garrett. "The Structure of Joel." *JETS*, 28 (1985): 289–97.

Pablo R. Adinâch. "The Locusts in the Message of Joel." *VT*, 42 (1992): 433–41.

Notes and Comments:

[1]Carl Sagan, *Pale Blue Dot* (New York: Random House, 1994).

[2]When the text of 1 Samuel 15:34–35 says that Samuel did not see (NIV, "go to see") Saul again until the day of his death, I take it to mean that he would not consult with Saul as God's prophet. He actually did see him when Saul pursued David to Ramah (1 Sam. 19:23–24). Yet, only on the literal day of his death did Saul "see" Samuel in the sense of getting a prophetic word from him (1 Sam. 28:11–20).

[3]Scholars generally make a distinction between classical and preclassical prophets. Preclassical prophets, like Samuel, Nathan, Elijah, and Elisha, are seen as primarily giving God's word to the king concerning guidance and rebuke. The writing prophets are labelled as classical prophets. They are seen as widening the prophetic ministry to speak directly to the people about social justice, warnings of judgment, and calls to repentance.

[4]Though the view that Jonah was disturbed because he would be viewed as a false prophet has a long and impressive following in the history of interpretation, it

seems a bit overdrawn. If Jonah already knew that God had an option to relent, then he obviously understood that the message of judgment in forty days was conditional. Is this any different from the message of Isaiah to Hezekiah (Isa. 38:1–6)? Isaiah informed Hezekiah that he would not recover from his illness. After Hezekiah's prayer, Isaiah is sent back to tell him that he has been given fifteen more years. Does this make Isaiah a false prophet? No, because the timing on the first prophecy had not run out before the new modification was given. The same would be true for Jonah. The forty days have not run their course, and God always has the right to change his actions—especially when there has been a change in those to whom the prophecy was directed. Jonah already suspects that God will change his word of judgment to compassion, but this does not make Jonah a false prophet, and it is hard to see how Jonah would think that it did.

[5]Dumbrell's comments on the view that Jonah was intended as a condemnation of Israelite particularism are appropriate. "Such a theme, however, is nowhere pronounced, and it detracts from the more general issues. . . . Equally, the book is not intended to resolve the difficult problems of the exilic period (i.e., mixed marriages and collaboration within the land with foreigners), for these matters are not brought up" (William J. Dumbrell, *The Faith of Israel*, 172).

[6]See ibid., 169, for a chart of the chiastic arrangement of this section that clearly brings out the emphasis on the various types and stages of fear for the Gentile sailors.

[7]The objection that Jonah's prayer in 2:10 is a thanksgiving psalm that should come after his arrival on dry ground, or that it should be a lament psalm praying for deliverance if it is offered in the belly of the fish, misses the significance of both the placing and the type of psalm, as Kohlenberger observes. Jonah already prayed his prayer for help (lament) while drowning (cf. 2:2–6). When he finds himself conscious in the fish's belly, he recognizes that his prayer is being answered and offers his thanksgiving with the promise of future sacrifice and vows (2:9). John R. Kohlenberger III, *Jonah and Nahum* (Chicago: Moody, 1984), 45–55.

[8]Some object to a prophet marrying a harlot, yet the Law only proscribes a priest from such a marriage. The real question is the analogy in the book. Is Israel presented as unfaithful before she was married to Yahweh by covenant at Sinai? Or is she accused of unfaithfulness only afterward? Cf. Walter Kaiser, *Toward an Old Testament Theology*, 197–98, for a vigorous defense of later unfaithfulness only. Cf. Thomas Edward McComiskey, "Hosea," *The Minor Prophets*, ed. Thomas Edward McComiskey, 2 vols. (Grand Rapids: Baker, 1992), 1:13–16. McComiskey not only argues, as do many others, for Gomer's being a prostitute when Hosea married her but also suggests two groups of children. The three in chapter one are Hosea's, but others from Gomer's past must have been adopted by Hosea. The basis for this suggestion is the use of the plural "sisters" in 2:3. The two brothers in chapter 1 apparently have only one sister by Hosea.

[9]C. Hassell Bullock, *An Introduction to the Old Testament Prophetic Books*, (Chicago: Moody, 1986), 98, provides an alternative interpretation to the reference to Jacob. He sees it, along with the other examples in the context, to be a negative

reference—citing the tendency of Israel to struggle with God going back to Jacob's precedent-setting problems with faith.

[10]Summaries of arguments for a ninth century B.C. date for Joel during the minority of Joash (c. 835 B.C.) as well as a post-exilic date of c. 400 B.C. may be found in Hobart E. Freeman, *An Introduction to the Old Testament Prophets* (Chicago: Moody, 1968), 147–49, who favors the early date, and R. K. Harrison, *Introduction to the Old Testament* (Grand Rapids: Eerdmans, 1969), 876–79, who slightly favors a post-exilic date. More recently Richard D. Patterson, "Joel," *EBC* (Grand Rapids: Zondervan, 1985), 7:231–33, has argued persuasively for an early eighth-century date.

[11]The interpretation of Joel centers around three crucial interpretive decisions. First, has the initial plague of chapter one already occurred, or is the description a warning of a future plague? With most commentators it seems best to understand Joel as giving the reason for a locust invasion that has already occurred. Second, is the invasion of chapter two a future greater locust invasion, or is Joel using the locust plague as a metaphor for a future invasion of an army? Here commentators are divided. Certainly it is at least a greater plague of locusts. The argument against a human army is that the locusts are pictured as being like an army. Would a writer use an army as a simile for describing locusts that were themselves to be symbolic for an army? It sounds confusing, but such a reversal could be an effective literary device. The third interpretive decision is the most crucial: Does "Then afterward, I will pour out my Spirit . . ." in 2:28 begin the timing of the ultimate future blessing, or is it connected to the more immediate relief? It would seem best to take it with what follows (especially 3:1: "in those days") as the beginning announcement of Israel's ultimate blessing. Cf. Duane A. Garrett, "The Structure of Joel," *JETS*, 28 (1985): 289–97; Pablo R. Adinách, "The Locusts in the Message of Joel," *VT*, 42 (1992): 433–41.

[12]As noted by Hill and Walton, *A Survey of the Old Testament*, 367, Joel 2:18–19 should be translated as past tense, showing that relief from the immediate locust destruction has been granted.

[13]Note Waltke's discussion of the expression translated as "ancient days" or "days of eternity" in the messianic prophecy of Micah 5:2. Bruce K. Waltke, "Micah," *The Minor Prophets*, ed. Thomas Edward McComiskey, 2:704–5. He concludes that it refers to ties of Messiah to the ancient establishment of the Davidic Covenant. So also Ralph L. Smith, *Micah–Malachi*, WBC (Waco, Tex.: Word, 1982), 43. Kaiser, *Toward an Old Testament Theology*, 203, agreeing with von Orelli, takes it to refer to Messiah's beginnings being rooted in God's ancient plan of redemption.

[14]The meaning of a sign in the Old Testament is of a near-term prophecy or miracle used to confirm a prophet as bringing God's message (e.g., 1 Sam. 3:34). Additionally, the son produced by the virgin is born and still is a boy when the lands of Israel and Syria are laid waste. This means the boy must be born in Ahaz's lifetime. Initially, these observations seem to cast doubt on Matthew's claim (Matt. 1:23) that the sign of Isaiah was fulfilled in Jesus' conception by the virgin Mary. However, such a conclusion misses other compelling observations. Namely, that this is only the first of births in these oracles (8:3, 18; 9:6) and that the name Immanuel runs throughout the section (8:8, 10), finally culminating in the birth of an ultimate child

("For to us a child is born, to us a son is given, and the government shall be upon his shoulders"). This Davidic King bears divine titles ("Mighty God," "Father of eternity," 9:6) and is, therefore, Immanuel. Isaiah's initial sign, then, is only the acorn out of which grows longer-term prophecies about "God with us" (cf. 8:8, 10) At first God is with them in judgment (8:10). This is signified by Isaiah's second child (8:1–4). Then finally, there is the child of 9:1–6, the deliverer who will bring the light of salvation first to northern Galilee of the Gentiles, will be the ultimate righteous King, will bear divine titles (be "Immanuel"), and will establish David's throne forever. So the original sign in 7:14–16 may well have been a virgin in Ahaz's household who was the beginning of an immediate time span. (Marriage + pregnancy + birth + child grows to know right from wrong = ? months + 9 months + c. 4 years; see 8:3–4 for a similar method of marking a time span.) Her son's boyhood would witness the demise of the Aram and Israel, yet the sign is also the thematic seed for Isaiah's continuing oracle that produces the ultimate Immanuel who would reestablish David's throne forever. Is it so strange that Matthew saw Jesus as fulfilling this role announced in germinal form in that initial sign? Is it strange that he would see further significance to this connection when God produces a miracle so that with this ultimate child, a virgin actually produces a son without knowing a man or marrying first? How could he or his Jewish readers miss the significance that Jesus is the Ultimate Immanuel—the Immanuel, not of God with us in judgment, but God with us in bringing the light of salvation?

[15]Sometimes "Mighty God" is interpreted as a figurative expression for a great leader, but Isaiah uses this term in this same oracle for God himself (10:21).

[16]The theories concerning fulfillment of the sign of Isaiah 7:14 are many. Many see double fulfillment—a local sign that is fulfilled in a fuller and more literal way in the New Testament as happens with some of the psalms of David's sufferings. Cf. Herbert M. Wolf, *Interpreting Isaiah: The Suffering and the Glory of the Messiah* (Grand Rapids: Zondervan, 1985), 90–92, who cites a Ugaritic parallel where the announcement "a virgin will give birth" as an announcement of an upcoming marriage and expectation of blessing on the marriage. Wolf takes the local sign to be fulfilled in Isaiah's son in chapter 8. Kaiser, *Toward an Old Testament Theology*, 208–9, holds out for an immediate fulfillment in the birth of Hezekiah, though all modern chronologies would have Hezekiah as nine years old at the time of the prophecy. A ten-year problem in the chronologies of the northern kingdom suggests this possibility to him. Hezekiah would become for Kaiser the near-term shadow (type) of the ultimate Immanuel. Others take the "sign" to be an exception to the immediate nature of a sign, as a play on the word *sign* when Ahaz refuses one. The "sign" then goes far beyond unbelieving Ahaz in the first place—looking only at the ultimate King or Messiah. Others see a mixture of present and future in the sign. The time descriptions in the passage that relate to the immediate future are explained as something that Isaiah does in his prophecies—includes a timescale for the present in longer-term prophecies (cf. Bullock, *Prophetic Books*, 135–37). My own preference in note 14 above, is based upon the study of C. H. Dodd, who found that often NT quotes that seem initially out of context are based on the larger block of Scripture

and contain the thematic elements of that larger block. When the larger block is studied and the verse not seen as a "proof-text" but the initiator of these larger themes, then the justification for the quote is clear. The writer (Matthew in this case) was aware of the larger thematic context. Though Dodd did not study Matthew 1:23, I suggest that his findings would work particularly well here, as the initial sign language becomes the theme of the whole section that does yield an ultimate long-term prophecy of a coming Immanuel. Cf. C. H. Dodd, *According to the Scriptures* (New York: Scribner's, 1953). As to the meaning of *'almāh*, in its few usages in the Old Testament, all clear cases involve someone presumed to be a virgin (see Bullock, *Prophetic Books*, 136) and the LXX translators so translate it before Jesus ever appeared on the scene.

[17]Those who take chapters 40–66 to represent the appended prophecies of a Second Isaiah, see the prophet as speaking during the Exile. The best of these views is that of Childs, *Introduction to the Old Testament*, 328–30, who fully recognizes the ties to the earlier part of the book and concludes that Second Isaiah could only have been written with the purpose of integrating it with First Isaiah—not as a separate prophecy. As many have pointed out, however, chapters 40–66 reflect as much of the neo-Assyrian period as they do the neo-Babylonian period. The extensive sections on idolatry reflect Canaanite practices that would be unknown and irrelevant to a Second Isaiah. Cf. Bullock, *Prophetic Books*, 151–52, and Harrison, *Introduction to the Old Testament*, 777–80.

[18]Kaiser, *Toward an Old Testament Theology*, 212–19; Bullock, *Prophetic Books*, 147–48, see chapters 40–66 as subdivided into three equal sections, whereas some critical scholars see a third prophet ("Third Isaiah") penning chapters 55–66. Rikki E. Watts, in "Consolation or Confrontation? Isaiah 40–55 and the Delay of the New Exodus," *TB*, 41 (1990): 31–59, sees the divisions as 40–48, 48–55, and 56–66. More significant is his observation (among many significant suggestions) that much of the language is confrontational and challenging of the nation's doubt.

[19]Further justification for this identification of the Suffering Servant with the Davidic King is found in the similar metaphor for the origins of this person. In 53:2 the Servant is like "a root out of dry ground"; in 11:1 the Davidic King is a shoot "from the stump of Jesse." In addition there is a similar interchange in the Psalms between the King and the nation as the one speaking. The Davidic King represents and acts for the nation. This shifting between individual and group has been noted by many. Kaiser, *Toward an Old Testament Theology*, 216, summarizes it well: "The apparent ambivalence is the same type of oscillation found in all the collective terms previously observed in the promise. . . . They were all-inclusive of all Israel, but they were simultaneously always focused on one representative who depicted the fortunes of the whole group for that present time and the climactic future. The connection was to be found not in some psychological theory of personality but in the 'everlasting covenant,' even the 'sure loyal love for David' (Isa. 55:3; 61:8; cf. 2 Sam. 7)."

[20]For a stimulating discussion of themes and their integration in Isaiah see J. Alec Motyer, *The Prophecy of Isaiah: An Introduction and Commentary*, esp. 13–25. Cf. Richard J. Clifford, "The Unity of the Book of Isaiah and Its Cosmogenic Language," *CBQ*, 55 (1993): 1–17.

chapter fourteen

The Prophets
of Judah and Exile

It's All Downhill from Here

Until you see it visually, the words of the history books seem tame when they review the causes and battles of the Civil War. Seeing it over nine days in the miniseries, "The Civil War," on PBS brings home the awful, awful carnage.[1] Time after time, we were confronted with skulls, bones, and old battlefields full of skeletons upon which new battles were fought. Yet for me, having taken in all of that, Lincoln's Second Inaugural Address was the climax. In a short speech that could not have lasted five minutes, Lincoln recognized the hand of divine providence in a way that no modern president ever could. Not unlike the prophets, Lincoln speaks with a keen sense of divine justice as he sees the Almighty working out the just results of the evils of slavery for both sides.

> Both [North and South] read the same Bible. Both pray to the same God: and each invokes his aid against the other. It may seem strange that any men should dare to ask a just God's assistance in wringing their bread from the sweat of other men's faces; but let us judge not that we be not judged. The prayers of both could not be answered; that of neither has been answered fully. The Almighty has his own purposes. . . . Fondly do we hope—fervently do we pray—that this mighty scourge of war may speedily pass away. Yet, if God wills that it continue, until all the wealth piled by the bond-man's two hundred and fifty years of unrequited toil shall be sunk, and until every drop of blood drawn with the lash, shall be paid by another drawn with the sword, as was said three thousand years ago, so still it must be said "the judgments of the Lord, are true and righteous altogether."[2]

Wow! To accept the carnage and the economic cost to both North and South as a divine balancing of the books for both sides (*lex talionis*!) would take political courage that no politician could muster in today's climate.

When we are victorious or suffer defeat as a nation, we credit it to our strategy and judgment. We also pray for divine aid, of course, but fail to see why we as a society might endure any losses. We like to think of God as a "grandfather in the sky" shorn (like all modern educated people) of all harshness, endued in "niceness," and dedicated to the proposition that we deserve happiness without facing any consequences for our own departures from God's standards. The God of the Bible is the one who claims the right to judge injustice. He carries out the vengeance due because of man's inhumanity to man and national sins that weaken the social fabric. So prophets such as Nahum, Habakkuk (much to his horror), and Jeremiah come to proclaim judgment, even against the nation founded in true liberty under the covenant law of God.

PROPHETS BEFORE THE EXILE

Following the destruction and exile of the northern kingdom of Israel by Assyria in 722–721 B.C. and the repopulation of the region with foreign peoples, the remaining southern kingdom of Judah went on under Hezekiah. It lasted more than a century before succumbing to a series of exiles to Babylon and the destruction of Jerusalem in 587–586 B.C.

As in the early neo-Assyrian period, prophets warned of the need for Judah to return to the Lord in truth. After Hezekiah, only the reforms of Josiah held promise of such a return. This turned out to be "too little, too late" as the heart of the nation was untouched.

Nahum—Vengeance on Assyria

The prophet Nahum appropriately begins our tour of the prophets of this period because he announces the doom of Nineveh and the King of Assyria. Because Nahum mentions the fall of Thebes (3:8), the book must be dated after that event in 663 B.C. As the fall of Nineveh is anticipated in the book, our prophet must predate that event of 612 B.C. And so, Nahum prophesied roughly a century after the fall of Samaria to the brutal Assyrians.

This book is the counterpoint to the book of Jonah. In Jonah, Yahweh was shown to be the One Who Is Compassionate to Ninevah, in line with the significance of his own proclamation of his Name in Exodus 34:6–7. The full text reads:

> Yahweh, Yahweh, the compassionate and gracious God, slow to anger, abounding in love and faithfulness, maintaining love to thousands, and forgiving wickedness, rebellion and sin. Yet he does not leave the guilty unpunished; he punishes the children and their children for the sin of the fathers to the third and fourth generation.

Now is the time to add Yahweh as the One Who Does Not Leave the Guilty Unpunished.

Literary Flow

Nahum presents both features—Yahweh's goodness and his anger—in the very first address (1:2–11).

> The LORD is slow to anger and great in power;
> > he will not leave the guilty unpunished (1:3).
>
> The LORD is good,
> > a refuge in times of trouble.
> He cares for those who trust in him,
> > but with an overwhelming flood
> he will make an end of Ninevah;
> > he will pursue his foes into darkness (1:7–8).

In our own times God is allowed to be good, but not to judge. For Nahum, nature shakes before Yahweh, the sovereign Creator, who carries out vengeance as righteous retribution (1:2–6). No one is able to stand before his anger. Specifically in this case, Yahweh, who is good, judges Nineveh as one "who plots evil" (1:7–11).

"This is what the LORD says," introduces God's judgment on Nineveh in the remainder of the book, which may be stylistically arranged in a chiastic or mirrored-image arrangement (see outline).[3] Nineveh, having chosen to continue in false worship rather than to follow Yahweh and his righteous ways is pronounced "vile" (1:14). She is "the city of blood, full of lies, full of plunder, never without victims" (3:1). When the Lord of Armies proclaims "I am against you" (2:13; 3:5), your doom is sure. Nineveh will surely be judged to the third and fourth generation (forever), and disappear off the stage of history (2:13–19)

Figure 14.1

Outline of Nahum
Title (1:1)
I. Yahweh's Vengeance Against Nineveh (1:1–11)

II. Yahweh's Judgment Proclaimed (1:12–3:19)
   A. Nineveh's demise; Judah's salvation and celebration (1:12–15)
      B. Call to alarm (2:1–10)
         C. Taunt (2:11–12)
            D. Announcement of judgment (2:13–3:7)
         C'. Taunt (3:8–13)
      B'. Call to alarm (3:14–17)
   A'. Nineveh's demise; all nations rejoice (3:18–19)

Because of Nineveh's demise, the land of Israel can regain her splendor that had been destroyed by Assyria (2:2). Judah will be free from the shackles of Assyria (1:12).

Nahum closes the pages of history on Assyria with an address to the king of Assyria (3:18–19):

> Nothing can heal your wound;
>   your injury is fatal.
> Everyone who hears the news about you
>   claps his hands at your fall,
> for who has not felt
>   your endless cruelty?

Themes and Theology

Yahweh is slow to anger, but as sovereign Creator/Judge who is also great in power, he will bring vengeance on those who reject him and his righteous ways.

Zephaniah—The Universal Day of the Lord

This prophet, a contemporary of Jeremiah and King Josiah, interlocks the Day of the Lord, the nations, and Jerusalem, so much so that it is hard to outline the book! It starts with a clean sweep of the earth—men, animals, birds, and fish (1:2–3).

Literary Flow

In contrast to Amos, where the nations are first addressed for their sins, here judgment begins at the house of God! Judah and Jerusalem are first indicted for their pagan practices and worship (1:4–9). With biting irony, the Lord announces his own sacrifice with the leaders who have adopted pagan worship and dress being the sacrificial victims! Also, they have coupled unjust profit with complacency about God's justice ("The Lord will do nothing, either good or bad"). Such people will be plundered themselves (1:10–13). This precipitates "the great day of the Lord [that] is near—a day of wrath ... distress and anguish ... trouble and ruin ... darkness and gloom ... clouds and blackness ... trumpet and battle cry" (1:14–18). This day will come, not only upon Jerusalem, but "in the fire of his jealousy the whole world will be consumed." Quickly, however, the prophet again turns to the "shameful nation" of Judah, exhorting her to national assembly to "Seek the Lord," "Seek righteousness, seek humility." Perhaps then they would be "sheltered on the day of the Lord's anger."

Shifting back to the nations, in quick order, the Philistines, Moab and Ammon, Cush, and Assyria meet their judgment on this day of wrath (2:4–15). In the case of the first three nations, the future remnant of Judah is also mentioned. They will inherit these territories. Additionally, after the second judgment oracle, future "nations on every shore" are seen as coming to worship the Lord after they see his victory over the false gods of these lands (2:11). There is universal judgment, but there is international worship as a result!

Self-sufficient Assyria with its "carefree city" of Ninevah turned into a ruin is the last among the nations to be condemned, and the prophet turns to the carefree and proud city of Jerusalem under the title "the city of oppressors" (3:1–8). The city, however, is not identified as Jerusalem. The hearers and readers would continue to read as if Ninevah was being addressed. We can see them nodding in agreement at the condemnation of such a city of oppression, only gradually grasping that the prophet was now addressing their own sins.[4] Rulers, prophets, and priests are all seen as ravenous and treacherous. "Morning by morning" the Lord's justice is available. The God of Israel is not the problem. He is still "within her . . ., yet the unrighteous know no shame." Yahweh's judgments on the nations were intended to warn his own city to save her from a similar ruin. "But they were still eager to act corruptly in all they did." Therefore, Yahweh will judge.

Switching back to the nations, Yahweh announces his intention to assemble the nations to pour out his wrath on them and consume the whole world (3:8). Yet not for total destruction, but for total purity. "Then I will purify the lips of the peoples, that all of them may call on the name of the LORD and serve him shoulder to shoulder" (3:9). Offerings will come from distant nations (3:10). And (back to Jerusalem), Zion will also be purified (3:11–13). Only the humbly obedient remain, purged of the deceit of false worship. Such restoration calls for rejoicing (3:14–20). Jerusalem should sing, rejoicing in forgiveness and safety. Yahweh himself will respond in joyful song as he delights in his future people. So, the people will be regathered and brought home to Zion and receive "honor and praise among all the peoples of the earth" (3:20).

Themes and Theology

The zigzagging track of Zephaniah, though hard to reduce to a simple outline, is plain enough in its intention. Zephaniah predicts a *universal Day of the LORD* as a day of wrath for Judah and Jerusalem as well as for the whole earth. This day of darkness and distress, however, also has a positive purpose. It opens the eyes of the nations to the reality of the true God, purges them and Zion of the arrogant, and initiates *restoration of Jerusalem* as the center of delight, blessing, and universal worship of Yahweh. This takes us back to the language and expectation of the *Abrahamic Covenant* in which "all peoples on earth will be blessed through you" (Gen. 12:3).

Habakkuk—Faith Facing Disaster

Habakkuk, like Jonah, is a prophet with a problem. He prophesied during the declining years of Judah, either before Josiah's reforms (640–628 B.C.) or much later in his reign or that of his son Jehoiakim (609–598 B.C.). He, like most prophets, was concerned at the wickedness and injustice in Judah and wants to know when the Lord will answer his call for help.

Literary Flow

The book develops around Habakkuk's two complaints. His first complaint (1:2–4)—that his cry for help against Judah's injustice is not being answered—is answered. The Lord is raising up the ruthless Babylonians who are bent on violence to sweep across the land (1:5–11).

Habakkuk objects to the answer to his prayer! His complaint this time is that God is too holy to tolerate the Babylonians (1:12–17). Though God is using them for judgment, they are more wicked at the same sins that Judah commits. Besides, as idolaters, they do not worship Yahweh and as oppressors they need judgment themselves.

Habakkuk waits as a watchman upon his tower for the Lord's answer. And, come it does (2:1–20). Habakkuk is told to write it clearly on tablets to proclaim it to all who come by. The revelation is yet to come, it may not be soon, but if one waits it will not prove false (2:1–3). It predicts judgment for the instrument of judgment. Because Babylon is not upright in motive but is arrogant, greedy, and violent, six woes are proclaimed against her for her sins (2:6–20). For Babylon and divine justice, what goes around comes around. As she has done to others, so it will be done to her.

Habakkuk's psalm closes the book (3:1–19). He remembers the Lord's deeds in the beginning of Israel's history when God revealed his glory and power in plague and pestilence on the nations, in the parting of waters, in the prolongation of the day, and surprising victory over enemies. His prayer is that these will be renewed in his day, "in wrath remember mercy" (3:2). And while he waits for the answer to his prayer, he will also "wait patiently for the day of calamity" (3:16). Such is the prophet's faith that

> Though the fig tree does not bud
>> and there are not grapes on the vines,
> though the olive crop fails
>> and the fields produce no food,

> though there are no sheep in the pen
> > and no cattle in the stalls,
> Yet I will rejoice in the LORD,
> > I will be joyful in God my Savior.
> The Sovereign LORD is my strength;
> > he makes my feet like the feet of a deer,
> he enables me to go on the heights.

Themes and Theology

Like Job, Habakkuk qualifies as a theodicy—a defense of God. In airing the prophet's problem, the book addresses the problem of injustice. The prophet, concerned about injustice in Israel, could not understand the use of a more unjust people to bring judgment on God's people. God reveals that he uses nations with evil motives and unjust methods to accomplish his will. Yet, because of their motives and methods, they, too, will face divine wrath. For all that effort is spinning of wheels:

> Has not the LORD Almighty determined
> > that the people's labor is only fuel for the fire,
> > that the nations exhaust themselves for nothing?
> For the earth will be filled with the knowledge of the glory of the LORD,
> > as the waters cover the sea (2:13–14).

As the six woes establish, when it comes to divine justice, you reap what you have sown. Yet that is not the final story. When God finally intervenes, the wheels will stop spinning and his glory will be ultimately manifest. But for now, let humanity recognize the true and sovereign God.

> The LORD is in his holy temple;
> > let all the earth keep silent before him (2:20).

And what is the proper human response to such fearful reality as God's judgment? *Faith must win out over fear.* The circumstances of divine chastening must not quench the faith of the righteous saint in his God, his only Savior. Just so, the righteous will live through it all by faith and in faithfulness.

Jeremiah—The Harsh Path to a New Covenant

The Prophet and His Time

If Hosea was called to have a painful family life, Jeremiah had none at all. Beginning his ministry during the reign of Josiah and continuing it through the decline and destruction of Jerusalem, Jeremiah was called to register the disaster ahead for wives and children by foregoing marriage altogether (Jer. 16:1–4). And, it was just as well. It would have been less than fair to ask a partner to share in the extraordinary trials and tensions of this prophet. More of Jeremiah's struggles—inner and outer—are given to us than any other prophet. He not only struggled over the state of the nation, as did Habakkuk, but he struggled with opposition and persecution. Opposition was multiple—kings, priests, their temple prophets, even Jeremiah's own village. Conditions were ugly. He was beaten, threatened by family and neighbors, put into stocks, placed under house arrest, charged with being a traitor, imprisoned in a muddy cistern, and finally taken as an exile to Egypt. The emotional stress comes through—tears and all. At one point the prophet wrestles with depression and despairs of life (20:14–18). Yet for all this, Jeremiah is driven by an inner compulsion to continue to speak Yahweh's Word. He cannot do otherwise—and he trusts in Yahweh's protection (20:9–12). A master of the prophetic object lesson, Jeremiah at one point lay on his side for more than a year.

Flow of the Book

Scholars have struggled with the arrangement of Jeremiah's oracles. They are not chronological, and it is difficult to discover a topical pattern—except for chapters 46–51 which are prophecies against the nations. In addition, the Greek version (LXX) differs from the Hebrew Bible. Most notably chapters 46–51 are found after 26:1–13, and five other passages are not found in the Greek text (17:1–5a; 29:16–20; 33:14–26; 39:4–13; 51:44b–49; 52:27b–30).[5]

We should remind ourselves, as John Bright points out, that prophetic books differ from epistles and narrative books as the oracles were normally delivered individually at various times by the prophet.[6] Then they were gathered into a book. They can be gathered in a way that presents a continuous argument, or they can simply be gathered as an anthology. This latter may be the case with Jeremiah. We may be attempting too much when to try to see a pattern. A collection of prophetic speeches still presents a unity of message and outlook.

On the other hand, most scholars recognize that along with chapters 46–51, chapters 30–33 also are a unit. It centers around the final future under the New Covenant. In addition, we are told that Jeremiah dictated to his scribe, Baruch, a collection of all his prophetic messages from the time of Josiah to the fourth year of Jehoiakim (36:1–3, 32). Many see chapters 1–25 as being that collection with a few later prophecies added.[7] Others see chapters 1–20 as the initial unit with Jeremiah's wish that he had died in the womb (20:17–18) forming an *inclusio* with God's setting him aside for the prophetic task while he was yet in the womb (1:4). This division also matches with the effort of Paul House, who approaches the book from the perspective of plot development.[8] He suggests that the oracles have been generally arranged to develop the plot, conflict, and resolution. The elements for the plot are all introduced in 1:1–19 with 1:10 summarizing the themes: judgment, renewal or salvation after judgment, and denunciation of sin. In chapters 2–20 the rebellion of the people is announced, proclaimed, and experienced by the prophet himself. Each major group (prophets, priest, king, people) is shown to be contributing to the downfall. The nation's idolatry is astounding as they have exchanged the glory of the true God for idols.

> Has a nation ever changed its gods?
>> (Yet they are not gods at all.)
> But my people have exchanged their Glory
>> for worthless idols.
> Be appalled at this, O heavens,
>> and shudder with great horror (2:11–12).

The turn from Yahweh brought a turn from covenant justice.

> Does a maiden forget her jewelry,
>> a bride her wedding ornaments?
> Yet my people have forgotten me,
>> days without number.
> How skilled you are at pursuing love!
>> Even the worst of women can learn from your ways.
> On your clothes men find
>> the lifeblood of the innocent poor,
>> though you did not catch them breaking in (2:32–34).

The message in these chapters pronounces the judgment but gives time to repent although repentance is not expected (cf. 7:3–7, 27; 36:1–3).[9]

Chapters 21–29 describe the rising crisis as God helps the prophet survive and Jeremiah proclaims the need to surrender and a definite exile in Babylon for an extended time (cf. 27:12–15; 29:1–15) and we come to the brink of the national crisis. Chapters 30–33 on the New Covenant moves to resolution of the conflict by giving the ultimate future resolution, and chapters 34–51 bring us back to the present and the problem of bringing Israel and the nations to that future point. Only by going through the judgment and exile that chapters 34–44 catalog will the nation ultimately come to the restoration in view in chapters 30–33. Thus, Jeremiah's message of the necessity of submission to Babylon is confirmed.

Themes and Theology

Jeremiah, after all, is not a traitor. His message of exile, so unwelcome by Judah's leadership, proclaimed the only way forward for a nation whose idolatry and injustice made it as impossible to restore as a smashed clay jar. The object lesson of good and bad figs proclaims this ironic twist. The group taken to exile will be the good figs who are the key to Israel's future in the land through God's chastening and restoration. Those who stayed in the Land of Promise would ironically turn out to be bad figs without a future (24:1–9). A chastening judgment for her long-term sins of idolatry and injustice was necessary. *God's Covenants* with David as king (Davidic) and Israel as his people (Mosaic), and the Levites as priests are also secure, even though the throne in Zion would be vacant, the temple demolished, and the people exiled. But Jeremiah's message hinges on the New Covenant.

> The issue throughout is how there may be a future for the people of God in view of their refusal to meet the covenant demands. . . . Judgment must ensue, *as a means* of the relationship continuing (21–24). . . . The idea of God *enabling* the obedience is precisely Jeremiah's answer to the basic problem. . . . It is the theology of the New Covenant . . . which enables the transition to hope.[10]

Obadiah—Curse and Blessing

Obadiah proclaims the death warrant of Edom. This national prophecy against Edom summons the nation to judgment, announces the indictment, and gives the verdict. "Her crimes shall return upon her own head"—*lex talionis* ("an eye for an eye" or "you reap what you sow").[11]

Exactly when Obadiah proclaimed this death warrant, however, is uncertain. Most modern commentators would place Obadiah as shortly after the fall of Jerusalem, though some would place him as the earliest among these books of prophets. The whole issue hinges on the indictment in verses 10–14 where Edom is accused of standing by and rejoicing while Jerusalem was sacked as well as during the cutting down of those who fled. Besides the well-known sack of Jerusalem by Nebuchadnezzar with which most modern commentators connect the book, a lesser-known pillage by the Philistines and Arabs occurred during Jehoram's reign at about 845 B.C. (2 Chron. 21:8–9, 16–17; cf. 2 Kings 8:20–22).[12]

Literary Flow

Obadiah's message starts with an announcement from Yahweh Sabaoth (Yahweh of Armies). As the Ruler with the ultimate power Yahweh announces the destruction of Edom (vv. 1–4). Edom's pride is her downfall.

By it, she has been deceived and believed herself impregnable and answerable to no one. Her eagle-like soaring will bite the dust. Her destruction will be total (vv. 5–9). She will be destroyed by her allies. Her vaunted wisdom will prove unable to help.

The cause for her judgment is her treatment of Jerusalem (vv. 10–14). She has fallen under the covenantal curse of Abraham (Gen. 12:3). Her sins against Jerusalem are listed from lesser to greater. She not only stood aside and rejoiced over the looting of Jerusalem but also partook in the looting itself, and finally engaged in the horror of cutting down those who tried to escape.

Figure 14.2

Outline of Obadiah
I. Edom's Destruction Announced (1–4)
II. The Destruction Described (5–9)
III. Reasons for Destruction (10–14)
IV. The Day of the LORD for All Nations (15–18)
V. The Kingdom of Yahweh (19–21)

Edom's judgment is a prefiguration of the Day of the LORD, when Yahweh will judge all the nations in righteousness (vv. 15–18). The sins of the nations will come before him and, "as you have done, it will be done to you"—justice (*lex talionis*) will finally come to earth. The House of Jacob will consume the House of Esau. The Day of the LORD's presence in judgment also suggests the ultimate blessing for Israel and Zion in the extended land of promise as promised to Abraham (vv. 19–21). The covenantal hope is secure: "The kingdom will be the LORD's" (v. 21).

Themes and Theology

Several themes comprise this little book of judgment on Edom. *Yahweh's sovereignty* is foremost. The pride and arrogance of Edom before Yahweh matches the original temptation in Eden—to attempt to be self-sufficient in wisdom. Now it is not the original, but the final sin for this nation. The *Abrahamic Covenant* as traced through Jacob stands in the foreground of this book as another major theme. Edom fails to find its blessing through Jacob, Esau's brother, but rather places itself under the curse of the covenant by her actions. Jacob's seed, Israel, in spite of the immediate pillage, will ultimately experience rest in the land when the kingdom is Yahweh's. These early themes lead to the final and climactic theme: *the Day of the LORD*, the future and final period of judgment on rebellious nations and also blessing with its secure hope of the kingdom.

Lamentations—A Lament for Jerusalem

The book of Lamentations is entitled "Ah, how" in the Hebrew Bible, following the practice of using the first word of the book as the title. The Greek Bible uses the title "Wailings," and traditional Judaism called it

"Laments." It is ascribed to Jeremiah, the prophet, by both Jewish tradition and the Greek Old Testament, which begins: "And it came to pass, after Israel was led into captivity and Jerusalem laid waste, that Jeremiah sat weeping and lamented with this lamentation over Jerusalem and said. . . ."

For the Hebrew Bible, however, our book is anonymous. If we were guessing, though, Jeremiah would not be a bad choice. The book must have been written shortly after the fall of Jerusalem with its eyewitness type of description. Its theology for the fall of Jerusalem is in line with the prophets. Jeremiah wrote both prose and poetry as well as lamentations over the death of King Josiah (2 Chron. 35:25). Jeremiah's feeling for his people and their desperate sin would match the feeling expressed in this book. That Jeremiah argued that the presence of the temple did not guarantee the safety of Jerusalem does not mean that he would not have sorrowed over the destruction of temple and city. If not Jeremiah, then someone from his time and someone like him.

Literary Flow

The book is made up of five poems (one per chapter) written largely but not exclusively in what has been called dirge (*qinah*) or dropping meter (three beats in the first line and two in the second). Such dropping meter can give a sense of letdown or sorrow. Thus it is appropriate in a funeral lament or dirge. The poems, however, are not simply dirges. Parts of them reflect the individual lament or complaint pattern (chap. 3) that we saw in the psalms. Group or community lament (chap. 5) is also present.

The first four poems are alphabetic acrostics. The first two use a successive letter of the twenty-two-letter Hebrew alphabet for each verse of normally three lines in length.[13] The third poem is approximately the same length as the first two but has sixty-six verses of one line each with each line beginning with the same Hebrew letter for three lines each. The fourth poem reverts to a twenty-two-verse acrostic of only two lines each. And the fifth poem drops the use of the alphabet, but follows the pattern of twenty-two with twenty-two verses of only one line each. No one knows why.

Why use acrostics? Some have suggested that it adds limits and control to expressing grief. Others have proposed that the completeness of the alphabet has been used to affirm that all has been said that could be. ("We covered it from A to Z.")[14]

The central poem is the high point and focus of the five. *Poem 1* sets the stage with a dirge lamenting Zion as a widowed queen; her temple desecrated by pagan nations; destitute because of her many sins (1:5, 8, 14, 18, 20, 22). She prays for a similar day of God's anger upon the fierce nations. *Poem 2*, another funeral dirge, stresses that it is the Lord who has done it.

"Like an enemy" he has wreaked total havoc (palaces, temple, wall, and gates; elders, young women, children, and infants) and shocking disaster. ("Should women eat their offspring? . . . Should priest and prophet be killed in the sanctuary?") It is "the day of Yahweh's anger" for sure!

Poem 3 as the apex of the book contains the response of the righteous person "who has seen affliction by the rod of his wrath." The affliction is described as broken bones, dwelling in darkness, weighed with chains, mangled, a target for arrows, broken teeth, and lacking peace. Yet in the midst of depression, the righteous person takes hope in Yahweh's great love "for his compassions never fail. They are new every morning; great is your faithfulness." The exiles are counseled to hope in Yahweh and to wait for his ultimate salvation.

> For men are not cast off
> > by the Lord forever.
> Though he brings grief, he will show compassion,
> > so great is his unfailing love.
> For he does not willingly bring affliction
> > or grief to the children of men (3:31–33).

Both Yahweh's sovereign control and the sin of the people is again accentuated. This remarkable individual lament closes with the recital of the expected answer to his plea for help ("You came near to me when I called you, and you said, 'Do not fear.'/ O Lord you took up my case; you redeemed my life.") and closes with a prayer for Yahweh's vengeance on the invaders.

The book begins to wind down with Poem 4. Is this the reason each poem becomes shorter? This dirge further documents the awful circumstances of the siege ("The infant's tongue sticks to the roof of his mouth. . . . Compassionate women have cooked their own children"), but with a final word of hope: "O Daughter of Zion, your punishment will end; he will not prolong your exile. . . ." Though Poem 3 is the high point of hope, Poem 5, is the appropriate finish. The shortest of all, it is a communal lament that brings the disgrace of the people before Yahweh, confesses their sin, and calls upon him, the King whose throne even now "endures from generation to generation," to restore and return them "unless you have utterly rejected us and are angry with us beyond measure." This is the appropriate response to be modeled by the remnant in exile.

Theme and Theology

Running through each lamentation is the recognition that this is the day of the Lord's anger as the judgment predicted by the prophets for Israel's violation of her Covenant. Additionally, there is recognition that Yahweh's standard is righteous, that sin and rebellion is the cause, and that Yahweh has acted after great patience and extended warning. Even so, a *hope of restoration built on Yahweh's faithful love and compassion* is possible. He will not cast off his people forever. He is still the sovereign King who has not been overcome by the tragedy. Given community confession of sin in line with the Deuteronomic blessings and cursings, Yahweh will not be angry with his righteous ones beyond measure. "His compassions never fail. They are new every morning; great is your faithfulness."

PROPHETS OF THE CAPTIVITY

Ezekiel—The Glory of Yahweh

Ezekiel is the counterpoint to Jeremiah. Jeremiah was God's prophet in Palestine to pronounce doom on Jerusalem. Ezekiel did the same for the exiles, who hoped to see the nation survive. Jeremiah was not allowed to marry, as a sign of the approaching terror. Ezekiel married, but lost his wife, so that his lack of mourning might be a pattern for exiles not to mourn God's righteous judgment on Jerusalem.

God did not leave his exiled people without a prophet. As exiles they were desperate to know their fate and the fate of their beloved Jerusalem. Taken to Babylon by Nebuchadnezzar in 597 B.C. with King Jehoiachin, these 10,000 exiles wanted to know how it would all turn out. Oddly enough, in the fifth year of Jehoiachin's exile (593 B.C.)[15] God called an unemployed priest to be a prophet. Ezekiel would never have his time to minister in the temple, but he would predict a new temple. A second career as a prophet sounds like an exciting alternative, but instead of the majestic ceremony and glory of Solomon's temple, Ezekiel found himself digging through clay walls, cooking food over dung, and performing other often difficult acts of symbolic pantomime to communicate God's message.

Literary Pattern and Flow

Unlike the book of Jeremiah, the order to Ezekiel's oracles is not difficult to discover. They fall into four clear groupings: (1) From Ezekiel's call to the siege of Jerusalem (chaps. 1–24); (2) against the nations (chaps. 25–32); (3) reversal following judgment (chaps. 33–39); (4) the restored temple and land (chaps. 40–48). Many of Ezekiel's prophecies are dated. All dated prophecies are in chronological order, except those in section two, concerning the nations, where oracles are grouped for each nation.[16]

Ezekiel's first vision and call (1:1–3:15) open the first section (chaps. 1–24). Like Isaiah's call and vision, much of the thematic thrust of the book is here. Certainly of interest is the vision of the throne—gyroscopic wheels within wheels and living many-faced cherubim over which a crystal platform supported a sapphire throne. High above sits one with the appearance of a man of glowing metal and fire surrounded by a shining rainbow spectrum. "This was the appearance of the likeness of the glory of the LORD" (1:28). It is God's throne, easily able to move in any direction and not limited to one locality. Unlike Isaiah's vision, it is not fixed over Jerusalem's temple. The point: God's sovereignty extends even to the land of captivity. God's rule just as easily takes place by the Kebar Canal of the exiles as in Zion. Like Isaiah, Ezekiel falls facedown. His call follows. As with Isaiah, Ezekiel is sent to a "rebellious house." He eats a double-sided scroll of God's Word—a message of "lament and mourning and woe."

Like a child playing with toy soldiers and tanks, seven days later Ezekiel is instructed to draw the city of Jerusalem on a clay tablet and set up siege works, a ramp, camps, and battering rams around it—thus symbolizing the fate of Jerusalem under siege for her many sins (3:16–5:17). Ezekiel has been commissioned as a watchman—guilty if he gives no warning but free from responsibility if his warning falls on deaf ears. Ever working with pantomime, Ezekiel cooks his own food as if under the famine conditions predicted for the city and shaves his head and beard, dividing the hair according to the method of death for Zion's population. Only a few strands are saved in the folds of his garment. With the next two oracles the judgment extends to the mountains of Israel with their high places of false worship and the "four corners of the land" with its detestable practices (6:1–14; 7:1–27).

Curious to Bible scholars is the instruction that Ezekiel will be shut up in his house, bound with cords, and "I will make your tongue stick to the roof of your mouth so that you will be silent and unable to rebuke them, though they are a rebellious house" (3:26). This silence is lifted when word comes of the fall of Jerusalem (33:21–22; cf. 24:26). But how is Ezekiel mute and yet able to give all of these messages that are dated before the siege of Jerusalem? As the first twenty-four chapters are filled with pantomime that typically followed the formula: "This is what the Sovereign LORD says," perhaps we should take seriously 3:27: "But when I speak to you, I will open your mouth and you shall say to them, 'This is what the Sovereign LORD says.'" In other words, Ezekiel was not able to speak for the normal affairs of personal life or give his own rebuke to the people. In addition, in his mute state he often was instructed to use pantomime to initiate the message from God. Then, he was granted speech only at those times when he was given a direct Word from God, which he normally introduced by the prophetic formula: "This is what the Sovereign LORD says." Only after news of the fall of Jerusalem was Ezekiel able to return to a normal life of speech.[17]

Another unique and crucial vision is the Temple Vision of Ezekiel 8–11. Grasped by the hair, Ezekiel is snatched up in vision from his model siege in his home and taken to the temple in Jerusalem. In this temple vision, he again encounters the majestic throne and the glory that fills the temple—reminiscent of God's glory at the original filling of the tabernacle following the Exodus. Yet abominations fill the temple now! So, the temple is abandoned by the glorious Presence. The throne first hovers above the eastern gate, then moves to the Mount of Olives east of Jerusalem. Only those who grieve such detestable practices are marked for salvation. The unrighteous in Jerusalem may believe that they are the future Israel because they are still in the land; but God declares that those in exile, who Jerusalemites consider to be "far away from the LORD," ultimately will be the future nation in the land (8:14–17). Similar to Jeremiah's pronouncement of a New Covenant, those restored will be given "an undivided heart" and "a new spirit." "Then they will follow my decrees and be careful to keep my laws. They will be my people, and I will be their God" (8:19–20).

The remaining prophecies of Ezekiel 12–24 finish out the details of God's judgment on Jerusalem, its king (12:12–13), false prophets, and idolaters at heart (13:1–15:8). Israel's long litany of sins (18:1–32) and unfaithful conduct (16:1–63; 20:1–49; 23:1–48) are in contrast with God's choice of Israel at the Exodus and his faithfulness to the nation (16:1–63). Though current proverb suggests that they were being punished for their father's sins, God was perfectly willing to assess judgment on an individual basis—"the soul who sins is the one who will die." Even heartfelt repentance would bring forgiveness at this late date "for I take no pleasure in the death of anyone, declares the Sovereign LORD. Repent and live!" (18:19–32). All for naught. Yet Yahweh still promises to restore the nation after exile and reconstitute his covenant with them (16:59–63; 20:33–44). But for now, Jerusalem is a cooking pot of judgment (24:1–13). The siege of Jerusalem by Nebuchadnezzar commences by the end of this section and Ezekiel's wife dies (24:14–26).

The book then turns to the nations and God's judgment on them (chaps. 25–32). As other prophets have announced Yahweh's Day of the LORD upon the nations as necessary before final eschatological world peace under Zion's rule, so Ezekiel also prophesies judgment against the nations—especially those who have looked with vengeance on Israel in her destruction. Just as the judgment on Judah and Jerusalem will teach them "that I am the LORD," so the nations will also ultimately learn that Yahweh is the only true and living God who will judge malice against his people. Just as Pharaoh learned that "I am Yahweh" in the original Exodus, so Pharaoh and the other nations (Ammon, Moab, Edom, Philistia, Tyre) must, along with Israel, relearn this lesson.[18]

Reversal of earlier judgment dominates the third section (chaps. 33–39). Reminders of Ezekiel's earlier prophecies abound. We are reintroduced to Ezekiel's role as a watchman (33:1–9; cf. 3:16–21); reminded that the individual who is righteous or turns away from his wickedness will live (33:10–20; cf. 18:1–32); told of Ezekiel's recovery of speech when the message of the fall of Jerusalem arrives (33:21–22; cf. 24:26); and promised again that "they will know that a prophet has been among them" (33:33; cf. 2:5).[19] At the fall of Jerusalem, the Sovereign Lord has cut off the shepherds who have fleeced the flock, and will shepherd his scattered flock himself, rescue and regather them to the pasture of Israel, and "place over them one shepherd, my servant David." Then "they will know that I am the LORD" (34:27, 30). Edom, though related closely to Israel through Esau, will find no similar restoration due to her non-brotherly conduct (35:1–15).

Line by line, the judgment is reversed. Now the mountains of Israel, once judged for the high places of idolatry (6:1–14), will be blessed with produce, animals, and population (33:1–21). The sin-cursed land (7:1–14) will be rebuilt when Yahweh gathers them, cleanses them, and gives them "a new heart" and "a new spirit" (36:22–37). The "dry bones" of this dead people will come to life again as a nation (37:1–14) and the "two sticks" of the divided kingdom will be joined together again. And, "My servant David will be king over them. . . . I will make a covenant of peace with them; it will be an everlasting covenant. . . . My dwelling place will be with them; I will be their God, and they will be my people. Then the nations will know that I the LORD make Israel holy" (37:24–28). The prophecy of Gog and Magog caps this section of reversal of judgment (38:1–39:29). Unlike the earlier judgments on nations, this one is set after the return of Israel to the land and these nations will not be successful in victimizing God's people.[20] In the future, following God's Covenant of peace, when foes from the north come against his people, they will be secure. This final eschatological battle will vindicate Yahweh, the God of Israel, as the true God so that both the nations and the people of Israel "will know that I am the LORD [Yahweh] their God" (38:23; 39:6, 7, 21, 28).

Ezekiel's second temple vision rounds out the book (chaps. 40–48). The first temple vision (chs. 8–11) had been one of defilement and loss of God's glorious Presence. This vision is also a reversal. Like the pleasure of contemplating the architecture and layout of a future dream home, the future temple is intricately described and measured for the exiles. Its furnishings and worship requirements are detailed. But most importantly, the Glory returns and fills the temple (43:1–5)! Additionally, a life-giving river flows from this temple to the Dead—now Alive—Sea. The river is lined with fruit trees that bear fruit monthly. The leaves of the trees provide healing, overcoming the death curse of Eden's tree. Also important are the boundaries of the restored land and tribal borders as well as a description of the new Zion. Such detail of the future temple, city, and land may seem tedious to us, but it adds concrete reality to the hope of the exiled Israelite. Would God give such extensive detail if he did not intend to bring it to pass?

Themes and Theology

Ezekiel takes us back to the Exodus and, like the book of Exodus, its primary theme is "*I am Yahweh.*" More than sixty times the book declares that they "will know that I am Yahweh" and ten additional times repeats "I am Yahweh" or other similar forms. For Ezekiel, Israel has left her high calling and her recognition of Yahweh, who redeemed her out of the land of Egypt, constituted her as his people and nation, and brought her into the land promised to the patriarchs. But Yahweh is not through. Through the judgment of exile, Yahweh will purge his people, return them to the land, put a new spirit in them, and vindicate himself as the living God. Both Israel and the nations will finally and fully "know that I am Yahweh."

Crucial to this final arrangement is the "everlasting covenant" or "covenant of peace" which, like Jeremiah's New Covenant, grants "a new spirit" and "a new heart" which overcomes the failure of the nation before. This is similarly described as the pouring out of Yahweh's Spirit (39:29).

Alongside this restoration and covenant is the fulfilling of the Davidic Covenant by placing one Davidic ruler on the throne over the reunited Israel and Judah. For Ezekiel, this king is called "my servant, David" (34:24; 37:25).

Finally, the importance of the Glory of Yahweh and his Presence as in Exodus is critical to this book. Again we are reminded of the coming of the presence of Yahweh to the original tabernacle. The Glory of God's Presence and Rule is not limited to the land of Israel. Neither can it stay in a temple of abominations. Yet the Glory will return following God's restoration of his people. The renewed land will be redivided and the city of Zion rebuilt. And those final words of Ezekiel tell the whole story of glad tidings for Israel and the whole earth concerning that future Zion: "The LORD [Yahweh] is there" (48:35).

Daniel—God's Sovereignty Under Foreign Rule

It must have been difficult for these first exiles. Even before the major exile in 597 that took Ezekiel into captivity, Daniel, his three companions, and others from the best and brightest of Jerusalem were taken to Babylon. This smaller and earlier exile apparently occurred as part of Nebuchadnezzar's campaign against Egypt after defeating their forces at Carchemish. The Babylonian chronicle places the defeat of Egypt in August, 605, and records "at that time Nebuchadrezzar conquered the whole area of Hatti" (Syria and Palestine).[21] From Egypt he hurried home to take the throne at the death of his father, Nabopolasar.

Everything was new: food, clothes, even names. How would they adapt in a foreign land? Could they worship Yahweh in another god's land? How much culture should they adopt? Would they lose their identity as a people? In short: How should they act in a foreign land? No one could provide these answers for these young men. It was clearly the intent of the Babylonians to train them for civil service and to transform them into the religious-political-cultural learning that was Babylon.

In short, these men were pioneers. Daniel, as civil servant and receiver of visions and interpretations, lived and prospered under four kings and two foreign powers.[22] The answers they forged in the daily crucible of Babylonian culture would provide direction for coming generations destined to live under Gentile rule. To complicate the picture, these men did not deserve exile. Under corporate judgment as part of a nation doomed to captivity, even the faithful experience it. And, in the providence of God, these righteous men encounter the challenges first and provide a model for the faithful to follow.

Literary Pattern and Flow

Several elements contribute to the development of the book of Daniel. Daniel is unique in that it is written in two languages. The book begins in Hebrew (1:1–2:4a). Then it switches to Aramaic, the commercial and governmental language of the time (2:4b–7:28). Finally, it returns to Hebrew for the remaining visions (8:1–12:13). Of course, this language switch has provided fodder for academic debate. If it relates to content, it may be significant that chapters 2–7 relate primarily to the progress and response of foreign powers to God's sovereignty, whereas the initial chapter and the visions of chapters 8–12 relate more specifically to Jewish religious and national concerns.[23]

The book contains ten units. Some are story narratives. Some are visions. Some include both. Fortunately for the English reader, these units follow our chapter divisions, except for the last unit, which begins in chapter 10 and runs for three chapters. These units may further be grouped as two halves. The first six chapters are narrative about Daniel and friends as they interact with the Babylonian government, beginning at the first year of Nebuchadnezzar and running to the first year of Darius the Mede.[24] The second half, chapters 7–12, consists of four visions, starting back at the first year of Belshazzar[25] and running to the third year of Cyrus. The first half deals primarily with the question of how to live in exile, and the visions of the second half prepare the Hebrews for what the future holds.

Themes and Theology

The narratives of the first half of the book provide a practical theology for exile. Through the experiences of Daniel and the three Hebrews (Hananiah, Mishael, and Azariah) the readers learn that Yahweh is still sovereign even in the land of captivity. Yahweh is no merely local god, but in our book is the God of heaven, superior to Marduk and the whole Babylonian pantheon. God honors Daniel's desire to avoid polluted food.[26] He not only delivers Daniel and friends from the threat of extinction along with the incompetent Chaldean wise guys and magicians, but Yahweh exalts these Jewish men by giving supernatural knowledge (chap. 2) and deliverance (chaps. 3 and 6). Even pagan kings must recognize the superiority of their God and seek him through these Hebrew young men (2:46–47; 3:28; 4:37; 6:25–28). The self-exaltation of prideful kings who promote their own glory and dominion along with their own idolatrous creations (chaps. 3, 4, 5; cf. 8:9–10; 11:37–38) reminds us of the standard satanic temptation from Eden onward (cf. Gen. 3; Isa. 14; Ezek. 28).[27] Always a temptation of ancient kings, such pride is abased by the God of heaven (chs. 3, 4), who is the God of gods (2:47), the Most High (4:34), and the King of heaven (4:37).

For exiled Hebrews, then, Yahweh must be exclusively worshiped and idolatry shunned at whatever cost—even the threat of death. The God of Heaven is able to deliver, though deliverance is not to be presumed. The proper stance is that of the three Hebrews before the king: "The God we serve is able to save us.... But even if he does not, we want you to know, O king, that we will not serve your gods or worship the image of gold" (3:17–18). Faith and faithfulness are the keys to living in exile under the sovereign God of Heaven.

Nebuchadnezzar's vision of future kingdoms (2:31–45) provides the framework for the visions of chapters 7–12 which prepare the Jewish people for the difficult future that follows. Chapter 7 repeats the four empire framework under the figure of beasts. The focus is on the last empire and the vision of "one like a son of man" who stands before the Ancient of Days. Like kings he is given authority and dominion. Unlike what is allowed for merely human kings, he is universally worshiped! As the stone of chapter two destroyed all prior kingdoms and established the kingdom of God, so this Son of Man will eventually rule forever as the only truly human(e), nonbeastly kingdom. In the interpretation that follows, this authority is shared by the saints of the Most

High, who will undergo persecution, yet finally rule (7:25–27).[28] In spite of this good news, the vision deeply troubles and physically affects Daniel. Why? Isn't this news encouraging? No, Daniel sees nothing short of a crushing holocaust for his people preceding the arrival of the final kingdom.

Chapter 8 adds more devastating detail to the Greek period by describing a ruler who will "destroy the mighty men and the holy people" (8:24). Though the ruler will be destroyed, Daniel is ill and appalled by the vision (8:27). The program of seventy sevens (9:20–27) fills in another unexpected blank. Reading Jeremiah's prophecy of seventy years of captivity, Daniel anticipates the possibility of return, but is concerned about the readiness of the exiles. The need for national confession of sin and full repentance as a prerequisite to a successful return motivates Daniel's prayer (9:1–19). Yet, a program of—not seventy years—but seven times seventy years of domination by foreign powers is prescribed! It finally culminates in a sixfold package which ushers in the final kingdom (9:24), but such an extensive period of national struggle beyond a seventy-year exile and before the coming of God's anointed Ruler is not the best of news![29]

Further details of the struggle envisioned for the Greek period following Alexander the Great (chaps. 10–12) traces so closely the campaigns of Antiochus IV Epiphanes that some insist on dating the book of Daniel after these events![30] The effect of these visions is to push back the timing for independent nationhood under a Davidic king—so important to the prophetic hope—to a time long past the life of Daniel himself. And so, to Daniel and the faithful comes the message of 12:1–13. Though they will long be placed in the dust before these days, those who live wisely will shine like the stars of the sky. They will be raised from the dust to receive their inheritance! They will not miss out! And so, the theme of both halves of the book is ultimately the same: Tough times are ahead, but faithful, wise living will be rewarded under the sovereign plan of the God of heaven.

THE FULFILLMENT OF THE PROPHETS' HOPE

When Jesus announced his coming death to his disciples at the celebration of the Passover, he took two common elements of the meal, the bread and the wine, and proclaiming them as standing for his body and blood about to be sacrificed, encouraged the disciples to eat and drink. Using the language of Jeremiah, he took the cup of wine and proclaimed: "This is my blood of the covenant which is poured out for many" (Mark 14:24). Thus, like the Passover of old, the new way of deliverance again involves forgiveness marked by sacrificial action. The establishment of the final means, however, could not be accomplished by vicarious animal sacrifice. As the writer of Hebrews puts it "the better covenant" must be implemented by "better sacrifices" (Heb. 10:23–28). And so, the vicarious suffering visualized by the animal sacrifice of the Mosaic Covenant comes to completion by the sacrifice of the Son of God himself for humanity, demonstrating God's willingness to take the penalty on himself through incarnation and suffering.

But this is not the only facet of Jesus' message which reflects these prophets. Jesus' proclamation of "living water" also has its roots here. For Ezekiel's water, which runs from under the throne of Yahweh in the restored temple, provides living water for the healing of the nations. Jesus proclaims himself to be that living water, which even before the final appearing of the kingdom can be experienced by his followers:

> On the last and greatest day of the Feast, Jesus stood and said in a loud voice, "If a man is thirsty, let him come to me and drink. Whoever believes in me, as the Scripture has said, streams of living water will flow from within him." By this he meant the Spirit, whom those who believed in him were later to receive. Up to that time the Spirit had not been given, since Jesus had not yet been glorified (John 8:37–39).

In his picture of the future kingdom, John the revelator gives us a final glance of the establishment of such worldwide healing and peace under the vision of such a stream proceeding from Zion, lined with fruit and leaves for the healing of the nations (Rev. 22:1–2).

And so will the visions of the prophets ultimately come to fruition. Jesus, the living water, now provides such eternal life to those who believe and will return as King to rule over a peaceful and healed world. Jesus, through his death has provided the means of bringing in the promised new and better covenant that ultimately will yield worldwide knowledge of God in the kingdom of Messiah. Jesus, the Son of Man, has entered into the human family, is able to stand before the Ancient of Days representing the saints, and is worthy of worship as the Divine King. Jesus will bring in the final Day of the LORD, first in judgment on the rebellious nations, but then in glorious peace and justice—a justice that has eluded all the efforts of humanity to date.

SUGGESTED SCRIPTURE READING:

Nahum 1; Habakkuk 1–3
Zephaniah 1–3
Jeremiah 1, 11, 13:1–11; 16; 19:1–20:6; 30–33
Lamentations 3
Ezekiel 1–4; 9–10; 33–34; 37; 44:1–4; 47:1–12
Daniel 1–3, 7–9, 12

For Interaction and Discussion:

1. What elements do the prophets include in "the Day of the LORD"? Are there stages to that day? How does it affect the nations and Israel?

2. How does the book of Habakkuk address the problem of judgment and faith for the righteous? How does it compare to the book of Daniel as a manual for exiles?

3. How would the book of Daniel and its prophetic messages affect those in exile and those who returned under Cyrus? To what extent would their expectations be modified?

4. In what ways do Ezekiel's temple visions relate to judgment and hope? What other factors in Ezekiel involve elements of judgment and then hope?

5. What themes are common to more than one prophetic book? How important are these themes to our overall understanding of the Old Testament? How do these themes converge on the New Testament as a time of fulfillment?

For Further Reading:

(See also books on the minor prophets listed with chapter 13).

Derek Kidner. *Love to the Loveless: The Message of Hosea*. Downers Grove, Ill.: InterVarsity, 1981. Highly readable and practical, yet academically sound.

David W. Barker. *Nahum, Habakkuk, Zephaniah*. TOTC. Downers Grove, Ill.: InterVarsity, 1988. Another solid addition to a Hebrew-based series accessible to English readers.

Ralph Alexander. "Ezekiel." *EBC*. Grand Rapids: Zondervan, 1986, 6:737–996. Careful detailed exposition.

Joyce Baldwin. *Daniel*. TOTC. Downers Grove, Ill.: InterVarsity, 1978. Solid English commentary based on the Hebrew text.

Gleason L. Archer, Jr. "Daniel." *EBC*. Grand Rapids: Zondervan, 1986, 7:3–157. Helpful with pertinent archeological information.

Ehud Ben Zvi. "Understanding the Message of the Tripartite Prophetic Books." *Restoration Quarterly*, 35 (1993): 93–100. An important scholarly contribution.

Leo G. Purdue. "Jeremiah in Modern Research: Approaches and Issues." *A Prophet to the Nations, Essays in Jeremiah Studies*. Ed. Leo. G. Purdue, Winona Lake, Ind.: Eisenbrauns, 1984, 10–14. A scholarly review of academic issues.

R. K. Harrison. *Jeremiah and Lamentations*. TOTC. Downers Grove, Ill.: InterVarsity, 1973. Another solid commentary in this series for English readers.

J. Gordon McConville. "Jeremiah: Prophet and Book." *TB*, 42 (1991):, 80–95. Especially helpful with message and theology.

Paul R. House. "Plot, Prophecy and Jeremiah." *JETS*, 36 (1993): 297–306. Helpful for plot development

Richard D. Patterson. "Of Bookends, Hinges, and Hooks: Literary Clues to the Arrangement of Jeremiah's Prophecies." *WTJ*, 51 (1989): 109–131. Literary and academic.

Norman K. Gottwald. *Studies in the Book of Lamentations*. London: SCM, 1962. The classic academic treatment.

Notes and Comments:

[1]Geoffrey C. Ward, Ric Burns, and Ken Burns, "The Civil War," *PBS TV Miniseries*, 9 parts (Alexandra, Va: PBS, 1989).

[2]Abraham Lincoln, "Second Inaugural Address," *Abraham Lincoln: Speeches and Writings*, ed. Don E. Fehrenbacher (New York: The Library of America, 1989), 686–87.

[3]The outline of Nahum with slight modifications follows that of Robert B. Chisholm, Jr., *Interpreting the Minor Prophets* (Grand Rapids: Zondervan, 1990), 165–67. For insight into this chiastic arrangement, Chisholm credits his colleague, Gordon Johnston.

[4]Barker has pointed out this rhetorical device of Zephaniah. Additionally, he suggests that by first treating neighboring peoples, "the audience would agree that they deserved what God was giving them" and not anticipate hearing their own sins. David W. Barker, *Nahum, Habakkuk, Zephaniah*, TOTC (Downers Grove, Ill.: InterVarsity, 1988), 110–11. Cf. the insightful analysis of Ehud Ben Zvi, "Understanding the Message of the Tripartite Prophetic Books," *Restoration Quarterly*, 35 (1993): 93–100. He demonstrates that the common thread behind the specific charges against the nations in Zechariah is the assumption that they know that Yahweh is Israel's God and that their actions fail to demonstrate the recognition that Yahweh is THE GOD.

[5]In addition to these passages, the LXX of Jeremiah differs from the Hebrew text in omitting numerous other single verses and parts of verses as well as following a different ordering of the prophecies against the nations that occur after 25:13a in the LXX. The text of the LXX is approximately 12% (about 2700 words) shorter than the Hebrew text. Both the short and longer texts have been found at Qumran. For more specifics see Leo G. Purdue, "Jeremiah in Modern Research: Approaches and Issues," *A Prophet to the Nations, Essays in Jeremiah Studies*, ed. Leo. G. Purdue (Winona Lake, Ind.: Eisenbrauns, 1984), 10–14; Bullock, *Prophetic Books*, 206–7; R. K. Harrison, *Introduction*, 817–19.

[6]John Bright, "The Book of Jeremiah," *Int*, 9 (1955): 277.

[7]Arguing for chapters 1–25 (or 1–24) as a unit (based on the book that was compiled according to Jeremiah 36) has a difficulty: These chapters include some dated oracles after the fourth year of Jehoiakim—the terminal date for the book as described (36:1–3). Those who hold this position see 25:1–14, which also men-

tions the scope of Jeremiah's ministry down to the fourth year of Jehoiakim, as the end of one book or the beginning of another. For this position, chapters 1–25 include the book of Jeremiah 36 plus some oracles added later. If chapters 1–20 are viewed as a unit as I have suggested, they possibly could be that book of oracles (or largely so) as all the dated prophecies after the fourth year of Jehoiakim occur after chapter 21, although many scholars date a few of these oracles after Jehoiakim's fourth year based on content (such as 10:17–18, 25; 13:15–19). Charts that place the oracles under the appropriate kings may be found in R. K. Harrison, *Jeremiah and Lamentations* (Downers Grove, Ill.: InterVarsity, 1973), 33; also William S. LaSor, David A. Hubbard, and Frederic W. Bush, *Old Testament Survey* (Grand Rapids: Eerdmans, 1982), 428–30. Harrison finds no dated oracles in chapters 1–20 later than Jehoiakim, though in the commentary he identifies the king and queen mother in 13:17–18 as Jehoiachin and Nahushta in 597 B.C. (cf. 2 Kings 24:8). LaSor et al. find several undated oracles in chapters 1–20 that they would date after Jehoiakim. A number of these passages, however, are in the warning parts of oracles where exile or destruction is being graphically pictured, but may not have already occurred. (Cf. 10:17–18 where the people under siege are told to gather their belongings to leave for exile.) For outlines using chapters 1–25 as the larger unit, see Bullock, *Prophetic Books*, 196–99; Harrison, *Jeremiah and Lamentations*, 45. For a broad summary of approaches to Jeremiah see Leo G. Purdue, "Jeremiah in Modern Research: Approaches and Issues," *TB*, 42 (1991): 1–32; J. Gordon McConville, "Jeremiah: Prophet and Book," *TB*, 42 (1991): 80–95.

[8]Cf. Paul R. House, "Plot, Prophecy and Jeremiah," *JETS*, 36 (1993): 297–306. I have adapted House's analysis to fit the literary observation of many scholars that Jeremiah 1–20 is a unit. House prefers to combine chapters 2–29 as a larger unit inclusive of three subunits—one of which breaks after chapter 20. This does not affect the substance of House's argument. Another noteworthy approach is that of Richard D. Patterson, "Of Bookends, Hinges, and Hooks: Literary Clues to the Arrangement of Jeremiah's Prophecies," *WTJ*, 51 (1989): 109–131. Patterson, following literary clues, believes he has a pattern which follows known semitic compositional techniques. His conclusions lead to a major break at chapter 24. On the other hand, the analysis of William L. Holladay, *The Architecture of Jeremiah 1–20*, (Cranbury, N.J.: Associated University Presses, 1976), 13–20, supports the earlier work of Lundbom in seeing a great *inclusio* between 1:5 and 20:14–18 as support for a chapters 1–20 grouping (cf. J. R. Lundbom, *Jeremiah—A Study in Ancient Rhetoric* [Missoula, Mont.: Scholars, 1976], 28. In addition, it may be significant that Babylon is not mentioned by name until chapter 20, though it occurs very frequently through the remainder of the book. In the prophecies of chapters 1–19 the potential judgment is pictured as coming "from the north." This supports the notion that prior to chapter 20, the focus is on a final call to repent of national sins, to avoid disaster. The hardness of the nation is clearly established by the end of the section when the judgment is no longer potential and the enemy vague. Jeremiah may then state directly to the priest who ordered him beaten and put in stocks that he will experience exile to Babylon along with the city and nation.

[9]It is possible to suggest from 36:1–3 that the fourth year of Jehoiakim is viewed as the critical year when the proclamation of disaster from the north and exile changed from a final formal opportunity to repent and stay in the land (7:1–8) to a word that insisted on submission and exile to Babylon as Yahweh's route of necessary chastening and future blessing (23:1–8; 24:1–9).

[10]J. Gordon McConville, "Jeremiah: Prophet and Book," 92–93.

[11]As pointed out by Hill and Walton, *Survey*, 381.

[12]For discussion of dating see R. K. Harrison, *Introduction*, 901–2.

[13]After the first poem in Lamentations, the alphabetical order is slightly altered with the *Ayin* and *Pe* reversed.

[14]Norman K. Gottwald, *Studies in the Book of Lamentations* (London: SCM, 1962), 29–31. "The author . . . selected the external principle of the acrostic to correspond to the internal spirit and intention of the work. He wished to play upon the collective grief of the community in its every aspect, 'from *Aleph* to *Taw*' so that the people might experience an emotional catharsis. He wanted to bring about a complete cleansing of the conscience through a total confession of sin . . . . By intimately binding together the themes of sin, suffering, submission and hope, he intended to implant the conviction of trust and confidence in the goodness and imminent intervention of Yahweh. That this is the case is evident in the third poem where the acrostic form is intensified at precisely the point where hope becomes the strongest" (30).

[15]The book of Ezekiel starts with a mysterious reference to "the thirtieth year" but without stating the starting point for that date. The third year, apparently referring to the same day (note the "fifth day" in each), states the year to be the fifth year of the exile of King Jehoiachin—which would be 593 B.C. Two primary suggestions are made for "the thirtieth year." It could refer to the year of Ezekiel's birth, thus being the year he would normally have begun his priestly ministry. Or, it could refer to the year of Josiah's reform. "Indeed, if one counts back from the fifth year of exile thirty years according to the regnal years given in the book of Kings one arrives at year 18 of Josiah, in which the Torah book was found and the great reform undertaken." Moshe Greenberg, *The Anchor Bible: Ezekiel 1–20* (New York: Doubleday, 1964), 39–40. Greenberg himself rejects this suggestion, however, because dating from an event is unparalleled. Cf. Bullock, *Prophetic Books*, 234–35, for other suggestions.

[16]The dating of oracles in Ezekiel in the first section runs from 593 (1:1–2) to the beginning of the siege of Jerusalem in 588 B.C. (24:1; cf. 3:16; 8:1; 20:1–2). In the second section against the nations, the oracles are arranged topically per nation and are not in exact chronological order (26:1 Tyre, 587–586 B.C.; 29:1 Egypt, 587 B.C.; 29:17 Egypt, 571 B.C.; 30:20 Egypt, 587 B.C.; 31:1 Egypt, 587 B.C.; 32:1 Egypt, 585 B.C.; 32:17 Egypt 586/585 B.C.). Ezekiel 33:21 picks up the chronology after the siege with the arrival of the fugitive declaring the fall of Jerusalem in 585 B.C. Ezekiel 40:1 concerning the Temple Vision is dated as 573 B.C. See Ralph Alexander, "Ezekiel," *EBC* (Grand Rapids: Zondervan, 1986), 6:888–89, for a discussion of the reasons for the thematic rather than chronological arrangement of the Egyptian oracles.

[17]Other theories of Ezekiel's mute state are summarized in Bullock, *Prophetic Books*, 232–34. Many of the theories speculate about editorial redaction either elim-

inating 3:26 (muteness) as Ezekiel's situation or 3:27 (delivering oracles) as a later addition, often failing to see that 3:27 could serve as a subset and qualification to the general situation of 3:26.

[18]Many of the nations in Ezekiel 25–32 are judged for their malice against Israel, especially for gloating and vengeance upon the city after its fall.

[19]These repetitions and reminders convince R. K. Harrison, *Introduction*, 848–49, that Ezekiel is a bifid book—i.e., it is written on two scrolls with important items (watchman function; individual judged for his own righteousness or wickedness) from the first scroll begin the second, so that the second scroll may operate as a self-contained unit. It seems to me that repetitions or parallels continue throughout the rest of the book, as I suggest in the text, and thus the second two sections of the book (chaps. 33–48) constitute in general a mirror image of reversal to the first half (chaps. 1–32).

[20]Childs, *Introduction*, 367, notes the distinction of Gog and Magog from the earlier judgment on nations: "Significantly, the prophecies against Gog and Magog (chs. 38–39) have not been included within the framework of chs. 25–32, but these nations are explicitly envisioned as attacking the restored and forgiven Jerusalem. The eschatological hope thus expressed is closely akin to that of Joel 3 and Zech. 14."

[21]Cited in Bullock, *Prophetic Books*, 282.

[22]Daniel is not included in the prophetic section of the present Hebrew Bible, but is found in the Writings. Conservatives generally explain this by pointing out that Daniel did not have a normal prophetic ministry but received visions more after the pattern of Joseph—thus he may not have been regarded as having the "office" of a prophet. Nonconservatives have generally argued that Daniel ended up in the last section, the Writings, because of a later, Maccabean date of origination. This later dating has become increasingly difficult with the discovery of the Qumran scrolls, leaving little time for distribution before the date of extant copies we now possess. Josephus apparently knew Daniel to be in the second division of the prophets in his Hebrew canon, reserving only four books that "contain hymns to God, and the precepts for the conduct of human life" for the third division (Against Apion, 1. 8). For an evaluation of all views, cf. Daniel Lockwood, "A Theological Defense for the Closing of the Canon," unpublished Th.M. thesis, Dallas Theological Seminary, Dallas (May, 1976).

[23]Gleason L. Archer, Jr., "Daniel," *EBC* (Grand Rapids: Zondervan, 1986), 7:6.

[24]The identity of Darius the Mede (9:1; 5:30; 6:1) is still considered an historical difficulty. Some believe he should be identified with the first Babylonian governor, Guburu. Others think it is another titular name for Cyrus (cf. 10:20; 11:1). In view of other historical difficulties in the book that have later been shown to be more accurate than our then-current information (see note 25, below), judgment should be postponed.

[25]The mention of Belshazzar as king was another point of attack on the historicity of the book of Daniel. The contention being that Nabonidus was ruler after Nebuchadnezzar and, according to extrabiblical sources, ruled until the fall of Babylon. The discovery of cuneiform oath tablets from the twelfth year of Nabonidus that associated Belshazzar, his son, with him on an equal status, changed

all this. The writer of Daniel was obviously aware of this arrangement as seen in the offer to Daniel of "third ruler" in the kingdom by Belshazzar (5:16, 29). "It became startling apparent that the writer of Daniel was much more accurately informed about the history of the 540s in Babylonia than Herodotus was in 450 B.C." Archer, "Daniel," 16.

[26]The author of Daniel does not specify whether the problem with the special diet for Daniel and friends was that it violated the dietary restrictions of the Law or that it was offered to idols. Perhaps he did not specify so that the reader could apply the lesson to any legitimate conviction.

[27]Cf. John H. Walton, "The Decree of Darius the Mede in Daniel 6," *JETS*, 31 (1988): 279–86. Was Darius actually promoting himself as a god or as a mediator to all gods? In the light of Persian practices, Walton suggests that the first option is dubious.

[28]Again, as with the Servant of Isaiah, in Daniel 7 we see a corporate unity between the Son of Man and the saints.

[29]Some see these seventy weeks of Daniel 9:24–27 as only a general apocalyptic figure for an extended period beginning with the Decree of Cyrus and extending to the ministry of Messiah. Others take them as straightforward chronology dating the first period of seven weeks (49 years) from the decree of Artaxerxes to the complete restoration of Jerusalem. The middle sixty-two sevens run from that restoration to Christ's ministry. The last seven years are often reserved for the yet-future period of the Antichrist, who will accomplish the eschatological "abomination of desolations" in the temple similar to that of Antiochus IV (cf. Dan. 11:31; Matt. 24:15). Others associate this last week with Christ's death. Though discussion continues, the yet-future view has the advantage of interpreting the terminology "put an end to sacrifice" and "desolation" associated with "abominations" of 9:27 in the same way as they are used elsewhere in the book (11:31). Some see the six goals of 9:24 as having been secured at the first advent of Messiah. Others see the last three as remaining to be completed at the Second Coming. Cf. John F. Walvoord, *Daniel, The Key to Prophetic Revelation* (Chicago: Moody, 1971), 219–37, and E. J. Young, *The Prophecy of Daniel* (Grand Rapids: Eerdmans, 1949), 191–221. For totally different identifications see Ronald W. Pierce, "Spiritual Failure, Postponement, and Daniel 9," *Trinity Journal,* 10 NS (1989): 211–22.

[30]Childs, *Introduction*, 611–18, summarizes the development of the critical view that Daniel belongs to the Maccabean period as "prophecies-after-the-event" (*vaticinia ex eventu*) written in 165 B.C. He bemoans the fact that the theological insights of such critical scholars into the book of Daniel have not kept pace with the history of critical research. In fact, "One could almost wonder if there is a reverse ratio" (613). Perhaps a belief in the historic authenticity and genuineness of the book has more to do with an interest in its theology than critics care to admit! Childs' own unique approach is to see the later visions (chaps. 7–12) as being a further interpretation for later times of the vision of chapter 2 from Daniel himself, confirming the earlier prophecy and identifying the outworking in their own history. LaSor et al. critique Childs and others for dating chapters 1–6 earlier than chapters 7–12,

pointing out that all concur that the Hebrew of Daniel is closer to that of the Chronicler than to Qumran and that the Aramaic is closer to Ezra than Qumran, but fail to recognize that the "Aramaic section continues through chapter 7, which is of the same age as the Aramaic of 2–6; and the Hebrew of chapters 7–12 is identical with that of chapters 1–2," LaSor, Hubbard, and Bush, *Survey*, 666.

Figure 14.3
Chart of the Writing Prophets and Themes

Prophets of the Divided Kingdom		
Prophet	**Theme or Themes**	**Date**
Jonah	The compassion of the Sovereign Creator	782–745
Amos	The Sovereign Creator requires covenant justice	762–750
Joel	The Day of the LORD	?
Hosea	Yahweh's unconditional covenant love	753–715
Micah	Israel's violation of covenant Law; God's faithfulness to the Abrahamic Covenant	740–710
Isaiah	The Holy One of Israel; The Ideal King and Servant; The Restoration of Zion	740–680
Prophets of the Remaining Kingdom of Judah		
Nahum	Yahweh's righteous vengeance on Ninevah	660–630
Zephaniah	The universal Day of the LORD	640–615
Habakkuk	The righteous will live by faith even when facing disaster	640–628 or 609–598
Jeremiah	Judgment is necessary for chastening, but a New Covenant is coming	626–585
Obadiah	Covenantal curse on Edom; The ultimate Day of the LORD	586 or 845
Ezekiel	"I am Yahweh;" The Glory of Yahweh as the Ruler	593–571
Daniel	Yahweh is the God of heaven and will be faithful to those who are faithful to him even though extended tribulation is ahead	605–537
Prophets of the Return From Babylon		
Haggai	The House of David and the House of God	520
Zechariah	The nation must return to God before Jerusalem's full restoration and the reign of the promised Davidic King in victory over the nations	520–516?
Malachi	God's covenantal love and blessing or cursing	Between 500–430

Part Five

RESTORATION
AND
HOPE

Not unlike Sherman's march to the sea, Nebuchadnezzar's destruction of Judah and Jerusalem left the land in shambles—so much so that Jeremiah pictured Palestine as returning to the earth's original chaotic state: "formless and empty" (Jer. 4:23–26).

As the Jews were evacuated they apparently were gathered for transport at Ramah, near enough Rachel's tomb for the prophet to picture that mother of Israel "weeping for her children and refusing to be comforted, because her children are no more" (Jer. 31:15). The Jews, nevertheless, prospered in the land of their captivity. Though not free, they were not prisoners either. They were allowed to have their own community organization and elders, and could build houses, farm, and earn a living.[1]

The Babylonian empire soon developed its own problems. After King Nebuchadnezzar's death, the sprawling empire deteriorated rapidly, helped along by the rise of Cyrus the Mede to head the Persian empire. In the autumn of 539, Babylon fell without a struggle. She had been weighed on God's sovereign scales and found too slim on justice (Dan. 5:27). This Cyrus, Isaiah had predicted, would be brought to power by Yahweh himself to return God's exiled people, allowing them to rebuild Jerusalem (Isa. 45:1–6, 13).

Figure 15.1

Persian Kings	
Cyrus	539–530
Cambyses	530–522
Darius I	522–486
Xerxes	486–465/4
Artaxerxes I	464–423
Darius II	423–404
Artaxerxes II	404–359
Artaxerxes III	359/58–338/37
Arses	338/37–336/35
Darius III	336/35–331

The new Persian policy toward captive peoples was more humane than any of its predecessors. The Assyrians, who captured northern Israel in 722 B.C., had not only exiled nations but also replaced them in their land with other displaced peoples—a kind of international shell game. This resulted in foreigners populating the region of Samaria. These people, after a number of disastrous episodes, decided to worship Yahweh as well as their own gods (cf. 2 Kings 17:24–41). The Babylonians, the next world power after Assyria, had maintained puppet governments and exacted tribute; but an especially rebellious territory like Judah would be taken into exile. The Persians under Cyrus reversed all this. They returned captive peoples to their own land and restored the worship of each nation's gods. This was good insurance for king and empire. How better to earn the favor of so many gods?

Such is the scene when a few Jewish survivors return from exile to restore their community in Jerusalem and Judah, as recorded in the books of Ezra and Nehemiah.

chapter fifteen

A Peg
in the Holy Place
(Ezra–Nehemiah, Chronicles, Esther)
Concerns of Ezra and Nehemiah

My first three years of academics took place in a one-room schoolhouse. My mind has preserved mental snapshots of those rows of desks—each row to the left representing a year of progress. Central heating was supplied by a single stove in the rear of the room.

When the winds of progress inevitably prevailed, our school consolidated with a larger district in the nearest town. Eventually the property was sold, but whatever plans the buyer had went awry. Brush grew up in the playground. The merry-go-round broke down. The building deteriorated.

Some time ago, several of us returned to that site of earlier misadventures. Thirty years had taken its toll, but we entered and tried to match our memories to the scene before us. The room was much smaller than our childhood eyes recalled—especially the cloakroom where my sister, Janet, spent many exiled hours learning in isolation away from people-oriented distractions. Most difficult to match, however, was our remembrance of a clean, tidy, orderly room with the shambles lying before us. Though we fully expected such conditions, a sense of depression clouded our homecoming mood.

How much worse it must have been for Israel's first returning exiles. No drop-in visit here. Like pioneers, they left security for a new, yet old, land. They were not on a brief nostalgic journey. They were returning to stay and to restore the worship of Yahweh in Jerusalem. How the rubble must have depressed them!

RETURNS AND REFORMS—EZRA AND NEHEMIAH
The Exiles Return—538 B.C.

Actually, the books of Ezra and Nehemiah record three returns. The first return follows the edict of Cyrus (538 B.C.), which allows the Jews to return to their homeland, supplies them with the captured temple treasures, and calls for neighborly contributions to the project so the temple may be restored (Ezra 1). The Jews who returned worked under Zerubbabel, a descendant of King David, to restore sacrificial worship (Ezra 3) and rebuild the temple.[2]

Opposition to the project from other residents and local officials brought the project to a standstill for fifteen years (Ezra 4:1–5, 24).[3] One protest too many, however, reversed the trend. King Darius, recently come to the throne of Persia (522 B.C.), ordered a search of the archives and found a memorandum outlining Cyrus's original decree. Officials were then ordered to aid the project by supplying expenses and sacrificial animals. The threat of finding oneself impaled on a beam from his own destroyed house encouraged cooperation (Ezra 6:11).

Ezra—Priest and Scribe

The initial return did not involve Ezra at all. Ezra 7 introduces us to this unique man. The time (458 B.C.) is nearly eighty years after the first return

Figure 15.2
The Cylinder of Cyrus

The Cylinder of Cyrus that gives the royal decree allowing conquered peoples to return to their homelands (Copyright British Museum)

and nearly sixty years after the temple's completion.[4] Ezra desires to teach Israel to live according to the Law of Moses so God can bless and fully restore Israel (Ezra 7:1–10). King Artaxerxes, the reigning Persian, also has an interest in the Jews' obeying "the Law of your God" as well as "the law of the king" (Ezra 7:25–26): If he did not allow the God of the Jews to be worshiped properly, what might this God do against the king of the Persians (Ezra 7:23)? Artaxerxes knew how to cover all the bases!

Ezra didn't have to be much of a detective to find abuses of the Law among the returned community. Intermarriage with heathen neighbors was epidemic—not only among the people in general but even among leaders and priests. The rest of the book of Ezra chronicles Ezra's successful yet painful effort to reverse this trend that threatened to wipe out the Jews as a distinctive people for Yahweh (Ezra 9–10).

Nehemiah the Governor—445–432 B.C.

Nehemiah comes next, thirteen years after Ezra (445 B.C.), in the book that bears his name and contains a personal account of his own experiences. Nehemiah occupied the close and trusted position of king's cupbearer, yet his life-interest was not personal advancement but the welfare of Jerusalem and the returned exiles. The news that Zion's faraway city walls were still in ruins left him nearly despondent. Always a man of prayer, he turns to God. He admits Israel's wickedness but focuses on God's promise of deliverance and prays for success. Always a man of action, he successfully seeks from Artaxerxes a leave of absence along with supplies for rebuilding the wall of Jerusalem (Neh. 1–2).

Figure 15.3
Map of Babylonian Empire and Returns

From *The NIV Study Bible* (Zondervan, 1985), map 7b of color maps.

Like Zerubbabel, Nehemiah faces opposition from surrounding peoples and officials. In his case, the threats are more physical than legal. Sentence prayers to his God carry him through the personal abuse and potential discouragement that threatened completion of the project (4:4–5, 9; 5:19; 6:9, 14).

Jerusalem's wall is complete in fifty-two days despite ridicule ("If even a fox climbed up on it, he would break down their wall of stones!" 4:3), attempt at assassination ("Come, let us meet together . . . on the plain of Ono," 6:2–3), and fifth-column intrigue (6:10–13).

Like Ezra, Nehemiah was concerned about the spiritual health of the Jews. The rest of the book focuses on spiritual reforms (Neh. 8–13). The upcoming national festival in the seventh month provides an opportunity. Appropriately enough, Ezra's reading of the Law of Moses is the fuse that lights the reform (8:1–9). The immediate response is a full celebration of the very feast they are attending, the Feast of Booths, following precisely the Law's instruction (8:13–17). Next comes confession of Israel's repeated failure before a faithful and just God (9:5–37). The people recognize their need to be faithful to the Mosaic Law before God can fully remove the punishment of exile. They covenant together to do just that (9:38–10:39). Leaving nothing to chance, they list their most frequent failings:

- intermarriage with heathen peoples
- failure to keep the Sabbath
- failure to provide for the needs of temple worship
- failure to recognize God's right to the firstborn
- failure to tithe

Talk about specific application! How often is spiritual growth dependent on a willingness to be specific and honest about weaknesses? This profitable time together ends with arrangements for sufficiently populating Jerusalem, the dedication of the finished walls, and the exclusion of Ammonites and Moabites from the community (11:1–13:3). The people go home and Nehemiah reports back to Artaxerxes. All is well.

Or is it? When Nehemiah returns he finds that promised reforms have been neglected (chap. 13). The influential Tobiah, governor of the Ammonite province, has been given a room in the temple itself![5] Temple supplies were neglected, and the Levites had returned to their own fields to support themselves. Men worked on the Sabbath, marketing their goods right in Jerusalem. To top everything, people had reverted to square one and were intermarrying with heathen peoples. Nehemiah, the man of prayer and action, strengthens his resolve by prayer and forcefully acts to stop these practices once again.

Surely these men—Zerubbabel, Ezra, and Nehemiah, along with the prophets Haggai, Zechariah, and Malachi—made their impact on the

The Book of Chronicles

The two books of Chronicles form a single book in the Hebrew Bible. The Greek Bible divided it, and that pattern is followed in our English versions. For many, Chronicles is a rerun of the history of Samuel and Kings — except that it starts with a genealogy from Adam onward that makes even thinking about reading the book a difficult task.

Though Chronicles in our English Bibles is placed after 1 and 2 Kings, it really belongs in the postexilic period. It summarizes the history of Israel for those who returned from exile. Whereas Kings had emphasized why it was that the nation went out into exile, Chronicles emphasizes those historical ties, including genealogies, that are important to life after exile. A convenient outline follows:

I. Genealogies from Adam Through Saul (1 Chron. 1 – 9)
II. David's Reign (1 Chron. 10 – 29)
III. Solomon's Reign (2 Chron. 1 – 9)
IV. Kings of Judah to the Decree of Cyrus (2 Chron. 10 – 36)

Certain things are conspicuously absent from Chronicles. The events of the reign of Saul are excluded — only his death is important! The reigns of the kings of northern Israel are missing. The ministries of Elijah and Elisha, so prominent in Kings, are only briefly acknowledged. The anonymous Chronicler[6] has also been accused of neglecting David's shortcomings and Solomon's straying from Yahweh. All of these omissions, however, should not be taken as evidence of duplicity on the part of our writer. After all, his readers already had Samuel and Kings. He was hardly fooling anyone! Rather, he was gleaning the wholesome thread of the past — the part that modeled how to do it right! His "idealizing" of David and the successes of the past was not to deny frailty and failures but to highlight the positive contribution to the ongoing plan of God for the exiles.[7]

Certain things are also conspicuously present. These revolve around Davidic line, the Law, temple, and worship.[8] The Davidic Covenant and line are important to the continuing hope for a reestablishment of a theocratic nation and throne, whereas the kings of Israel have no such relevance or future. The building and place of the temple is the central focus — not only for worship, but because the temple is the earthly house of the real Ruler of Israel. Thus, the prime function of David and Solomon as kings is to build that house and encourage worship and full obedience to Torah. Yes, worship! Worship is a strong concern of the Chronicler. Priestly and levitical genealogies and roles are highlighted. Sacrifices and offerings, prayers and thanksgivings, fasting and feasting, New Moons and annual festivals, song and confession were to the Chronicler part of the vibrant life of Israel and crucial to the functioning and health of the returned people of God. Not as mere outer worship but as vital recognition of a faithful God:

"Give thanks to the LORD,
for his love endures forever" (20:21).

community of returned exiles. The very existence of these books shows that the Jews recognized their concerns as God's own concerns. The lesson for this people (and any people) is found in another book written for the exiles. The word spoken first to Asa needs to be heard again: "If you seek him [Yahweh], he will be found by you, but if you forsake him, he will forsake you" (2 Chron. 15:2).

UNDERSTANDING EZRA–NEHEMIAH

The Good Hand of God

Many supernatural events assured the Israelites they were God's people. Yahweh had vindicated himself in Egypt, had brought them through the Sea, had miraculously fed them in the desert, had brought them across the Jordan, defeated the Canaanites, and delivered them innumerable times since. If their time of punishment in Babylon—predicted as seventy years (Jer. 25:11–12; 29:10–14)—was indeed over, then expectation must have been high that Yahweh would intervene.

And intervene he did. "The LORD moved the heart of Cyrus king of Persia" (Ezra 1:1). Unlike Yahweh's ancient acts of deliverance, his actions in these books take place behind the scenes. He is the sovereign God of history who can bring things to pass without showing his hand. It is enough that God names Cyrus as the deliverer in advance (Isa. 44:28–45:7). Though no cloud of glory and no pillar of fire by night led these people, they nonetheless enjoyed fulfillment of his Word (Isa. 40:8). The classic Negro spiritual has it, "He's got the whole world in his hands." Just so, Ezra and Nehemiah recognize Yahweh's ability to bring to pass his will. They also recognize Yahweh's involvement in their own work when they are committed to his plan.

At every step when they desire to glorify God in their plans and a green light shows up, they perceive the hand of God. Does Ezra want to go to Jerusalem to teach the Law? He seeks permission from the Gentile ruler Artaxerxes. Permission is granted. This is "the hand of the LORD his God" (Ezra 7:6, 27–28).

Does Nehemiah want to help reestablish Jerusalem and Judah in the Land of Promise—a place where his heart is, though his feet stand in far-away Susa? He prays that God might allow it. He tells his desires to the king. Permission and more is granted. It is "the gracious hand of my God upon me". (Neh. 2:18).

It is this God of heaven who moved the heart of Cyrus, and who moved the hearts of those who returned under Zerubbabel, and who put it in the heart of Nehemiah to act for Jerusalem (Ezra 1:1, 5; Neh. 2:12; 7:5; cf. Ezra 8:18).[9] It is this same God who protects his people—whether from the perils of desert travel or from plotting officials (Ezra 8:21–23, 31; 4:5; Neh. 4:15, 20; 6:16).

The returnees no doubt could have wished for "instant success" and "instant fulfillment" of all the prophecies about God's ultimate salvation after exile—just as today many look for "instant maturity" and "instant perfection" through some new experience or quick fix. Even at the original entrance to the land, God tested Israel's response and faithfulness. Here, too, he would test her faithfulness—not in great battles, but in a struggling situation when his own activity seems less than spectacular.

Doing It Right

Every youngster needs to learn about doing it right. My father did his best to teach me about the right use of tools. I was most impressed with this lesson after I used one of his wood chisels to lop the head off a small metal bolt. Let's just say Dad got my attention that day.

Israel, too, needed the lesson of doing it right. Her neglect in following the directions of the Law had been total and nearly fatal. Hear the confession of Nehemiah:

> I confess the sins we Israelites, including myself and my father's house, have committed against you. We have acted very wickedly toward you. We have not obeyed the commands, decrees and laws you gave your servant Moses (Neh. 1:6–7; cf. 9:13–37; Ezra 9:6–7).

The reason for failure was recognized. So was the solution:

> Remember the instruction you gave your servant Moses, saying, "If you are unfaithful, I will scatter you among the nations, but if you return to me and obey my commands, then even if your exiled people are at the farthest horizon, I will gather them from there and bring them to the place I have chosen as a dwelling for my Name" (Neh. 1:8–9; cf. Deut. 30:1–10; 1 Kings 8:46–51).

This accounts for the primary emphasis in these books on obeying the Law of Moses. Far from being a new emphasis, this insistence on obedience for blessing takes us back to the basic principles of Israel's founding.[10] Just as she was oppressed in the period of Judges because of disobedience, so now exile had come. The solution is the same. She must turn back to Yahweh. And emphasis it is! On every page we are told that things are being prescribed "in accordance with what is written in the Law of Moses the man of God" (Ezra 3:2), or "according to the command of the God of Israel" (6:14; cf. Neh. 8:1, 14), and "according to what is written in the book of Moses" (Ezra 6:18; cf. Neh. 8:15). Ezra is recognized as "well versed in the Law of

Moses" and had "devoted himself to the study and observance of the Law of the LORD, and to teaching its decrees and laws in Israel" (Ezra 7:6, 10–11). It is the "wisdom of God" which he possesses (7:25–26).

The people recognize their sin as disregarding "the commands you gave through your servants the prophets" (9:10–11) and as unfaithfulness to God (10:2). How to set right the violation? "Let it be done according to the Law" (10:3). Based on the Law, usury was stopped, intermarriages with pagan peoples were dissolved, uncertified priests were excluded from temple duty, and pledges were given to live lives of commitment to God (Neh. 5:6–12; 7:64; 10:29–39). But the close of the book leaves in doubt whether the people will consistently obey. At Nehemiah's return from Persia he finds many of these same violations again. So the book's final concern is: Will God's people open themselves to the blessing of full restoration through obedience, or won't they?

Separation and Opposition

Another primary emphasis of Ezra–Nehemiah is the need to be a separate and distinct people. Intermarriage with peoples not exclusively devoted to worship of Yahweh would dilute and destroy true worship (Ezra 9:1–2). This is not a matter of pure bloodlines. Israel's history is dotted with those descended from other nations—Rahab and Ruth being two conspicuous examples. The concern is not with pure ancestry but with a pure people. There is a vast difference. Anyone can join this people, as Ezra 6:21 indicates, but to marry idolatrous peoples is to compromise faith with Yahweh. Solomon's foreign wives stand as a warning against this folly (Neh. 13:26–27). Divorce seems like a tragic and difficult option. But when God's directives have been disregarded, people often find themselves in a no-win situation. Their initial sin has made it impossible to cleanse themselves without causing more pain and suffering.

The questions the Corinthians asked the apostle Paul about their "mixed marriages" may well have been raised by reading Ezra and Nehemiah. Should marriages between believers and unbelievers be dissolved (1 Cor. 7:1, 12–16)? Paul says, "No." Though their situation looks similar to that of Nehemiah's day, he concludes that it is exactly the opposite. In Ezra's day the presence of an unbeliever in the marriage made the whole family "unclean" before God. But under the progress of the gospel, Paul says, it is just the reverse. The unbelieving spouse and the children are counted as "clean" or "sanctified" because of the believing mate. Why should this be? A moment's reflection shows the difference.

In the Old Testament, to marry an unbeliever was to defect from God. But this is far from the Corinthian situation. Paul had brought the gospel to the Corinthians. Many now believed and had come into relationship with God, yet their mates had not. Being tied to unbelieving mates does not indicate their movement away from God. Rather, their belief shows positively that God is at work in their family. No sin caused these "mixed marriages." They became "mixed" because salvation came to their house.

Just as intermarriage with surrounding peoples is prohibited by Ezra–Nehemiah, so is cooperative worship. Though these people claim to worship Yahweh, they do not worship him exclusively as the Law required (Ezra 4:1–3). These people were transplanted into Samaria by Assyria at the fall of the northern kingdom of Israel. They "worshiped the LORD, but they also appointed all sorts of their own people . . . as priests . . . . They worshiped the LORD, but they also served their own gods" (2 Kings 17:32–33). This is not true worship at all, as the historian of Kings points out (17:34–41).

Such "exclusiveness" as that demonstrated by Ezra and Nehemiah invariably brings opposition. It seems much nicer and not so narrow to teach that "there are many routes to heaven" or that people are "all worshiping the same God in their own way." This is all very polite, but it will hardly do for proof. Biblical history and the Jewish exile speak against it.

The Great, Mighty, and Awesome God

To many an exiled Jew it may have seemed God had gone underground—like a spy who cuts off all normal contacts. But this is not how Nehemiah views him. Nehemiah's prayers reveal a message about God that illumines everything else. Yahweh, God of heaven, is "the great and awesome God, who keeps his covenant of love with those who love him and obey his commands" (Neh. 1:5). Yahweh, Creator of all, is he who made a covenant with Abraham to give his descendants the land (9:7–8). His keeping this covenant shows his righteousness (9:8). Yahweh is a forgiving God, gracious and compassionate, even in the face of rebellion by his people (9:16–19, 30–31). He did not "put an end to them or abandon them" (9:30–31). Yahweh is faithful and just. "In all that has happened to us," Nehemiah prays, "you have been just; you have acted faithfully, while we did wrong" (9:33). Yahweh is "the great, mighty, and awesome God, who keeps his covenant of love" (9:32). If they are in distress, it is not Yahweh's fault. The God of heaven has moved kingdoms for them.

Prayers of Remembrance

Nehemiah's view of God explains his many prayers. The awesome God is able to come to his aid and is willing to involve himself with a people who recognize their failings and call upon him. Did Nehemiah invent the sentence prayer? We find them spread throughout the book. In a number of them, Nehemiah asks God to remember him, a request based on Nehemiah's understanding of God's justice. Nehemiah follows the prescription of the Law: "Do not seek revenge" (Lev. 19:18). Vengeance is the Lord's (Deut. 32:35). When Nehemiah is abused, he commits it to God and asks him to carry out justice (cf. Rom. 12:19).

On other occasions, Nehemiah asks God to remember his efforts. Sometimes, due to indifference, a ministry effort is unsuccessful and even misunderstood. Nehemiah knows that God alone is judge of our efforts. It is encouraging in difficult times to be able to commit such things to him (cf. 1 Cor. 4:1–5).

A New Exodus?

How do Ezra and Nehemiah view the situation of the returned exiles? Do they see the return from Babylon as a second Exodus, such as that predicted in Isaiah 40:1–11? Opinion is divided. Certainly some events suggest a parallel with the original Exodus—such as neighbors giving money to the returning Jews (Ezra 1:4) and the problem of intermarriage (Ezra 9:1–2; compare Moses' warnings in Deut. 7:1–4). Certainly the celebration of the Festival of Booths (Neh. 8:13–17), which recalled God's leading through the wilderness, would encourage the people to reflect on the first Exodus. These worshipers also had crossed a desert and entered the land. And in that great prayer of Nehemiah 9, the Exodus is labeled front-page news: "You made a name for yourself, which remains to this day" (9:10).

But in all this is not one clear indication that they saw themselves in a second Exodus.[11] In fact, the "parallels" make totally different points. Even the Feast of Booths is stressed not to suggest a new Exodus, but to show their joyful compliance with the Law as read by Ezra. There are clearer parallels to Solomon's temple building (cedars from Lebanon, begun in the second month, Davidic worship, and the nearly duplicated chorus; Ezra 3:7–11, cf. 2 Chron. 5:13) than to the Exodus.

If Ezra–Nehemiah does not proclaim a second Exodus, how does it view Israel's situation? The answer is clear and shows why they are unwilling to fully identify with a new Exodus. They are slaves (Ezra 9:9). They are subjects to a foreign king, the king of Persia. As much as God has moved his heart to aid them, they have not been freed as a people. The land is not theirs. The Davidic king is not on the throne. What has God done for them?

> But now for a brief moment grace has been shown from the LORD our God, to leave us an escaped remnant and to give us a peg in His holy place, that our God may enlighten our eyes and grant us a little reviv-

ing in our bondage. For we are slaves; yet in our bondage, our God has not forsaken us, but has extended loving kindness to us in the sight of the kings of Persia, to give us reviving to raise up the house of our God, to restore its ruins, and to give us a wall in Judah and Jerusalem (Ezra 9:8–9 NASB).

They have a "peg" or "stake" (NRSV) in Jerusalem. The word means "tent-peg" and refers to the place a wanderer pitches his tent.[12] God has given them an opportunity, something of a start—and Ezra is concerned that their renewed sin might wipe out this beginning: "Would you not be angry enough with us to destroy us, leaving us no remnant or survivor?" (Ezra 9:14).

The prayer of Nehemiah 9 arrives at the same bottom line:

> But see, we are slaves today, slaves in the land you gave our forefathers so they could eat its fruit and the other good things it produces. Because of our sins, its abundant harvest goes to the kings you have placed over us. They rule over our bodies and our cattle as they please. We are in great distress (9:36–37).

The judgment begun at the Exile has not been fully lifted. But they have a beginning. The Lord has moved the heart of Cyrus. The temple is rebuilt. They have their peg in the holy place.

THOSE WHO DIDN'T RETURN—THE BOOK OF ESTHER

If "the good hand of God" was upon those who returned, what about those who remained in exile? The book of Esther is a post-exilic history that deals with Jews who had not returned under Zerubbabel. The events of the book of Esther are to be dated between the time of the temple's completion (515 B.C.) and the returns of Ezra and Nehemiah (458 and 445 B.C.). These events relate to the Persian king, *Khshayarsha*, transliterated into Hebrew as Ahasuerus, and known to the world by the Greek name, Xerxes (485 B.C.).

The book seems to revolve around twin banquets or celebrations. Chapter 1 opens with two initial banquets. Vashti refuses to leave the banquet of women to become the entertaining object of the imbibing men. However justified, her refusal was quickly perceived as a threat to the authority of all husbands, from Xerxes to the lowest peasant. Vashti's position is to be given to another—enter candidates for Xerxes' harem and Esther.[13] Esther's journey of favor to the top, her uncle Mordecai's unveiling of an assassination attempt against Xerxes, and top administrator Haman's hatred for the Jews, all combine to bring us to the moment of crisis. Haman, a descendent of Agag the Amalekite (3:1; 1 Sam. 15:1–8),[14] casts the lot or *pur*[15] to mark the auspicious day for his Jewish pogrom. The story's turning point comes at Xerxes' insomnia, his subsequent review of the annals and his discovery that Mordecai's efforts had gone unrewarded (6:1). The unwinding of Haman's plot begins. Mordecai's challenge to Esther to risk approaching the king (4:12–16), followed by her own two banquets, unravels Haman and arouses Xerxes' wrath. The days of *pur* (pl., *purim*) now become days of extermination for those planning to attack the Jews. Two days of celebration result (9:18–19). The annual festival of *purim*, a day of fasting followed by two of joy and celebration, commemorates this great historical deliverance.

Several features of the book have raised questions about its theological perspective. It never mentions God. Though fasting is mentioned, prayer is not. There are no miracles, nor references to the Law. Even the critical verses could be read as a statement of fate as much as of divine providence: "Who knows but that you have come to royal position for such a time as this" (4:14).[16] It seems as if "coincidence" is the order of the day. Such concerns have led to a variety of suggestions. Perhaps the book writer is writing from the perspective of the Persian annals.[17] Perhaps it illustrates—not the happy intervention of God for his faithful people in exile—but the problem of God openly intervening for a people who were not interested in returning to the land. Perhaps they have adapted only too well to Persian culture and practice. After all, should Esther join a pagan harem? Avoid revealing her heritage? Partake of special food, which seems to have violated Jewish dietary laws (4:8–13)?[18]

On the other hand, the above features also add to the literary suspense. If God is not intervening directly, then he has still not disregarded his people. The name of the fast/feast, *purim*, is ironic commentary on the failure of fate and superstition to overcome God's care. The statement of Mordecai that deliverance will come, if not from Esther, then from another place, strongly suggests to the faithful that they know the place, even though such "coincidences" might seem to be happenstance. And, at the very center of the story is the "coincidence" of the king's sleepless night that led to his awareness of Mordecai.[19] Such "coincidences" are worth telling and worth celebrating. And, they ultimately fit the outlook of Ezra–Nehemiah: "the good hand of our God" has shown itself, even for those still in exile.

ON THE WAY: COMPLETION OF EXILE

Remember Jeremiah's picture of Rachel weeping for her children as they were marched off to exile (Jer. 31:15)? Matthew uses this scene with an entirely different situation. In Matthew 2 we find Herod, not Nebuchadnezzar, persecuting the Jews. In an effort to eliminate any competition, Herod orders a pogrom against the Jewish lads of Bethlehem. All boys two years of age and under are to be butchered, so that Herod can eradicate the one born "king of the Jews" (2:13–18; 2:2). Jesus escapes, but others die—as they often have under Pharaohs and Herods and Hitlers. The massacre of Bethlehem, Matthew says, fulfilled the words of the prophet Jeremiah.

> A voice is heard in Ramah,
> weeping and great mourning,
> Rachel weeping for her children
> and refusing to be comforted,
> because they are no more (Matt. 2:18).

But how can the deaths of these children of Bethlehem fulfill Jeremiah's words when Jeremiah was speaking of the Babylonian captivity over five centuries earlier (Jer. 31:15)?

The answer shows that Matthew views the return from exile in precisely the same way as did Ezra and Nehemiah. As we noted in our discussion of the Exodus, Matthew uses Hosea 11:1—"Out of Egypt I called my Son," a verse speaking of Israel's Exodus from Egypt—to show that Jesus is Israel's representative who will fulfill God's purposes for his people. Jesus will bring in the new and final Exodus. What God did for Israel at her beginning, he will bring to completion through his Son. This New Exodus would bring Jews back from their exile in Babylon and elsewhere and restore them to the land and nationhood (Isa. 49).

Is it then surprising that in this same context Matthew again uses a verse referring to Israel's history and teaches its fulfillment in Jesus? In the account of the Bethlehem massacre, Matthew quotes Jeremiah 31:15 to remind the Jews they still await restoration from the captivity that Nebuchadnezzar began. His use of this verse indicates that, like Ezra and Nehemiah, he believes the Jews are still slaves under Gentile rulers.

The Babylonian captivity was replaced by the rule of Persia. Cyrus allowed a contingent to return and rebuild the temple, but full restoration was not achieved. The next king of the hill was Alexander the Great of Greece, conqueror of the then-known world. After Alexander's early death and the division of his empire, the Jews rebelled against a despised Seleucid ruler, Antiochus IV. For a brief moment this revolt of the Maccabees gave Judea its freedom, but it produced no lasting kingdom. The Jews soon found themselves under Pax Romana—Roman "peace."

Herod, Caesar's local stand-in, appears as the latest of a long series of Gentile rulers. As Ezra confessed,

> We and our kings and our priests have been subjected to the sword and captivity, to pillage and humiliation at the hand of foreign kings, as it is today (Ezra 9:7).

That confession would hold equally good for any Jew of Jesus' day.

Rachel still cries. She cried when they went out under Nebuchadnezzar. Nearly six centuries later, she still is weeping. And in Matthew's day, Jeremiah's report of Israel's suffering is yet being fulfilled. But Jeremiah did not tell us about Rachel's crying to predict unending persecution for the Jews. In fact, he uses this grim picture as a backdrop for sketching a brighter day. Rachel will not always cry, says Jeremiah, because Yahweh will never abandon his people. Rachel's children will return and be restored, and God will give them a New Covenant more effective than the one given after the original Exodus. This covenant will produce in them a new heart—and Yahweh will never again have to chasten his people with judgment (Jer. 31:16–37).

Jesus, the promised Messiah, will complete the New Exodus—full restoration from the captivity of Babylon. Even now his herald is calling, "Repent, for the kingdom of heaven is near" (Matt. 3:2). This John the Baptist, Matthew says, is the messenger Isaiah predicted to announce the New Exodus.

> A voice of one calling in the desert,
> "Prepare the way for the Lord,
>   make straight paths for him" (Matt. 3:3; cf. Isa. 40:3).

Rachel's crying must cease. As surely as Jeremiah predicted Jewish suffering under captivity, he predicted future relief, restoration, and a New Covenant. Matthew says, "It's beginning. The King has arrived."

SUGGESTED SCRIPTURE READING:

Ezra 1, 3–6, 8–10:17
Nehemiah 1–2, 4–7:3, 8–9; 12:27–13:31
Jeremiah 31:5–34
Matthew 2:1–18

For Interaction and Discussion:

1. How does understanding that there were three returns from exile help put the book of Ezra–Nehemiah into proper perspective?

2. What are the specific sins that trouble the people at this time? What specific sins might God list if he were evaluating his people today?

3. Why is not the attitude of excluding foreigners in Ezra–Nehemiah a racist approach to salvation? How does the New Testament attitude about separating from unbelieving partners differ from what was prescribed here? Why?

4. How does God's activity in this period differ from his great acts of salvation in earlier periods? Which approach is closest to our own time?

What do the attitudes of Ezra and Nehemiah toward God's oversight suggest about God's guidance? What about the attitude of these men toward sin?

5. How do the themes of the book of Chronicles fit with Ezra and Nehemiah?

6. Consider our culture's "instant success" syndrome. How do desires, God's purposes, prayer, and action relate in Ezra–Nehemiah?

7. How does effort relate to prayer? What is to be our attitude when our efforts are misunderstood or opposed by others?

8. How is the book of Esther different from these other historical books? How is it similar?

9. How does the hope of a New Exodus fit in with the return from Babylon and with Jesus? Why is Rachel crying? Is she still crying?

For Further Reading:

William J. Dumbrell. *The Faith of Israel*. Grand Rapids: Baker, 1988, 266–79, 252–55.

Derek Kidner. *Ezra-Nehemiah*. TOTC. Downers Grove, Ill.: InterVarsity, 1979.

Joyce G. Baldwin. *Esther*. TOTC. Downers Grove, Ill.: InterVarsity, 1984.

James D. Newsome, Jr. "Toward a New Understanding of the Chronicler and His Purposes." *JBL*, 94 (1975): 201–17.

Sandra Beth Berg. *The Book of Esther*. SBL Dissertation Series. Atlanta: Scholar's Press, 1979. Academic study of literary parallels and arrangement.

Robert Gordis. "Religion, Wisdom and History in the Book of Esther—A New Solution to an Ancient Crux." *JBL*, 100 (1981): 359–88. Academic evaluation of Esther's historical roots.

Notes and Comments:

[1]John Bright, *A History of Israel*, 345–46. Biblical references that indicate the organization and community life of the exiles in Babylon include Ezekiel 3:15; 8:1, 14:1; 33:30ff; Jeremiah 29:5ff; Ezra 2:59; 8:17.

[2]Ezra 1:8 and 5:14 indicate that the return took place under "Sheshbazzar the prince of Judah." Much debate has taken place about the relationship of Sheshbazzar to Zerubbabel (Ezra 3:2, 5:2). It is interesting to note that only official documents use the name "Sheshbazzar." The narrative gives all the credit for actual activity to Zerubbabel. This observation supports the view that they are one and the same— "Sheshbazzar" being the official Persian name for Zerubbabel. This same tacit identification is present in Josephus as well (*Antiquities*, 11.11–13).

On the other hand, W. F. Albright identified Sheshbazzar as the same as Shenazzar of 1 Chronicles 3:18, seeing both as a corruption of a Babylonian name like Sin-ab-user (see *JBL*, 40 [1921]: 108–10). Cf. Bright, *A History of Israel*, 361–

64, for the implications of the latter view. F. F. Bruce, *Israel and the Nations*, 100–101, sees them as joint leaders with Sheshbazzar returning to Persia as soon as the altar is reestablished.

[3]Ezra 4:6–23 follows a common Hebrew literary pattern in choosing to complete the topic of opposition to building beyond the time of the events in the narrative. Thus, the biblical writer goes beyond the opposition to building during the rule of Cyrus and Darius and includes in these verses opposition under Artaxerxes as well. This opposition was against the building of the walls (4:16). The account returns to the time of Darius in verse 24.

[4]Much ink has been expended on the dating of Ezra's return. Bright, *A History of Israel*, 391–402, provides a good summary of the current views. We have followed the traditional view based on Ezra 7:7. We believe that Gleason Archer, *A Survey of Old Testament Introduction*, 396–98, has adequately answered Bright's hesitations about the traditional view that has Ezra preceding Nehemiah. Cf. F. Charles Fensham, *The Books of Ezra and Nehemiah* (Grand Rapids: Eerdmans, 1982), 6–9.

[5]The insidious influence of Tobiah was helped no doubt by the apparent fact that he was Jewish. His name ("Yahweh is good") attests at least a nominal adherence to Yahweh, as do the names of his sons. It is also possible that Sanballat claimed to be a Yahweh worshiper. Cf. Derek Kidner, *Ezra–Nehemiah* (Downers Grove, Ill.: InterVarsity, 1979), 101; R. K. Harrison, *Introduction to the Old Testament*, 1141–42.

[6]Regarding the authorship of the anonymous book of Chronicles, W. F. Albright argued for a single author of Chronicles and Ezra–Nehemiah with Ezra the scribe as the likely candidate in agreement with rabbinic tradition. More recent discussion has emphasized differences between Chronicles and Ezra–Nehemiah and suggested separate authors, notwithstanding the tie of the Decree of Cyrus at the conclusion of Chronicles and at the beginning of Ezra–Nehemiah. The extension of the genealogy of Zerubbabel in 3:21 has suggested to some a date at least as late as Ezra and perhaps as late as 400 B.C. (cf. Harrison, *Introduction to the Old Testament*, 1153–57, for a full discussion). In the latter case, rather than precede and provide historical justification for the efforts of temple rebuilding, the book would be intended to encourage the people at a later date to continue to support temple, worship, obedience to the Law, and a hope for full restoration of the New Israel (cf. Dumbrell, *The Faith of Israel*, 279).

[7]Against theories of suppression and misrepresentation of history by the Chronicler, Childs, *Introduction*, 646–47, rightly points out places where the writer assumes his readers know the other accounts or uses sources to make explicit references to such history. In addition, we should note that the writer actually makes more explicit the failure involved in the accounts he does see as important to his history. When he tells about David's purchase of the temple plot, he is quite explicit about David's sin in taking a census of potential military strength (1 Chron. 21:1–13). When he deals with Jehoshaphat, he is very direct in outlining the failure of this good king in aligning with Ahab (2 Chron. 19:1–3). The Chronicler is not guilty of "whitewashing" heros. There is simply no interest in stories that do not affect the temple or worship. Absalom's and Adonijah's rebellions, as unsettling as they were

and important to the writer of King's history of difficulties due to disobedience, did not in the end affect the orderly succession of the Davidic kingship.

[8]Cf. James D. Newsome, Jr., "Toward a New Understanding of the Chronicler and His Purposes," *JBL*, 94 (1975): 201–17.

[9]The unfortunate use of the word *heart* in our culture to refer primarily to non-rational "feelings" has led many readers to believe that this verse about God putting it in Nehemiah's heart vindicates God "speaking" to them through their feelings. The word primarily looks at our true inner thoughts and motivation. Here we are told that it was God who was the source of Nehemiah's motivation to rebuild the walls.

[10]It is popular among scholars to find the beginnings of Phariseeism and legalism here. This period is then viewed as one that has reversed the original purpose of the Law. Cf. Paul J. and Elizabeth Achtemeir, *The Old Testament Roots of Our Faith* (Philadelphia: Fortress, 1962), 75–78. We, however, see here no contradiction with the earlier view of the Law. Certainly, in Deuteronomy the Law was a gracious gift. But if there was to be blessing, it would have to be followed with all the heart, life, and strength. The later legalism, which saw the Law as a way of earning righteousness, was a development that perverted this needed emphasis of a return to the Law.

[11]Childs, *Introduction*, 634, also rejects a clear "Second Exodus" theme in Ezra–Nehemiah, though he does find it typologically in Chronicles.

[12]Fensham, *The Books of Ezra and Nehemiah*, 129–30.

[13]There is an historical problem with the identity of Vashti and Esther. Herodotus, the Greek historian, identifies Xerxes' Queen as Amestris, who exerts influence down into the reign of her son, Artaxerxes I. Amestris cannot be Esther, because Artaxerxes' birth (483 B.C.) preceded Esther's marriage to Xerxes. As the details of Amestris' exploits in Herodotus relate to early in the reign of Xerxes and then later in his reign and the reign of Artaxerxes I, some have concluded that Esther died or fell into disfavor, and Vashti reasserted herself. Joyce Baldwin, *Esther: An Introduction and Commentary*, TOTC (Downers Grove, Ill.: InterVarsity, 1984), 20–21, suggests that Vashti's official position as queen was maintained in the annals and that Esther was a secondary wife. The issue will have to remain open for the present. (Cf. Herodotus, *History*, 7.61, 114; 9.108ff.) The dating within the book shows a gap of four years between the first banqueting and the time of implementing the decree for choosing a wife (1:3; 2:16). This dating corresponds to the involvement of Xerxes in the disastrous Greek campaigns (482–479 B.C.). The first banquet, involving the nobles and officials of Persia, may have marked the occasion of planning for the Greek campaign. This tight historical fit, along with the accuracy of details concerning the background at Susa, bodes well for the historical awareness of the author and should provoke caution in declaring Esther herself to be fictitious. Cf. Harrison, *Introduction*, 1090–98. Robert Gordis, "Religion, Wisdom and History in the Book of Esther—A New Solution to an Ancient Crux," *JBL*, 100, 3 (1981): 359–88, esp. 379 ff., demonstrates the essential features of the book to be historical, though he is satisfied with the term "historical fiction" if the emphasis is on the adjective.

[14]It is interesting to consider whether Haman, the Amalekite and a descendent of Agag, might well be perpetuating the historical hatred of Amalek toward Israel

(Ex. 17:8–16; Deut. 25:17–19). King Saul was to carry out the judgment against Amalek for their mistreatment of Israel, but failed to do so (1 Sam. 15). Mordecai, a Benjamite and possible descendant of Saul (2:5), is ironically involved in this reversal against Haman and his anti-Jewish supporters.

[15]Cf. Baldwin, *Esther*, 22–23, for a description of the cube-shaped dice in the Yale collection dating to the time of Shalmaneser III, important for its inscription using the word *pûru* ("lot") twice. "The derivation of *purîm* in the book is vindicated on the extraordinary chance of archaeology that one dice . . . should come to light."

[16]The similarity of this phrase "for such a time as this" (4:14) to the Joseph story is striking (Gen. 45:5–7). Other possible parallels (Est. 3:4 and Gen. 39:10; Est. 6:11 and Gen. 41:42–43; Est. 8:6 with Gen. 44:34) suggest that the writer may intend to raise this background. If so, remembering the providential care and survival theme of the Joseph story would further support our conclusions regarding the theme of Esther. Cf. Baldwin, *Esther*, 25–26 for bibliography and summary of this issue. Of course, the parallels can be used to arrive at nearly the opposite conclusion—that individual intervention rather than total dependence on providence was important! Berg agrees with the thesis that "Esther was intended to counter any beliefs that the safety of the Jewish community rested solely with Yahweh" (142). Cf. Sandra Beth Berg, *The Book of Esther* (SBL Dissertation Series; Atlanta: Scholar's Press, 1979), 123–42.

[17]Robert Gordis, "Religion, Wisdom and History," 375–78.

[18]The view that the Jews still in exile are pictured negatively by the author of Esther as those who were not interested enough in God's purposes to return to the land runs into difficulty when the timing of Esther as prior to the returns of Ezra and Nehemiah is considered. Such a far-reaching judgment about those in exile then would apply equally to these two men and later returnees. In fact, those who have returned earlier were still part of the Persian empire and therefore under threat as well. Those in the land, perhaps unknown to them, were also delivered by this reversal of plots.

[19]Yahuda T. Radday, "Chiasm in Joshua, Judges and Others," *Linguistica Biblica*, 3 (1973): 9, cited by Baldwin, *Esther*, 30, and Berg, *The Book of Esther*, 108, suggests the following chiastic pattern for the book, which leaves 6:1 at the very center.

A. Opening and Background (chap. 1)
  B. The King's First Decree (chaps. 2–3)
    C. The Clash Between Haman and Mordecai (chaps. 4–5)
      Crisis: "On that night the king could not sleep" (6:1)
    C'. Mordecai's Triumph over Haman (chaps. 6–7)
  B'. The King's Second Decree (chaps. 8–9)
A'. Epilogue (chap. 10)

This center also occurs between the two banquets of Esther, the center banquets of the book. Mordecai's honoring, the first step in the unraveling of Haman (cf. 6:12–14) also occurs between the banquets. Preceding the first banquet is the critical theological outlook of the book (4:12–17), which leads to Esther's banquets.

Berg concludes, however, that "the sequence of events does not present a precise chiasm, the [series of] reversals are of a general nature. The 'antithesis' of each pair may occur at a point in the narrative preceding or following what would be its position in a strict chiasm" (109).

chapter sixteen

THE SECOND TEMPLE
(Haggai, Zechariah, and Malachi)

"Hope deferred makes the heart sick." So Solomon tells us in Proverbs 13:12. Unrealized hopes sack marriages, ruin careers, prompt suicides, and make midlife crisis a household term. To bet your life on someone or something and then lose is more than demoralizing. It can cripple. The prophets Haggai and Zechariah are called to minister to people who began with elevated hopes and dreams. This first group of returning exiles gave up what had become, surprisingly enough, a comfortable life in captivity. With the words of the earlier prophets in their minds and hearts, they headed home to the Land of Promise.

The predictions of exile by Jeremiah and others had not been popular; but now the people could claim the brighter prophecies of restoration (Jer. 30:1–31:40). Riches did not await them, but they could be the first generation to reenter the land and see God work. In Israel's history they could stand like those of Joshua's generation and see Yahweh do great and mighty things for them. Yet it was not to be. As we saw in the last chapter, the initial attempt to rebuild the temple was halted for fifteen years by opposition from non-Jewish residents and officials. The work barely had begun. Unlike Joshua's generation, the Jews had no command from God to exterminate the other peoples in the land, nor were they enabled to do so. They came not with might or with power. They came by permission of Cyrus.[1] Disillusion set in. Cynicism found fertile soil. Energies were turned to the business of making a living. Hope was placed on a dusty shelf to be reconsidered when more time was available. Enter Haggai and Zechariah.

HAGGAI—PROPHET OF PRIORITIES
Misplaced Priorities

Haggai is first to face the lethargy of the people. Some were saying, "The time has not yet come for the LORD's house to be built" (Hag. 1:2). Not good enough, says Haggai: "Is it a time for you yourselves to be living in your paneled houses, while this house [the temple] remains a ruin?" As often happens, living has become so important that living for a purpose has been pushed to the back of the bus. Take stock, says Haggai, what have you accomplished? Haven't you noticed that you've been caught in that most desperate of circles—the direct pursuit of things? What have you gained? You always seem to come up short. Your moneybag is full of holes. Has God been trying to tell you something (1:5–6)? The God who provided manna to that first generation is blowing away the crops of this one. Why? Because they put their comfort ahead of spiritual priorities. The temple still lies in ruins. Their delay in rebuilding the temple cannot be compared to debate today over building a new and larger sanctuary for a local assembly. Today's questions are merely issues of growth, convenience, and seating. But having a temple meant proper worship according to God's revealed Word. Not having it meant neglecting the ceremonies that announced God's forgiveness and care. If those responsible for rebuilding the temple have doubts about timing, they need doubt no more: Haggai's message to Zerubbabel the governor, Joshua the high priest, and the people is, "'I am with you,' declares the LORD" (1:13). With this, the people resume work on the temple.

A House with a Future

After building is resumed, each message from Haggai is increasingly positive. Do some feel like quitting because this temple, built from recycled rocks and common timber from nearby mountains, doesn't have the glory of Solomon's temple? Then they should know that God himself will make the temple a place of splendor, with gold and silver from the nations. Not only splendor but peace will finally come to this place, a peace never finally established even under the man of peace who built the first temple (2:1–9; cf. 2 Sam. 7:11–16).

Blessing Begun

When will God begin to bless them? God could not bless them with an incomplete temple in their midst. "The ruined skeleton of the Temple was like a dead body decaying in Jerusalem and making everything contaminated."[2] Even what was offered on the altar was considered by God to be defiled.[3] But now that they had begun to build, God's word to them is, "From this day on I will bless you" (Hag. 2:19).

Another House with a Future

With each prophecy, Haggai alternates between present and future perspectives.[4] His final prophecy (2:20–23), like the second (2:1–9), looks to the future fulfillment of God's promises. The "signet ring" of kingship will return to the descendant of David. The son of David, Zerubbabel, is now only a governor under King Darius of Persia, but it will not always be so. Yahweh "will overturn royal thrones and shatter the power of the foreign kingdoms." As at Israel's beginning, Yahweh will again fight for Israel. The house of David, like the house of God, has been chosen for future greatness. Haggai performs his task well. His messages get the people going. Straightforward and hard hitting, he deals with the immediate problems of lethargy and defeatism. He holds up the twin banners of the house of God and the house of David and starts the people marching.

ZECHARIAH—VISIONS OF HOPE

Zechariah delivers his first message one month before Haggai's last recorded words. Appropriately so! He takes up and enlarges on what Haggai had begun. With broader brush strokes and greater depth of field, he paints a picture of the future that God's people can ponder again and again. Haggai gave them the sketch. Zechariah gives them the oil.

Zechariah's Purpose

But first, Zechariah gives a message that is direct and definite. "Return to me, declares Yahweh of Hosts, and I will return to you" (1:3, my translation). This initial message sets the tone for all the rest. From the start, God's people must recognize there are no guarantees for this generation. If they do not avoid the evil practices of their fathers who were taken into exile, they can expect the same judgment. Their fathers are dead, as are even the prophets who brought God's message; but God's message itself came to pass. Haggai tackled immediate problems to get the temple started. But Zechariah wants to probe deeper. The people must realize that building the temple will not guarantee that the promises will be fulfilled. Unless they consistently follow the Lord, they cannot expect the hopes of this book to begin unfolding in their lifetime.[5]

Zechariah's Visions

One night, two months after Haggai's last message, Zechariah enjoys little sleep. He is kept alert by a series of complex scenes that pass before his red eyes (1:7–6:8). They are not the result of indigestion, nor should they be equated with the "visions" of leaders today. No, Zechariah's visions are appropriate to a prophet: They are revelations from God. Exciting ideas do not qualify. Zechariah is not merely "pumping sunshine" or using modern motivational techniques. Only divinely inspired revelation can produce truly inspired living. This one-night screening has some eye-catching features. Along with horses and chariots are a man with a measuring line, a woman in a basket, a flying scroll, a priest in dirty duds, and a golden menorah with automatic oil feed.[6] But what can it mean? These visual messages click off a number of crucial concepts. The visions begin and end with patrols that survey the earth and report back to the angel of the Lord (1:7–17; 6:1–8). The theme: Yahweh controls history and nations. He has judged Israel for her sin; now he will judge the nations. This is further spelled out by the second vision in which four craftsmen demolish four "horns" that stand for the nations that exiled Judah and Israel (1:18–21). But Jerusalem itself has a great future (2:1–13). The man who would measure Jerusalem is to inform Zechariah that the city will be larger than ever before—so large it will not be walled. She will not need walls. Yahweh, as in the days of the Exodus, will provide a wall of protecting fire around his people.[7] Yahweh's presence will cause other nations to become his people too. A vision of the filthy high priest introduces another theme (3:1–10). Looking more like a bum than God's high priest, Joshua's clothes picture the sin of Israel. Satan would demand punishment, but God announces grace. He will take away Israel's sin in a single day through his future servant, the Branch. Not only will her sin be removed and forgiveness granted, but justice will be guaranteed as the scroll of the Law flies throughout the whole land (5:1–4). This aerodynamic billboard searches out and removes the very sins that the Law placed under a curse. In this way the hidden apostasy of individuals would not be allowed to bring failure to the nation. Wickedness itself, pictured as a woman—perhaps a figurine idol—would be removed from Israel and sent back to its source, Babylon (5:5–11).[8] In addition to the high priest, a civil leader named Zerubbabel is brought into the visions (4:1–14). The golden menorah, the seven-stemmed lamp of the temple, represents Israel as God's light. Two olive trees joined to the lamp supply it with golden oil. These stand for the two anointed offices of priest and king, represented by Joshua and Zerubbabel (heir to the throne of David). God will use these two functions to sustain his people. Even now in this "day of small things" (4:10), when it seems as if nothing spectacular is happening, God's Spirit is at work. Completion of the temple will be the first step in the ultimate success of God's program.

A Crown in Jerusalem

This focus on priest and king is reaffirmed in a following message (6:9–15). Here a crown is made and placed on the head of Joshua, the high priest. Joshua again symbolizes the future servant, the Branch. The Branch—a name already used in Jeremiah 23:5 and 33:15 for the coming Messiah of David's line—will take his place on the throne. "He will be a priest on his throne" (Zech. 6:13). So the two offices of priest and king will become one in the Messiah. To place a crown on the head of Zerubbabel would signal rebellion against the Persian throne.[9] But this was not the time for rebellion. God would work by his Spirit at the proper time, without military might or power. Yet even now these prophets do not hesitate to predict the restoration of David's throne.

Aren't these visions enough to stir even the dullest of hearts? The Jews would not always be under the Persian throne. David's line and Israel's worship will last until even the nations themselves join Israel. God will pardon their sin and remove evil from among them. There is a future for Jerusalem! And in that ultimate hope there is forgiveness and a future for us all.

Feast or Fast?

Like a newsreel between two special features, chapters 7 and 8 lie between Zechariah's visions and prophecies—and answer a rather mundane question about keeping fasts. Four yearly fasts had been started by the Jews to mourn the fall of Jerusalem.[10] "Should these fasts continue?" a delegation from Bethel asks the priests (7:1–3). Glad you asked, says Zechariah. God has something to say about that. This little question provides an opportunity to reemphasize the main features of God's message through Zechariah. Check them out:

- Their fasting was over their own loss and not over the sin that caused that loss. They will need to start to do justice, not mourn God's righteous judgment of past failure (7:4–14).
- Jerusalem will be reestablished as God's great city complete with aged people and playing children (8:3–6).
- There will be a greater return of Israel to the land (8:7–8).
- Because rebuilding the temple has started, God will be able to bless them if they are careful to reverse their former injustice in the land (8:9–17).
- Periods of fasting will be changed into times of rejoicing, and other nations will want to worship at Jerusalem because of the news of God's blessing on Israel (8:18–23).

Jerusalem, the temple, God's blessing, returning to God, and conversion of the nations are all reaffirmed in answer to a question about fasting! Jesus provided an additional answer: When the Messiah himself is present, no one fasts (Mark 2:19).

Two Final Oracles (Zechariah 9–14)

There was upheaval in the empire before Darius was firmly established on the Persian throne. Undoubtedly the Jews hoped God would use this confusion to break up the empire and allow his people to begin their life again as an independent state. But it was not to be. The first vision (1:8–17) contained the discouraging report that all was quiet. When would God begin to move the political situation for the restoration of his people? These last two prophetic messages glimpse the future of Israel leading to a time of ultimate peace and fulfillment. Someone has said that God does not show each of us our future because we would not be prepared to accept it all at once. Reading Zechariah 9–14 is like that. Ultimate blessing is here, but so are rough times—the kind of times synonymous with the area of the world known as the Middle East.

Much like Psalm 2, these oracles predict the Lord's victory over the nations. The nations will gather against Jerusalem, but God will use her to judge them (12:1–9). The surrounding peoples will be conquered (9:1–8), and many, like the Jebusites of David's time, will become part of Israel (9:7). It is Yahweh who fights for them again (9:14–17). The final battle for Jerusalem will bring Yahweh himself to the Mount of Olives to aid Israel and bring plagues on the rebellious nations (14:2–15). Reading Zechariah 9–14 is much like singing a musical round. Half the fun is recognizing the repeated lines as they enter at alternate places. Just so, these prophetic episodes are not traced chronologically. Again and again, themes are repeated—yet modified.[11] Zechariah gives us not an event-by-event calendar of the future but pictures of events like pages in an album. Each page is dedicated to a particular slice of the future. One such page is God's action to deliver Israel from the nations while at the same time using her to cause many nations to recognize the true God. Another page includes snapshots of the Messiah. Like other Old Testament prophets, Zechariah does not separate events of Messiah's first coming (to suffer) from his second coming (to reign). Examples of both are found on the same page.

One great picture of the future Messiah is that of Zechariah 9:9–10. The righteous Messiah comes with salvation—a king who enters Jerusalem riding a purebred donkey. He is not arrogant as other shepherds of Israel have been (another theme of these prophecies—11:15–17; 13:2–6). Here is one who humbly follows Yahweh's word (cf. Isa. 66:2). This scene, of course, pictures Jesus' triumphal entry into Jerusalem; yet verse 10 awaits fulfillment at the Second Coming. Another Messianic scene is found in 13:7–9. Following the discussion of false prophets (13:2–6), Yahweh's own shepherd is introduced. But astonishingly enough, Yahweh calls on his sword of judgment to kill his shepherd (13:7). Moreover, Yahweh calls this shepherd My Associate (NASB; NIV: "who is close to me"). This word translated "associate" is used elsewhere only in the Law of Moses where it is translated "neighbor" or "brother." ("Do not have intercourse with your neighbor's wife," Lev. 18:20.) It looks at an equal, a comrade, a fellow citizen with equal standing.[12] The Messiah, the man equal in standing with Yahweh, will suffer Yahweh's righteous judgment. Again, readers of the New Testament will recognize that Jesus applied this verse to himself. In his crucifixion God brought judgment on his own Shepherd, that a fountain might be opened to cleanse us from sin and impurity (Zech. 13:1; Matt. 26:31).

MALACHI—MESSENGER OF THE COVENANT

If Haggai and Zechariah faced disillusionment and cynicism, Malachi experienced no less at least half a century later. People and priests had fallen victim to the discouraging drudgery of living in a "nothing's happening" time. As with politicians, people soon begin asking of God: "What have you done for me lately?"

> Zerubbabel and Joshua, whom Haggai and Zechariah had indicated as God's chosen men for the new age, had died. True the Temple had been completed, but nothing momentous had occurred to indicate that God's presence had returned to fill it with glory, as Ezekiel had indicated would happen (Ezk. 43:4). The day of miracles had passed with Elijah and Elisha. Where was the God of their fathers? Did it really matter whether one served him or not?[13]

The book of Malachi pictures a functioning temple and priesthood, along with a people having lost the zest for worship and the idealistic vision of living as God's people. They struggled on the edge of poverty. This picture places the timing of Malachi long after the rebuilding of the temple and either before, in between, or after the reforms of Ezra and Nehemiah toward the middle or late fifth century B.C.

The name, Malachi, means "my messenger"—a fact that suggests to many that it is not the name of the prophet at all, only the function of one. The opening verse should then read: "An oracle: The word of the LORD to Israel through my messenger." If so, the book would be the only anonymous book in the Twelve, though there is really no substantial reason to reject "Malachi" as a proper name.[14]

Malachi's Method

Those of us in the United States of America, who were force-fed what the media calls "the trial of the century," are all too familiar with the words, "I object." Every move of the prosecution, every line of argument, every piece of evidence faces immediate objection. So it is with each of Malachi's five messages. Each begins with a statement or charge from God. What immediately follows? The disputing question Malachi expects from his spiritually insensitive audience.

Malachi's Hard-hitting Messages

- Message One: the Lord's covenantal love is disregarded (1:2–5).
- Message Two: Yahweh is disrespected by priests who offer inappropriate sacrifices, yet respond with wide-eyed innocence (1:6–2:9).
- Message Three: Divorce and intermarriage with idolaters breaks faith with both covenantal partner and covenantal God (2:10–16).
- Message Four: God is wearied with blind injustice (2:17–3:5). They desire blessings from the predicted Messenger of the Covenant, but they will not be able to avoid the purging fire of that day.
- Message Five: An unresponsive attitude follows Yahweh's call to "Return to me, and I will return to you" (3:6–12). They have cursed their own blessings by cutting short tithes and offerings.
- Message Six: The charge that no blessing comes from following God and that the wicked are allowed to prosper is countered by the promise that those who do fear and walk with Yahweh will be rewarded as his treasured possession in that day (3:13–4:3). That day will also bring fiery judgment on the arrogant.
- Final Exhortation: Follow the law of Moses and look for a future Elijah as the last prophetic chance for reconciliation (4:4–6).

Malachi's Themes

Covenant is the major theme of Malachi. Virtually all the covenants are represented. The book begins with God's choice of Jacob over Esau to form his covenant people, Israel, as the great nation of the *Abrahamic Covenant*. It is only because they are descendants of Jacob and that Yahweh doesn't change or go back on his word that they are not destroyed—certainly not because of their obedience (3:6–7). The *Messenger of the Covenant* is expected in the future, along with the Lord's return to his temple (3:1). The *covenant with Levi* as the priestly tribe has been violated by lack of reverence and faulty instruction by the priests (2:1–9). The *"covenant of our fathers"* has been violated by the broken faith of divorce as well as idolatrous marriages, even though the offender still comes to worship (2:10–16).

The theme of *blessings and cursings* (1:14; 2:2; 3:9–12; 4:6) reinforces this covenantal theme. The Deuteronomic promise of blessing for believing obedience of the Mosaic Covenant and cursings upon the land for departing from the Lord is still valid (Deut. 28). The very set of curses that drove the nation out into exile, now holds up ultimate blessing of the returnees! How can priest and people expect to see their day be a day of God's abundant working when they are so insensitive to his ways? They seek happiness their own way by holding back produce, trading in marriage partners, giving inferior sacrifices, and cheating others. This effectively cuts off their opportunity to be truly blessed. They see their compromising tokenism as a case of having tried it but it didn't work. "It is futile to serve God. What did we gain by carrying out his requirements and going about like mourners before the LORD Almighty?" (3:14). Their try was half a loaf and halfhearted. Yet true to the human condition, they saw themselves as having done their part for God.

Though Malachi is concerned with Israel's response to God's covenants, he is also aware of *God's plan for the nations*—a third related theme. "Great is the LORD—even beyond the borders of Israel" (1:5)! Yahweh is a great king "and my name is to be feared among the nations" (1:14). God's covenant with Abraham was to bring blessing upon all nations through Abraham and his descendants (Gen. 12:1–3). An obedient and blessed nation would gain the attention of the surrounding peoples. "Then all the nations will call you blessed, for yours will be a delightful land" (3:12). Their continued failure effectively postponed the day of blessing on all nations until the coming of the Messenger of the Covenant.

THE OUTLOOK OF THE POST-EXILIC PROPHETS

Our overview of the themes of Haggai and Zechariah makes plain the outlook of the prophets after the Exile: The house of David and the house of God, so tightly combined in the original Davidic Covenant (2 Sam. 7:11–16), are still the hope of the future. "Then suddenly the Lord you are seeking will come to his temple; the messenger of the covenant, whom you desire, will come" (Mal. 3:1). Yahweh's presence with the nation once again, predicted in Ezekiel 44:4, is her only hope of restoration and salvation.

The other concern is like the old chorus sung by Sunday school children: "Will you be ready when Jesus comes?" Malachi, after announcing the coming of Messiah to his temple, continues: "But who can endure the day of his coming? Who can stand when he appears? For he will be like a refiner's fire or a launderer's soap" (Mal. 3:2). Zechariah's call for repentance is reissued by Malachi. Unfaithfulness to the temple and injustice to fellow Israelites still predominate. But make no mistake about the Cause of their salvation. Yahweh of Hosts (or armies) is his name. This is the favorite name for God in these books (translated "LORD Almighty" in the NIV). This name is appropriate in worship settings where "hosts" refers to the angels who surround God's throne (Isa. 6:1–5). It is also used for God's power to deliver through heavenly armies of angels (Ps. 46:7, cf. Josh. 5:14). Yahweh of Armies is the awesome God they are to worship and to whom they look for deliverance. He is in control of all the earth, which his angelic army patrols.

Hope has been proclaimed, but there is a gauntlet to run. The returned exiles may despise "the day of small things"—no glory, no fire, no military victories—yet there is a great future for Judah and also for Ephraim (Zech. 10:6–12), neither of which were yet fully restored. The temple project is the first signal that God would restore his people. If they return faithfully to him, they can be part of a great movement leading ultimately to the promised kingdom under the restored line of David. Perhaps a Jew of Zerubbabel's time could have seen it as Paul did: "I consider that our present sufferings are not worth comparing with the glory that will be revealed in us" (Rom. 8:18). It sure beats finishing life with a bag full of holes!

FULFILLMENT OF HOPE: THE DAY OF SALVATION

As Jesus rode that purebred donkey into Jerusalem, he was riding an animal favored by ancient kings but long since supplanted by the horse as the steed of choice. His kingship was recognized by the crowd that accompanied him with shouting (Matt. 21:1–11): "Hosanna to the Son of David!" "Blessed is he who comes in the name of the Lord!" "Hosanna in the highest!" Did not the prophet say to shout at this event (Zech. 9:9)? And what did they shout? None other than the words of Psalm 118:25–26.

What is it about this psalm that singles it out for use on such an occasion? Psalm 118 celebrates a great event, an unexpected victory over the enemies of Israel who are pictured as swarming around Israel's leader like bees. The celebration makes its way to the temple where the leader asks entrance to give his thanks to Yahweh (vv. 19–21). He is allowed to enter and offer his praise, praise that begins with a proverb: "The stone the builders rejected has become the capstone" (v. 22). The praise continues:

> The LORD has done this,
>> and it is marvelous in our eyes.
> This is the day the LORD has made;
>> let us rejoice and be glad in it (vv. 23–24).

What could he mean by the rejected stone becoming the capstone? The capstone finishes the building (Zech. 4:7). Because the leader is entering the temple, this saying must be about the temple itself—most likely the second temple.[15] A stone from the rubble of Solomon's temple, rejected earlier by the builders, is found to be just the right stone for the final, honored spot. What could the leader mean by applying this proverb to himself? He sees his situation as parallel. He was rejected and yet now has been elevated to a place of honor. Verses 17–18 of the psalm confirm this:

> I will not die but live,
>> and will proclaim what the LORD has done.
> The LORD has chastened me severely,
>> but he has not given me over to death.

Because the leader in Psalms is usually the king of David's line and represents the people of Israel in his actions, the conclusion of Perowne seems most likely:

> They [Israel] had been despised by their heathen masters, but now, by the good hand of their God upon them, they had been lifted into a place of honour. They, rejected of men, were chosen of God as the chief stone of that new spiritual building which Jehovah was about to erect.[16]

Israel and her kingly line had been counted out. Declared a national has-been. Washed up on the sands of time. Yet her captivity was not an end but a beginning. She may celebrate her deliverance in the language of those kings that Yahweh delivered before her. But she must also pray for deliverance (118:25) because she has not yet seen Yahweh's full salvation:[17]

> O LORD, save us;
>> O LORD, grant us success (v. 25).

In the same way, the Jews of Jesus' time still looked for salvation, though they were living in the land of their forefathers with the temple completed and some of the riches of the nations adding to its splendor. Yet Yahweh's full salvation had not yet come. They are subjects, no longer of the Persians, but of the Romans.

Hosanna

"Hosanna!" the crowds shouted as Jesus headed toward the temple. This cry repeats the Hebrew words in Psalm 118:25—"Save now." Here comes the King! They expect him to deliver. Only later did they recognize that the words true of Israel once before would also be true of Israel's final King: "The stone the builders rejected" is the one God places at the top of the building. Peter boldly declares of Jesus, "He is the stone you builders rejected, which has become the capstone." This means that "Salvation is found in no one else, for there is no other name under heaven given to men by which we must be saved" (Acts 4:12).

The Day

> This is the day the LORD has made;
> let us rejoice and be glad in it (Ps. 118:24).

Christians sing these lines today as if they speak of each new day provided by God. "Let's rejoice in another day God has given us" is the common thought. But Psalm 118 is not exhorting us to find something joyous about every day. It is speaking of a special day of victory when God delivers. Yahweh makes such a day by his intervention. A day of victory! A day of celebration! The psalm looks and prays for another such day—a day of ultimate salvation.

Isaiah 49 predicted that kind of day for the exiles. Not only will Yahweh's Servant restore the tribes of Israel, but he will be "a light for the Gentiles, that you may bring my salvation to the ends of the earth" (v. 6). God says to Israel,

> In the time of my favor I will answer you,
> and in the day of salvation I will help you (v. 8).

In Christ, that day of salvation has arrived! The New Testament declares, "God was reconciling the world to himself in Christ, not counting men's sins against them" (2 Cor. 5:19). As Christ's ambassadors we implore others, "Be reconciled to God." Reconciliation is possible because "God made him who had no sin to be sin for us, so that in him we might become the righteousness of God" (5:20–21). Quoting Isaiah 49:8, Paul concludes: "I tell you, now is the time of God's favor, now is the day of salvation" (2 Cor. 6:2). We are living in the day of salvation! Christ has come and provided light not only to the Jews, but also to the Gentiles. Rejected by rulers, he nonetheless is God's answer. We await his return to complete all that the prophets have spoken; but today we may celebrate. Sing it with me:

> This is the day that the Lord has made,
> We will rejoice and be glad in it!

> ## SUGGESTED SCRIPTURE READING:
>
> *Haggai 1–2*
> *Zechariah 1–6; 9:9–17; 12–14*
> *Malachi 1–4*
> *Psalm 118*
> *2 Corinthians 5:17–6:2*

For Interaction and Discussion:

1. How did changing priorities keep the returned exiles from fulfilling their original purpose? What unhealthy priority took first place? What actions resulted? In what ways is this experienced in today's culture?

2. What dual promise and hope are held up in the book of Haggai? Why are these so important to these people?

3. How does Zechariah's basic message differ from Haggai's? What possible misconception does he correct? What response does he want from the people? How does Malachi's message tie in?

4. How do the visual images in Zechariah clarify what God will do for his people?

5. What is the message about Yahweh's Shepherd? How does he compare with the other shepherds of Israel? What specifics about this Shepherd tie in to Jesus? What other features of the future can you gather from these books?

6. What is the "day of salvation"? What is meant by "now is the day of salvation" (2 Cor. 6:2)? What glorious message does this make available?

For Further Reading:

Walter C. Kaiser, Jr. *Malachi: God's Unchanging Love*. Grand Rapids: Baker, 1984. Practical exposition for the English reader.

John D. W. Watts. "Zechariah," *The Broadman Bible Commentary*, vol. 7. Nashville: Broadman Press, 1972.

Joyce Baldwin. *Haggai, Zechariah, Malachi*. TOTC. Downers Grove, Ill.: Inter-Varsity, 1972.

Merrill F. Unger. *Unger's Bible Commentary: Zechariah*. Grand Rapids: Zondervan, 1963. Academic discussion of Hebrew text.

Notes and Comments:

[1]This observation that the Jews did not return "by might and power" but by permission of Cyrus is that of Yehezkel Kaufmann, *The Religion of Israel*, IV (New York: KTAV, 1977), 286.

[2]Joyce Baldwin, *Haggai, Zechariah, Malachi*, TOTC (Downers Grove, Ill.: Inter-Varsity, 1972), 33.

[3]Kaufmann, *The Religion of Israel*, 261, argues that the discussion of ritual uncleanness here is not intended as a parallel to the moral sins or injustice of the people, but that the incomplete temple made everything ritually unclean because it was impossible to carry out the prescribed rites acceptably with just an altar.

[4]Kaufmann (ibid., 254) observes that Haggai contains two sets of two prophecies each. The first set is prior to the laying of the foundation (1:1–2:9), the second on the day it was laid (2:10–23). The first prophecy of each set deals with the present tem-

ple situation, the second is messianic. The first messianic prophecy (2:6–9) deals with the temple, the second messianic prophecy (2:21–23), the house of David.

[5]Zechariah's insistence of moral repentance before Yahweh would return to his Temple reminds us of Judges 10:6–16 when God was so weary of their repeated failure that he would not deliver them until after they had demonstrated their willingness to serve him exclusively. Also similar is our earlier observation that God did not give final rest to Joshua's generation, apparently requiring that more than one generation be faithful. A look at Ezra, Nehemiah, and Malachi suggests that the returned exiles never fulfilled this requirement.

[6]Zechariah's visions (1:7–6:8) are grouped by twos, except for the first and the last which as a pair bracket the whole section. Joyce Baldwin, *Haggai, Zechariah, Malachi*, 80, 85, 93, has suggested a chiastic arrangement for these paired visions. In addition to these suggestions, however, it should be noted that the second and third visions are also closely connected to the first in that 2:6–13 contains exhortations depending upon the united message of the first three visions, not just the third.

[7]David L. Peterson, "Zechariah's Visions: A Theological Perspective," *VT*, 34 (1984): 201, calls attention to the city of Pasargadae, an unwalled ritual capital built by Cyrus during the period 545–530 B.C. This city was without walls and had fire altars on its perimeter. Yahweh's protection surely addressed the issue of the security normally handled by walls, which Jerusalem did not have. But, Kaufmann is correct when he cautions that the vision does not argue that no walls should be constructed. "The measurer goes to measure this great Jerusalem of the future whose extent no man now knows. This greater Jerusalem will have no walls; the Lord will be its shield. The messianic vision does not indicate any stance with respect to the building of the real wall" (*The Religion of Israel*, 277).

[8]John D. W. Watts, "Zechariah," *The Broadman Bible Commentary* (Nashville: Broadman, 1972), 7:327, has noted that "the ephah basket would be much too small for a full-sized person. The vision either has a very small woman or a womanlike figure, that is, an idol" (328). This conforms very nicely to setting it up on its base in Babylon.

[9]The oddity of having the high priest wear the crown and be called the Branch (6:9–15) has occasioned much discussion. For the view followed in the text see Merrill F. Unger, *Unger's Bible Commentary: Zechariah* (Grand Rapids: Zondervan, 1963), 110–18; and Joyce Baldwin, *Haggai, Zechariah, Malachi*, 133–35. An alternate interpretation finds both Joshua and Zerubbabel present. A crown is placed on the head of Joshua. To avoid problems of implied revolt, no crown is placed on Zerubbabel's head, but the predictions that follow are addressed alternately to Joshua and Zerubbabel as the two leaders. Zerubbabel represents the Branch of David's line who will build the Temple and sit on his throne (6:13a). The subject shifts now to Joshua: "And he will be a priest on his throne" (13b); then to the conclusion: "And there will be harmony between the two (king and priest)." The shift of reference within one verse without clearly identifying the person in view is taken as necessary by the political situation. Cf. Kaufmann, *The Religion of Israel*, 294–96; Watts, "Zechariah," 329–30. The use of "throne" in both places works against this view.

[10]Regarding the fasts of Zechariah 7–8, the main fast was that of the fifth month which marked the destruction of the Temple (2 Kings 25:8). The tenth month was the month that Nebuchadnezzar began the siege of Jerusalem (2 Kings 25:1–2). The fourth month saw the army break through the city wall (2 Kings 25:3–4; Jer. 39:2) and the seventh month memorialized the murder of Gedeliah, the governor (2 Kings 25:25). Cf. Unger, *Zechariah*, 122.

[11]Baldwin, *Haggai, Zechariah, Malachi*, 77–81, here follows the work of P. Lamarche, *Zacharie IX–XIV, Structure Litteraire et Messianisme* (Paris: Gabalda, 1961), translating his headings into English. Lamarche has suggested that four essential themes are repeated in chiastic arrangement in Zechariah 9–14. These are: (1) judgment and salvation of neighboring peoples; (2) the king shepherd and false shepherds; (3) Israel's war and victory; and (4) judgment on idols. Whatever the merits of the details of Lamarche's literary analysis, the observation that there is repetition of several major themes is very helpful as is the suggestion that each time a theme is renewed, a new perspective is added. Also helpful is Baldwin's observation that the writer "in the manner characteristic of apocalyptic, is using past events to typify a supremely important future event. Just as successive armies swept through Syria and Palestine and claimed a right to each territory, so finally the Lord will see every proud city capitulate to Him" (158). A threat to Lamarche's chiastic arrangement comes from Paul Hanson, *The Dawn of Apocalyptic* (Philadelphia: Fortress, 1975), 315–16, who sees Zechariah 9 as following the format of an ancient warrior hymn. See also Elmer A. Martens, *God's Design: A Focus on Old Testament Theology* (Grand Rapids: Baker, 1981), 203–5.

[12]For a full discussion of the word *associate*, cf. E. W. Hengstenberg, *Christology of the Old Testament* (Grand Rapids: Kregel, 1956 [1872–78]), 4:96–98. Some avoid the conclusion that Messiah is equal to God by taking the verse to be a judgment of the false shepherd. Cf. Eli Cashdan, "Zechariah," *The Twelve Prophets*, Soncino Books of the Bible, ed. A. Cohen (London: Soncino Press, 1948), 325.

[13]Baldwin, *Haggai, Zechariah, Malachi*, 211.

[14]Cf. ibid., 211–12, for a brief but sensible response to the arguments concerning the name *Malachi*.

[15]Franz Delitzsch, *Biblical Commentary on the Psalms* (Grand Rapids: Eerdmans), 3:223–24, identifies this psalm as "without any doubt a post-exilic song." He decides in favor of the dedication of the second temple as the psalm's setting. J. J. Perowne, *The Book of Psalms* (Grand Rapids: Zondervan, 1966 [1878–79]), 2:338–39, also sees it as post-exilic, but identifies it with the celebration in Nehemiah 8. More recent interpreters are greatly divided on its setting (cf. Leslie C. Allen, *Psalms 101–150*, WBC [Waco, Tex.: Word, 1983], 122–24). The more recent recognition of the king as a main speaker in songs of praise for victory, especially those which are singular or shift from singular to plural (king to nation), accounts for some identifying this psalm with pre-exilic worship. Its present place in the Psalms, however, identifies it as being used in the post-exilic community. Perhaps an earlier psalm of victory was adapted and applied to the situation at the time of

the second temple. It would not be out of place in the mouth of the Davidic heir, Zerubbabel.

[16]J. J. Stewart Perowne, *The Book of Psalms,* 2:343, and A. Cohen, *The Psalms,* Soncino Books of the Bible (New York: Soncino, 1945), 392, both take Psalm 118 as post-exilic and Israel being rejected by the nations. A similar view is taken by Delitzsch, *Biblical Commentary on the Psalms,* 3:229, though he identifies the rejecters as chiefs and members of Israel itself.

[17]Ronald E. Clements, *Old Testament Theology: A Fresh Approach* (Atlanta: John Knox Press, 1978), 151, believes that hope for the future restoration during the post-exilic period caused them to include royal psalms. Psalms originally speaking of a specific victory in the past for the Davidic king would, read through the eyes of God's promise of restoration, be sung as prophetic about what Yahweh would do in the future.

chapter seventeen
THEMES FOR THE FUTURE: NEW TESTAMENT UPDATE

If you've come this far with me, perhaps your notion of the bigger half of the Bible has changed. The Hebrew Scriptures have long been viewed by many as containing some interesting stories and some meaningful psalms and proverbs, but also a lot of dusty dry history along with a complex set of laws. I hope you've noticed a few important realities about what Christians call "the Old Testament."

It's going somewhere. It's headed toward a goal. Hope and promise are prominent. It is not about a bunch of static laws and dry history. It's about an ideal creation that God initiated. Humanity has stumbled and stuttered, but God has not given up on his plan or people. He will bring in the kingdom of peace, love, and justice under a final Davidic king. Yet this program is incomplete by the end of the Hebrew Scriptures. There is more to come.

It's characterized by a growing set of promises. God's plan of reversal and redemption of fallen humanity is progressive. The Abrahamic Covenant assures us that through Abraham's descendants, ultimate blessing will come on the world. The Mosaic Covenant initiates that nation through whom world redemption would come and gives her just laws so that she might live as a light of God's blessing in the midst of the nations. The Davidic Covenant specifies the tribe and line through which the ultimate King, the Messiah, would come. The New Covenant of Jeremiah tells how God will enable his people to respond positively. The promises have become more specific and the outline of fulfillment is filled in as we go.

It involves a network of themes. Old Testament scholars have suggested a number of themes as candidates for the central theme of the Old Testament. Yet it is difficult to see the same central theme as the theme of each and every book. Suggested central themes include: promise, covenant, kingdom, rule of God, "I am Yahweh," God himself, the plan of redemption or history of salvation, and Messiah. A quick look at these suggestions and one thing becomes apparent: They overlap. In fact, I have ordered these suggestions in pairs. Each pair (such as promise and covenant) is similar. In addition, the rest of the themes are interlocking parts of each other. How can we talk of covenant or promise and not talk of kingdom and vice versa? How can we talk about the history of salvation without promise and God's rule over his people? How can we think about kingdom without Messiah? In other words, these scholars really are all looking at the same Bible! They are just looking at this jewel of God's revelation from different angles and starting with a different facet of the whole jewel. It seems best to see all these themes as interlocking or intertwining. Like a rope, each strand is running in the same direction and contributing to the whole. Each Old Testament book is free to focus on one strand or another and make its own contribution to the whole. Each of these themes is relevant for understanding the Bible. Each of them, and more than these, must come to fulfillment.

One thing is obvious. The Old Testament is not a finished book! It looks forward to fulfillment. Christians believe that fulfillment started with Jesus of Nazareth and that the New Testament and its Gospel or "Good News" is the capstone of completion for the Old Testament. Let's briefly see how the New Testament sees the fulfillment of these growing promises and themes and how it also points us forward to a final future and hope.

THEMES FOR THE FUTURE

A web of unrealized expectations still awaits fulfillment as we enter the pages of the New Testament. And, as we saw in the prophets, the exact outworking of time and manner for these promised events is left unspecified. These things would *unfold* and God's plan would become clearer. Let's look at several of the events that are tied together by the New Testament.

A New Covenant

One crucial event is the installation of a new covenant as predicted by Jeremiah the prophet. Even though he was announcing the catastrophe of captivity, Jeremiah trumpeted a message of hope to those on their way out of the land. As we saw earlier, he pictures Rachel, the mother of Israel, weeping for her children as they leave and "are no more" (Jer. 31:15). But this nation that was no more was not forgotten by God. Jeremiah does not end his prophecy on this note of despair. In fact, he tells them to dry their tears because the exiles "will return from the land of the enemy" (31:16). Weeping provides the background to the announcement of a new covenant (31:31–34). The old covenant that shaped Israel when she left Egypt is found inferior "because they broke my covenant, though I was a husband to them." The failure of the old covenant is not in its laws but in its inability to guarantee heartfelt obedience. The New Covenant will remedy this failure.

> I will put my law in their minds
>> and write it on their hearts.
> I will be their God,
>> and they will be my people.
> No longer will a man teach his neighbor,
>> or a man his brother, saying, "Know the LORD,"
> because they will all know me,
>> from the least of them to the greatest,
>>> declares the LORD.
> For I will forgive their wickedness
>> and will remember their sins no more.

Universal knowledge of Yahweh, forgiveness, and spiritual enablement are the hallmarks of the coming New Covenant. The New Covenant will guarantee the restoration of God's people. Because it will overcome the weak link of human frailty, achieve forgiveness, and produce a response of gratitude and obedience, there is a blessed future for Israel's descendants (31:35–37). But how will God accomplish this?

Born by Water and Spirit

The prophet Ezekiel also prophesies of Israel's restoration and describes the same enablement that Jeremiah announced as part of the New Covenant.

> I will sprinkle clean water on you, and you will be clean; I will cleanse you from all your impurities and from all your idols. I will give you a new heart and put a new spirit in you; I will remove from you your heart of stone and give you a heart of flesh. And I will put my Spirit in you and move you to follow my decrees and be careful to keep my laws. You will live in the land I gave your forefathers; you will be my people, and I will be your God. I will save you from all your uncleanness (Ezek. 36:25–29).

No wonder Jesus told Nicodemus that "unless a man is born of water and the Spirit, he cannot enter the kingdom of God," and chided that teacher of Israel for not understanding these things (John 3:5–12). Without cleansing from God and the promised new heart and the work of God's Spirit within, no restoration can last. With these things, we are looking at none other than the arrival of the promised kingdom.

The Pouring Out of the Spirit

The work of the Holy Spirit of God, promised in Ezekiel, is also the subject of Joel 2:28–32:

> And afterward,
>> I will pour out my Spirit on all people.
> Your sons and daughters will prophesy,
>> your old men will dream dreams,
>> your young men will see visions.
> Even on my servants, both men and women,
>> I will pour out my Spirit in those days.
> I will show wonders in the heavens and on the earth,
>> blood and fire and billows of smoke.
> The sun will be turned to darkness
>> and the moon to blood
>> before the coming of the great and dreadful day of the LORD.
> And everyone who calls
>> on the name of the LORD will be saved;
> for on Mount Zion and in Jerusalem
>> there will be deliverance,
>> as the LORD has said,
> among the survivors
>> whom the LORD calls.

This prophecy looks for Israel's universal experience of the Spirit of God. In the past, the Spirit spoke through the prophets. In the future, everyone will speak God's word and see visions from God. Communication with God will be direct.

The Prophetic Combination

When we combine these aspects of the future hope of Israel with those we saw in Zechariah and Haggai, we arrive at the following picture:

- Israel is looking for an ultimate restoration under the Davidic Messiah who will reign as King and Priest.
- Israel's restoration will be effective because God will initiate a new covenant to replace the old one (which failed because it did not supernaturally change men's hearts, as the New Covenant will).
- This change will involve forgiveness, cleansing, and a new spirit produced by the work of God's Spirit.
- God's Spirit will be universally experienced and everyone will know God.

- The nations will oppose Israel, but Yahweh will deliver her by direct intervention. Many from the nations will be drawn to worship Yahweh at Jerusalem.

Such is the package of hope as we close the Old Testament. And in spite of disappointment at waiting years with no national restoration, it is still the hope of the faithful as we open the pages of the New Testament. Here we find priests and teachers able to name the place of Messiah's birth (Matt. 2:5–6) and to question John the Baptist about his place in the prophetic scheme (John 1:19–21). How many, like Simeon, were "waiting for the consolation of Israel" (Luke 2:25)? Apparently old Anna's devotion and expectation were such that she never left the temple precincts (Luke 2:36–38). Nor did she have difficulty finding those "who were looking forward to the redemption of Jerusalem" so she could tell them the news of Jesus' birth (Luke 2:38).

NEW TESTAMENT UPDATE

The New Testament brings some surprises, however. In the Gospel records of Jesus' life there is no rise of this Son of David to an earthly throne and kingdom, no overthrow of the Gentile rulers, and no intervention by Yahweh for the final deliverance of Jerusalem. What has happened? How does the New Testament relate the life of Jesus to these hopes and expectations?

Two Advents

Predictions, when fulfilled, often happen in a way that—dare I say it—are unpredictable. Or to put it another way, while futuristic prophecy often tells us what will occur, how it comes to pass may surprise us. I suspect that many best-selling books on prophecy will blush (were it possible) when prophecies "as clear as the headlines in your daily newspaper" actually come to pass. The details surrounding fulfilled prophecy are recognized when they happen, not before. This does not mean prophecy is less than exact. Micah 5:2 predicted that the Messiah would be born in Bethlehem. And he was. But who would have predicted that a manger would be his first cradle and that his parents, in the kingly line of David, would be there only temporarily because of a Roman edict about a census?

One of these unpredictable items facing the Jewish believer during Jesus' lifetime was the Bible's silence concerning the fact that Messiah would come twice, not just once. The Old Testament told of both a suffering Messiah (Isa. 53; Zech. 13:7) and a victorious and reigning Messiah (Isa. 9; 11). The idea that Messiah would deliver them from Gentile rule and establish the kingdom dominated Jewish thinking in the New Testament period. That Messiah would come without restoring Israel to nationhood was unthinkable.

From a human perspective, the Israeli people saw their problem as a lack of freedom from Gentile rule and the absence of a restored Davidic monarchy. From the divine standpoint, however, the greatest problem was the human need to solve the sin problem. Messiah needed to achieve spiritual redemption for humanity before physical redemption could be meaningful and lasting. For God, the prerequisite for restoration was the establishment of the New Covenant with its payment for sin and ability to change hearts. That must come first. And that is what the First Advent is all about. If Israel was granted a restored kingdom no different from great Gentile kingdoms, what would be gained? Even a restored kingdom as righteous as the past monarchy would not do.

Just as we saw the notion of *telescoping* of prophecy with the Old Testament prophets, Jesus revealed that fulfillment would actually come in two stages. Not everything was fulfilled during Christ's first advent. Much is still future. Though this new knowledge about two comings helps clarify the timing of Old Testament fulfillment, it also causes problems. Take God's sending of the Holy Spirit in Acts 2. Peter quotes Joel 2 to explain to his audience what was happening at Pentecost. Yet it is obvious that Pentecost does not fulfill all the features of Joel's prophecy. Where are the signs in the heavens, the sun turning to darkness and the moon to blood?[1] Even more, where is the gift of universal prophecy? It is quite clear that prophecy and knowledge are not universal in the church, even if gifts of the Spirit are (1 Cor. 12:29). In fact, apart from receiving the Spirit himself, there is little similarity between Pentecost and Joel 2.

Partial Fulfillment

Experiencing part of a fulfillment, yet not to the full extent of the original prophecy, has gathered a variety of labels. Some call it partial fulfillment. Others use the term *double fulfillment*, suggesting that a prophecy can be fulfilled more than once. Still others see all such cases as token fulfillments that look forward to a full and final fulfillment. But the label is not so important. What is important is the reason we need these labels. We have this problem because Messiah's two comings were unforeseen in the Old Testament. Therefore some predicted events and blessings that began at the first coming await ultimate and universal fulfillment at Christ's return, when he sets up his kingdom in full operation.

Already, But Not Yet

In fact, there is a whole list of predicted blessings that believers enjoy today.

- We have the promised Spirit of God (1 Cor. 6:19; Rom. 8:9).

- We are under the benefits of the New Covenant, rather than the limitations of the Mosaic Covenant (Heb. 8:6–13).
- We are new creatures in Christ Jesus, part of the new creation yet to be fully revealed (2 Cor. 5:17).
- We are citizens of the promised Kingdom (Col. 1:12–14).
- We have every spiritual blessing provided by Messiah, who now sits at the right hand of the Father in the place of authority and power (Eph. 1:3, 18–23).

The Jews spoke of the present age and the age to come. Jesus, in his death and resurrection, provided forgiveness of sins and made available the power of the age to come (Eph. 1:19–21). The only requirement for an individual who wishes to enjoy this powerful salvation is faith in Jesus as the Messiah (Eph. 2:7–10). This means that we are already in "the last days" spoken of by the prophets. We are in the time of fulfillment—the end times, if you please (Heb. 1:2; 1 Peter 1:20; 1 Cor. 10:11). We who believe already experience the age to come by being united to Messiah, by being under the New Covenant, and by experiencing the power of the promised Spirit.

The age to come is here; yet it is not fully revealed. Already . . . but not yet. Believers may enjoy it individually now, but all the earth will experience it at Christ's return. The time of fulfillment has begun. The Rule of Messiah has commenced. He has been given the position of authority and power (Eph. 1:21–22). Yet he sits at the right hand of the Father, waiting for the time when all things are subject to him (Ps. 110:1; Heb. 10:12–13). The Kingdom has begun, but the Kingdom has not yet been fully revealed.[2]

Gentiles and the Church

Another difficulty: What is the period like between these two comings of Christ? This era is unseen by the prophets. This telescoping that we saw in the prophets has been well illustrated by a diagram of two mountain peaks, one behind the other. These two peaks represent the two comings of Christ. From the distance of the Old Testament, they appear as one peak with no hint of a gap in between.

So what is the period in between the two comings like? The people of God in this period are called the church. The church is "in Christ," the Greek word for Messiah. It has entered into the work of Messiah, for it has been forgiven of its sins through his sacrificial death on the cross and operates as his representative on earth by the power of the Spirit.

But what about Gentiles or nations? May they be considered part of the people of God? Or can only Israelites be full citizens under Israel's king?

The Mystery Revealed

Understandably, Jewish believers were reluctant to accept Gentiles as fully part of Christ without becoming part of Israel. But the fact that God gave to the Gentiles the promised gift of the Holy Spirit when they believed in Jesus as Messiah was convincing evidence that God had accepted them (Acts 10; 11:15–17; 15:1–3). The "mystery" or "secret," unknown in the Old Testament, but now revealed through apostles and prophets, is that "one new man" has been formed in Christ. That new man is made up of both Jew and Gentile, all who believe in Christ (Eph. 2:11–3:6).

The New Covenant Experienced

The New Covenant promised by Jeremiah is now made available to Jews and Gentiles through the blood of Christ (Luke 22:20; Heb. 9:15). Paul is a minister of the New Covenant, and all who trust in Christ participate in the New Covenant's benefits (2 Cor. 3:6–18). Kingdom life, eternal life—may now be had by those who have believed in Christ, whether Jew or Gentile. But a question arises: How can Gentiles participate in a covenant promised specifically to the Jews? We Gentiles had no covenant, old or new. We were "foreigners to the covenants of the promise, without hope and without God in the world" (Eph. 2:12). How do we get a "new" covenant?

Because the idea of covenant is like a contract today, perhaps an example from modern business will make clear what has happened: The head of a manufacturing firm has two plants in different states. One is unionized; the other is not. Workers in the unionized plant, who are under a contract with management, go out on strike for additional pay and benefits. After negotiation, a settlement is reached that gives workers in the unionized plant a ten-percent raise and better medical coverage. Union members refer to this settlement as the "New Contract." To the workers in the other plant, nothing new is promised at all. They never even had an "Old Contract." But shortly after the union shop returns to work, the owner of the firm travels to his nonunionized plant, calls the workers together, and makes an announcement: "You may have heard that my other plant has negotiated a New Contract. I know you were not part of that arrangement. I have no obligation to you under either the Old Contract or the New Contract. But I am giving you the same New Contract I promised them." That is what the New Testament says about the New Covenant. Gentiles who had no covenant promises are accepted when they believe in Christ and come under the New Covenant. The New Testament has a name for this: It's called GRACE.

> For the grace of God has appeared, bringing salvation to all men, instructing us to deny ungodliness and worldly desires and to live

sensibly, righteously and godly in the present age, looking for the blessed hope and the appearing of the glory of our great God and Savior, Christ Jesus; who gave Himself for us, that He might redeem us from every lawless deed and purify for Himself a people for His own possession, zealous for good deeds (Titus 2:11–14 NASB).

And this is the place to end our trip. It has brought us to "Jesus, the author and perfecter of our faith, who for the joy set before him endured the cross, scorning its shame, and sat down at the right hand of the throne of God" (Heb. 12:2).

SUGGESTED SCRIPTURE READING:

John 3:1–21
Acts 2
Ephesians 2:1–3:6

For Interaction and Discussion:

1. How has this trip through the bigger half of the Bible sharpened your focus on the future?

2. What aspects of the future has Jesus already made available to individuals who belong to his Kingdom? What difference does this make?

3. Why did Jesus not set up a restored kingdom on earth at his first coming?

4. What is the mystery that was not known in the Old Testament? Why is this so important to Gentiles? How does it relate to God's promise to Abraham?

5. Why do Gentiles experience the benefits of the New Covenant when it was promised to Israel?

6. Can any individual become a member of the coming Kingdom of Jesus? How?

7. With the New Testament look forward, how does hope affect your outlook and life choices?

For Further Reading:

F. F. Bruce. *New Testament Development of Old Testament Themes*. Grand Rapids: Eerdmans, 1968. The treatment that originally encouraged me to think of fulfillment along the lines of themes.

John S. Feinberg. *Continuity and Discontinuity: Perspectives on the Relationship Between the Old and New Testaments*. Westchester, Ill.: Crossway, 1988. Debate among evangelical scholars over the nature of New Testament fulfillment along several major categories.

R. T. France, *Jesus and the Old Testament*, Downers Grove, Ill.: InterVarsity, 1971. Coverage of specific texts where Jesus cites the Old Testament.

Darrell Bock. "Evangelicals and the Use of the Old Testament in the New." *BSac*, 142 (1985): 209–23, 306–19. A helpful academic overview of the different views about the New Testament's use of the Old. Academic treatments of these views follow below.

Elliot E. Johnson. "Author's Intention and Biblical Interpretation." *Hermeneutics, Inerrancy and the Bible*, ed. Earl D. Radmacher and Robert D. Preus, Grand Rapids: Zondervan, 1984, 409–29. One of the views discussed by Bock that maintains that the authorial intent of the Old Testament text is not violated by New Testament authors.

Richard N. Longenecker. "'Who is the Prophet Talking About?' Some Reflections on the New Testament's Use of the Old," *Themelios* (1987): 4–8. An advocate of New Testament use of rabbinic hermeneutical method, a view in contrast to my own in the text.

J. Douglas Moo. "The Problem of Sensus Plenior." *Hermeneutics, Authority, and Canon*, ed. D. A. Carson and John D. Woodbridge. Grand Rapids: Zondervan, 1983. An evaluation of another major approach.

S. Lewis Johnson, Jr. *The Old Testament in the New*. Grand Rapids, Zondervan, 1980. The author was my professor who stirred my interest in the use of the Old Testament in the New.

Walter C. Kaiser, Jr. *The Uses of the Old Testament in the New*. Chicago: Moody, 1985. Strong advocate of a literal, contextual use of the Old Testament in the New.

Notes and Comments:

[1] F. F. Bruce, *The Book of Acts* (Grand Rapids: Eerdmans, 1954), 68–69. Bruce suggests these natural signs may have had some significance to those who had seen the unnatural darkness at the crucifixion nearly two months earlier. He recognizes as well, however, that this is at best a beginning of fulfillment (cf. Rev. 6:12).

[2] Ibid., 35. Cf. George E. Ladd, *A Theology of the New Testament* (Grand Rapids: Eerdmans, 1974), 550–52.

Scripture Index

SUBJECT INDEX